# Practice *Planner*

Arthur E. Jongsma, Jr., Series Editor

# *Helping therapists help their clients...*

**Treatment Planners** cover all the necessary elements for developing formal treatment plans, including detailed problem definitions, long-term goals, short-term objectives, therapeutic interventions, and DSM-IV™ diagnoses.

- ❏ The Complete Adult Psychotherapy Treatment Planner, Fourth Edition........978-0-471-76346-8 / $55.00
- ❏ The Child Psychotherapy Treatment Planner, Fourth Edition........................978-0-471-78535-4 / $55.00
- ❏ The Adolescent Psychotherapy Treatment Planner, Fourth Edition..............978-0-471-78539-2 / $55.00
- ❏ The Addiction Treatment Planner, Fourth Edition...........................................978-0-470-40551-2 / $55.00
- ❏ The Couples Psychotherapy Treatment Planner, Second Edition...................978-0-470-40695-3 / $55.00
- ❏ The Group Therapy Treatment Planner, Second Edition...............................978-0-471-66791-9 / $55.00
- ❏ The Family Therapy Treatment Planner, Second Edition...............................978-0-470-44193-0 / $55.00
- ❏ The Older Adult Psychotherapy Treatment Planner .....................................978-0-471-29574-7 / $55.00
- ❏ The Employee Assistance (EAP) Treatment Planner .....................................978-0-471-24709-8 / $55.00
- ❏ The Gay and Lesbian Psychotherapy Treatment Planner ...........................978-0-471-35080-4 / $55.00
- ❏ The Crisis Counseling and Traumatic Events Treatment Planner ...............978-0-471-39587-4 / $55.00
- ❏ The Social Work and Human Services Treatment Planner ...........................978-0-471-37741-2 / $55.00
- ❏ The Continuum of Care Treatment Planner...................................................978-0-471-19568-9 / $55.00
- ❏ The Behavioral Medicine Treatment Planner ...............................................978-0-471-31923-8 / $55.00
- ❏ The Mental Retardation and Developmental Disability Treatment Planner ...978-0-471-38253-9 / $55.00
- ❏ The Special Education Treatment Planner......................................................978-0-471-38872-2 / $55.00
- ❏ The Severe and Persistent Mental Illness Treatment Planner, Second Edition....978-0-470-18013-6 / $55.00
- ❏ The Personality Disorders Treatment Planner ..............................................978-0-471-39403-7 / $55.00
- ❏ The Rehabilitation Psychology Treatment Planner .......................................978-0-471-35178-8 / $55.00
- ❏ The Pastoral Counseling Treatment Planner..................................................978-0-471-25416-4 / $55.00
- ❏ The Juvenile Justice and Residential Care Treatment Planner ....................978-0-471-43320-0 / $55.00
- ❏ The School Counseling and School Social Work Treatment Planner ...........978-0-471-08496-9 / $55.00
- ❏ The Psychopharmacology Treatment Planner ...............................................978-0-471-43322-4 / $55.00
- ❏ The Probation and Parole Treatment Planner................................................978-0-471-20244-8 / $55.00
- ❏ The Suicide and Homicide Risk Assessment & Prevention Treatment Planner ..978-0-471-46631-4 / $55.00
- ❏ The Speech-Language Pathology Treatment Planner.....................................978-0-471-27504-6 / $55.00
- ❏ The College Student Counseling Treatment Planner .....................................978-0-471-46708-3 / $55.00
- ❏ The Parenting Skills Treatment Planner .........................................................978-0-471-48183-6 / $55.00
- ❏ The Early Childhood Education Intervention Treatment Planner .................978-0-471-65962-4 / $55.00
- ❏ The Co-Occurring Disorders Treatment Planner ...........................................978-0-471-73081-1 / $55.00
- ❏ The Sexual Abuse Victim and Sexual Offender Treatment Planner .............978-0-471-21979-8 / $55.00
- ❏ The Complete Women's Psychotherapy Treatment Planner .......................978-0-470-03983-0 / $55.00
- ❏ The Veterans and Active Duty Military Psychotherapy Treatment Planner ...978-0-470-44098-8 / $55.00

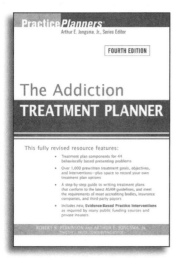

The **Complete Treatment and Homework Planners** series of books combines our bestselling *Treatment Planners* and *Homework Planners* into one easy-to-use, all-in-one resource for mental health professionals treating clients suffering from the most commonly diagnosed disorders.

- ❏ The Complete Depression Treatment and Homework Planner..................978-0-471-64515-3 / $48.95
- ❏ The Complete Anxiety Treatment and Homework Planner .......................978-0-471-64548-1 / $48.95

# Practice*Planners*®

**Homework Planners** feature dozens of behaviorally based, ready-to-use assignments that are designed for use between sessions, as well as a disk or CD-ROM (Microsoft Word) containing all of the assignments—allowing you to customize them to suit your unique client needs.

**Progress Notes Planners** contain complete prewritten progress notes for each presenting problem in the companion Treatment Planners.

**Client Education Handout Planners** contain elegantly designed handouts that can be printed out from the enclosed CD-ROM and provide information on a wide range of psychological and emotional disorders and life skills issues. Use as patient literature, handouts at presentations, and aids for promoting your mental health practice.

# The Family Therapy Progress Notes Planner

## PracticePlanners® Series

### Treatment Planners

*The Complete Adult Psychotherapy Treatment Planner, Fourth Edition*
*The Child Psychotherapy Treatment Planner, Fourth Edition*
*The Adolescent Psychotherapy Treatment Planner, Fourth Edition*
*The Addiction Treatment Planner, Fourth Edition*
*The Continuum of Care Treatment Planner*
*The Couples Psychotherapy Treatment Planner, Second Edition*
*The Employee Assistance Treatment Planner*
*The Pastoral Counseling Treatment Planner*
*The Older Adult Psychotherapy Treatment Planner*
*The Behavioral Medicine Treatment Planner*
*The Group Therapy Treatment Planner*
*The Gay and Lesbian Psychotherapy Treatment Planner*
*The Family Therapy Treatment Planner, Second Edition*
*The Severe and Persistent Mental Illness Treatment Planner, Second Edition*
*The Mental Retardation and Developmental Disability Treatment Planner*
*The Social Work and Human Services Treatment Planner*
*The Crisis Counseling and Traumatic Events Treatment Planner*
*The Personality Disorders Treatment Planner*
*The Rehabilitation Psychology Treatment Planner*
*The Special Education Treatment Planner*
*The Juvenile Justice and Residential Care Treatment Planner*
*The School Counseling and School Social Work Treatment Planner*
*The Sexual Abuse Victim and Sexual Offender Treatment Planner*
*The Probation and Parole Treatment Planner*
*The Psychopharmacology Treatment Planner*
*The Speech-Language Pathology Treatment Planner*
*The Suicide and Homicide Treatment Planner*
*The College Student Counseling Treatment Planner*
*The Parenting Skills Treatment Planner*
*The Early Childhood Intervention Treatment Planner*
*The Co-Occurring Disorders Treatment Planner*
*The Complete Women's Psychotherapy Treatment Planner*
*The Veterans and Active Duty Military Psychotherapy Treatment Planner*

### Progress Notes Planners

*The Child Psychotherapy Progress Notes Planner, Third Edition*
*The Adolescent Psychotherapy Progress Notes Planner, Third Edition*
*The Adult Psychotherapy Progress Notes Planner, Third Edition*
*The Addiction Progress Notes Planner, Third Edition*
*The Severe and Persistent Mental Illness Progress Notes Planner, Second Edition*
*The Couples Psychotherapy Progress Notes Planner*
*The Family Therapy Progress Notes Planner, Second Edition*
*The Veterans and Active Duty Military Psychotherapy Progress Notes Planner*

### Homework Planners

*Employee Assistance Homework Planner, Second Edition*
*Family Therapy Homework Planner, Second Edition*
*Grief Counseling Homework Planner*
*Group Therapy Homework Planner*
*Divorce Counseling Homework Planner*
*School Counseling and School Social Work Homework Planner*
*Child Therapy Activity and Homework Planner*
*Addiction Treatment Homework Planner, Fourth Edition*
*Adolescent Psychotherapy Homework Planner II*
*Adolescent Psychotherapy Homework Planner, Second Edition*
*Adult Psychotherapy Homework Planner, Second Edition*
*Child Psychotherapy Homework Planner, Second Edition*
*Parenting Skills Homework Planner*

### Client Education Handout Planners

*Adult Client Education Handout Planner*
*Child and Adolescent Client Education Handout Planner*
*Couples and Family Client Education Handout Planner*

### Complete Planners

*The Complete Depression Treatment and Homework Planner*
*The Complete Anxiety Treatment and Homework Planner*

**PracticePlanners®**

Arthur E. Jongsma, Jr., Series Editor

# The Family Therapy Progress Notes Planner
# Second Edition

*David J. Berghuis*

*Arthur E. Jongsma, Jr.*

**WILEY**

JOHN WILEY & SONS, INC.

ISBN 978-0-470-44884-7(paper)
ISBN 978-0-470-63837-8 (ebk)
ISBN 978-0-470-63838-5 (ebk)
ISBN 978-0-470-36839-2 (ebk)

Printed in the United States of America

10  9  8  7  6  5  4  3  2  1

To Lucy Berghuis and Tom Ranney, who have helped to complete our family.

*– David J. Berghuis*


To Justin, Carter, Kaleigh, and Tyler—grandchildren who enrich our family circle with their energy and love.

*– Arthur E. Jongsma, Jr.*

# CONTENTS

# PRACTICE*PLANNERS*® SERIES PREFACE

Accountability is an important dimension of the practice of psychotherapy. Treatment programs, public agencies, clinics, and practitioners must justify and document their treatment plans to outside review entities in order to be reimbursed for services. The books and software in the Practice*Planners*® series are designed to help practitioners fulfill these documentation requirements efficiently and professionally. The Practice*Planners*® series includes a wide array of treatment planning books including not only the original *Complete Adult Psychotherapy Treatment Planner*, *Child Psychotherapy Treatment Planner*, and *Adolescent Psychotherapy Treatment Planner*, all now in their fourth editions, but also *Treatment Planners* targeted to specialty areas of practice, including:

- Addictions
- Co-occurring disorders
- Behavioral medicine
- College students
- Couples therapy
- Crisis counseling
- Early childhood education
- Employee assistance
- Family therapy
- Gays and lesbians
- Group therapy
- Juvenile justice and residential care
- Mental retardation and developmental disability
- Neuropsychology
- Older adults

- Parenting skills
- Pastoral counseling
- Personality disorders
- Probation and parole
- Psychopharmacology
- Rehabilitation psychology
- School counseling
- Severe and persistent mental illness
- Sexual abuse victims and offenders
- Social work and human services
- Special education
- Speech-Language pathology
- Suicide and homicide risk assessment
- Women's issues
- Veteran's and active duty military

In addition, there are three branches of companion books which can be used in conjunction with the *Treatment Planners*, or on their own:

- *Progress Notes Planners* provide a menu of progress statements that elaborate on the client's symptom presentation and the provider's therapeutic intervention. Each *Progress Notes Planner* statement is directly integrated with the behavioral definitions and therapeutic interventions from its companion *Treatment Planner*.

- *Homework Planners* include homework assignments designed around each presenting problem (such as anxiety, depression, chemical dependence, anger management, eating disorders, or panic disorder) that is the focus of a chapter in its corresponding *Treatment Planner*.

- *Client Education Handout Planners* provide brochures and handouts to help educate and inform clients on presenting problems and mental health issues, as well as life skills techniques. The handouts are included on CD-ROMs for easy printing from your computer and are ideal for use in waiting rooms, at presentations, as newsletters, or as information for clients struggling with mental illness issues. The topics covered by these handouts correspond to the presenting problems in the *Treatment Planners*.

The series also includes:

- **Thera*Scribe*®**, the #1 selling treatment planning and clinical record-keeping software system for mental health professionals. Thera*Scribe*® allows the user to import the data from any of the *Treatment Planner*, *Progress Notes Planner*, or *Homework Planner* books into the software's expandable database to simply point and click to create a detailed, organized, individualized, and customized treatment plan along with optional integrated progress notes and homework assignments.

Adjunctive books, such as *The Psychotherapy Documentation Primer* and *The Clinical Documentation Sourcebook*, contain forms and resources to aid the clinician in mental health practice management.

The goal of our series is to provide practitioners with the resources they need in order to provide high quality care in the era of accountability. To put it simply: We seek to help you spend more time on patients, and less time on paperwork.

ARTHUR E. JONGSMA, JR.
*Grand Rapids, Michigan*

# ACKNOWLEDGMENTS

This book builds on the revised work done on the new edition of the *Family Therapy Treatment Planner* (2010) by Sean Davis, Frank Dattilio, and Art Jongsma. They highlighted evidence-based interventions that already existed in the previous edition and added new research supported content where needed. Two new chapters were also added to the new edition of the *Treatment Planner*: Reuniting Estranged Family Members and Interfamilial Disputes over Wills and Inheritance. Since this *Progress Notes Planner* follows the *Treatment Planner*, those new chapter titles are also found in this volume. We thank those authors of the *Treatment Planner* for their work on the new edition.

We also thank the production staff at John Wiley & Sons for their help in revising this new edition of the *Family Therapy Progress Notes Planner*. Digging out old files and integrating new material can be a challenge in manuscript management.

Finally, we thank the editorial staff at John Wiley & Sons for their ongoing support for this Practice*Planner* project. Special thanks to Marquita Flemming, Judi Knott, and Margaret Alexander, who have guided us for many years.

ARTHUR E. JONGSMA, JR.
DAVID J. BERGHUIS

# INTRODUCTION

## ABOUT PRACTICE*PLANNERS*® PROGRESS NOTES

Progress notes are not only the primary source for documenting the therapeutic process, but also one of the main factors in determining the client's eligibility for reimbursable treatment. The purpose of the *Progress Notes Planner* series is to assist the practitioner in easily and quickly constructing progress notes that are thoroughly unified with the client's treatment plan.

### Each *Progress Notes Planner:*

- Saves you hours of time-consuming paperwork.
- Offers the freedom to develop customized progress notes.
- Features over 1,000 prewritten progress notes summarizing patient presentation and treatment delivered.
- Provides an array of treatment approaches that correspond with the behavioral problems and *DSM-IV* diagnostic categories in the corresponding companion *Treatment Planner*.
- Offers sample progress notes that conform to the requirements of most third-party payors and accrediting agencies, including The Joint Commission, COA, CARF, and NCQA.

## HOW TO USE THIS *PROGRESS NOTES PLANNER*

This *Progress Notes Planner* provides a menu of sentences that can be selected for constructing progress notes based on the behavioral definitions (or client's symptom presentation) and therapeutic interventions from its companion *Treatment Planner*. All progress notes must be tied to the patient's treatment plan-session notes should elaborate on the problems, symptoms, and interventions contained in the plan.

Each chapter title is a reflection of the client's potential presenting problem. The first section of the chapter, "Client Presentation," provides a detailed menu of statements that may describe how that presenting problem manifested itself in behavioral signs and symptoms. The numbers in parentheses within the Client Presentation section correspond to the numbers of the Behavioral Definitions from the *Treatment Planner*.

The second section of each chapter, "Interventions Implemented," provides a menu of statements related to the action that was taken within the session to assist the client in making progress. The numbering of the items in the Interventions Implemented section follows exactly the numbering of Therapeutic Intervention items in the corresponding *Treatment Planner*.

All item lists begin with a few keywords. These words are meant to convey the theme or content of the sentences that are contained in that listing. The clinician may peruse the list of keywords to find content which matches the client's presentation and the clinician's intervention.

It is expected that the clinician may modify the prewritten statements contained in this book to fit the exact circumstances of the client's presentation and treatment. To maintain complete client records, in addition to progress note statements that may be selected and individualized from this book, the date, time, and length of a session; those present within the session; the provider; provider's credentials' and a signature must be entered in the client's record.

## A FINAL NOTE ABOUT PROGRESS NOTES AND HIPAA

Federal regulations under the Health Insurance Portability and Accountability Act (HIPAA) govern the privacy of a client's psychotherapy notes, as well as other protected health information (PHI). PHI and psychotherapy notes must be kept secure and the client must sign a specific authorization to release this confidential information to anyone beyond the client's therapist or treatment team. Further, psychotherapy notes receive other special treatment under HIPAA; for example, they may not be altered after they are initially drafted. Instead, the clinician must create and file formal amendments to the notes if he or she wishes to expand, delete, or otherwise change them. Our Thera*Scribe*$^{TM}$ software provides functionality to help clinicians maintain the proper rules concerning handling PHI, by giving the ability to lock progress notes once they are created, to acknowledge patient consent for the release of PHI, and to track amendments to psychotherapy notes over time.

Does the information contained in this book, when entered into a client's record as a progress note, qualify as a "psychotherapy note" and therefore merit confidential protection under HIPAA regulations? If the progress note that is created by selecting sentences from the database contained in this book is kept in a location separate from the client's PHI data, then the note could qualify as psychotherapy note data that is more protected than general PHI. However, because the sentences contained in this book convey generic information regarding the client's progress, the clinician may decide to keep the notes mixed in with the client's PHI and not consider it psychotherapy note data. In short, how you treat the information (separated from or integrated with PHI) can determine if this progress note planner data is psychotherapy note information. If you modify or edit these generic sentences to reflect more personal information about the client or you add sentences that contain confidential information, the argument for keeping these notes separate from PHI and treating them as psychotherapy notes becomes stronger. For some therapists, our sentences alone reflect enough personal information to qualify as psychotherapy notes and they will keep these notes separate from the client's PHI and require specific authorization from the client to share them with a clearly identified recipient for a clearly identified purpose.

# ACTIVITY/FAMILY IMBALANCE

## CLIENT PRESENTATION

### 1. Tension Due to Outside Activities (1)*

A. The family has experienced tension due to a family member's excessive time given to outside activities.

B. A parent spends an excessive amount of time at work away from home, resulting in arguments and tension within the family.

C. A family member spends a great deal of time involved in sports activities, resulting in tension about the lack of time spent with other family members.

D. A family member spends a great deal of time involved in activities away from the family, resulting in tension about lack of time with other family members.

E. Family members often experience arguments and conflicts when they try to resolve the activity/family imbalance.

F. Family tension has decreased as family members have developed a greater balance regarding activities outside of the home.

### 2. Priorities Questioned (2)

A. Family members often question other family members' priorities because of the unusual amount of time that is dedicated to outside activities.

B. Family members are uncertain about how important they are to other family members due to the unusual amount of time that is dedicated to outside activities.

C. Family members have become more at ease with the level of importance of the family within all family members' lifestyles.

### 3. Shift of Duties (3)

A. Some family duties and responsibilities have been unfairly shifted to other family members due to the time absorbed by the external activities.

B. Family members experience conflicts and tension due to the unfair shifting of responsibilities.

C. Family members have become more understanding about how their outside activities affect others and have become more responsible for their own duties around the home.

D. The family has prioritized responsibilities in a different manner, which has reduced the conflict and tension within the family.

### 4. Jealousy and Envy (4)

A. Family members often experience feelings of jealousy and envy due to the increased amount of time dedicated to external activities.

B. Accusations of favoritism have arisen among family members.

---

*The numbers in parentheses correlate to the number of the Behavioral Definition statement in the companion chapter with the same title in *The Family Therapy Treatment Planner*, Second Ed. (Dattilio, Jongsma, and Davis) by John Wiley & Sons, 2010.

C. Feelings of jealousy and envy often lead to arguments and conflict between family members.

D. As family members have begun to resolve concerns related to jealousy and envy, conflict has decreased.

E. Family members report no further feelings of envy or jealousy.

### 5. Competition for Absent Family Member's Time (5)

A. Family members often feel as though they are in competition with each other for the absent family member's available time.

B. Family members display attention-seeking behaviors to obtain time with the frequently absent family member.

C. Family members often disagree about how they can use the absent family member's available time.

D. As activity/family imbalance issues have been worked out, family members are able to obtain adequate time with the previously unavailable family member.

### 6. Mental Illness (6)

A. A family member's excessive involvement with activities away from the family appears to be related to mental illness.

B. Bipolar disease appears to be the precipitating cause of the activity/family imbalance issues.

C. As the family member's mental illness has been treated, the activity/family imbalance issues have been resolved.


## INTERVENTIONS IMPLEMENTED

### 1. Obtain All Family Members' Opinions (1)*

A. Each family member was allowed to express opinions about who is absent too often from the family.

B. Family members were encouraged to provide open, honest opinions about family members being overly committed to outside activities.

C. Family members were redirected when they tried to argue or deny other family members' opinions.

D. It was reflected to the family that they have very similar opinions about the activity/family imbalance issues.

E. Family members were noted to have quite varied opinions about the activity/family imbalance issues, and these differences in perception were summarized.

### 2. Facilitate Ventilation of Feelings (2)

A. Family members were asked to express their feelings regarding the activity/family imbalance pattern.

B. Family members were provided with support and encouragement when they openly expressed their feelings regarding the activity/family imbalance issues.

---

*The numbers in parentheses correlate to the number of the Therapeutic Intervention statement in the companion chapter with the same title in *The Family Therapy Treatment Planner*, Second Ed. (Dattilio, Jongsma, and Davis) by John Wiley & Sons, 2010.

C. Family members were redirected when they attempted to deny or invalidate the family members' emotions about the activity/family imbalance.

D. Family members were guarded about their feelings related to the activity/family imbalance and were encouraged to open up about these emotions when they felt safe to do so.

### 3. Encourage Ownership of Feelings and Behavior (3)

A. All family members were encouraged to take ownership of their own feelings and behavior.

B. All family members were encouraged to identify and express their feelings.

C. Each family member was directed to identify the behaviors they have that contribute to the conflicts over activity/family imbalance.

D. Family members were supported as they took ownership of their feelings and behavior.

E. Family members tended to blame others for their feelings and behavior and were provided with feedback about this pattern.

### 4. Define Problem Clearly (4)

A. The family was asked to clearly define the problem of activity/family imbalance.

B. The family was assisted in developing specific information about the problem of activity/family imbalance.

C. When family members fell into vague generalizations, they were redirected to be more specific.

D. Family members' descriptions of the problem areas of activity/family imbalance were redefined in behavioral terms.

### 5. Review Evolution of the Problem (5)

A. The family was assisted in identifying how the activity/family imbalance problems evolved.

B. It was noted that the activity/family imbalance appeared to start because of emotional concerns.

C. It was noted that the activity/family imbalance seemed to begin due to logistical considerations.

D. It was noted that the activity/family imbalance appeared to begin with financial problems.

E. It was noted that the activity/family imbalance started with family-of-origin pressures.

F. The family was uncertain about why the activity/family imbalance started and was provided with tentative examples of how these patterns begin.

### 6. Use Assessment Techniques (6)

A. Objective assessment techniques were used to help define the activity/family imbalance problem and its historical roots.

B. *The Family-of-Origin Scale* (Hovestadt et al.) was used to help define the activity/family imbalance problem and its historical roots.

C. *The Family-of-Origin Inventory* (Stewart) was used to help define the problem and its historical roots.

D. The results of the objective assessment techniques were reflected to the family.

### 7. Solicit Opinions about Energy Directed Outside the Family (7)

A. Each family member was asked to provide an opinion about why excessive energy is directed to activities outside of the family.

B. Each family member's opinion was validated and honored in regard to perceptions about why excessive energy is directed to activities outside of the family.

C. The family's opinions regarding the excessive energy that is directed to activities outside of the family were summarized and reflected to the family.

### 8. Identify Each Family Member's Priorities (8)

A. Each family member was asked to express personal priorities regarding how time is spent.

B. Each family member was requested to rank his/her activities as to how much time is spent with them.

C. Family members' priorities were reflected to them, including similarities and differences.

### 9. Explore Differences in Priorities (9)

A. Family members were asked to compare their list of priorities.

B. Family members were asked to discuss how their priorities differ from each other.

C. Family members were asked to identify the reasons why their priorities have become divergent.

D. It was reflected to the family members that they have come to a greater understanding of each other's priorities as a result of discussing the differences in their priorities and the etiologies of those differences.

E. Family members were provided with feedback about how and why their priorities are different.

### 10. Develop Family Priorities (10)

A. The family was assisted in developing a list of priorities endorsed by all members.

B. Family members were urged to compromise in order to develop a list of priorities suitable to all family members.

C. Family members were reinforced for developing a set of priorities that are acceptable to all family members.

D. Family members failed to develop a set of priorities for the family as a whole and were provided with redirection in this area.

### 11. Explore Barriers to Cohesive Priorities (11)

A. The family was questioned about issues that may interfere with the cohesive, rank-ordered list of priorities endorsed by all members.

B. Family members were assisted in identifying worries or fears that may affect the cohesiveness of the list of family priorities.

C. Family members were helped to identify logistical concerns that will affect the family's list of priorities.

D. Family members were helped to identify how avoidance of conflict affects family priorities.

E. Family members were unable to identify possible barriers to the cohesive set of priorities for the family and were provided with tentative examples of possible barriers.

## 12. Develop Healthy Intervention Technique (12)

A. Family members were assisted in finding healthy ways to address issues that interfered with the rank-ordered list of priorities.

B. Family members were encouraged to use assertive communication techniques.

C. Family members were taught about how to replace aggressive and passive-aggressive communication with healthy communication.

D. Family members were reinforced for their healthy pattern of communication; specific examples were highlighted.

E. Family members were redirected when they used unhealthy communication.

## 13. Explore Perceived Expectations (13)

A. Family members were asked to verbalize their perceptions of what other family members expect of them.

B. Perceived expectations were compared to family members' actual expectations of one another.

C. It was reflected to the family members that they often perceive others to expect much more of them than what is actually expected.

D. It was reflected to the family members that their perceptions of what others expect of them are quite accurate.

## 14. Suggest Helpful Communication Techniques (14)

A. Family members were taught helpful communication techniques to more effectively express their disagreement over the activity issue.

B. Family members were taught the use of "I" statements.

C. Family members were urged to stay calm and respectful in tone when discussing the activity issue.

D. Family members were reinforced for their use of calm, respectful, and direct communication techniques.

E. Family members have not used respectful communication techniques and were reminded to do so.

## 15. Objectively Assess Relationships (15)

A. An assessment inventory was used to objectively define the nature of the relationships within the family.

B. The Index of Family Relations (Hudson) was used to assess the nature of the relationships within the family.

C. The results of the objective assessment of the relationships within the family were presented to the family members.

### 16. Discuss Inventory Results (16)

A. The results of the assessment inventory were discussed with the family.

B. The assessment inventory results indicated that family members do not feel close to one another.

C. The assessment inventory results indicated that family members do feel close to one another.

D. The family was helped to process the results of the objective assessment of family relationships, and the implication of this information was reviewed.

### 17. Discuss Home-Based Duties (17)

A. Family members were asked to discuss how home-based duties have been assigned to individual family members.

B. Each family member was asked to provide feedback on what would be the fairest distribution of duties and responsibilities, and why duties should be distributed in this manner.

C. Family members were assisted in synthesizing how home-based duties and responsibilities should be assigned.

D. It was reflected to the family members that they have very divergent beliefs about how home-based duties should be assigned.

### 18. Delineate Underlying Beliefs (18)

A. The family was asked to identify their beliefs about the basis for delegation of household chores.

B. Family members were asked about how chores should be delegated in regard to income earners versus non-income earners.

C. Family members were asked their opinion about how chores should be delegated based on age levels.

D. The family was assisted in clearly defining the underlying beliefs that form the basis for the delegation of household chores.

### 19. Develop a Fair Method for Assigning Chores (19)

A. The family was assisted in developing a fair method for assigning chores for various family members.

B. It was suggested to the family to use a lottery drawing to randomize the assignment of chores.

C. Family members were assisted in fine-tuning the selected method of assigning chores.

### 20. Confront Laziness (20)

A. Family members who were attempting to shirk their household chore responsibilities were directly confronted.

B. An emphasis was placed on the need for all family members to take responsibility for their own behavior.

C. Working for the good of the family was prioritized above working for the good of one's self.

D. The family was assisted in respectfully confronting those who have shirked news based responsibilities.

E. Family members who have increased their level of responsibility within the family were reinforced.

F. Family members continued to tend to shirk their responsibilities and require other family members to take over for them; treatment focus was changed to address this issue.

## 21. Explore Jealousy/Envy (21)

A. Family members were asked about their level of jealousy and envy in regard to the activity/family imbalance.

B. Family members were supported as they expressed their feelings regarding the activity/family imbalance.

C. Family members were provided with examples of situations in which they might experience jealousy or envy.

D. Family members denied any pattern of jealousy or envy and were urged to be aware of this dynamic.

## 22. Focus on Time-Allocation Arguments (22)

A. The family was asked to identify the specific arguments that they have over time allocation.

B. The family was assisted in identifying how time-allocation disagreements have developed.

## 23. Facilitate Emotional Ventilation (23)

A. Family members were asked to express their feelings regarding the lack of time that they are able to have with each other.

B. Family members were asked to express their feelings regarding the great amount of time spent with a specific family member.

C. Family members were encouraged to openly express their feelings; when other family members attempted to suppress the healthy expression of emotion, they were redirected to allow this necessary ventilation.

D. Family members were very guarded about expressing their feelings and were urged to be more open as they felt safe to do so.

## 24. Probe for Avoidance (24)

A. Family members were questioned about whether they may be using external activities as a way to avoid contact or closeness with the family.

B. Family members were noted to be avoidant of closeness with other family members by remaining overly involved in external activities.

C. The avoidant family member was provided with support as the pattern of avoidance was processed and reviewed.

## 25. List Pros and Cons of Closeness (25)

A. Each family member was asked to list the pros and cons of being a close-knit family unit.

B. Family members were assisted in clarifying the positive aspects of being a close family unit.

C. Family members were assisted in clarifying the negative side of being a close family unit.

D. It was reflected to the family that all family members seem to be seeking a close-knit family unit.

E. It was reflected to the family members that they are not unified in their desire to obtain a more close-knit family unit.

### 26. Suggest Intimacy Builders (26)

A. Ways to increase family intimacy were suggested to the family.

B. The family was encouraged to engage in social and recreational activities together.

C. The family was encouraged to play *The UnGame* (Zakich) as a way to build mutual understanding.

D. The family was reinforced for using specific activities to build family intimacy.

E. The family has not used activities to build family intimacy and was redirected in this area.

### 27. Assess Family Mental Health History (27)

A. The often-absent family member's extended family was assessed for the presence of mental health concerns.

B. It was noted that there are mental health problems within the family-of-origin of the too-often-absent family member.

C. It was reflected that there is no history of mental health illness within the too-often-absent family member's history.

### 28. Assess for Mental Health Issues (28)

A. The family member who is often spending excessive time outside of the home was assessed for a mental health issue.

B. The too-often-absent family member was assessed for any obsessive or compulsive symptoms.

C. The too-often-absent family member was assessed for addiction concerns.

D. The too-often-absent family member was assessed for severe and persistent mental illness concerns, such as bipolar disorder.

E. Mental health problems were identified for the too-often-absent family member, and an appropriate referral was initiated.

F. Upon assessment, no significant mental health concerns were identified for the too-often-absent family member, and this was reflected to the family.

### 29. Suggest Further Evaluation (29)

A. The too-often-absent family member was referred to another mental health professional (e.g., clinical psychologist or psychiatrist) for an in-depth assessment of mental health needs.

B. The too-often-absent family member has followed through on the referral for further evaluation, and the results of this assessment were reviewed.

C. The too-often-absent family member has not followed up on a referral for a more in-depth evaluation, and the reasons for this resistance were processed and resolved.

**30. Discuss Treatment Options (30)**

A. The various treatment options available for the mentally ill family member were discussed.

B. The family was provided with specific information regarding treatment available for the mentally ill family member.

C. A specific referral was made for treatment for the mentally ill family member's needs.

D. The family has followed up on treatment for the mentally ill family member, and the benefits of this treatment were reviewed.

E. The family has not followed up on treatment for the mentally ill family member and was redirected to do so.

**31. Develop Support for Mentally Ill Family Member (31)**

A. Ways in which the family can support the mentally ill family member were identified.

B. Family members were asked to commit to helpful ways in which they can assist the mentally ill family member in recovery.

C. Family members were reinforced for the support provided to the mentally ill family member.

D. Family members have not been supportive of the mentally ill family member and were reminded about how helpful this can be.

**32. Use Buddy System (32)**

A. The buddy system was suggested as a way for family members to obtain peer support.

B. Family members were encouraged to use a peer support model in the family, attending treatment or support groups together, or holding each other accountable.

C. Family members were encouraged to seek out others outside of the family who can provide support regarding the family member's mental illness concerns.

D. Family members' use of peer support/buddy system concepts was reviewed.

E. The family has not used peer support or the buddy system to gain support in coping with the mental illness in the family and was reminded about these helpful resources.

**33. Confront Denial (33)**

A. The family was confronted for their denial of the mental illness concerns.

B. The mentally-ill family member was confronted for denying the mental illness concerns.

C. The nonmentally-ill family members were confronted about their pattern of denial of mental illness within the family.

**34. Uncover Enabling (34)**

A. Family members were taught about how enabling can exacerbate mental illness concerns.

B. Family members were confronted for their pattern of enabling the mentally ill family member.

C. Positive reinforcement was provided to the family members for decreasing their enabling behaviors.

# ADOLESCENT/PARENT CONFLICTS

## CLIENT PRESENTATION

### 1. Conflicts with Adolescent Child (1)*

A. The parents reported experiencing conflicts with their adolescent child.

B. The conflicts with the adolescent child have been so severe and persistent as to interfere with the family's overall functioning.

C. The parents and their adolescent child experience frequent arguments that affect the day-to-day functioning of the family.

D. As treatment has progressed, the conflicts between the parents and their adolescent child have decreased, and the family is functioning better.

### 2. Disagreements Regarding Parenting Strategies (2)

A. The parents described a lack of agreement regarding strategies for dealing with various types of negative adolescent behaviors.

B. One partner advocates for stricter parental controls, while the other partner endorses a more permissive approach.

C. The parents' variable pattern of disciplinary response is ineffective in managing their adolescent's behavior.

D. As communication has increased, the parents have gained an agreement regarding strategies for dealing with various types of negative adolescent behaviors.

### 3. Resentment about Conflict (3)

A. Family members complain about the time and attention that the adolescent-centered conflict takes from other family members and responsibilities around the home.

B. There is increased tension in the home due to the adolescent-centered conflict.

C. As the adolescent-centered conflict has been decreased, the resentment and tension in the home have also decreased.

### 4. Parents Feel Loss of Control (4)

A. The parents feel a loss of control over their adolescent.

B. The adolescent seems to be empowered by the parent's dilemma and loss of control.

C. The adolescent resists parental intervention.

D. As treatment has progressed, the parents feel more in control and the adolescent is more compliant to the parents' interventions.

*The numbers in parentheses correlate to the number of the Behavioral Definition statement in the companion chapter with the same title in *The Family Therapy Treatment Planner*, Second Ed. (Dattilio, Jongsma, and Davis) by John Wiley & Sons, 2010.

## 5. Substance Abuse (5)

A. The adolescent has acted out in the area of substance abuse.

B. The adolescent has dabbled in drugs and alcohol.

C. The adolescent has regularly been abusing drugs and alcohol.

D. As treatment has progressed, the adolescent has discontinued substance abuse.

## 6. Sexual Acting Out (5)

A. The adolescent has acted out in a sexual manner.

B. The adolescent is involved in age-inappropriate sexual activity.

C. The adolescent's sexual activity is against general family norms or expectations.

D. As treatment has progressed, the adolescent's sexual acting out has diminished.

## 7. Poor School Performance (5)

A. The adolescent has displayed poor school performance.

B. The adolescent's school performance has decreased significantly.

C. As treatment has progressed, the adolescent's school performance has improved.

## 8. Delinquency (5)

A. The adolescent has acted out with delinquent behavior.

B. The adolescent has experienced legal problems due to his/her delinquent behavior.

C. As treatment has progressed, the adolescent's delinquent behavior has ended.


# INTERVENTIONS IMPLEMENTED

## 1. Share Perceptions/Feelings about Adolescent's Behavior (1)*

A. Time was provided for each of the family members to share their perceptions about the adolescent's behavior and to discuss their feelings.

B. Family members were supported as they openly and honestly discussed their perceptions and feelings about the adolescent's behavior.

C. Family members appeared to be quite guarded about discussing the adolescent's behavior and were urged to be more open in this area.

## 2. Assess Stability of Acting-Out Behavior (2)

A. An assessment was made regarding the adolescent's acting-out behavior in regard to transience versus a more stable pattern.

B. The adolescent's acting-out behavior was judged to be transient.

C. The adolescent's acting-out behavior was judged to be a stable pattern of behavior.

## 3. Direct Parents to Share Philosophy and Expectations (3)

A. The parents were asked to share their philosophy on parenting.

B. The parents were asked about the expectations that they have for their child.

*The numbers in parentheses correlate to the number of the Therapeutic Intervention statement in the companion chapter with the same title in *The Family Therapy Treatment Planner*, Second Ed. (Dattilio, Jongsma, and Davis) by John Wiley & Sons, 2010.

C. Active listening skills were used as the parents described their philosophy on parenting and the expectations that they have for their child.

D. The parents were uncertain about how to describe their parenting style and expectations and were provided with assistance in clarifying their views.

**4. Administer Questionnaire/Inventories (4)**

A. Questionnaires and inventories were used to assess the specific areas of conflict and how the family may be contributing to the problems.

B. The Adolescent Coping Orientation for Problem Experiences (A-COPE) by McCubbin and Thompson was used to assess specific areas of conflict and how the family may be contributing to the problems.

C. The results of the adolescent conflict assessment were discussed with the family.

**5. Assess Belief Systems about Behavior (5)**

A. Family members' belief systems about appropriate versus inappropriate behavior were assessed.

B. Interviews and questionnaires were used to assess what behaviors the family members see as appropriate versus inappropriate.

C. The Family Beliefs Inventory (Roehling and Robin) was administered.

D. The Parent-Adolescent Questionnaire (Robin, Koepk, and Moye) was administered.

E. The results of the assessment regarding the family members' belief systems were shared with the family.

**6. Explore for Exacerbating Dynamics (6)**

A. The family interactional patterns were explored for dynamics that may be exacerbating the conflict between the adolescent and the parents.

B. Family members were assessed regarding underlying conflicts, family-of-origin issues, unrealistic expectations, marital problems, and other dynamics that may be exacerbating the conflicts between the adolescent and the parents.

C. The familial interactional patterns and dynamics that are exacerbating conflict between the adolescent and parents were pointed out to the family members.

D. Family members were supported as they accepted interpretations regarding dynamics that exacerbate the conflict between the adolescent and the parents.

E. The family was quite reluctant to accept the dynamics that may be exacerbating the conflict between the adolescent and the parents and were urged to watch for evidence that may support or disprove these patterns.

**7. Explore for Environmental Stressors (7)**

A. Family members were assessed regarding any environmental stressors that may be exacerbating the conflicts between the adolescent and the parents.

B. The environmental stressors that are exacerbating conflict between the adolescent and parents were pointed out to the family members.

C. Family members were supported as they accepted interpretations regarding environmental dynamics that exacerbate the conflict between the adolescent and parents.

D. The family was quite reluctant to accept that environmental dynamics may be exacerbating the conflict between the adolescent and the parents and were urged to watch for evidence that may support or disprove these interpretations.

## 8. Role-Play Problem (8)

A. The parent and adolescent were asked to role-play a problem to assess how the parents solve the problem.

B. A role-play was conducted with the parents to assess their ability to solve problems.

C. Feedback was provided to the parents regarding the strengths and weaknesses of their approach to problem solving with their adolescent.

D. Modify strengths and weaknesses

E. The parents were taught how the adolescent's strengths can be augmented.

F. The parents were taught ways in which the adolescent's weakness can be diminished.

## 9. Recommend Reading on Parenting Techniques (9)

A. The parents were encouraged to read books on parenting techniques.

B. The parents were directed to read *The Five Love Languages of Teenagers* (Chapman).

C. The parents were directed to read *Parents, Teens and Boundaries: How to Draw the Line* (Bluestein).

D. The parents were directed to read *Parents and Adolescents: Living Together* (Patterson and Forgatch).

E. The parents were directed to read *Raising an Emotionally Intelligent Child* (Gottman and Declaire).

F. The parents were directed to read *Parenting Teens with Love and Logic* (Cline and Fay).

G. The parents have read the assigned material on parenting and key points were processed.

H. The parents have not read the assigned material on parenting and were redirected to do so.

## 10. Assign Monitoring of Adolescent's Activities (10)

A. The parents were assigned to coordinate monitoring of their adolescent's activities, keeping track of where the adolescent is, who the adolescent is with, what the adolescent is doing, and when the adolescent will be home.

B. The parents have coordinated monitoring of their adolescent's activities on a regular basis.

C. The parents have not monitored their adolescent's activities and deficiencies in this area were reviewed.

## 11. Review Monitoring Efforts (11)

A. The parents were assigned to record their joint monitoring efforts.

B. The parents have regularly recorded joint monitoring efforts of the adolescent, and this record was reviewed.

C. The parents were asked to discuss the successes that they have had at monitoring the adolescent's whereabouts.

D. The partners were asked to identify times and situations where their monitoring of the adolescent's whereabouts needs to be improved.

E. The parents were unable to identify any ways in which their monitoring of the adolescent needs to be improved, and their thorough record of monitoring the adolescent was noted to be consistent with this assessment.

F. The parents were unable to identify any areas in which they needed to improve their monitoring of the adolescent, but were confronted with examples of where they have not been able to successfully monitor the adolescent, as indicated in the record that they have kept.

G. The parents have not regularly recorded their monitoring activities of the adolescent and were redirected to do so.

**12. Investigate Behavior Pattern to Increase (12)**

A. The parents were asked to identify one of their adolescent's positive behaviors that they would like to increase.

B. The parents were assigned to record the occurrence of their adolescent's positive behavior every day for a week.

C. The couple was asked to note the situations that precede the identified positive behavior (i.e., antecedents) and follow the behavior (i.e., consequences).

D. The parents have regularly identified the occurrence of the adolescent's positive behavior, antecedents, and consequences and were encouraged to continue this.

E. The parents have not regularly recorded the occurrence, antecedents, and consequences of the identified positive behavior pattern and were redirected to do so.

**13. Identify and Practice Rewards (13)**

A. The parents were directed to identify an appropriate reward (e.g., praise, use of the car, increase of allowance) to reinforce the adolescent's positive behavior.

B. The parents were provided with assistance in identifying an appropriate reward to reinforce the adolescent's positive behavior.

C. The parents were asked to rehearse praising a positive behavior pattern in the session.

D. The couple was provided with feedback about their practice of praising positive behavior.

E. The parents were directed to seek input and agreement from the adolescent for the rewards for positive behavior.

**14. Review Behavioral Contract Implementation (14)**

A. The implementation of the behavioral contract was reviewed.

B. The family was supported as they gave examples of successes and failures in the implementation of the behavioral contract.

C. The successes in the family's implementation of the behavioral contract were reinforced.

D. Redirection was provided for situations in which the family did not succeed with the use of the behavioral contract.

### 15. Increase Recreational Activity (15)

A. A list of topics and activities that could be initiated between the adolescent and parents was solicited.

B. The parents were assigned to increase their amount of focused, adolescent-centered activity.

C. The couple was provided with feedback regarding their changes in recreational activity with the adolescent experiencing difficulty.

D. The parents were refocused on to using recreational activities that are more adolescent-centered.

### 16. Identify and Practice Negative Consequences (16)

A. The parents were directed to identify an appropriate negative consequence (e.g., loss of privilege, five-minute work chore) to discourage the adolescent's negative behavior.

B. The parents were provided with assistance in identifying an appropriate consequence to discourage the adolescent's negative behavior.

C. The parents were asked to rehearse implementation of the negative consequence in the session.

D. The parents were provided with feedback about their use of negative consequences.

### 17. Contract Change in Own Behavior (17)

A. The parents' own modeling of the behavior that they would like to extinguish in their adolescent was reviewed with the parents.

B. The parents admitted their own modeling of the behaviors that they are trying to extinguish in the adolescent (e.g., yelling, being sarcastic, smoking) and were urged to change their own behavior.

C. The parents were reinforced for contracting to change their own behavior before trying to change the same behavior in the adolescent.

### 18. Teach Anger Control (18)

A. The parents were taught anger control techniques to better mediate conflict.

B. Role-play was used to help the parents internalize the anger control techniques.

C. Positive feedback was provided to the parents for their clear understanding of anger control techniques.

D. *The Anger Aggression Workbook* (Liptak, Leutenberg, and Sippela) was recommended to the parents.

E. *The Anger Tray* (Carter).

F. The parents do not seem to understand the use of the anger control techniques and were provided with remedial assistance in this area.

### 19. Role-Play Discussions for Adolescent's Negative Behavior (19)

A. The parents were directed to role-play discussions that they will have when the adolescent displays negative behavior.

B. The supportive parent was prompted to ask the other partner in a supportive, nonthreatening manner the specifics about the adolescent's misbehavior.

C. The supportive parent was prompted to ask, in a supportive, nonthreatening manner, how the other partner dealt with the adolescent's misbehavior.

D. The supportive parent was prompted to ask about ways to help the other partner in the future.

E. The benefits of providing nonthreatening support regarding dealing with adolescent misbehavior were reviewed.

F. Feedback was provided to the parents about the role-play of discussions that they would have when the adolescent displays negative behavior.

### 20. Contract about Not Interfering (20)

A. The partners were asked to contract to support each other's parenting by not interfering during the other's parent-adolescent interactions and by not interfering with the other's decisions (i.e., avoiding splitting up parents' unity).

B. The partners agreed to support each other by not interfering during parent-adolescent interactions or with each other's decisions and were urged to maintain this contract.

C. The partners were provided with examples of how not interfering with the other's parent-adolescent interactions can be supportive and helpful.

D. The couple was provided with examples of how interfering with parent-adolescent interactions and decisions can be disruptive and split the parents' unity.

### 21. Teach Communication and Problem-Solving Skills (21)

A. The parents were taught communication skills.

B. The parents were taught problem-solving skills.

C. The parents were urged to use their communication and problem-solving skills with the adolescent as well as with each other.

D. The parents were taught the following problem-solving sequence: problem definition, brainstorming of solutions, evaluation of alternatives, solution enactment, and enactment evaluation.

### 22. Help Identify Nonconstructive Criticism (22)

A. The parents were assisted in identifying when they are engaging in criticism of the other parent in a nonconstructive manner.

B. Gentle confrontation was used in sessions when parents were engaging in criticizing their partner in a nonconstructive manner.

### 23. Direct Parents to Meet in Private (23)

A. The parents were assisted in establishing the practice of meeting in private to discuss parenting decisions, coming to a mutual agreement, and then presenting it to the adolescent.

B. The parents were assisted in brainstorming how to implement the regular use of private meetings to discuss parenting decisions.

C. Positive feedback was given as the parents reported that they regularly use private meetings to discuss parenting issues.

D. The parents reported that they have not used private meetings to discuss parenting issues and were reminded about this helpful technique.

## 24. Identify Thoughts and Emotions during Problematic Situations (24)

A. The couple was asked to track their thoughts and emotional reactions during problematic situations with their adolescent.

B. The couple expressed their thoughts and emotional reactions during problematic situations with their adolescent, and these were reviewed and accepted.

C. The parents' cognitive messages were reviewed for distortions.

D. The parents have not tracked their thoughts and emotional reactions during problematic situations with their adolescent and were redirected to do so.

## 25. Identify/Challenge Unreasonable Assumptions (25)

A. The partners were assisted in identifying unreasonable assumptions about their adolescent through a request to provide evidence of the assumption and persuasively illuminating the illogical premise involved.

B. The partners were provided with a specific example of an unreasonable assumption (i.e., "If my daughter stays out late, she will become pregnant or a drug addict," can be replaced by "I can make my opinions and house rules known, but ultimately her behavior is up to her.").

C. The partners were provided with positive feedback for their identification and challenge of unreasonable assumptions.

D. The partners have not identified and challenged unreasonable assumptions and were provided with additional feedback in this area.

## 26. Assign Family Meeting (26)

A. The parents were assigned to initiate regularly scheduled family meetings for constructive problem solving and evaluation of earlier contracts.

B. The family was urged to make the family meetings time-limited and to establish ground rules to be observed.

C. The couple was directed to page 117 of *Parents and Adolescents: Living Together* (Patterson and Forgatch) for detailed information about running family meetings.

D. The couple has initiated regularly scheduled family meetings, and the benefits of these were reviewed.

E. The couple has struggled with how to conduct family meetings, and the issues in this area were problem solved.

F. The partners have not scheduled family meetings and were redirected to do so.

## 27. Set Respectful Expectations for Family Meetings (27)

A. The couple was urged to use and expect respectful communication during family meetings.

B. Examples of respectful communication were provided, including taking turns talking, treating each other with respect, and no lecturing.

C. The parents were directed to page 118 of *Parents and Adolescents: Living Together* (Patterson and Forgatch) to identify respectful expectations during family meetings.

D. Role-play techniques were used to help teach respectful communication during family meetings.

E. The family reported respectful communication during family meetings and the benefits of this were reviewed.

F. The partners reported disrespectful communication during the meetings, and this was problem solved.

### 28. Brainstorm Alternative Styles of Parenting (28)

A. The parents were asked to list alternative styles of parenting that they have learned as a result of their assigned material, observing other parents, or attending previous family therapy sessions.

B. The parents were assisted in listing all of the other styles of parenting of which they are aware.

### 29. Direct Experimentation with Alternative Parenting Styles (29)

A. The parents were asked to try alternative parenting styles in order to evaluate their effectiveness.

B. The parents were directed to provide each other with critical feedback about how they perceived the alternative parenting style to work.

C. The parents were assisted in critiquing and summarizing their assessments about the alternative parenting styles.

### 30. Direct Discussion about Reasonable Adolescent Behavior (30)

A. The parents and adolescent were assisted in listing what they each believe is reasonable and unreasonable adolescent behavior.

B. The parents and adolescent were assisted in maintaining their focus and not interrupting each other as they described what they believe to be reasonable and unreasonable behavior in adolescence.

C. It was noted that the parents and adolescent have very similar beliefs about what is appropriate adolescent behavior.

D. It was reflected that the parents and adolescent have very divergent beliefs about what is reasonable and unreasonable adolescent behavior.

### 31. Establish House Rules for Family Meetings (31)

A. The parents were supported for developing clear expectations regarding house rules for family meetings.

B. The family was asked to identify the consequences for rule violations and for compliance.

C. The family was directed to modify and negotiate rules within the family meeting, if necessary.

D. The parents have not established and maintained house rules for family meetings and this was problem solved.

### 32. Reinforce Follow-Through on Rules and Consequences (32)

A. The parents were reminded about the need for follow-through on praise for following rules, as well as consequences for not following rules.

B. The parents were reinforced for following through on praise when the rules were followed, as well as providing consequences for not following rules.

C. The parents were gently confronted when they described situations in which they did not follow through on praise or consequences.

## 33. Discuss Family Dinners (33)

A. The partners were assisted in discussing the feasibility of the family eating together, the frequency that eating together can occur, and the expectations for attendance by the adolescent.

B. The partners were supported for agreeing on the frequency and feasibility of family dinners and expectations for attendance by the adolescent.

C. *The Intentional Family* was recommended to the family.

D. The family has read and implemented techniques from the assigned reading and the benefits of such were reviewed.

E. The family has not read the assigned material and were redirected to do so.

## 34. Encourage Parents' Time Alone (34)

A. The parents were encouraged to have one or two nights per week out alone with each other, or with adult friends.

B. The parents were directed not to have children be the focus of conversation or the relationship when spending time out together.

C. The parents were reinforced for their use of time out together.

D. The parents have not spent time out together, and were redirected to use this helpful resource.

# ADOPTION ISSUES

## CLIENT PRESENTATION

### 1. Infertility (1)*

A. The parents are struggling with the issue of infertility.

B. The parents are considering contacting a child adoption agency.

C. The parents are considering making a private adoption arrangement.

D. The parents have decided to aggressively pursue medical solutions to infertility.

E. The parents have decided not to pursue medical solutions to infertility, but to accept the situation.

### 2. Disconnectedness with Adopted Child (2)

A. The parents describe a poor relationship with their adopted child, due to the lack of a biological link.

B. The parents struggle with a sense of failure and disconnectedness with the adopted child.

C. The parents have begun to feel more connected and successful with their adopted child.

D. The parents have discontinued focusing on the lack of a biological link as a significant factor in their level of success and connectedness with their adopted child.

### 3. Uncertainty about Disclosure of Adoption (3)

A. The parents struggle with whether they should inform their child about being adopted.

B. The parents have become overprotective and overindulgent due to worries about how disclosure of the adoption would affect their child.

C. The parents have decided to inform their child about being adopted, but struggle about when this should be done.

D. As treatment has progressed, the parents have been able to work through the issue of the disclosure of the adoption to their child.

E. The parents have resolved their concerns regarding informing their child about the adoption, are appropriately protective, and are no longer overindulgent.

### 4. Feeling Different (4)

A. The adopted child identified feeling different from the parents and siblings due to the adoption.

B. The adopted child often feels isolated from the rest of the family.

C. The adopted child described feeling removed or as a second-class citizen in comparison with the parents and siblings.

D. As the family has strengthened and the adopted child has felt more accepted, included, and connected with the parents and siblings.

---

*The numbers in parentheses correlate to the number of the Behavioral Definition statement in the companion chapter with the same title in *The Family Therapy Treatment Planner*, Second Ed. (Dattilio, Jongsma, and Davis) by John Wiley & Sons, 2010.

## 5. Abandonment Issues (4)

A. The adopted child has many questions about why the biological parents renounced their parental rights.

B. The adopted child often feels responsible for the biological parents' decision to release for adoption.

C. The adopted child fears abandonment by the adopted family and others.

D. As treatment has progressed, the adopted child has developed a better understanding of why biological parents might allow their child to be adopted and feels less abandoned.

E. The adopted child celebrates being selected by the adoptive parents, rather than grieving being released by the biological parents.

## 6. Parents' Lack of Connection (5)

A. The parents report that they feel less connected with their adopted child as opposed to their biological children.

B. The parents often focus on physical differences and other characteristics that are different for their adopted child as opposed to their biological children.

C. As treatment has progressed, the parents have felt more connected with their adopted child, commensurate with their connection to their biological children.

## 7. Tension between Biological and Adopted Children (6)

A. A feeling of tension exists between the biological and adopted children.

B. The adopted child often experiences badgering and ridicule from the siblings.

C. The extended family-of-origin members have directly or inadvertently discounted the adopted child.

D. As treatment has progressed, the sense of tension has decreased between the biological and adopted children.

## 8. Questions about Biological Parents (7)

A. The adopted child questions the whereabouts of the biological parents.

B. The adopted child has made comments about wanting to search for the biological parents.

C. The adoptive parents are threatened by the adopted child's quest for information about the biological parents.

D. Family members have become more at ease about the questions regarding the biological parents.

## 9. Idealization of Biological Parents (8)

A. The adopted child often fantasizes about who the biological parents might be.

B. The adopted child often idealizes the biological parents, dreaming that life with them would be perfect.

C. As treatment has progressed, the adopted child has become more realistic about what the biological parents might be like.

## 10. Adoptive Parents Threatened by Search for Biological Family (9)

A. The adopted child has made overtures to search for the biological parents and/or siblings.

B. The adoptive parents feel a sense of threat regarding the adopted child's overtures to seek the biological family.

C. The adoptive parents believe that the adopted child's overture to search for the biological family is a personal rejection, abandonment, and betrayal.

D. As treatment has progressed, the parents have become more at ease with the adopted child's overtures to search for the biological family.

## 11. Reconnection to Biological Parents (10)

A. The adopted child has successfully located the biological parents.

B. The adopted child has successfully contacted biological siblings or other family members.

C. The adopted child has begun to form a bond with the biological family.

D. Friction occurs between the adoptive family members due to the adopted child's successful location of biological family members.

E. As treatment has progressed, the adoptive family members have become more at ease with the adopted child's connection to the biological family.

## 12. Rejection from Biological Parents (11)

A. The adopted child has encountered a cold and/or rejecting reception from biological parents.

B. The adopted child has experienced negative emotions due to experiences with the biological parents.

C. The adoptive family has provided support and encouragement for the adopted child through the process of finding the biological family.

D. The adopted child has developed a greater sense of connection with the adoptive family due to the cold or rejecting reception from the biological family.

## 13. Tension between Adoptive and Biological Parents (12)

A. The adoptive parents have met with their adopted child's biological parents.

B. The adoptive and biological parents have experienced tension.

C. The adopted child experiences tension due to the difficulties that the adoptive parents and biological parents have in getting along together.

D. As treatment has progressed, the adoptive parents and biological parents have developed a better understanding, resulting in less tension for all parties involved.

## INTERVENTIONS IMPLEMENTED

### 1. Allow Ventilation of Emotions (1)*

A. The couple was allowed to ventilate about the hardship of enduring infertility.

B. The couple was encouraged to express their emotions regarding the hardship of infertility.

*The numbers in parentheses correlate to the number of the Therapeutic Intervention statement in the companion chapter with the same title in *The Family Therapy Treatment Planner*, Second Ed. (Dattilio, Jongsma, and Davis) by John Wiley & Sons, 2010.

C. The couple was supported as they expressed feelings of shame, anger, blame, uncertainty, and frustration regarding infertility.

## 2. Explore Stress and Strain of Infertility (2)

A. The ways in which infertility has stressed and strained the couple's relationship was explored.

B. The dynamics of how stress and strain may be precluding the couple's ability to conceive were reviewed.

C. The couple was recommended to read *Infertility and Identity* (Deveraux and Hammerman).

D. The couple has read assigned material on infertility and the key points were reviewed.

E. The couple has not read the assigned material on infertility and was reminded about this helpful resource.

## 3. Refer to an Infertility Support Group (3)

A. The couple was referred to an infertility support group.

B. The couple was directed to find and offered an infertility support group via the American Red Cross.

C. The couple was directed to find and offered an infertility support group via their obstetrician or gynecologist.

D. The couple has followed through on the referral to attend an infertility support group and the benefits were reviewed.

E. The couple had not followed through on the referral to attend an infertility support group and was redirected to do so.

## 4. Educate about Failure to Conceive (4)

A. The couple was educated on the biological factors involved in their failure to conceive.

B. The couple was referred to infertility experts to help identify and educate the couple on the biological factors that keep them from conceiving.

C. The couple was directed to read *The Long-Awaited Stork* (Glazer).

D. The couple was noted to report increased knowledge and support through reading, meeting with experts, and involvement in a support group.

## 5. Discuss the Big Picture of Parenting (5)

A. A discussion was held with the parents regarding the notion that giving birth to a child is only a small part of the picture of parenting.

B. It was emphasized that parenting is independent of birthing.

C. The parents were reassured that a strong bond can form irrespective of the biological connection.

D. The parents were supported and reinforced as they displayed a more complete understanding of the place of birthing within the full spectrum of parenting and bonding.

E. The parents continued to overemphasize the importance of the biological connection and were provided with additional feedback in this area.

### 6. Allow Adopted Child to Vent (6)

A. The adopted child was allowed to vent feelings regarding the adoption within the family therapy session.

B. The focus was on productively processing the adopted child's feelings.

C. Invalidating responses by the parents toward the adopted child were redirected.

D. The adopted child struggled to identify emotions and was provided with tentative examples in this area.

### 7. Teach Commonality of Adopted Children's Emotions (7)

A. Family members were taught about the common emotions that adopted children might experience.

B. Anger, isolation, acting-out behaviors, and depression were identified as common responses for an adopted child.

C. The family was helped to identify how the adopted child's specific emotions are consistent and common.

D. Family members were reinforced when they were able to support the adopted child's expression of emotion.

E. Family members were redirected when they tended to invalidate or overrule the adopted child's emotions.

### 8. Encourage Re-Bonding Family Activities (8)

A. The family was encouraged to participate in activities that will promote the re-bonding of the adopted child to the parents and siblings.

B. The parents were urged to engage in nurturing behaviors.

C. The family was encouraged to engage in playing games, family outings, or doing one-to-one activities with the adopted child.

D. Positive feedback was provided as the family has focused on developing a greater bond with the adopted child.

E. The family has not focused on activities to help promote the re-bonding of the adopted child and was redirected in this area.

### 9. Normalize Curiosity about Biological Parents (9)

A. The adoptive parents were advised about how common it is for adopted children to be curious about their biological parents.

B. The parents were reinforced for their acceptance of their adopted child's normal curiosity about the biological parents.

### 10. Reinforce Meaning about Inquiries about Biological Parents (10)

A. It was reinforced with the parents that the child's inquiries about the biological parents are not an overture of rejection.

B. It was emphasized that the adopted child's inquiries about the biological parents are a quest for meaning, existence, and origin.

C. The parents were reinforced for accepting their biological child's inquiries about the biological parents.

D. The parents continued to be very guarded and defensive about their adopted child's inquiries about the biological parents and see this as a rejection; they were provided with remedial feedback in this area.

## 11. Normalize Family Feelings (11)

A. Family members were reassured that their feelings are not unusual.

B. The fear of rejection and guilt issues experienced by the family were identified as very common.

C. It was reflected that the family was better equipped to accept their feelings.

## 12. Use Stress Inoculation and Coping Skill Techniques (12)

A. Stress inoculation techniques were used to prepare the family for any potential negative experiences.

B. Specific coping skills were identified as advanced preparation for any potential negative experiences when meeting the adopted child's biological family members.

C. Family members were assisted in brainstorming their potential reactions to meeting the biological parents.

D. A role play of the initial meeting with the biological parents was conducted.

E. It was reflected to the family members that they have developed a healthy level of preparation for the meeting with the biological parents.

## 13. Review Pros, Cons, and Timing of Telling the Child (13)

A. The parents were assisted in reviewing the pros and cons of telling the child about the adoption.

B. The parents identified specific arguments for telling the child about the adoption (e.g., not having the child learn from someone else accidentally), and these were reviewed.

C. The parents identified specific arguments regarding not telling the child about the adoption (e.g., risking the child's withdrawal from the adopted family to search for biological parents), and these were reviewed.

D. The parents were referred to *The Adoption Resource Book*, 4th ed. (Gilman).

E. The parents have read the assigned book on adoption, and key points were reviewed.

F. The parents have not read the assigned book on adoption and were redirected to do so.

## 14. Assist in Decision about Informing the Child (14)

A. The parents were assisted in deciding whether or not the child should be told about the adoption.

B. The parents were assisted in deciding when the child would be old enough to understand about the adoption.

C. The parents were assisted in identifying what it is they would like to tell the child about the adoption.

D. It was emphasized to the parents that the decision to tell or not to tell the child about the adoption is not carved in stone and can be reevaluated and changed at a later date.

### 15. Recommend Books on the Emotions of the Adopted Child (15)

A. The child and parents were encouraged to read books on how it feels to be adopted.

B. The child and parents were directed to read *How It Feels to Be Adopted* (Krementz).

C. Reading material on how it feels to be adopted was reviewed and processed.

D. The child and parents have not read material on how it feels to be adopted and were redirected to do so.

### 16. Process Guilt about Not Informing the Child about the Adoption (16)

A. The parents were supported as they expressed feelings of guilt about failing to inform the child of the adoption and the child's experience of anger and rage about not being told.

B. The parents were helped to express and process their guilt feelings over not having informed the child of the adoption.

C. The parents' feelings of guilt over not telling their child of the adoption were normalized.

D. The parents have been guarded about their feelings of guilt about failing to inform the child of the adoption and were provided with tentative examples of how many parents have felt in this situation.

### 17. Process Original Decision Not to Inform the Child about Adoption (17)

A. The reasons behind the parents' original decision not to inform the child about the adoption were reviewed and processed.

B. The child was assisted in gaining a better understanding about the parents' logic that supported their decision not to tell the child about the adoption.

C. Positive feedback was provided as the child showed a greater understanding of the reasons why the parents had decided not to tell about the adoption.

D. The parents were reinforced as they have accepted the responsibility for the child learning about the adoption from a source outside the immediate adoptive family.

### 18. Facilitate Meeting with Older Adopted Child (18)

A. The family was urged to coordinate a meeting between their child struggling with adoption issues and an older adopted child, outside of the immediate family, who has accepted being adopted.

B. The family was provided with resources of older adopted children who have accepted being adopted.

C. The contact between the child struggling with adoption issues and an older adopted child was processed.

D. The child struggling with adoption issues has not connected with an older adopted child and was redirected to do so.

### 19. Identify Factors Influencing Different Levels of Bonding (19)

A. It was reflected to the parents that they seem to have a different level of bonding with their adopted versus their biological children.

B. The parents were assisted in identifying possible factors that could contribute to differences in bonding with their adopted versus their biological children.

C. The parents were assisted in processing some of the factors that they believe contribute to differences in bonding with their adopted versus their biological children.

D. The parents were unable to identify possible factors that influence a different level of bonding with adopted versus biological children and were provided with tentative examples (e.g., lack of physical resemblance, absence of time in utero).

### 20. Resolve Parents' Differences in Feelings (20)

A. The parents were supported as they were able to identify differences in their feelings for their adopted versus their biological children.

B. The parents were assisted in developing a better understanding about how differences in feelings for their adopted versus their biological children will affect the family.

C. The parents were assisted in resolving any differences they may experience in their feelings between their adopted and their biological children.

D. Individual psychotherapy was recommended to assist the parents in resolving differences in their feelings between their adopted and their biological children.

### 21. Suggest Couples Meeting (21)

A. It was suggested to the parents that a separate couple's meeting take place to address the issue of a lack of bonding with their adopted child.

B. The therapist and the couple have met in a separate meeting to address the lack of bonding with their adopted child.

C. The parents declined any meeting to address the lack of bonding with their adopted child and were encouraged to consider this option at a later date.

### 22. Address Tension between Biological and Adopted Children (22)

A. The tension between the biological and adopted children was brought up for the entire family to work on.

B. Subtle parental messages or conflicts that support the tension between the adopted and biological children were sought.

C. The children were assisted in mediating their tensions or feuds regarding their differences.

D. The children were reinforced for decreasing tension between themselves.

### 23. Discuss How to Accept Biological Parents' Rejection (23)

A. The parents and children were directed to discuss how they could support one another in the event that the biological parents reject any inquiry from the adopted child.

B. Positive feedback was provided for a healthy plan of support by the parents and children should the biological parents reject inquiries about the adoption.

C. The parents and children were assisted in developing a more comprehensive plan for how to support each other in the event of rejection by the biological parents.

### 24. Promote Acceptance of Decision to Re-Bond with Biological Family (24)

A. The parents and family members were assisted in accepting the adopted child's decision to re-bond with the biological family-of-origin.

B. The parents and family were assisted in processing their emotions regarding the child's decision to re-bond with the biological family-of-origin.

C. It was reflected to the family that they are providing loving support to the adopted child by allowing time to re-bond with the biological parents.

# ALCOHOL ABUSE

## CLIENT PRESENTATION

### 1. Use of Alcohol (1)*

A. A family member frequently abuses alcohol.

B. Multiple family members frequently abuse alcohol.

C. The abuse of alcohol has been so severe as to meet a diagnosis of alcohol dependence.

D. The abuse of alcohol has led to interference with family members functioning at work and school, a pattern of ignoring the dangers to health, vocational or legal problems, and family/marital conflict.

E. As treatment has progressed, the family member's alcohol abuse has decreased or been eliminated.

### 2. Verbal/Physical Abuse (2)

A. The alcohol-abusing family member has engaged in periodic episodes of violence or threats of physical harm.

B. The alcohol-abusing family member has often been verbally abusive to others when intoxicated.

C. Serious conflict has arisen between family members due to the verbal or physical abuse associated with the abuse of alcohol.

D. The family member being abused has taken steps to leave the abusive relationship.

E. Family members who have been abused by the client with an alcohol abuse problem have taken steps to reduce that family member's access to them.

F. Physical violence or verbal abuse has been terminated.

### 3. Broken Promises (3)

A. The alcohol-abusing family member has made many promises to quit or significantly reduce the frequency and quantity of drinking.

B. The alcohol-abusing family member has consistently failed to keep promises to quit or significantly reduce the frequency and quantity of drinking.

C. The alcohol-abusing family member's failure to keep promises about the frequency and quantity of drinking has led to friction within the family relationships.

D. As the alcohol-abusing family member has attained sobriety, the family reports less friction within the family relationships and an increased sense of trust.

### 4. Threats/Violence (4)

A. Family members described periodic episodes of violence or threats of physical harm, especially when the abusive family member has been intoxicated.

*The numbers in parentheses correlate to the number of the Behavioral Definition statement in the companion chapter with the same title in *The Family Therapy Treatment Planner*, Second Ed. (Dattilio, Jongsma, and Davis) by John Wiley & Sons, 2010.

B. Family members described periodic episodes of violence or threats of physical harm, especially when the client has been intoxicated.

C. The abused family member has taken steps to leave the abusive relationship.

D. The physical violence and threats of physical harm have been terminated.

### 5. Communication Deterioration (5)

A. Family members described a pattern of deterioration within the relationship, including little or no communication and reduced levels of familial interaction.

B. Family members seem to simply coexist without any cohesiveness as a family.

C. Family members rarely attempt to meet each other's emotional needs.

D. Family members have taken steps to increase communication and spend quality time together.

E. Family members reported that relationships have been significantly reestablished, with better communication, shared recreation, and a sense of cohesiveness within the family.

### 6. Enabling (6)

A. Family members who do not abuse alcohol consistently enable the family member with an alcohol abuse problem by making excuses for the other's drinking, doing anything to please the drinking person, and denying the seriousness of the problem.

B. Enabling family members have been disparaged or abused repeatedly without offering assertive, constructive resistance.

C. Family members without alcohol abuse problems have acknowledged being enablers and are beginning to take steps to change this pattern.

D. As the family members without alcohol abuse problems have terminated the pattern of enabling, the dynamics within the relationships have changed.

### 7. Denial (7)

A. All family members engage in denial of the seriousness of the alcohol abuse and the effects that this has had on the family dynamics.

B. Family members tend to minimize the negative consequences of the alcohol abuse done by family members, in spite of direct feedback from others about the negative impact of the substance abuse.

C. Family members' denial is breaking down as the family is acknowledging that substance abuse has created problems in their lives.

D. Family members are now able to openly admit the severe negative consequences in which substance abuse has resulted.

### 8. Severe Financial Distress (8)

A. Family members described severe indebtedness and overdue bills that exceed their ability to meet the monthly payments, due to the pattern of alcohol abuse, squandering money, loss of jobs and/or low-wage employment.

B. Family members have developed a plan to reduce financial pressures through increasing income and making systematic payment, as well as the discontinuation of substance abuse.

C. Family members have begun to reduce the pressure of indebtedness and financial pressures and are making systematic payments.

D. Family members have significantly reduced their financial pressures.

### 9. Social Isolation (9)

A. The alcohol-abusing family member is away drinking too frequently and/or spending time with fellow alcohol abusers.

B. The alcohol-abusing family member has been emotionally unavailable to the sober family members.

C. Nondrinking family members have become passively withdrawn.

D. As treatment has progressed, the family member with an alcohol abuse problem has decreased relationships with fellow alcohol users and increased contact with the sober family members.

E. The alcohol-abusing family member continues to spend time only with alcohol abusers, but other family members have become more socially involved with others.

### 10. Children React to Lack of Structure and Boundaries (10)

A. A lack of structure and poor boundaries has occurred within the family due to the pattern of alcohol abuse.

B. Children in the family tend to act out due to the lack of structure and poor boundaries within the family.

C. As treatment has progressed, the parents have developed a healthier pattern of structure and boundaries for the family.

D. Children's acting out behavior has decreased due to the adequate structure and boundaries within the family.

### 11. Overlook Children's Alcohol Use (11)

A. Alcohol-abusing parents tend to overlook their children's alcohol use.

B. Parents inadvertently reinforce early substance-abusing patterns for their children.

C. As the alcohol-abusing parents have gained their sobriety, they have decreased their reinforcement and/or overlooking of the children's alcohol use or substance-abusing patterns.

### 12. Isolation from Extended Family and Friends (12)

A. The alcohol-abusing family member has been avoided or become unwelcomed by the extended family.

B. The alcohol-abusing family member's immediate family has been isolated by the extended family as a result of the alcohol-abusing family member's behavior.

C. The extended family has become more accepting of the nonabusing family members, but continue to isolate the alcohol–abusing family member.

D. As the alcohol-abusing family member has gained sobriety, the extended family has become more open and accepting.

## 13. Financial Problems (13)

A. Bills are often not paid due to the alcohol abuse within the family.

B. Family members have bounced checks due to the pattern of alcohol abuse.

C. Family members often fail to follow through on daily responsibilities due to their persistent use of alcohol.

D. As treatment has progressed, financial and daily responsibilities have become a greater priority for all family members.

## 14. Shame and Humiliation (14)

A. Family members have experienced shame and humiliation due to the alcohol abuser's behavior.

B. Family members often make excuses for the alcohol abuser's behavior.

C. Family members have become healthier in their understanding of the alcohol abuser's responsibility for irrational behavior.

D. Family members have discontinued making excuses for the alcohol abuser's behavior.

# INTERVENTIONS IMPLEMENTED

## 1. Gather Family Members' Perspectives on Negative Effects of Alcohol Abuse (1)*

A. Each family member was asked to provide their perspective on the negative effects that the alcohol abuse has had on family members and the general family dynamics.

B. Individual sessions were held with family members to provide them with a safe environment in which they can explore the negative effects that the alcohol abuse has had on family members and the general family dynamics.

C. Family members were asked to focus on the destructive effects of the alcohol abuse on the abuser, as well as the impact that denial has played in this process.

D. The effects of intimidation and denial were decreased by exploring the negative effects of alcohol abuse on the family, the abuser, and the relationships.

E. Family members tended to minimize the effects of alcohol abuse on the relationships within the family and were urged to focus on this in a more realistic manner.

F. Family members were realistic about the effects of alcohol abuse on the relationships within the family and were supported for their honesty.

## 2. Administer Inventory/Rating Scales (2)

A. Inventories were used to evaluate the family members' attitudes toward alcohol.

B. Rating scales were used to identify the effects of alcohol abuse on the quality of the alcohol abuser's functioning and the family's life.

C. Family members were administered the *Alcohol Beliefs Scale* (Connors and Maisto).

D. The results of the inventories were shared with the family members.

---

*The numbers in parentheses correlate to the number of the Therapeutic Intervention statement in the companion chapter with the same title in *The Family Therapy Treatment Planner*, Second Ed. (Dattilio, Jongsma, and Davis) by John Wiley & Sons, 2010.

### 3. Coordinate Controlled Drinking Contract (3)

A. The alcohol-abusing family member was directed to sign a controlled drinking contract that stipulates the frequency of drinking allowed per week (e.g., twice) and the maximum number of drinks per instance (e.g., three in two or more hours).

B. The Sobell Method for controlled drinking (as described in *Behavior Treatment of Alcohol Problems*) was used.

C. Positive feedback was provided to the alcohol-abusing partner for signing the controlled drinking contract.

D. The alcohol-abusing partner has followed the controlled drinking contract, and the positive effects of this pattern were reviewed with the family members.

E. The alcohol-abusing client has broken the controlled drinking contract and was directed to sign a nondrinking contract.

F. The alcohol-abusing partner has signed the nondrinking contract and the implications of this were processed.

### 4. Record Alcohol Use (4)

A. The alcohol-abusing family member was asked to track the frequency and quantity of alcohol use on a daily basis.

B. Family members were asked to record the alcohol abuser's frequency and quantity of alcohol use on a daily basis.

C. The daily record of alcohol use was reviewed, and confirms that the alcohol abuser is able to consistently control the intake of alcohol.

D. The daily record of the frequency and quantity of alcohol use was noted to confirm an inability of the alcohol abuser to control alcohol intake.

E. The client was recommended to read *How to Cut Down on Your Drinking* (National Institute on Alcohol Abuse and Alcoholism).

### 5. Assign Controlled Drinking Information (5)

A. The alcohol-abusing partner was assigned to read information on alcoholism.

B. The alcohol-abusing partner was assigned to read the National Institute on Alcohol Abuse and Alcoholism pamphlet: *Alcoholism: Getting the Facts.*

C. The alcohol-abusing family member was assigned to read *Controlling Your Drinking* (Miller and Munoz).

D. *Overcoming Alcohol Use Problems* (Epstein and McGrady) was assigned to the alcohol abuser and family members.

E. The alcohol-abusing partner has read the information on alcohol abuse, and key points were processed.

F. The alcohol-abusing partner has not read the information on alcohol abuse and was redirected to do so.

### 6. Facilitate Discussion about Written Information (6)

A. Family members have read the assigned material on alcoholism and a discussion about the information that they have read was facilitated.

B. Family members have not read the information on alcohol abuse and were redirected to do so.

C. The different perceptions of family members were highlighted.

D. Family members were assisted in exploring how different perceptions of the alcohol abuse severity and impact contribute to the overall problem of substance abuse.

### 7. Develop Attendance Contract (7)

A. A contract was developed regarding all family members attending all sessions unless ill, and that they will be completely free of mood-altering substances (not including legitimate prescription medications).

B. Family members were directed to sign the joint family contract agreeing to attend sessions free of substances.

C. Family members were supported for their agreement to attend all sessions sober.

D. Family members were reinforced for their regular attendance at sessions free of mood-altering substances.

### 8. Develop Substance-Free Session Contract (8)

A. A contract was presented to all family member that they will be free of mood-altering substances at all sessions (including prescribes medications).

B. Family members were reinforced for signing and adhering to the non-use contract.

C. Family members have not complied with the contract to be substance-free during sessions, and the focus of treatment turned to this issue.

### 9. Assign Abstinence Contract (9)

A. The alcohol abuser has broken the controlled drinking contract, and has been asked to sign an agreement regarding abstaining from all alcohol use.

B. The alcohol abuser was supported for signing an agreement to abstain from all alcohol use.

C. The alcohol-abusing family member was asked to sign an agreement to attend a support group (e.g., AA) or group psychotherapy for substance abusers.

D. The alcohol-abusing family member has discontinued alcohol use and is regularly attending a support group; positive feedback was provided for this progress.

### 10. Refer to Physician (10)

A. As drinking has continued despite psychological interventions, the alcohol-abusing partner was referred to a physician for Antabuse treatment.

B. The alcohol-abusing partner was referred for an evaluation for psychotropic medication.

C. The alcohol-abusing partner has followed-up on referrals for additional treatment, and the benefits of this treatment were reviewed.

D. The alcohol-abusing partner has not followed up on additional treatment and was redirected to do so.

### 11. Use Nonviolence Contract (11)

A. All family members were directed to sign a nonviolence contract that prohibits the use of physically assaultive contact, weapons, or threats of violence.

B. Family members were provided with positive feedback when they signed a nonviolence contract.

## 12. Develop Safety Plan while Treating Anger (12)

A. The alcohol-abusing family member was provided with individual treatment for anger issues prior to conjoint treatment.

B. Supportive counseling was provided to the sober family members to address anxiety and self-blame related to the domestic violence.

C. A safety plan was developed to provide a means of escape from family violence.

## 13. Teach Anger-Management Techniques (13)

A. The alcohol-abusing family member was taught anger-management techniques (e.g., time-out, thought stopping, positive thought substitution, counting down serial sevens from 100).

B. The alcohol-abusing family member was reinforced for regular use of anger-management techniques, which has led to decreased anger and decreased urges to abuse substances.

C. The alcohol-abusing family member has not implemented the anger management techniques, continues to feel quite stressed in anxiety-producing situations, and was redirected to use these techniques.

## 14. Teach Time-Out Steps (14)

A. Family members were taught the five steps to time-out (self-monitoring, signaling, acknowledgment, separation, and return).

B. Family members were reinforced for their understanding of the time-out strategies.

C. Family members were reinforced for their use of time-out strategies.

D. Time-out strategies have not been used by family members and they were redirected to do so.

## 15. Teach Assertiveness (15)

A. Family members were referred to an assertiveness training group that will teach and facilitate assertiveness skills.

B. Role-playing, modeling, and behavioral rehearsal were used to train family members in assertiveness skills.

C. Family members were reinforced for demonstrating a clearer understanding of the difference between assertiveness, passivity, and aggression.

D. Family members were referred to appropriate reading material (e.g., *Your Perfect Right* by Alberti and Emmons) to learn about assertiveness.

## 16. Discuss Necessity of Family, Couples, or Individual Treatment (16)

A. The appropriateness of providing individual, family, or couples treatment was discussed.

B. As the level of violence is severe and has caused injury and/or significant fear, individual treatment was recommended.

C. As severe violence and intimidation were not occurring, family or couples treatment was recommended.

D. The acting-out family member was referred to another provider for individual or group treatment of explosive disorder.

### 17. Probe Benefits Sought through Alcohol Abuse (17)

A. The alcohol-abusing partner was probed regarding the benefits being sought in becoming intoxicated (e.g., reduced social anxiety, altered mood, lessened family demands).

B. The benefits that the alcohol-abusing partner is seeking in becoming intoxicated were identified and reviewed.

C. The alcohol-abusing partner was assisted in identifying healthier ways to get satisfaction of needs.

D. The alcohol-abusing partner failed to identify the reasons for abusing substances, has not been able to replace the substance abuse with healthier alternatives, and was provided with confrontation and suggestions.

### 18. Trace Alcohol Abuser's History (18)

A. The alcohol abuser's history was traced to help identify how this behavior has been reinforced at home and in the community.

B. Positive feedback was provided as the alcohol abuser and other family members were able to identify how this behavior has been reinforced at home and in the community.

C. Family members had a difficult time identifying how the alcohol abuser's behavior has been reinforced at home and in the community and were provided with tentative examples in this area.

### 19. Emphasize Constructive Alternatives (19)

A. The alcohol abuser was helped to develop techniques that will produce the results sought in becoming intoxicated without using mood-altering substances.

B. The alcohol abuser was assisted in verbalizing increased understanding of how to get good things out of life without using mood-altering substances.

C. The alcohol abuser rejected the concept of using constructive behavioral alternatives to produce the results sought in becoming intoxicated and was redirected in this area.

D. The alcohol abuser was provided with tentative examples about how to obtain the benefits of drinking without the bad side effects (e.g., meditation, relaxation, social skills, assertiveness).

### 20. Teach Anxiety and Stress Reduction Techniques (20)

A. The alcohol abuser was taught the use of stress-reduction techniques (e.g., deep muscle relaxation, aerobic exercise, verbalization of concerns, positive guided imagery, recreational diversions, taking a hot bath).

B. The alcohol abuser was assigned to relax twice a day for 10 to 20 minutes.

C. The alcohol abuser reported regular use of relaxation techniques, which has led to decreased anxiety and decreased urges to abuse substances; this progress was reinforced.

D. The alcohol abuser has not implemented relaxation techniques and continues to feel quite stressed in anxiety-producing situations; these techniques were encouraged.

### 21. Model/Role Play Assertiveness and Social Skills (21)

A. Modeling techniques were used to teach family members assertiveness and social skill techniques.

B. Role-play techniques were used to teach assertiveness and social skills techniques.

C. The alcohol abuser was assisted in weighing the pros and cons of using assertiveness and social skills techniques.

D. Positive feedback was provided as the alcohol abuser has increased the use of assertiveness and social skills techniques.

E. Remedial feedback was provided to the family members who are not using assertiveness and social skill techniques.

### 22. Measure Progress in Assertiveness and Social Skills Training (22)

A. Measurement scales were used to assess any progress made as a result of the assertiveness and social skills training.

B. The alcohol abuser has been administered the *Assertiveness Self-Report Inventory* (Herzberger, Chan, and Katz).

C. The alcohol abuser was administered the *Social Problem-Solving Inventory* (D'Zurilla and Nezul).

D. Feedback was provided to the alcohol abuser on the progress made through the use of social skills and assertiveness training.

### 23. Assign Caring Days (23)

A. Each family member was assigned to do small favors that would be appreciated by the other family members (e.g., help with or do a chore, run an errand, purchase a small present).

B. The alcohol-abusing family member has completed small favors for the other family members, and the benefits of this were reviewed.

C. Family members without a drinking problem have completed small favors for the family member with the drinking problem, and the benefits of this were reviewed.

D. Family members have not completed small favors for each other and were redirected to do so.

E. Reasons for the family members not completing small favors for each other were identified and problem-solved.

### 24. Encourage Non-Alcohol Social Activity (24)

A. Family members were encouraged to plan social activities with other families in which alcohol will not be consumed.

B. Church, hobby, recreational groups, or work associates were identified as possible opportunities for social outreach.

C. Family members were provided with positive feedback as they have participated in social activities where alcohol was not consumed.

D. Family members have not developed social contacts where alcohol is not consumed, and were redirected to do so.

### 25.  Schedule a Recreational Activity (25)

A.  Family members were encouraged to engage in shared recreational activities (e.g., a family outing, visiting friends together).

B.  Family members were requested to stipulate who is responsible for what steps in implementing the recreational activities.

C.  Family members were assisted in brainstorming a list of recreational activities that might be enjoyed by the family, through the use of the *Inventory of Rewarding Activities* (Birchler).

D.  Family members have increased their involvement in shared recreational activities, and the benefits of this were reviewed within the session.

E.  Family members have not increased involvement in shared recreational activities and were redirected to do so.

### 26.  Review Outcome of Social/Recreational Assignment (26)

A.  Family members were assigned to choose one social or recreational activity.

B.  Family members were helped to assess how they fared on the outcome of the chosen social or recreational activity.

C.  Family members were directed to keep notes on what they enjoy about the activity and what they do not enjoy about the activity.

D.  The enjoyable and non-enjoyable aspects of the activity were assessed within the session.

### 27.  Identify Communication Interfering Behavior (27)

A.  Family members were requested to describe the ways that each interferes with the communication process in the relationship (e.g., raises voice, walks away, refuses to respond, changes subject, calls family member names, uses profanity, becomes threatening).

B.  Each family member was encouraged to describe their own ways of interfering with the communication process in the family.

C.  Family members' interference in the relationship communication process was focused on, identified, and reviewed.

D.  Family members were provided with positive feedback for their insight into the ways that each interferes with the communication process in the family relationships.

E.  Family members tended to minimize the ways in which each interferes with the communication process and were provided with feedback about this defensive reaction.

### 28.  Explore Etiology of Communication Styles (28)

A.  Family members were assisted in self-exploration about their own communication style and how they have learned such styles from their family-of-origin experiences.

B.  Family members were provided with positive feedback as they displayed insight into how they may have learned their communication styles from their family-of-origin experiences.

C.  Family members displayed a poor understanding of how they may have learned their communication styles from their family of origin and were provided with additional feedback.

### 29. Review Rules for Communication (29)

A. Family members were assisted in developing rules for communication, both for the speaker and for the listener.

B. Rules for communication were reviewed, including techniques such as taking turns talking, paraphrasing, reflecting, respect, and not lecturing.

C. Family members were referred to the book *Fighting for Your Marriage* (Markham, Stanley, and Blumberg).

D. Positive feedback was provided to family members for their identification and implementation of rules for communication.

E. Remedial feedback was provided to the family members to assist them in developing healthy rules for communication.

### 30. Work Out Conflict in Session (30)

A. Family members were requested to choose a relationship conflict topic and discuss it in the session.

B. Family members were provided with feedback about their listening and communication styles to improve healthy, accurate, effective communication.

C. Family members were given positive feedback as they displayed a healthy pattern of conflict-resolution skills.

D. A variety of communication suggestions were made to help the family members discuss conflict topics.

### 31. Reinforce Positive Communication (31)

A. Positive communication experiences between the family members that occurred since the last session were reviewed.

B. Positive feedback was provided for healthy communication experiences between the family members that occurred since the last session.

C. Family members were unable to identify positive communication experiences, and additional effective communication skills were reviewed.

### 32. Teach the Five Steps of Conflict Resolution (32)

A. Family members were taught how to define the interpersonal problem.

B. Family members were taught to generate many solutions for each problem, even if some are not practical, allowing for creativity.

C. Family members were assisted in how to evaluate the pros and cons of the proposed solutions.

D. Family members were taught how to obtain agreement on a proposed solution.

E. Family members were directed to implement the solution identified.

F. Positive feedback was provided to family members for their use of problem-solving techniques.

G. Family members were provided with remedial feedback as they have struggled to correctly implement the problem-solving techniques.

### 33. Suggest Family Meetings (33)

A. Family members were requested to choose a relationship conflict topic and problem solve it in the session via a family meeting.

B. Family members were provided with feedback about their problem-solving style in order to improve healthy, accurate, effective communication.

C. Family members were given positive feedback as they displayed a healthy pattern of conflict resolution.

D. A variety of communication suggestions were made to help the family members discuss conflict topics.

E. The family was assigned the homework of using the problem-solving techniques.

F. Family members have completed the homework using the problem-solving techniques, and this was reviewed within the session.

G. Family members have not participated in the assigned homework and were redirected to do so.

### 34. Review Problem-Solving Techniques (34)

A. Family members were asked to use the problem-solving techniques in real-life situations between the sessions.

B. A review and critique was provided regarding the family members' reported instances of implementing problem-solving techniques at home since the last session.

C. Positive feedback was provided for the effective use of problem-solving techniques at home.

D. Family members have failed to consistently use the problem-solving techniques and were redirected to do so.

### 35. Encourage Making Amends (35)

A. The alcohol abuser was encouraged to make amends by apologizing to each family member for specific behaviors that have caused distress.

B. The alcohol abuser has made amends and this was processed with that family member.

C. Family members without alcohol abuse problems were requested to provide feedback about the manner in which the alcohol-abusing family member has made amends.

D. The alcohol abuser has not yet made amends to family members and was redirected to do so.

### 36. Obtain Closure to Ritual of Apology (36)

A. Family members were helped to process the ritual of apology to closure.

B. Positive feedback was provided when family members were able to help bring closure to the ritual of apology.

C. It was emphasized that bringing closure to the ritual of apology may help to minimize barriers to the alcohol abuser's future progress.

D. Family members were noted to be blocking closure of the ritual of apology and were redirected in this area.

### 37. Identify Relapse Triggers (37)

A. Family members were assisted in identifying situations that trigger relapses of drinking episodes.

B. Family members identified a variety of triggers for drinking relapses, and these were processed.

C. Family members failed to identify many situations that trigger relapses of drinking episodes and were provided with tentative examples in this area.

### 38. Develop Coping Strategy Index Cards (38)

A. The family was directed to develop index cards with alternative strategies for coping with the stimuli that trigger relapse.

B. Family members have developed a variety of strategies for coping with alcohol abuse in the face of stimuli that trigger relapse, and were provided with support and encouragement for this progress.

C. Family members were provided with common alternative coping strategies for the stimuli that trigger relapse (e.g., connecting with sponsors at AA support groups, using stress inoculation techniques).

D. Family members have not developed index cards with alternative strategies for coping with relapse triggers and were redirected to do so.

### 39. Confront Enabling (39)

A. Family members who were not alcohol abusers were confronted regarding behaviors that support the continuation of abusive drinking by other family members (e.g., wanting to cover up for the drinker's irresponsibility; minimizing the seriousness of the drinking problem; taking on most of the family responsibilities; tolerating the verbal, emotional, and/ or physical abuse).

B. Family members who were not alcohol abusers were provided with positive feedback regarding identifying the pattern of enabling.

C. Family members who were not alcohol abusers failed to identify the pattern of enabling and were provided with additional feedback in this area.

### 40. Practice Refusing to Enable (40)

A. Modeling and role-playing were used to help family members practice examples of how a non-alcohol-abusing family member can refuse to accept responsibility for the behavior and/or feelings of the alcohol-abusing family member.

B. Encouragement was provided as the non-alcohol-abusing family members displayed an understanding of how to refuse to accept responsibility for the behavior and/or feelings of other family members.

C. Family members who were not alcohol abusers were reinforced for regularly refusing to accept responsibility for the behavior and/or feelings of other family members within the home setting.

D. Family members who were not alcohol abusers have continued to enable the other family members and were provided with redirection in this area.

### 41. Review Successful Avoidance of Enabling (41)

A. Family members were asked to identify situations in which they have avoided enabling behaviors.

B. The pattern of family enabling behaviors was reviewed and processed.

C. Positive feedback was provided for family members who have avoided enabling behaviors.

D. Family members identified continued enabling and were provided with redirection in this area.

### 42. Brainstorm Constructive Responses to Enabling Triggers (42)

A. Family members were assisted in identifying the triggers that have previously precipitated enabling behaviors.

B. Family members were assisted in brainstorming how to more constructively respond to situations that previously precipitated enabling behaviors.

C. Positive feedback was provided, as the family members were able to identify a variety of situations that have previously precipitated enabling behaviors, as well as more constructive responses to the situations.

D. Family members were provided with examples of more constructive responses to situations that previously precipitated enabling behaviors (i.e., not making excuses for broken promises or unfulfilled responsibilities, telling the truth regarding intoxication even if it brings painful consequences, reporting physical abuse to the police).

### 43. Explore Individual Family Members' Stressor (43)

A. Family members were assisted in identifying stressors facing each member of the family.

B. Each family member was encouraged to provide complete information about the stressors being faced.

C. Support and encouragement were provided as each family member discussed stressors.

D. Family members were guarded about stressors each may face, and were provided with additional encouragement in this area.

### 44. Develop Strategies for Identified Stressors (44)

A. Family members were assisted in identifying strategies for dealing with each of the identified stressors.

B. Family members were assisted in ways that they can restructure their finances.

C. Family members were provided feedback about job search techniques.

D. Family members were assisted in how to make apologies to friends, neighbors, or extended family members.

E. Family members were assisted in how to obtain tutoring assistance.

F. Family members were provided with positive feedback for the strategies that they have developed for each individual stressor.

G. Family members have not developed comprehensive strategies for dealing with each of the identified stressors and were redirected to elaborate on these concerns.

### 45. Investigate Factors That Facilitate Alcohol Abuse (45)

A. The emotional factors that tend to facilitate alcohol abuse were investigated.

B. The social factors that tend to facilitate alcohol abuse were investigated.

C. The genetic factors that facilitate alcohol abuse were investigated.

D. The need for abstinence was reinforced.

## 46. Teach about Roles Adopted by Children of Alcoholic Parents (46)

A. Family members were taught about the roles usually adopted by children of alcoholic parents.

B. Family members were taught about different roles, including the family hero, the scapegoat, the lost child, and the mascot.

C. Relevant information from *Families under the Influence* (Elkin) and *Bradshaw on the Family* (Bradshaw) was reviewed with family members.

D. Each child was asked to identify the role or roles that have been adopted.

E. Family members were provided with feedback about the roles that have been adopted by them.

## 47. Encourage Giving Up Unhealthy Roles (47)

A. The children were encouraged to give up their unhealthy role assumptions.

B. The children were encouraged to express their needs, feelings, and desires directly and assertively.

C. Positive feedback was provided as the children have avoided using the roles common to children of an alcoholic parent.

D. The children were gently redirected when they used unhealthy role assumptions.

## 48. Brainstorm Alternative Roles (48)

A. The children were assisted in brainstorming how they can develop alternative behaviors rather than unhealthy role assumptions.

B. Positive feedback was provided as the children identified healthy behaviors instead of unhealthy role assumptions.

C. The children have not developed alternative behaviors for the unhealthy role assumptions and were provided with additional feedback in this area.

# ANGER MANAGEMENT

## CLIENT PRESENTATION

### 1. Explosive, Destructive Outbursts (1)*

A. Family members described a family pattern of loss of temper in which family members have destroyed property in fits of rage.

B. Family members identified a family member with an anger control problem, including breaking objects or destroying property during fits of rage.

C. The family member's pattern of anger outbursts dates back to childhood, involving verbal outbursts as well as property destruction.

D. The family member displaying anger problems often makes threats to other family members.

E. The family reports no recent incidents of explosive outbursts that have resulted in any destruction of property or intimidation.

### 2. Violating Space/Silent Treatment (1)

A. Family members identified a pattern of violating each other's individual space.

B. Family members often refuse to speak to each other.

C. Family members identified that one family member uses intimidation tactics, such as invading others individual space or refusing to speak to other family members as a way to express anger.

D. The family reports no recent incidents of anger as displayed in refusing to speak to other family members or violating each other's individual space.

### 3. Anger as Intimidation (2)

A. The family reported a history of threats or intimidation, as a way to force other family members into relinquishing their rights.

B. Family members became verbally threatening during today's family therapy session.

C. Family members report a mild reduction in the frequency of anger as a way to intimidate and coerce the relinquishing of rights.

D. The family has recently displayed good anger control and reports that threats and intimidation do not occur.

### 4. Hostile, Aggressive Behavior (3)

A. Family members reported a pattern of hostile, aggressive behavior that tends to alienate neighbors, extended family members, and school personnel, as well as nuclear family members.

B. Family members appeared angry, hostile, and irritable during today's family therapy session.

*The numbers in parentheses correlate to the number of the Behavioral Definition statement in the companion chapter with the same title in *The Family Therapy Treatment Planner*, Second Ed. (Dattilio, Jongsma, and Davis) by John Wiley & Sons, 2010.

C. Family members report that others tend to avoid specific family members due to their hostile and aggressive behavior.

D. Family members report a sense of isolation, due to neighbors, extended family members, and others feeling intimidated by the family.

E. The family has started to show greater control of hostile and aggressive behavior and does not react as quickly or intensely when angry or frustrated.

F. Family members reported a significant reduction in the frequency and intensity of anger outbursts.

## 5. Demeaning, Disrespectful Anger Expression (4)

A. Family members acknowledged a pattern of verbal abuse of others that is demeaning, threatening, or disrespectful.

B. Family members identified that a family member has a pattern of expressing anger in a demeaning, threatening, or disrespectful manner.

C. Significant others within the family have indicated that they have been hurt by family members' frequent verbal abuse.

D. The angry family member has shown little empathy toward others for the pain caused by verbal abuse.

E. The angry family member reports a greater awareness of the effects of demeaning, threatening, or disrespectful expressions and has decreased the pattern of these types of anger outbursts.

F. There have been no recent incidences of verbal abuse by family members.

## 6. Disagreement about Threat (5)

A. Family members disagree about the level of threat inherent in the family member's outburst.

B. Some family members view other family members as overreacting to the anger outbursts.

C. Some family members are frustrated by the limited negative reaction made by other family members to the anger outbursts.

D. The family has become more unified in their criticism of the anger outbursts and the inherent level of threat.

## INTERVENTIONS IMPLEMENTED

### 1. Teach Anger as a Natural Signal (1)*

A. Family members were taught that the purpose of anger control is not to eliminate anger because anger is an important, natural signal that something important is at stake.

B. Examples were provided to help family members understand the use of anger as a natural signal.

C. Family members were reinforced for displaying an increased understanding of the appropriate place for anger.

*The numbers in parentheses correlate to the number of the Therapeutic Intervention statement in the companion chapter with the same title in *The Family Therapy Treatment Planner*, Second Ed. (Dattilio, Jongsma, and Davis) by John Wiley & Sons, 2010.

D. Additional information was provided as family members failed to grasp the appropriate place for anger as a natural signal.

## 2. Review Positive Uses of Anger (2)

A. Today's session focused on the positive uses of anger.

B. Anger as a natural reaction to a perceived threat was highlighted.

C. The use of anger as a way to communicate that some personal violation has occurred was identified as a positive use.

D. The positive uses of anger identified by family members were processed and reinforced.

E. Family members were provided with additional ideas regarding the positive use of anger.

## 3. Educate about Expressing Feelings to Obtain a Positive Outcome (3)

A. The family was educated on the need for anger management as a method of more aptly expressing one's feelings to obtain a positive outcome.

B The family was directed to read portions of *The Anger and Aggression Workbook* (Liptak, Leutenberg, and Sippola).

C. The family was directed to read *The Anger Trap* (Carter).

D. The family was assigned to read *Don't Sweat the Small Stuff with Your Family* (Carlson).

E. The family was reinforced as they displayed understanding of the need for anger management to more appropriately express their feelings and obtain a positive outcome.

F. Family members were provided with remedial feedback regarding the issue of anger control as a method of more aptly expressing their feelings.

## 4. List Counterproductive Nature of Uncontrolled Anger Expression (4)

A. Each family member was asked to describe the ways in which anger has been destructive to self or to the relationships within the family on a short-term basis.

B. Each family member was asked to describe ways in which anger has been destructive to self or the family relationships in the long term.

C. Family members were assisted in describing ways in which anger is counterproductive for themselves and for other family members.

D. Family members were assisted in identifying the negative effects of uncontrolled anger (fear, withdrawal, guilt, revenge, etc.).

E. Family members' experiences of the negative effects of anger were processed.

## 5. Review Misinterpretations of Anger (5)

A. Family members were asked to take turns volunteering and explaining examples of how their anger has been misinterpreted.

B. Family members were assisted in identifying ways in which one family member's de-escalating strategies have been perceived as a provocation to another family member (e.g., one family member's withdrawal is perceived as a provocative rejection by the other family member).

C. Family members were questioned about what message they were attempting to convey when they were misinterpreted as expressing anger.

D. Family members were provided with positive feedback as they identified how one family member's de-escalation strategies have been perceived as provocation to another family member.

E. Additional examples were provided to the family members about how de-escalation strategies can sometimes be perceived as provocation by another family member.

### 6. Identify Secondary Gain (6)

A. The family members were taught about secondary gain that may derive from uncontrolled anger.

B. Family members were assisted in identifying the secondary gain that occurs during uncontrolled anger in the family.

C. Family members were provided with tentative examples of secondary gain, such as acquiescence to demands, fear-based service, and so on.

### 7. Review History of Positive and Negative Anger Expression (7)

A. Each family member was asked about ways in which anger has been managed or de-escalated appropriately in the past.

B. Each family member was asked about the counterproductive ways in which anger had been expressed in the past.

C. The family was provided with feedback and encouragement as they identified ways of managing or de-escalating anger in the past.

D. Support was provided as family members identified counterproductive anger experiences.

### 8. Contract Regarding Anger Responsibility (8)

A. Family members were focused on the need to accept responsibility for managing their own anger, instead of managing the partner's anger.

B. Family members were asked to verbally contract to accept responsibility for managing their own anger instead of managing the other's anger.

C. A written contract was used to focus the family members on taking responsibility for their own anger rather than the other's anger.

D. Positive feedback was provided as the family members accepted the responsibility for managing their own anger rather than other family members' anger.

E. Family members were confronted as they tended to focus on managing other family members' behavior rather than their own anger.

### 9. Discuss Methods for Instituting Family Support Systems (9)

A. The family was led in a discussion of how to institute family support systems in helping each other control their anger levels.

B. Family members were provided with examples of family support systems to assist in controlling anger levels (signaling time-out, breathing cues, etc.).

C. The family agreed on specific methods for instituting family support systems and helping each other control anger levels; positive feedback was provided.

### 10. Discuss Dilemma of Anger Expression (10)

A. It was emphasized that each family member needs to express anger, but in an appropriate, constructive fashion.

B. The dilemma of finding the difficult balance of expressing anger appropriately was highlighted.

C. Positive feedback was provided to the family members as they displayed a clear understanding of the need to balance expressing anger with how to do it appropriately.

D. Specific examples of balanced anger expression were reviewed.

E. Family members were redirected when they tended to downplay the need for expressing anger.

### 11. Evaluate Anger-Control Techniques (11)

A. Specific techniques for controlling anger were evaluated.

B. The family was assisted in evaluating the thought stopping, controlled breathing, counting to 10, self-talk, and other anger-control techniques.

C. Each family member was helped to identify which types of anger-control techniques were best suited to that family member.

### 12. Assign Paradox of Trying to Become Angry (12)

A. Paradoxical intention techniques were used by instructing family members to focus on cues that cause them to become angry.

B. Family members' experience of attempting to become angry on purpose were reviewed.

C. It was highlighted to the family how difficult it is to become angry when we deliberately attempt to provoke it in ourselves.

### 13. Explore Primary Reasons for Anger (13)

A. Each family member was asked to list three primary reasons for becoming angry.

B. Each family member was assisted in identifying primary reasons for becoming angry.

C. Family members were urged to assist each other in identifying things that make each family member angry.

D. Family members failed to identify issues that make each other angry and were provided with tentative suggestions in this area.

### 14. Identify Anger as Manipulation (14)

A. Family members were oriented to the concept of anger being used as a means of manipulation.

B. Family members were asked to identify incidences when their expression of anger was used as a means of manipulation.

C. Positive feedback was provided as family members were able to honestly identify situations in which they have used anger as a means of manipulation.

D. Family members were guarded about admitting to the use of anger as a means of manipulation and were provided with tentative examples of how this occurs.

## 15. Teach Alternative Methods to Achieve Goals (15)

A. Modeling and role-playing techniques were used to teach alternative methods to achieve goals, without manipulating each other with anger.

B. Family members were taught the use of "I" messages as an alternative to manipulating each other with anger.

C. Family members were taught about making calm, respectful requests for change as an alternative to manipulating each other with anger.

D. Positive feedback was provided as family members displayed an understanding of alternative methods to anger.

E. Family members failed to grasp the use of alternative methods, such as "I" statements or making calm, respectful requests and were provided with remedial feedback in this area.

## 16. Identify Anger to Assert Independence (16)

A. Family members were asked to verbally identify episodes in which their anger was used to assert independence (i.e., anger that results from perceptions that the other family member is trying to exert control over one's life or actions).

B. Feedback was provided as the family members identified episodes in which their anger was used to assert independence.

C. Family members were provided with additional examples of the use of anger to assert independence.

D. Family members were assisted in discussing their use of anger in order to assert independence.

## 17. Distinguish Unassertive, Assertive, and Aggressive Patterns (17)

A. Family members were assisted in differentiating between unassertive (i.e., not standing up for one's wishes or rights), assertive (i.e., appropriately asserting one's wishes or rights without infringing on the rights of others), and aggressive (i.e., asserting one's wishes and rights without regard to the rights of others).

B. Family members' use of unassertive, assertive, and aggressive patterns were identified and reviewed.

C. Family members were provided with positive feedback for their reported increase in assertive responses.

D. Additional feedback was provided to the family as they struggled to identify the differences between unassertive, assertive, and aggressive actions.

## 18. Direct Assertive Communication Regarding Independence (18)

A. Family members used role-playing to practice assertive communication skills for "declaring" desired outcomes.

B. Family members were encouraged to identify the specific behaviors that trigger the perceptions of being controlled.

C. Family members were reinforced for understanding the specific behaviors that trigger the perceptions of being controlled and for using assertive communication about those behaviors.

D. Additional, direct feedback was provided to family members regarding identifying specific behaviors that trigger the perception of being controlled and how to assertively express this.

### 19. Identify Cues at Home and in Public (19)

A. Family members were assisted in identifying internal and external cues for anger in the home setting.

B. Family members were assisted in identifying internal and external cues for anger in public settings.

C. Family members were assisted in comparing and contrasting the internal and external cues for anger both at home and in public.

### 20. Emphasize Public Anger Control as Evidence of Skill (20)

A. Family members were assisted in identifying ways in which anger is controlled in public but uncontrolled at home.

B. It was emphasized to family members that being able to control anger while in public is evidence of the ability to control anger, even when at home.

### 21. Review Passive-Aggressive Behavior (21)

A. Passive-aggressive behavior was clearly defined to the family members.

B. Family members were provided with a variety of examples of passive-aggressive behavior.

C. Family members were asked to recall specific examples of their past behaviors that have been passive-aggressive.

D. Family members were assisted in developing ways to redirect passive-aggressive behavior into appropriate assertiveness.

E. Family members struggled to identify any instances of their own passive-aggressive behavior and were provided with tentative examples based on the family's previous descriptions.

### 22. Teach about SUDs (22)

A. Family members were taught about the Subjective Units of Discomfort (SUD) scale.

B. Family members were taught how to use the SUD scale from 0 to 100 as a barometer for measuring anger.

C. Family members were reinforced for their understanding of the SUD scale.

D. Family members were assisted in applying the SUD scale to describe their level of anger.

### 23. Teach about Cues for Anger (23)

A. Family members were taught about how to identify the cognitive, affective, behavioral, and physiological cues of anger.

B. Family members were recommended to read *Angry All the Time* (Potter-Efron).

C. Family members were assisted in differentiating low, moderate, and high levels of anger.

D. Family members were reminded to focus on verbal as well as nonverbal cues related to anger.

E. Family members were reinforced as they were able to identify various cues of anger.

F. Family members failed to correctly identify the cues of anger and were provided with remedial assistance in this area.

## 24. Teach Time-Out Techniques (24)

A. Family members were taught about the six components of time-out techniques (i.e., *self-monitoring* for escalating feelings of anger and hurt, *signaling* to the partner that verbal engagement should end, *acknowledging* the need of the partner to disengage, *separating* to disengage, *cooling down* to regain control of anger, and *returning* to controlled verbal engagement).

B. Positive feedback was provided as family members displayed understanding of the time-out technique.

C. Family members were advised about the potential for misuse and manipulation of the time-out technique if used to avoid arguments or manipulate the other partner.

D. Family members have misused the time-out technique and were provided with additional feedback in this area.

E. Family members were reinforced for their reports of successful use of the time-out technique.

## 25. Practice Time-Outs (25)

A. The family practiced time-out techniques in the session, and was coached about these practice attempts.

B. Positive feedback was provided to the family as they appropriately used time-out in session practice attempts.

C. The family was provided with additional feedback about how to use the time-out technique.

D. The family was assigned to practice the time-out technique at home.

E. Family members were reinforced for their reports of successful use of the time-out technique.

## 26. Develop Agreement to Talk about Angry Feelings Early (26)

A. Family members were assisted in developing an agreement to begin talking about angry feelings and thoughts in the early stages of anger.

B. Family members were encouraged to talk about angry feelings prior to reaching the level of intense behavioral expression, passive-aggressive maneuvers, or manipulative behaviors.

C. Family members endorsed the need to talk about angry feelings early and were supported in the use of these techniques.

D. Family members have not followed their agreement to begin talking about angry feelings earlier and were reminded about this commitment.

## 27. Teach the "Turtle" Technique (27)

A. Family members were taught about the use of the "turtle" technique, in which family members imagine themselves individually retreating into their shells until they cool down.

B. Family members were assisted in identifying cues that indicate that they should use the turtle technique.

C. Positive feedback was provided as family members reported successful use of the turtle technique.

D. Family members have not used the turtle technique at appropriate times and were provided with feedback about when and how to use this technique.

**28. Assign Anger-Tracking Homework (28)**

A. Family members were asked to track their level of anger.

B. Family members were asked to track the precursors to anger, along with the accompanying emotions and behaviors that fuel it.

C. Family members have regularly tracked their anger, and the results of this information were processed within the session.

D. Family members have not tracked their anger and were redirected to do so.

# ANXIETY

## CLIENT PRESENTATION

### 1. Excessive Worry (1)*

A. Family members described symptoms of preoccupation with worry that something dire will happen.

B. Family members showed some recognition that the excessive worry or perceived threat is beyond the scope of rationality, but are unable to control it.

C. Family members described worries about issues related to family, personal safety, health, and employment, among other things.

D. Family members report that worries about life's circumstances have diminished, and they are experiencing more of a sense of peace and confidence.

### 2. Poor Role Fulfillment (1)

A. The anxious family member's experience of perceived threat and worry impede the fulfillment of important roles.

B. The anxious family member has failed to complete typical tasks within relationships due to the worry and anxiety.

C. As the anxious family member's anxiety level has decreased, there has been an increased fulfillment of important role functions.

D. Family member is no longer anxious and is able to normally fulfill important role tasks.

### 3. Autonomic Hyperactivity (2)

A. Family members report the presence of symptoms such as heart palpitations, dry mouth, tightness in the throat, and shortness of breath.

B. Family members report jitteriness, restlessness, insomnia, and high-level autonomic activity.

C. Family members have reported periods of nausea and diarrhea when anxiety levels escalate.

D. Family members have experienced tension headaches that occur along with their anxiety-related symptoms.

E. Family members' anxiety-related symptoms have diminished as new coping skills have been developed.

### 4. Concessions Because of Undue Distress (3)

A. One family member's symptoms of anxiety have caused undue distress within the family.

B. The stress within the family has become so severe that concessions are often made to one family member due to the level of anxiety that that family member is experiencing.

C. Family members are unable to complete basic family tasks due to the concessions that must be made to the anxious family member.

*The numbers in parentheses correlate to the number of the Behavioral Definition statement in the companion chapter with the same title in *The Family Therapy Treatment Planner*, Second Ed. (Dattilio, Jongsma, and Davis) by John Wiley & Sons, 2010.

D. Arguments and jealousy have erupted due to the concessions that have been made to the anxious family member.

E. As the distress level of the anxious family member has decreased, the family's functioning has improved.

F. As the family has become healthier in their response to the anxious family member, the level of undue distress has decreased.

## 5. Agitation and Alienation (4)

A. The anxiety-ridden family member often ruminates or engages in controlling behaviors toward other family members.

B. Other family members have become agitated with the controlling and ruminating behaviors done by the anxiety-ridden family member.

C. Family members have become alienated from each other due to the experience of anxiety within the family.

D. As treatment has progressed, the anxiety-ridden family member has decreased the pattern of rumination or controlling behavior.

E. Family members report a greater sense of satisfaction and closeness with each other.

## 6. Intergenerational Anxiety Effects (5)

A. A parent experiences anxiety symptoms.

B. The anxiety of a parent has led to a child's dysfunctional behavior.

C. A child within the family is attempting to compensate for a parent's anxiety symptoms in a dysfunctional manner.

D. A child within the family is mirroring the parent's anxiety symptoms.

E. As treatment has progressed, anxiety symptoms within the family have decreased, and the child's dysfunctional behavior has decreased.

## 7. Irrational Phobic Fears (6)

A. One or more family members experience limitations on their behavior due to irrational phobic fears.

B. Family members often have had to modify their travel plans due to the irrational phobic fears.

C. The phobic family member has shown a willingness to begin to encounter the phobic travel stimulus and endure some of the anxiety response that is experienced.

D. The phobic family member has been able to tolerate the previously phobic travel stimulus without debilitating anxiety.

E. The phobic family member reports no longer being fearful during an encounter with phobic travel stimuli.

F. The family has discontinued making travel allowances for the family member with a phobia.

## INTERVENTIONS IMPLEMENTED

### 1. List Symptoms and Avoidance Behaviors (1)*

A. The anxious family member was directed to list specific symptoms and avoidance behaviors.

B. The anxious family member was administered an anxiety inventory to help list specific symptoms and avoidance behaviors.

C. The anxious family member was directed to take the *Beck Anxiety Inventory* (Beck and Steer).

D. The anxious family member was directed to take the *Body Sensations Questionnaire* (Shambles, Caputo, and Bright).

E. The anxious family member was asked to take the *State-Trait Anxiety Inventory* (Spielberger).

F. The results of the anxiety inventory were reviewed with family members.

G. The anxious family member has not taken the assigned anxiety inventory and was redirected to do so.

### 2. Gather Information on Anxiety Development (2)

A. The anxious family member's recollections of how anxiety developed was reviewed.

B. Family member's reports and observations about the development and maintenance of anxiety were collected.

C. The symptomatic effects of anxiety for the anxious family member were reflected to other family members.

D. Family members were reinforced for their understanding of the symptoms of anxiety for this anxious family member.

E. Family members were not supportive or understanding in regard to the symptomatic effects of anxiety for the anxious family member and were provided with additional information in this area.

### 3. Add Family Members' Perspectives (3)

A. The non-anxious family members' perspectives about the anxious family member's pattern of anxiety and avoidance were gathered.

B. Information that was not mentioned by the anxious family member was collected from the non-anxious family members.

C. It was noted that the anxious family member's description of anxiety and avoidance is commensurate with the non-anxious family members' perspectives in this area.

D. It was noted that the anxious family member's description of anxiety and avoidance patterns was quite divergent from those gathered from the non-anxious family members.

*The numbers in parentheses correlate to the number of the Therapeutic Intervention statement in the companion chapter with the same title in *The Family Therapy Treatment Planner*, Second Ed. (Dattilio, Jongsma, and Davis) by John Wiley & Sons, 2010.

### 4. Encourage Expression about Anxiety Impact (4)

A. Each family member was asked to characterize the impact that the anxiety disorder has had on that family member and on the family as a whole.

B. Family members were encouraged to select modes of expression to help characterize the impact of the anxiety disorder, including dramatization, written, or artistic expression.

C. Each family member's characterization of the impact of the anxiety disorder was reviewed within the family session.

D. Family members have not worked to characterize the impact that the anxiety disorder has had and were redirected to do so.

### 5. Ascertain Current Stress-Coping Skills (5)

A. The current stress-coping skills of each family member were assessed.

B. Family members' stress-coping skills were assessed to determine which coping mechanisms have been effective.

C. Feedback was provided to family members about their effective stress-coping skills.

### 6. Request Description of Support (6)

A. Non-anxious family members were asked to describe how they have each tried to be supportive of the anxious family member.

B. Family members were assisted in identifying ways in which they have been supportive of the anxious family member.

C. Family members were assisted in brainstorming additional ways to support the anxious family member.

D. Positive feedback was provided as family members described a variety of ways in which they have tried to be supportive of the anxious family member.

E. Family members were provided feedback regarding their attempts to be supportive of the anxious family member.

F. Family members were unable to identify ways in which they have been supportive of the anxious family member and were provided with tentative examples in this area.

### 7. Identify Specific Incidences of Resentment (7)

A. Each non-anxious family member was asked to identify specific incidences in which they have experienced resentment as a result of the side effects of another family member's anxiety.

B. Family members were supported as they described situations in which they felt resentment due to another family member's anxiety.

C. Family members were assisted in strategizing ways in which to reduce conflict and resentment due to a family member's anxiety.

D. Family members struggled to identify ways in which they have felt resentment as a result of the side effects of another family member's anxiety and were provided with tentative examples in this area (i.e., family members having to forfeit activities due to the anxiety).

### 8. Discuss Effects and Roles Used (8)

A. Family members were asked to discuss how the anxiety disorder has affected them.

B. Family members were asked to identify what role they have adopted in response to the anxiety.

C. Family members were provided with examples of roles used to respond to the family member's anxiety (e.g., supporter, antagonist, spectator, martyr, comforter).

### 9. Explore Etiology of Roles (9)

A. Each family member was assisted in exploring how he or she developed his or her role within the family.

B. Some family members were noted to have selected their own role within the family.

C. Family members were noted to have been assigned roles by another family member.

D. Support and encouragement were provided as family members displayed a better understanding of the roles within the family.

### 10. Teach about the Proper Role of Anxiety (10)

A. Family members were informed of the specific role that anxiety plays in every human being's system.

B. Anxiety was presented as a survival mechanism that can, at times, be misinterpreted to the point of causing distress and debilitating symptoms.

C. Young children within the family were provided with simplified information regarding the role that anxiety plays in every human being's system.

D. *The Worry Cure* (Leahy) was assigned to the family.

E. Family members were reinforced as they displayed an understanding of how anxiety can be helpful.

F. Family members did not display an understanding of the role that anxiety plays in every human being's system and were provided with remedial feedback in this area.

### 11. Teach Anxiety as Fluctuating and Manageable (11)

A. Family members were taught that anxiety is a survival mechanism.

B. Family members were taught that anxiety is not a dichotomous entity, but one that fluctuates in intensity.

C. Family members were focused on the concept of managing anxiety.

D. Family members were reinforced for their clear understanding of the nature of anxiety as a survival mechanism.

E. Family members did not display a clear understanding of the nature of anxiety as a survival mechanism and were provided with additional feedback in this area.

### 12. Reinforce Confrontation of Anxiety (12)

A. The notion that the anxious family member must consistently confront the anxiety in order to reduce it was presented.

B. Family members were reinforced for their acceptance of the family member's need to confront anxiety in order to reduce it to a manageable level.

C. Family members eschewed the idea that the anxious family member must consistently confront the anxiety to reduce it and were provided with additional examples and rationale for this approach.

### 13. Discuss Methods to Encourage Recovery (13)

A. A discussion was held regarding specific methods that family members could use to encourage the anxious family member to follow the anxiety-reducing treatment plan.

B. Family members identified a variety of ways in which they can encourage the anxious family member to follow the treatment plan, and these were reviewed and reinforced.

C. Family members were uncertain about how to encourage the anxious family member to follow the treatment plan and were provided with tentative examples (e.g., words of affection, encouragement, nonenabling behaviors).

### 14. Develop Coaching (14)

A. Non-anxious family members were encouraged to serve as a coach to the anxious family member.

B. Since more than one family member is anxious, a "buddy system" was employed to provide support.

C. Family members were assisted in developing helpful ways to be a coach to the anxious family member.

### 15. Brainstorm about Potential Problems with Coaching (15)

A. Potential problems or pitfalls when one family member is used as a coach or support to an anxious family member were brainstormed.

B. Family members identified potential problems or pitfalls, and these were reviewed, processed, and problem solved.

C. Family members were oblivious to any potential problems or pitfalls for using family members as coaches and supporting agents and were provided with tentative examples (i.e., parentification of a child, secondary gain).

D. Family members were reinforced for identifying and developing solutions to possible pitfalls to coaching and supporting each other.

### 16. Encourage Use of Educational Materials (16)

A. Family members were encouraged to read educational materials to learn more about anxiety, with a focus on the interplay between physiology, cognition, affect, and behavior.

B. *The Anxiety and Phobia Workbook* (Bourne) was recommended to family members.

C. Family members were encouraged to read *Mastery of Your Anxiety and Worry* (Craske, Barlow, and O'Leary).

D. Family members have read educational materials about anxiety, and key information was reviewed.

E. Family members have not read educational material about anxiety and were redirected to do so.

### 17. Explore Internal Anxiety-Producing Stimuli (17)

A. The anxious family member was taught how internal stimuli can be anxiety producing (e.g., catastrophic thoughts).

B. The anxious family member's cognitive, anxiety-mediating messages were identified.

C. The anxious family member was assisted in developing positive, realistic, alternative thoughts that could mediate confidence, self-assurance, and relaxation.

D. As the anxious family member has learned to implement positive self-talk, the anxiety level has been noted to diminish.

### 18. Identify Overestimation and Catastrophization (18)

A. The anxious family member's propensity to overestimate the threat inherent in anxious situations was identified.

B. The catastrophization of anticipated situations or events was diplomatically pointed out to the anxious family member.

C. The anxious family member was supported for accepting how overestimation and catastrophizing has occurred.

D. The anxious family member denied any pattern of overestimation or catastrophizing of anticipated situations or events and was provided with additional feedback and examples in this area.

### 19. Develop Positive Cognitions (19)

A. The anxious family member was assisted in replacing distorted, negative thoughts with positive, realistic thoughts that counteract anxiety.

B. The anxious family member was recommended to read *Mastering Your Anxiety and Panic-Patient's Workbook* (Craske and Barlow).

C. The anxious family member has used the recommended workbook on replacing distorted, negative thoughts with positive, realistic thoughts, and the key points identified in these exercises were reviewed.

D. As the anxious family member has learned positive self-talk and has implemented it into daily activities, anxiety has been noted to diminish.

E. Positive reinforcement was provided as the anxious family member reported increased self-confidence since instituting positive self-talk.

F. The anxious family member was provided with remedial feedback about how to replace distorted, negative thoughts with positive, realistic thoughts.

### 20. Model Cognitive Restructuring (20)

A. The anxious family member was helped to learn about cognitive restructuring of catastrophic thoughts and distortion through modeling.

B. The anxious family member was assisted in identifying how to restructure and reframe events.

C. Positive feedback was provided as the anxious family member displayed an understanding of how to restructure catastrophic thoughts and distortions.

### 21. Transfer Role Modeling to Other Family Members (21)

A. Family members were taught about the use of cognitive restructuring and reframing of thoughts and events.

B. Family members were provided with role-playing examples of how to restructure and reframe catastrophic thoughts and events.

C. Family members were urged to take over responsibility for role modeling, restructuring, and reframing thoughts and events in coaching situations.

### 22. Teach SUDS (22)

A. The family was taught to use the Subjective Units of Discomfort Scale (SUDS) in which the anxious family member rates perceived anxiety on a 0–100 scale.

B. Positive feedback was provided as the family displayed a clear understanding of the use of the SUDS.

C. Remedial information was provided as the family failed to grasp the use of the SUDS, including information from *Anxiety Free: Unravel Your Fears Before They Unravel You* (Leahy).

### 23. Direct Discussion of SUDS Score (23)

A. The anxious family member was directed to describe the current SUDS score to the non-anxious family members.

B. The anxious family member was directed to identify the elements of the situation that are affecting the SUDS score and what internal cues are being used to determine the SUDS score.

C. A discussion of the use of the SUDS score was facilitated.

D. The anxious family member was provided with feedback regarding the use of the SUDS score.

### 24. Teach Behavioral Techniques for Reducing Anxiety (24)

A. Family members were taught about various methods of behavioral techniques for reducing anxiety (e.g., deep breathing and progressive relaxation).

B. Family members were urged to read *The Relaxation and Stress Reduction Workbook* (Davis et al.).

C. Family members have read the assigned information about behavioral anxiety-reduction techniques, and the key points were reviewed.

D. Family members were urged to use behavioral anxiety-reduction techniques to better understand the techniques and to help the anxious family member to not feel like the identified patient.

E. Positive feedback was provided as all family members displayed a clear understanding of the behavioral techniques used to reduce anxiety.

F. Family members have not gained a clear understanding of how to use the behavioral techniques and were provided with remedial feedback in this area.

## 25. Assign Practice of Breathing Retraining and Relaxation Methods (25)

A. Family members were assigned to practice breathing retraining and relaxation methods for at least 10 to 15 minutes several times per day.

B. Family members were provided access to audio- or videotapes to assist them in practicing breathing retraining and relaxation methods.

C. Family members were taught how the breathing retraining and relaxation methods can help their personal health and stress reduction.

D. Family members were urged to use the breathing retraining and relaxation methods as a way to support and coach the anxious family member.

E. Positive feedback was provided as all family members have been using the breathing retraining and relaxation methods.

F. Family members have not regularly used the breathing retraining and relaxation methods and were redirected to do so.

## 26. Assign Anxiety Journal (26)

A. A written journal was assigned to identify the situations that trigger anxiety as well as the thoughts and behaviors that occur during anxiety-eliciting situations.

B. *Progressive Muscle Relaxation* (Dattilio) was recommended to the family members.

C. The anxiety journal was reviewed, and the pattern of situations, thoughts, and behaviors were processed.

D. Positive feedback was provided as family members showed increased insight regarding anxiety-eliciting situations.

E. The anxiety-tracking homework has not been completed, and the family was redirected in this area.

## 27. Develop Hierarchy of Feared Situations (27)

A. The anxious family member was asked to identify feared situations.

B. The anxious family member was asked to generate estimated SUDS scores for each feared situation.

C. A hierarchy of situations feared by the anxious family member was generated.

## 28. Conduct Imagined Exposure (28)

A. Within the session, beginning at the lower end of the hierarchy, imagined exposure was conducted regarding the feared situations for the anxious family member.

B. Family members without anxiety were taught how to ask for SUDS ratings every several minutes.

C. Modeling was used to teach the non-anxious family members how to give encouragement to the anxious family member.

D. Positive feedback was provided to the anxious family member as comfort was displayed moving through the hierarchy of anxious situations.

E. The anxious family member displayed significant difficulties while practicing exposure to the anxiety-eliciting situations and was taught more coping skills to enhance relaxation.

### 29. Assign *In Vivo* Exposure (29)

A. The anxious family member was assigned to complete *in vivo* desensitization contact with the anxiety-producing stimulus object or situation.

B. Family members were taught the principles of desensitization and encouraged to have the anxious family member encounter the anxiety-producing stimulus in gradual steps, utilizing relaxation to counterattack any anxiety response.

C. Positive feedback was provided as the anxious family member described successful use of the *in vivo* exposure and coping techniques.

D. The anxious family member reported failure when *in vivo* techniques were tried and was provided with additional coping skills for this task.

E. The anxious family member did not practice the *in vivo* desensitization techniques and the reasons for this failure were brainstormed and redirection was given.

### 30. Reinforce Continued Anxiety-Inoculation Techniques (30)

A. Family members were reinforced for their continued use of anxiety-inoculation techniques.

B. Reverse role-playing and modeling were used within the therapy session to teach how potential anxiety situations may be addressed.

C. The anxious family member was assisted in using anxiety-inoculation techniques to move through the hierarchy of anxious situations.

### 31. Teach Thought-Stopping Techniques (31)

A. The anxious family member was taught thought-stopping techniques that involve thinking of a stop sign and replacing negative thoughts with a pleasant scene.

B. The anxious family member was taught thought-stopping techniques that involve shouting "stop" within one's mind and replacing negative thoughts with a pleasant scene.

C. The anxious family member was taught the technique of snapping a rubber band on the wrist to interrupt negative thoughts and control anxiety symptoms.

D. The anxious family member's implementation of the thought-stopping techniques was monitored, and success with these techniques was reinforced.

E. The anxious family member reported that the thought-stopping techniques have been beneficial in reducing the preoccupation with anxiety-producing cognitions and was urged to continue to use this technique.

### 32. Assess/Refer for Medication (32)

A. The need for anti-anxiety medication was assessed.

B. The anxious family member was referred to a physician to be evaluated for psychotropic medication to reduce symptoms of anxiety.

C. The anxious family member has completed an evaluation by the physician and has begun taking anti-anxiety medications; the benefits of this treatment were reviewed.

D. The anxious family member has resisted the referral for anti-anxiety medication evaluation and does not wish to take any medication to reduce anxiety level.

### 33. Monitor Medication Effectiveness (33)

A. The anxious family member's compliance with the prescription for psychotropic medication was monitored as to the medication's effectiveness and side effects.

B. The anxious family member reported that the medication has been beneficial in reducing the anxiety symptoms, and this was reflected to the prescribing physician.

C. The anxious family member reported that the medication does not seem to be helpful in reducing anxiety symptoms, and this was reflected to the prescribing physician.

D. A consultation was held with the prescribing physician to discuss the anxious family member's reaction to the psychotropic medication, and adjustments were made in the prescription.

# BLAME

## CLIENT PRESENTATION

### 1. Blaming for Relationship Problems and Dissatisfaction (1)*

A. Family members repeatedly blame each other for the relationship problems.

B. Spouses repeatedly blame each other for dissatisfaction with the relationship.

C. Family members often make comments about how family life would be better if the other family members would make certain changes.

D. As treatment has progressed, family members have ceased blaming each other.

### 2. Dissatisfaction with the Relationship (2)

A. Family members have expressed dissatisfaction with the family relationships.

B. Family members often blame each other for the level of dissatisfaction that each experiences with the relationship.

C. As communication has increased, dissatisfaction within family relationships has been decreased.

D. Family members have expressed satisfaction with family relationships.

### 3. Resistance to Examining Role in Conflict (3)

A. The blaming family member does not see any personal contributions to the conflict.

B. The blaming family member is resistant to examining the contributors to the conflict.

C. The blaming family member often makes comments about how family difficulties are the other family members' problems.

D. As treatment has progressed, the blaming family member has become more accepting of the fact that all family members contribute to the relationship problems.

E. The blaming family member has become more open to examining personal contributions to the conflict.

### 4. Projection of Responsibility (4)

A. Responsibility is often projected onto the other family members for the blaming family member's behavior.

B. Responsibility is often projected onto the other family members for the blaming family member's thoughts.

C. Responsibility is often projected onto the other family members for the blaming family member's feelings.

---

*The numbers in parentheses correlate to the number of the Behavioral Definition statement in the companion chapter with the same title in *The Family Therapy Treatment Planner*, Second Ed. (Dattilio, Jongsma, and Davis) by John Wiley & Sons, 2010.

D. The blamed family members have refused to take responsibility for the blaming family member's thoughts, feelings, or behavior.

E. The blaming family member has terminated the projection of responsibility onto the other family members regarding personal thoughts, feelings, or behavior.

## 5. Blame Replaces Honest Self-Examination (5)

A. Virtually all family discussions result in a pattern of blaming rather than honest, open self-examination.

B. Family members react to perceived shortcomings with blaming rather than honest, open self-examination.

C. As communication has increased, family members are more open to honest self-examination.

## 6. Decreased Communication and Cohesiveness (6)

A. The chronic blaming behavior in family members has significantly affected communication and cohesiveness within the family.

B. Family members report that they have decreased communication with blaming family members due to the expectation that more blaming will occur.

C. Family members report that they do not feel very close to each other.

D. Family members experience a cycle of blaming, frustration, and termination of communication that leads to more blaming.

E. As the family members have progressed in treatment, blaming has decreased and communication and cohesiveness have increased within the family.

## 7. Low Self-Esteem/Poor Interpersonal Skills (7)

A. Family members who engage in various degrees of externalization of blame also verbalize low self-esteem and demonstrate poor interpersonal skills.

B. The blaming family members tend to compensate for their low self-esteem by diverting attention to other's faults or presumed faults.

C. As treatment has progressed, blaming family members have improved in regard to self-esteem and demonstrated better interpersonal skills, which has decreased the need to blame others.

## INTERVENTIONS IMPLEMENTED

### 1. Describe Relationship Problems (1)*

A. An individual session was held with each family member so each could describe the problems in the family relationships.

B. Family members were confronted about and discouraged from placing blame solely on other family members.

*The numbers in parentheses correlate to the number of the Therapeutic Intervention statement in the companion chapter with the same title in *The Family Therapy Treatment Planner*, Second Ed. (Dattilio, Jongsma, and Davis) by John Wiley & Sons, 2010.

C. When family members described problems as having a basis in all family members' behavior, reinforcement was provided.

D. Paraphrasing was used to review each family member's description of the problems in the family relationships.

## 2. Assess for Other Problems (2)

A. The family was assessed for the presence of other problems that might be the basis of most of the blaming in the family relationships.

B. Evidence of chemical dependence was uncovered, and the treatment focus was switched to this concern.

C. Evidence of physical abuse was uncovered, and the treatment focus was switched to this concern.

D. Evidence of sexual abuse was uncovered, and the treatment focus was switched to this concern.

E. Evidence of an extramarital affair was identified as the basis for most of the blaming in the marital relationship and treatment was focused on this area.

F. It was reflected to family members that alternative bases for the blaming in the relationship were assessed, but none were uncovered.

## 3. Encourage/Reinforce Taking Responsibility (3)

A. Family members were encouraged to take personal responsibility for how they each contribute to the problems rather than projecting all the blame onto other family members.

B. Reinforcing comments were made each time a family member took responsibility for a personal contribution to the problems.

C. Family members were encouraged to read *Beyond Blame* (Lukeman and Lukeman) and *The Language of Letting Go* (Beattie).

D. Family members have read the material related to letting go of blame and key points were processed.

E. It was reflected to family members that they have increased taking responsibility for their personal contributions to the problem rather than projecting all blame onto other family members.

F. Family members have not read the material related to letting go of blame and were redirected to do so.

## 4. Emphasize Equal Responsibility for Level of Satisfaction (4)

A. Each family member was encouraged to take responsibility for the satisfaction as well as the dissatisfaction in the family.

B. Family members were validated and reinforced when they took equal responsibility for satisfaction or dissatisfaction within the family.

C. Each family member was directed to sign a therapeutic agreement indicating partial responsibility for satisfaction and/or dissatisfaction in the relationship.

D. Family members were reinforced for taking written responsibility for the satisfaction and/or dissatisfaction in the relationship.

E. Family members have resisted taking responsibility for satisfaction or dissatisfaction within the family and were redirected to situations in which they could do this.

## 5. **Direct Division of Responsibility for Problems (5)**

A. Family members were asked to cite a typical example of a conflict within the family, and to take responsibility for their contribution to the conflict.

B. Active listening techniques were used to support all family members as they presented on problems for which they feel they can admit partial responsibility.

C. Positive reinforcement was provided as family members agreed to make constructive changes.

D. The blaming family members failed to identify even minor problems for which they could accept partial responsibility and were provided with tentative examples in this area.

## 6. **Emphasize Noninflammatory Communication (6)**

A. The use of noninflammatory communication was emphasized to the family.

B. Role-playing techniques were used to shape constructive behaviors to facilitate family members in adopting noninflammatory communication.

C. The use of noninflammatory communication was modeled to the family members.

D. Positive reinforcement was provided when family members used noninflammatory communication with each other.

E. The incompatibility of noninflammatory communication and blaming was emphasized.

## 7. **Teach "I" Messages (7)**

A. Family members were taught about the use of "I" messages (i.e., stating first what thoughts and feelings were experienced before stating the family member's behavior that seemed to trigger those thoughts and feelings).

B. Role-playing and modeling were used to teach family members how to use "I" messages.

C. The reduction in blaming inherent in "I" statements was highlighted.

D. Family members were reinforced for using "I" messages.

E. Family members have not used "I" messages and were redirected to do so.

## 8. **Encourage Rituals of Forgiveness (8)**

A. As anger issues have been worked through, the family was encouraged to work on rituals of forgiveness.

B. Family members were encouraged to use physical embraces, written letters of forgiveness, and other rituals for working through forgiveness of old hurts.

C. Family members were recommended to read *Forgiveness: The Healing Gift We Give Ourselves* (Carson).

D. Family members were encouraged to read *Forgive and Forget* (Smedes).

E. Family members were assisted in processing what they learned through their reading and experiences regarding forgiveness.

F. Family members have not read the material related to forgiveness and were redirected to do so.

G. Family members have not used rituals to assist in the process of forgiveness and were reminded about these helpful techniques.

### 9. Model and Reinforce Responsibility for Thoughts, Feelings, and Behaviors (9)

A. Modeling techniques were used to teach family members about accepting responsibilities for their own thoughts, feelings, and behaviors.

B. Emphasis was placed on how each family member has a myriad of choices in reacting to the other family members' behaviors.

C. Family members were reinforced for accepting responsibility for their own behaviors, thoughts, and feelings in the context of multiple choices as a reaction to the others' behaviors.

D. As family members reviewed specific examples of acceptance of responsibility, the decreased blame toward others was emphasized.

### 10. Identify Pleasing Behavior (10)

A. Family members were assisted in identifying two or more pleasing behaviors that each of the other family members could engage in.

B. Each family member's list of pleasing behaviors was identified and processed.

C. Family members were encouraged to use pleasing behaviors, including their own ideas and others' ideas.

### 11. Assign Pleasing Behaviors as Homework (11)

A. Family members were provided with specific homework exercises that will allow them to benefit from pleasing behaviors on a *quid pro quo* basis.

B. Family members were taught about the concept of caring days adapted from *Helping Couples Change* (Stuart).

C. Family members have used the pleasing behaviors on a *quid pro quo* basis, and their experience was processed.

D. Family members have not completed homework exercises regarding pleasing behaviors and were redirected to do so.

### 12. Assign Reinforcing Expressions of Appreciation (12)

A. Each family member was asked to express appreciation for two things each day that are pleasing about another family member's behavior.

B. Family members' use of appreciative comments were reviewed and reinforced.

C. The benefits of appreciative comments were reviewed and emphasized.

D. Family members have not regularly expressed appreciation for two things each day that are pleasing about another family member's behavior and were redirected to do so.

### 13. Review Compliments (13)

A. The blaming family member was asked to review occasions when compliments have been provided to other family members.

B. The blaming family member was reinforced for shifting from a position of criticism to a position of praise.

C. The benefits of complimenting the blamed family member were reviewed.

D. The blaming family member has not shifted from a position of criticism to a position of praise and was redirected to do so.

### 14. Identify Triggers for Blaming (14)

A. Family members were assisted in identifying specific words or behaviors that trigger blaming.

B. Positive feedback was provided as family members identified many behaviors or words that seem to trigger blaming.

C. Family members struggled to identify specific words or behaviors that might trigger blaming and were provided with tentative examples in this area.

### 15. Identify Alternatives When Blaming Is Triggered (15)

A. The family was taught about constructive alternatives to blaming when common blaming triggers occur.

B. The family was taught about using "I" messages in response to common blaming triggers.

C. The family was taught to use assertiveness techniques in place of blaming.

D. The family was taught to reinforce an incompatible behavior to extinguish common triggers to blaming.

E. Family members have used constructive alternatives to blaming and were provided with positive feedback for this success.

F. The family has not instituted constructive alternatives to blaming and was reminded about these helpful techniques.

### 16. Teach Problem-Solving Techniques (16)

A Family members were taught the six steps of problem solving: (1) Define the problem in specific terms; (2) brainstorm alternatives; (3) list the pros and cons of each alternative; (4) choose a mutually-acceptable alternative; (5) develop a plan to put the chosen alternative into practice, including a fall-back plan; and (6) evaluate the success of the chosen alternative.

B. Family members were provided with examples of how to use the six steps to problem solving.

C. Family members have used the six steps to problem solving, and their experience was reviewed and processed.

D. Family members have not used the six steps to problem solving and were redirected to use this helpful technique.

### 17. Encourage *Quid Pro Quo* (17)

A. Family members were encouraged to agree to *quid pro quo* contracts to promote cooperation.

B. Family members were encouraged to explicitly identify the reward or compensation used for completion of specific actions.

C. The use of *quid pro quo* contracts was reviewed with the family.

### 18. Focus on Anger Reduction (18)

A. Anger and resentment were identified as interfering with the blaming family members' ability to change.

B. The focus of treatment was shifted to anger reduction.

C. The blaming family member was taught anger management techniques to help work through the causes for anger and to help restructure thoughts to reduce distortions.

D. The angry, resentful, blaming family member was urged to write letters to explain feelings of hurt.

E. Positive feedback was provided to family members as they processed their hurt and resentment, thereby reducing it.

F. Family members have not decreased the pattern of hurt and resentment and were redirected in this area.

### 19. Reemphasize Assertiveness (19)

A. The use of assertiveness to circumvent aggressive, passive, or passive-aggressive behaviors was emphasized.

B. Family members were asked to provide examples of how they have used assertiveness rather than aggressive, passive, or passive-aggressive behaviors.

C. Family members were provided with examples of how to replace aggressive, passive, or passive-aggressive behaviors with assertiveness.

D. Family members were assisted in listing needs or desires that other family members can meet.

### 20. Emphasize Family Members' Choices (20)

A. Family members were taught about how they have specific choices as to the quality of their family life and the comfort of their own lives.

B. Emphasis was placed on how family members can chose to perform pleasing actions for each other as a way to fulfill their own needs.

C. Family members were accepting of how they have choices as to the quality of their family life and the comfort of their own lives and were reinforced for this.

D. Family members rejected the concept of performing pleasing actions for each other to fulfill their own needs and were asked to keep an open mind in this area.

### 21. Emphasize Rules of the Family (21)

A. The rules of the family were emphasized and codified.

B. Family members were urged to accept the rules of the family.

C. Family members seemed uncertain about the rules of the family and were provided with tentative examples in this area (e.g., the father should help put the children to bed; the mother should assist in the yard work; the children will make their beds or pick up their toys).

## 22. Clarify Response to Broken Rules (22)

A. Family members were asked about how the basic rules of the relationship are being broken.

B. The negative feelings evoked by the rule violations were identified and processed.

C. It was noted that family members displayed a clear understanding of the connection between rule violations and negative feelings.

## 23. Renegotiate Rules and Roles (23)

A. Family members were assisted in renegotiating rules and roles within the relationship that are agreeable to each as a means of reducing blaming behavior.

B. Family members were provided with feedback on their renegotiations of rules and roles.

C. An emphasis was placed on the reduced blaming behavior that occurs due to a renegotiated set of rules and roles.

## 24. Identify Hurt and Expected Mode of Expression (24)

A. Family members were individually asked to list specifically how they have been hurt by another family member's blaming.

B. Family members were asked to identify what future mode of expression (e.g., "I" message) should be followed to avoid blaming.

C. It was noted that family members have decreased blaming by expressing themselves in a healthier manner.

D. Family members continue to use blaming comments rather than more healthy ways of expressing themselves and were reminded about the healthy opportunities available to them.

## 25. List External Stressors (25)

A. Each family member was asked to list the external stressors that are putting pressure on the family relationships.

B. Active listening was provided as the family described the external stressors that are putting pressure on their relationship.

C. A discussion was held in regard to how family members can help each other to reduce the amount of external pressure on the family.

D. Family members failed to identify external stressors putting pressure on their relationships and were provided with tentative examples in this area.

# BLENDED FAMILY PROBLEMS

## CLIENT PRESENTATION

### 1. Discipline Arguments (1)*

A. The parent and stepparent often have arguments related to child-discipline differences.

B. The parent and stepparent display different child-discipline philosophies.

C. The parent and stepparent often disagree about how each disciplines the other's child.

D. As communication has increased, the parent and stepparent are more congruent in child-discipline techniques and are able to tolerate differences.

### 2. Loyalty to Absent Biological Parent (2)

A. The children within the family seem to have a great deal of ambivalence and uncertainty about attaching themselves to the stepparent.

B. The children have verbalized loyalty toward the biological, noncustodial parent.

C. The children have reported fear of hurting the feelings of the biological, noncustodial parent if an attachment were to be made to the stepparent.

D. As internal conflicts have been resolved, a sense of loyalty and belonging are beginning to develop between the children and the stepparent.

### 3. Behavioral/Emotional Problem Due to a Third Parent (3)

A. Behavioral and emotional problems have developed due to difficulty adjusting to a new third parent.

B. The child seems to be rejecting the stepparent's enforcement of rules and regulations.

C. The child appears to be confused and uncertain about how to respond due to the involvement of a new stepparent.

D. The child has become more accepting of the stepparent's enforcement of rules and regulations, and behavioral and emotional problems have decreased.

### 4. Non-Custodial Biological Parent Interference (4)

A. A biological parent living outside of the home often encourages the child to protest against the stepparent.

B. The biological parent living outside of the home tells the child that the stepparent does not have authority within the home.

C. The biological parent living outside of the home does not support the authority of the stepparent.

*The numbers in parentheses correlate to the number of the Behavioral Definition statement in the companion chapter with the same title in *The Family Therapy Treatment Planner*, Second Ed. (Dattilio, Jongsma, and Davis) by John Wiley & Sons, 2010.

D. Efforts to keep ex-spouses uninvolved in the new family's business have been unsuccessful and sabotaged by the children.

E. Efforts to keep ex-spouses uninvolved in the daily life of the new family have started to be effective, and the new family has started to solidify and become connected.

### 5. Arguments over Favoritism (5)

A. The parents often have arguments regarding perceived favoritism or financial support for biological versus nonbiological children.

B. A pattern of parental favoritism for biological versus nonbiological children is evident and causes conflict within the relationship.

C. The parents have identified a pattern of financial support that favors biological versus non-biological children.

D. The parents have acknowledged a pattern of favoritism for biological versus nonbiological children, and have committed to modifying this pattern.

E. The parents report a more balanced approach to the support of the biological and non-biological children.

### 6. Financial Pressures (6)

A. The family experiences financial pressures due to a reduction in or loss of child support.

B. Family members often verbalize resentment of the financial aspect of a previous divorce settlement or support arrangement.

C. Family members are often at odds with each other regarding the financial aspects of child support payments.

D. As the family has developed a more supportive approach to each other, financial pressures from divorce settlements and child support expectations become a less divisive issue.

### 7. Blended Sibling Rivalry (7)

A. The blended siblings have engaged in ongoing conflict with one another.

B. The sibling groups have clearly stated their dislike and resentment for one another.

C. The parents have indicated their frustration with the siblings' apparent attempt to sabotage their efforts to form a new family group.

D. The sibling groups have stopped their open conflict and started to tolerate and show respect for each other.

### 8. Jealousy/Insecurity Regarding Displays of Affection for Stepchild (8)

A. One parent has displayed affection for the stepchild, which has brought about jealousy and insecurity within the spouse.

B. Marital tension has occurred because of the jealousy and insecurity experienced as a result of a parent displaying affection for the stepchild.

C. The child feels guilty about the attention and affection displayed by the stepparent, and the struggles that this causes within the marriage.

D. Family members have openly discussed their concerns regarding the attention and affection displayed for a stepchild.

E. As the family has processed jealousy, insecurity, tension, and guilt issues regarding the attention and affection for a stepchild, these issues have been resolved.

## 9. Conflicts Regarding Visitation (9)

A. Conflict has risen between the noncustodial parent and the custodial parent over the child visitation schedule.

B. The noncustodial parent often usurps more visitation time than agreed on.

C. The ex-spouse deliberately undermines the wishes of the custodial parent.

D. An ex-partner's failure to show up for visitation, lateness in picking up a child, or entering the blended family's home to get the child has caused conflict between family members.

E. As better limits have been set, the ex-partner's failure to act appropriately regarding visitation and transportation has been decreased.

F. Family members have been more supportive of each other regarding visitation and transportation to a noncustodial ex-partner's home.

## 10. Ex-Spouse Interference (10)

A. An ex-spouse commonly interferes with the family issues that pertain to the blended family's lifestyle (e.g., curfew, rules, and regulations).

B. Family members often blame those most closely connected with the interfering ex-spouse for the problem caused by the ex-spouse.

C. Family members are working together to decrease the ex-spouse's interference with family issues that pertain to the blended family's lifestyle.

## 11. Personalization of the Child's Behavioral Problems (11)

A. The parents tend to internalize or feel overly responsible for their children's behavior problems.

B. The parents have supported each other in not taking the blame for a child's behavior problems.

C. Responsibility for a child's behavior rests clearly with the child, but both parents accept their role of guidance, discipline, and nurturance.

## 12. Children's Complaints of Unfair Treatment by Stepparent (12)

A. Children in the blended family often complain that they are being treated unfairly or ignored by the stepparent.

B. The stepparent acknowledges unfair treatment of the children.

C. The stepparent acknowledges ignoring the children within the blended family.

D. As treatment has progressed, the stepparent has begun to treat the children of the blended family in a fair manner.

E. The family processed the feelings of being treated unfairly or ignored by the stepparent, and came to understand that this was inaccurate.

### 13. Conflict over Financial Support of Grown Children (13)

A. Grown children living outside of the family-of-origin have asked for financial support.

B. Conflict has arisen among the blended family members regarding the financial support of grown children.

C. As decisions related to providing financial assistance for grown children have been made, the blended family has been able to process and come to terms with these decisions.

## INTERVENTIONS IMPLEMENTED

### 1. Establish a Neutral Zone (1)*

A. The therapy session was established as a neutral zone for family members to express themselves without fear of retaliation by other family members.

B. The need for freedom to express opinions was emphasized.

C. Retaliation against family members was confronted within the session.

D. Family members were reminded that retaliation after any session was not conducive to healthy treatment.

### 2. Use Metaphors or Family Sculpting (2)

A. Metaphors were used to facilitate family members talking openly about their feelings and emotions.

B. Family sculpting techniques were used to help family members talk about present conflict with one another.

C. The family was helped to process the issues that were brought up through the use of metaphors or family sculpting techniques.

### 3. Facilitate Dialogue (3)

A. A dialogue was facilitated between the disgruntled family and the new parent.

B. The child's feelings of disloyalty to his/her biological parent were acknowledged and explored.

### 4. Facilitate Release of Child's Feeling (4)

A. The child was assisted in releasing emotions that may be inhibiting acceptance of the stepparent's directives.

B. The child's fear of being controlled by the new stepparent was acknowledged and supported.

C. The child's fear of abandonment by the new stepparent was acknowledged as a common struggle.

D. The displaced anger toward an absent parent was identified as affecting the acceptance of the stepparent's directives.

---

*The numbers in parentheses correlate to the number of the Therapeutic Intervention statement in the companion chapter with the same title in *The Family Therapy Treatment Planner*, Second Ed. (Dattilio, Jongsma, and Davis) by John Wiley & Sons, 2010.

## 5. Assess Stepparent's Style and Alternatives (5)

A. The strictness or rigidity of the stepparent's style was assessed.

B. Feedback was provided to the stepparent about how strictness or rigidity may be interfering with acceptance by the children.

C. Role-playing and modeling were used to help the stepparent consider a more flexible, alternative method of parenting.

D. Positive feedback was provided as the stepparent was able to accept the need for modifying approaches to the children.

E. The stepparent was quite rejecting about any ideas of modifying the approach to the children and was provided with additional feedback in this area.

F. The stepparent's approach to the children was assessed, and it was reflected that the stepparent uses healthy, appropriate ways to interact with the children.

## 6. Assess for Scapegoating of Ex-Spouse (6)

A. The parent and stepparent were assessed for whether they too easily blame an ex-spouse for internal conflicts within the marriage and blended family.

B. Feedback was provided to the parent and stepparent for the ease with which they blame an ex-spouse for internal conflicts within the marriage and blended family.

C. It was reflected to the parent and stepparent that they do not easily blame an ex-spouse for internal conflicts within their marriage and blended family.

## 7. Resolve Biological Parents' Residual Feelings (7)

A. Conjoint sessions were held with the biological parents to resolve any residual feelings about their prior union.

B. Positive feedback was provided as the biological parents were able to resolve old feelings that have affected the functioning of the current families.

C. Although attempts were made to resolve residual feelings about the biological parents' prior union, their ongoing pattern of animosity toward each other was evident.

## 8. Teach Assertiveness and Communication Skills (8)

A. Assertiveness and communication skills were taught to the parents to strengthen the relationship and reduce the impact of an ex-spouse.

B. The parents were taught the use of "I" messages, empathetic listening, reflective responding, undivided attention, good eye contact, and respectful, controlled expression of emotions.

C. The parents were directed to read *Core Communications, Skills and Processes* (Miller and Miller).

D. The parents have read the recommended information on communication, and key points were reviewed.

E. Positive feedback was provided for the parents' increase in the use of assertiveness and communication skills.

F. The parents have not increased their use of assertiveness and communication skills and were provided with remedial feedback in this area.

### 9. Invite Ex-Spouse to Conjoint Session (9)

A. A conjoint session was coordinated between the biological parents to discuss differences in parenting philosophies, strategies, and misperceptions.

B. Both biological parents and stepparents were invited to a conjoint session to discuss differences in philosophies, strategies, and misperceptions.

C. The co-parenting group was urged to use a unified parenting program, such as the STEP or PET programs.

D. Positive feedback was provided as the parents and stepparents have come to an agreement regarding parenting philosophies and strategies.

E. The co-parents have not reached any agreement regarding parenting philosophies and strategies and were urged to set aside old differences to develop these strategies.

### 10. Address Underlying Emotional Needs (10)

A. A conjoint meeting was conducted with the parents of the blended family to address personal insecurities, feelings of loss of power, and needs to demonstrate favoritism.

B. Alternative methods for dealing with insecurities, loss of power, and favoritism needs were suggested.

C. The spouses were encouraged to be supportive of each other regarding the emotional concerns related to the blended family.

D. The parents were reinforced as they have reviewed and incorporated new techniques for addressing personal insecurities, loss of power, and needs to demonstrate favoritism.

E. The parents have not incorporated new techniques for dealing with issues related to the blended family and were reminded for the need for this type of resolution.

### 11. Assign Reading Materials on Conflict Resolution (11)

A. The parents were recommended to real information on conflict resolution in blended families.

B. The parents were recommended to read *Stepfamilies* (Bray and Kelly).

C. The parents have read the assigned information in conflict resolution, and key points were reviewed and processes.

D. The parents have not read assigned information on conflict resolution and were redirected to do so.

### 12. Use Role Exchange and Role Reversal (12)

A. The parents were urged to consider the advantages and disadvantages of behavioral change.

B. Role-exchange and role-reversal techniques were used to decrease parental conflicts and to help understand the stress that accompanies behavioral change.

C. After being helped to consider the effects of behavioral change, the parents are more understanding and have less conflict.

### 13. Address Child's Manipulation (13)

A. The idea that a child can play one parent against the other for power and territorial advantages was identified and discussed.

B. Parents were assisted in identifying ways in which the child has attempted to manipulate one parent against the other.

C. Positive feedback was provided for the healthy responses to a child attempting to manipulate one parent against the other.

D. The parents denied any pattern of manipulation or playing one parent against the other and were provided with tentative examples of how this occurs.

### 14. Discuss Effects of Reduction in Child Support (14)

A. It was noted that changes have been made in the pattern of child support provided.

B. The negative emotional reaction between family members regarding the financial effect of a reduction in child support was reviewed.

C. Family members were helped to process feelings such as anger and resentment due to the reduction in the amount of child support.

### 15. Encourage Children to Express Feelings Regarding Finances (15)

A. The children were encouraged to express their feelings regarding finances to both biological parents.

B. The children were assisted in identifying their emotions regarding finances.

C. The effect of the parents' comments about each other's finances was reviewed.

D. The children were assisted in processing their discussion about finances with the biological parents.

### 16. Brainstorm Solutions to Income Reduction (16)

A. Family members were assisted in brainstorming financial solutions to the change in income due to the reduction in child support payments (e.g., adding part-time jobs for family members).

B. Family members were assisted in identifying emotional solutions to the change in income due to the reduction in child support (e.g., more time spent in family activities that are free or low cost).

C. Family members were assisted in processing their ideas regarding how to deal with the change in income due to the reduction in child support.

### 17. Assess Effects of Affection (17)

A. The family was assessed to identify whether displays of affection by a parent to a stepchild may arouse anxiety, anger, suspicion, or jealousy in the biological parent.

B. It was reflected to the family that the displays of affection by a parent to the stepchild often arouse emotions for the biological parent.

C. The biological parent's own neglect or abuse in his/her family of origin was explored because this may relate to the negative emotional reaction to affection between the parent and stepchild.

D. Displays of affection by one parent to a stepchild do not appear to arouse anxiety, anger, suspicion, or jealousy in the biological parent, and this was reflected to the family.

## 18. Reframe Parent to Stepchild Affection (18)

A. The biological parent was assisted in dealing with insecurities regarding affection between the parent and stepchild.

B. The biological parent was urged to reframe the other parent's affection to the stepchild (e.g., "it's an honor to have my spouse show such fondness to my child").

C. Positive feedback was provided for the biological parent's ability to resolve insecurities regarding affection between the other parent and the stepchild.

D. The biological parent continues to have significant negative reactions to contact between the other parent and a stepchild and remedial assistance was provided in this area.

## 19. Reassure Children about Responsibility for Disagreement (19)

A. The children were reassured that they are not responsible for their parents' disagreements regarding visitation schedules.

B. The children were helped to see that their parents' disagreements do not reflect their parents' love for them.

C. The children were reinforced as they expressed acceptance of the concept that they were not responsible for the parents' disagreements regarding visitation scheduling.

D. The children continued to identify themselves as responsible for their parents' disagreements and were provided with remedial feedback in this area.

## 20. Suggest Conjoint Meeting Regarding Visitation (20)

A. A conjoint meeting was coordinated between the custodial and noncustodial parent to address the issue of visitation.

B. Both parties were willing to address the issue of visitation in a conjoint session and were reinforced for this willingness.

C. A conjoint session was held to work out issues related to visitation.

D. The custodial and noncustodial parents were not able to agree about issues related to visitation, and professional mediation was suggested.

## 21. Facilitate Children's Expression of Feelings Regarding Unfair Treatment (21)

A. The children were assisted in directly expressing their feelings of being treated unfairly by a stepparent.

B. The children were assisted in writing a letter to express the basis for their feelings of being treated unfairly by a stepparent.

C. Positive feedback was provided as the children expressed their feelings regarding being treated unfairly by a stepparent.

D. The parents seem to terminate the children's expression of their feelings regarding treatment by the stepparent and were urged to facilitate the expression of these feelings.

## 22. Explore Possible Ignoring of the Stepchildren (22)

A. The intentional or unintentional ignoring of the stepchildren by a parent was explored.

B. The stepparent identified a purposeful attempt to ignore the stepchildren, and the reasons behind this were processed.

C. The stepparent gained insight about an unintentional tendency to ignore the children and was supported for this insight.

D. Methods for increasing the parent's awareness of possible ignoring of the stepchildren were reviewed (e.g., suggest the use of reflective listening, evaluate parents' ability to listen to children).

E. A commitment from the parents to be more involved with the stepchildren was solicited.

### 23. Negotiate Fair Actions (23)

A. The children and the stepparent were assisted in negotiating actions that would be perceived as more fair to the stepchildren.

B. Positive feedback was provided to family members as they negotiated ways to increase the sense of fairness among the children.

C. Family members were not willing to accept a negotiated change in how the children are treated and were urged to consider this area.

### 24. Develop Relationship-Building Activities with the Nonbiological Child (24)

A. The parents were directed to facilitate involvement in relationship-building activities between the stepparent and the nonbiological child.

B. The nonbiological parent was directed to refrain from significant involvement in discipline until an appropriate relationship has been developed with that child.

C. The parents reported that the nonbiological parent has developed a more involved relationship with the child, and this was reviewed within the conjoint session.

D. The nonbiological parent has struggled to develop a relationship with the child, and the focus of the session was on how to increase this involvement.

### 25. Review Effects of Assisting Adult Offspring (25)

A. The pros and cons of giving money to adult offspring were reviewed.

B. The family members were assisted in brainstorming the potential resentment that may occur on the part of the spouse or other family members due to lending money or giving gifts to adult offspring.

C. Positive feedback was provided as the family members gave a realistic appraisal of the effects of lending money or giving gifts to adult offspring.

D. Family members were not realistic about the effects of assisting adult offspring and were given feedback in this area.

### 26. Vote on How to Assist Adult Family Members (26)

A. A family vote was taken on whether to assist adult family members.

B. A family vote was taken on how to assist adult family members.

C. The likelihood of guilt and anger that might arise due to assistance to adult family members was addressed, and the family was helped to identify how to deal with this tension.

D. Positive feedback was provided as the family has decided not to assist adult family members.

E. Positive feedback was provided as the family has agreed on how to assist adult family members.

### 27. Encourage Assertiveness (27)

A. Parents were encouraged to be assertive in the face of negative responses from children when they are refused financial assistance.

B. The long-term positive effects of assertiveness in the face of emotional blackmail were emphasized.

C. Positive reinforcement was provided to the parents for being assertive in not providing financial assistance to adult children.

D. The family members have continued to provide assistance to adult children despite their belief that they should not do this and were provided with remedial assistance on how to stick by their convictions.

# CHILD/PARENT CONFLICTS

## CLIENT PRESENTATION

### 1. Behavioral Problems (1)*

A. Children under the age of 13 have displayed behavioral problems (e.g., acting out, destructive behaviors, or refusal to go to school).

B. Behaviorally disordered children are often in a conflict with the parents.

C. Behaviorally disordered children are often in conflict with other members of the family.

D. As treatment has progressed, the children's behavioral problems have decreased.

### 2. Arguing between Parents (2)

A. The children's misbehavior tends to spark arguments and dissension between the parents.

B. The parents have become less effective with the discipline of the children due to ongoing arguments and dissension.

### 3. Power and Control Issue (3)

A. Boundaries between the parents' authority and the children's wishes have begun to weaken.

B. The children and parents appear to be vying for power and control within the family.

C. The parents have become decreasingly effective in their guidance of the children.

D. As treatment has progressed, the parents have strengthened their own boundaries and are more in control of guiding the family.

### 4. Community Problems (4)

A. The children's behavioral problems have spread to others within the community.

B. The neighbors have complained about the children's behavioral problems.

C. The children's behavioral problems have resulted in conflicts within the school setting.

D. The family's overall stress level has increased due to the children's behavioral problems in the community.

E. As treatment has progressed, the children have been better behaved within the community, which has helped to decrease the stress in the family.

### 5. Tension and Conflict (5)

A. The level of tension and conflict has risen within the home.

B. Family members are more irritable with each other due to the dysfunction in the home.

C. As treatment has progressed, family members have been less tense and less conflicted.

*The numbers in parentheses correlate to the number of the Behavioral Definition statement in the companion chapter with the same title in *The Family Therapy Treatment Planner*, Second Ed. (Dattilio, Jongsma, and Davis) by John Wiley & Sons, 2010.

C. Family members have developed plans for decreasing stress from external factors, and this plan was processed.

D. The family has not developed a plan to reduce the amount of stress from external factors and was redirected to this very important need.

## 8. Emphasize Support (8)

A. The parents were assisted in identifying methods for mutual support, rather than undercutting each other's attempts at setting limits on the children.

B. The parents were encouraged to support each other in setting limits on the children.

C. The parents were directed to review their differences of opinion regarding setting limits on the children in a private manner.

D. The parents identified several ways that they can support each other when setting limits on the children and were urged to implement these.

## 9. Role-Play Discipline (9)

A. Scenarios in which discipline is required were role-played, with appropriate support given to the parent who takes the lead for setting limits.

B. In processing the role-play, the helpfulness of support for the parent who is setting the limits was emphasized.

C. In role-play scenarios, the parents were noted to demonstrate mastery of discipline techniques and the need to support the limit-setting parent.

## 10. Assign Parenting Skills Material (10)

A. The parents were assigned readings and DVDs that may increase parenting skills.

B. The parents were assigned to review information from *Parenting Young Children* (Dinkmeyer, McKay, and Dinkmeyer).

C. The parents were encouraged to read *1-2-3 Magic* (Phelan).

D. The parents were assigned to read *Raising an Emotionally Intelligent Child* (Gottman and DeClaire).

E. The parents have reviewed the information related to parenting skills, and the key components were processed.

F. The parents have not reviewed the material related to parenting skills and were encouraged to do so.

## 11. Discuss Limiting Information about Disagreements (11)

A. The parents were urged to review the necessity of not allowing the children to have too much information about their disagreements.

B. The ways in which limiting information about parental disagreements can strengthen unity were reviewed.

C. The parents agreed on the need to limit information about their disagreements in order to strengthen their unity; this progress was reinforced.

D. It was emphasized to the parents that they review their disagreements in private, apart from the children.

## 12. Control Bickering (12)

A. Strategies for controlling bickering in front of the children were recommended to the parents.

B. The parents were encouraged to utilize self-talk or nonverbal signals to each other as a cue for curtailing bickering statements.

C. The parents were reinforced for using strategies to decrease their bickering in the presence of the children.

D. The parents continue to bicker significantly in the presence of the children and were reminded about techniques to curtail this pattern.

## 13. Solicit Examples of Negative Modeling (13)

A. Behaviors that are negative models for younger children were reviewed.

B. Family members identified behaviors that are negative models for younger children.

C. Family members failed to identify behaviors that are negative models for younger children and were provided with tentative examples in this area (e.g., temper tantrums, aggressive verbalizations, disrespectful name calling, ignoring another family member).

## 14. Role-Play Implementation of Healthy Alternatives (14)

A. Role-play techniques were used to help family members implement healthy alternatives to behaviors that serve as negative examples for the children.

B. Positive reinforcement was used as family members have displayed ways to replace their models for negative behavior.

C. Family members continued to model negative behavior and were provided with redirection in this area.

## 15. Contract for Positive Role-Modeling (15)

A. All family members were urged to contract to be a positive role model for younger family members.

B. Family members agreed to seek to implement positive alternative behaviors and to be positive role models for younger family members; positive feedback was provided for this commitment.

C. When family members failed to implement positive alternative behaviors or to be positive role models for younger family members, they were reminded about their commitment in this area.

## 16. Identify Distorted Cognition (16)

A. Family members were urged to track their thoughts and emotional reactions during problematic behaviors.

B. Family members were assisted in identifying distorted cognitions that promote problematic behaviors.

C. The pattern of distorted cognitions were reviewed with family members, with an emphasis on the extreme version of those cognitions, to help to reveal the illogical thought pattern.

D. Positive feedback was provided as family members were able to accept that their thinking was distorted.

### 17. Challenge Unreasonable Expectations (17)

A. Family members were helped to challenge unreasonable expectations regarding their child's behavior through persuasive illumination of the illogical premise involved.

B. Family members were supported as they identified unreasonable expectations.

C. Family members were unable to identify unreasonable expectations and were provided with specific examples (e.g., "This behavior will never change, and therefore my children are doomed to be social misfits.").

### 18. Provide Communication Training (18)

A. Family members were provided with basic communication training.

B. Family members were taught concepts from *Relationship Enhancement* (Guerney).

C. Family members were taught problem-solving skills.

D. Family members were taught concepts from *Parenting Young Children* (Dinkmeyer, McKay, and Dinkmeyer).

E. Family members were supported as they have used better communication and problem-solving skills.

F. Family members have not used better communication and problem-solving skills and were provided with additional feedback in this area.

### 19. Encourage Practice of Skills (19)

A. Family members were encouraged to role-play newly learned communication and problem-solving skills.

B. Family members' role-play of newly learned communication problem-solving skills was processed.

C. Family members were assisted in practicing problem definition, brainstorming solutions, evaluating alternatives in practice, solutions, and evaluating outcomes.

### 20. Rate Skills (20)

A. The parents were assisted in rating the effectiveness of the newly learned communication and problem-solving skills.

B. The positive and negative experiences that have occurred with the newly learned communication and problem-solving skills were processed.

### 21. Introduce Family Meeting Concept (21)

A. The parents were urged to hold family meetings on a regular basis in which all members express their thoughts and feelings.

B. The parents were assisted in establishing a set of basic rules to follow at the family meetings (e.g., length, frequency, attendance requirements, leadership, participation).

C. The family was assisted in problem-solving barriers to holding regular family meetings.

### 22. Assign Regular Family Meetings (22)

A. The family was assigned to hold family meetings on a regular basis.

B. Family members were asked to vote in session about the days and times for family meetings.

C. The use of family meetings was used and processed.

D. The family has not held family meetings and was redirected to use this helpful resource.

### 23. Recognize Inconsistency (23)

A. The parents were assisted in recognizing when there is inconsistency in their parenting.

B. The parents were encouraged to communicate with each other so that the children do not successfully manipulate them.

C. Positive feedback was provided as the parents identified ways in which they have communicated to resolve inconsistencies in their parenting.

D. The parents continued to be quite inconsistent in their parenting and were provided with additional feedback in this area.

### 24. Schedule Parenting Meetings (24)

A. The parents were asked to schedule parenting meetings with each other in order to review the children's behavior.

B. The parents were urged to develop plans during their parenting meetings for how to confront the children about their manipulations.

C. The parents have regularly met to review the children's behavior and develop plans for confronting them about their manipulations, and the benefits of this technique were reviewed.

D. The parents have not met to review the children's behavior and were redirected to do so.

### 25. Develop Awareness of Undercutting (25)

A. The parents were taught about the concept of undercutting each other, and that this was a natural response to frustration.

B. The parents were assisted in identifying how undercutting each other may inadvertently facilitate the children's manipulations.

C. The parents were supported as they have become more aware of how they are undercutting each other.

D. The parents did not identify ways in which they have been undercutting each other and were provided with examples in this area.

### 26. Facilitate Parents' Emotions (26)

A. The parents were assisted with getting in touch with their own emotions and frustrations associated with the trials of parenting.

B. The parents were assisted in normalizing their feelings regarding the trials of parenting.

C. The parents were encouraged when they freely expressed their emotions related to parenting.

D. The parents have been quite guarded about their feelings regarding parenting, and they were encouraged to be more open in this area.

### 5. Mind Reading (5)

A. Family members often rely on "mind reading" or "assumptions" to reach conclusions about the other family members' thoughts or feelings.

B. Family members often attribute specific thoughts or feelings to another family member based on nonverbal behaviors.

C. Family members are often incorrect in their conclusions based on "mind reading," "assumptions," or misinterpretation of nonverbal behaviors of other family members.

D. As treatment has progressed, the family has become more open in their communication and has decreased "mind reading."

### 6. Interruptions (6)

A. Family members often interrupt each other.

B. Family members often talk over each other.

C. The family tends to respond to the individuals who talk the loudest regardless of interruptions or other family members' comments.

D. Family members have decreased their pattern of interrupting or talking over each other.

## INTERVENTIONS IMPLEMENTED

### 1. Clarify Communication Problems (1)*

A. Definitions of communication problems were presented to the family.

B. Identifying techniques were used to provide examples of the family's communication problems.

C. The family was asked to present their own examples of communication problems.

D. The family was noted to have a good understanding of the nature of their communication problems.

### 2. Explore Family-of-Origin (2)

A. A genogram was developed to help explore communication problems from the parents' families-of-origin.

B. The *Family-of-Origin Inventory* (Stuart) was used to help explore communication problems that have trickled down from the parents' family-of-origin.

C. Family members were assisted in identifying the communication problems that have trickled down from the family-of-origin.

### 3. Reinforce Admission/Confront Denial (3)

A. Family members who readily admitted to communication problems were reinforced and encouraged.

B. Family members who denied communication problems were confronted with the reality of their problems.

*The numbers in parentheses correlate to the number of the Therapeutic Intervention statement in the companion chapter with the same title in *The Family Therapy Treatment Planner*, Second Ed. (Dattilio, Jongsma, and Davis) by John Wiley & Sons, 2010.

### 4. Identify Faulty Communication (4)

A. The family was asked to select a topical issue to discuss.

B. The family was observed, and specific feedback was provided regarding the faulty communication techniques used.

C. The family was videotaped in their discussion of a topical issue and were assisted in identifying times when they each engaged in faulty communication.

D. Family members were reinforced when they were able to identify faulty communication.

### 5. Contract "I" Statements (5)

A. Family members were contracted to shift away from blaming each other.

B. Family members were encouraged to use "I" statements.

C. Family members were assisted in role-playing the taking of responsibility for their own faulty communication skills.

D. Practicing taking responsibility for faulty communication skills was emphasized first with the parents and then with the resistant or oppositional children.

### 6. Discuss Recording Communication Success (6)

A. The idea of keeping a family record of when family members are successful in not blaming each other and taking personal responsibility was discussed.

B. The family was encouraged to monitor and document successes in communication.

C. The family record of successes in communication was reviewed.

D. The family has not kept a record of success in communication and was redirected to do so.

### 7. Teach Reflective Listening (7)

A. Family members were taught concepts related to reflective listening, rephrasing of confusing statements, and requesting clarification when something is not understood.

B. Reflective listening techniques were modeled to the family.

C. Family members were directed to specific speaker-listener techniques, as described in *Fighting for Your Marriage* (Markman, Stanley, and Blumberg) and *Core Communications, Skills and Processes* (Miller and Miller).

D. Positive feedback was provided for the healthy use of speaker-listener techniques.

E. The family has not used speaker-listener techniques in a healthy manner and was redirected to do so.

### 8. Confront Indirect, Unclear Communication (8)

A. The family was confronted about patterns of speaking indirectly, through other family members, or using only nonverbal communication.

B. Family members were encouraged to speak directly, clearly, and for themselves.

C. Family members' use of indirect communication was confronted.

D. Family members have continued to speak through other family members, or in nonverbal ways and were provided with specific redirection in this area.

### 9. Explore Underlying Dynamics (9)

A. Underlying dynamics that may be affecting the communication process were explored.

B. Underlying dynamics such as hidden resentment or avoidant behavior were reviewed.

C. Specific hidden dynamics affecting the communication process have been identified, and these areas have become the primary focus of family therapy.

D. No underlying dynamics were identified that may be affecting the communication process, but family members were encouraged to be aware of these types of dynamics.

### 10. Teach Cognitive Behavioral Techniques (10)

A. The family was taught cognitive-behavioral techniques to help family members reduce anger or frustration that results from problems in communication.

B. Family members were taught deep breathing and cognitive restructuring techniques to help decrease anger or frustration.

C. Family members were recommended to read *The Anger and Aggression Workbook* (Liptak, Leutenberg, and Sippola).

D. Family members were directed to read *The Anger Trap* (Carter).

E. Family members have learned cognitive-behavioral techniques for anger related to communication problems and were encouraged to use these.

F. Family members have struggled to learn the cognitive-behavioral techniques to cope with anger and frustration related to communication problems and were provided with remedial feedback in this area.

### 11. Encourage Alternative Ways to Vent Frustration (11)

A. Family members were encouraged to practice alternative behaviors for venting their frustration.

B. Family members were provided with specific examples of ways to vent their frustration (e.g., journaling, sports activities).

C. Family members were recommended to use books such as *Journalution* (Grason).

D. Family members were reinforced for their use of alternative frustration-venting techniques.

E. Family members have not used alternative frustration-venting techniques and were redirected to do so.

### 12. Teach Assertiveness Techniques (12)

A. Family members were trained in assertiveness techniques to counter passivity or aggression.

B. Family members were encouraged to read *Your Perfect Right* (Alberti and Emmons).

C. Family members have used assertiveness skills and were provided with support and encouragement.

D. Family members have failed to use assertiveness skills and were redirected to do so.

### 13. Teach the Problem-Solving Technique (13)

A. Family members were taught the six steps of the problem-solving technique.

B. Family members were encouraged to read information regarding problem solving in *Fighting for Your Marriage* (Marksman, Stanley, and Blumberg).

C. Family members were supported and reinforced for their use of the problem-solving technique.

D. The family has struggled to use the problem-solving technique and was provided with assistance in implementing this technique.

### 14. Reverse Roles (14)

A. Family members were instructed to reverse roles and review a problem from the other family members' perspective.

B. Family members were encouraged to provide each other with feedback about how well each is able to view the problem from other family members' perspective.

C. Family members were assisted in processing the experience of reversing roles.

### 15. Probe Regarding Desire for Closeness (15)

A. Family members were assisted in identifying how they have gravitated away from each other.

B. Family members were provided with specific examples of how they have tended to gravitate away from each other.

C. Family members were probed for a desire to increase their family connections.

D. It was reflected to family members that they have a great desire to be closer together.

E. It was reflected to family members that they have very little desire to be close to each other.

### 16. Explore Emotions (16)

A. Family members were assisted in exploring emotions that may contribute to isolation between family members.

B. Family members were helped to identify feelings of fear, anger, hurt, or depression.

C. Family members were assisted in identifying how the emotions contribute to isolation between family members.

D. Family members denied any emotional concerns that may contribute to isolation between family members and were encouraged to be aware of this dynamic.

### 17. Emphasize Time Needed for Cohesion (17)

A. The long period of time necessary to develop family cohesion was emphasized.

B. Empathy was given to the family regarding how cohesiveness may take time and feel different or unusual.

C. When family members attempted to have instant cohesion, the need for time for cohesion to build was emphasized.

### 18. Facilitate Emotions Related to Closeness (18)

A. Family members were encouraged to share their feelings about getting closer.

B. The pros and cons of a more cohesive family were focused on from each family member's perspective.

C. Family members' emotions regarding cohesiveness were characterized by anticipation and happiness.

D. Family members' emotions relating to cohesion were characterized by uncertainty and weariness.

### 19. Brainstorm Causes of Isolation (19)

A. Family members were assisted in brainstorming dynamics that might cause a family member to slide back into old habits of isolation.

B. Family members were supported as they identified a variety of dynamics that might affect family members and cause them to slide back into old habits of isolation.

C. Family members failed to identify dynamics that might cause backsliding into isolation and were provided with tentative examples (e.g., laziness, strength of old patterns, crisis).

### 20. Review Techniques for Backsliding (20)

A. Family members were assisted in reviewing techniques for how to avoid backslides into old habits.

B. Family members were supported and encouraged as they identified several techniques that may help them from backsliding into old habits.

C. Family members failed to identify techniques to avoid backslides and were provided with tentative examples in this area (e.g., monitoring, family meetings).

### 21. Assign Regular Family Meetings (21)

A. The family was assigned to hold family meetings on a regular basis.

B. Family members were asked to vote in session about the days and times for family meetings.

C. The use of family meetings was reviewed and processed.

D. The family has not held family meetings and was redirected to use this helpful resource.

### 22. Practice Initiating & Implementing Family Meetings (22)

A. Role-play and modeling techniques were used to assist the family in initiating and implementing family meetings.

B. The family was taught communication techniques (e.g., "I" statements, active listening, soft start-ups).

C. The family was reinforced for the implementation of family meetings.

D. The family has not implemented family meetings and was redirected to do so.

### 23. Reinforce Open, Respectful Communication (23)

A. Family members were reinforced when they contributed to open, respectful communication.

B. It was reflected to family members that their open, respectful communication has reduced the isolation between family members.

C. Family members have not contributed to open, respectful communication and were redirected to do so.

### 24. Model Providing Positive Feedback (24)

A. Modeling techniques were used to teach family members how to give positive feedback to one another.

B. Role-play techniques were used to teach the practice of giving positive feedback.

C. Family members were reinforced for providing positive feedback to one another.

D. Family members have not provided positive feedback to one another and were confronted about this need.

### 25. Assign Pleasing Behaviors (25)

A. The concept of "pleasing" behavior was discussed with the family members, with an emphasis on doing random acts of kindness for one another.

B. Family members were assigned to do "pleasing" behaviors for each other.

C. The positive, productive interaction developed through "pleasing" behaviors was reviewed and processed.

D. Family members often emphasized the inequity of family members' implementation of "pleasing" behaviors and were encouraged to focus on the positive family interactions that have occurred.

### 26. Plan Family Outings (26)

A. It was suggested to the family that they plan family outings or activities to strengthen family interaction.

B. Family members have been engaged in family outings or activities and were asked to discuss their reactions to this exercise.

C. Family members have struggled to work together to plan family outings and were assisted in developing these techniques.

### 27. Conduct Follow-Up Visits (27)

A. A follow-up visit was arranged with the parents to reinforce their role in supporting the family change.

B. A follow-up visit was conducted to help the parents focus on their role in supporting the family change.

# COMPULSIVE BEHAVIORS

## CLIENT PRESENTATION

### 1. Compulsive Activity Interferes with Daily Functioning (1)*

A. A family member engages excessively in a compulsive activity to the point that it interferes with daily functioning.

B. A family member's gambling behavior has begun to interfere with daily functioning of the family.

C. A family member's compulsive shopping has had an effect on the daily functioning of the family.

D. A family member's persistent Internet use has caused interference with the daily functioning of the family.

E. A family member's excessive involvement in health and exercise activities has created problems with the daily functioning of the family.

F. As treatment has progressed, the family member has been able to decrease the excessive involvement in a specific activity, which has helped to increase the functioning of the family.

### 2. Relationship Changes (2)

A. The response of family members to the compulsive individual's excessive behavior has led to a change in the pattern of relationships within the family.

B. Tension and conflict have increased because of the family members' response to the compulsive individual's excessive behavior.

C. Family members have begun to modify their responses to the compulsive behavior.

D. As treatment has progressed, the compulsive behavior has decreased and the level of tension and conflict has decreased within the family.

### 3. Abusive Response to Confrontation (3)

A. When the family member is confronted about the excessive behavior, verbal or physical abuse occurs.

B. The family member with compulsive behavior often becomes threatening or derides other family members when confronted about the excessive behavior.

C. The family member with compulsive behavior has been assaultive to other family members when confronted about the excessive behavior.

D. As the family member with compulsive behavior patterns has come to accept these behaviors as compulsive, the pattern of verbal or physical abuse has decreased.

*The numbers in parentheses correlate to the number of the Behavioral Definition statement in the companion chapter with the same title in *The Family Therapy Treatment Planner*, Second Ed. (Dattilio, Jongsma, and Davis) by John Wiley & Sons, 2010.

## 4. Enabling (4)

A. Family members without compulsive behaviors consistently enable the family member with compulsive behaviors by making excuses for the other's behavior, doing anything to please the compulsive family member, and denying the seriousness of the problem.

B. The enabling family members have been disparaged or abused repeatedly without offering assertive, constructive resistance.

C. The partner without compulsive behavior has acknowledged being an enabler and is beginning to take steps to change this pattern.

D. As the partner without compulsive behavior has terminated the pattern of enabling, the dynamics within the relationship have changed.

## 5. Negative Results of Excessive Behavior (5)

A. A pattern of dysfunctional communication has resulted from the excessive behavior pattern.

B. The family member with compulsive behavior has experienced a loss of employment.

C. The family member with compulsive behavior has lost financial support due to the pattern of excessive behavior.

D. Medication problems have resulted from the pattern of excessive behavior.

E. As treatment has progressed, the effects of the compulsive behavior have been decreased.

## 6. Children Acting Out (6)

A. A lack of structure or boundaries has occurred in the family environment as a consequence of the excessive behavior.

B. The children appear to be acting out as a result of the long-term effects of a lack of structure or boundaries in the environment.

C. As the excessive, compulsive behaviors have been remediated, structure and boundaries within the environment have improved.

D. Children have displayed more controlled behavior due to the structure and boundaries provided within the environment.

## 7. Social Isolation (7)

A. The family member with compulsive behavior is away from the family.

B. The family member with the compulsive behavior has been emotionally unavailable to the other family members.

C. The noncompulsive family members have become passively withdrawn.

D. As treatment has progressed, the family member with compulsive behavior has decreased time away from the family.

E. The family member with compulsive behavior continues to spend time away from the family, but the other family members have become more socially involved with others.

## 8. Daily Responsibilities Not Met (8)

A. The family member with the compulsive behavior pattern often fails to follow through on daily responsibilities.

B. Other family members are unable to follow through on daily responsibilities due to the effect of the compulsive family member's behavior.

C. Financial consequences have occurred (e.g., bills not being paid, checks bouncing) because of the time spent on the compulsive activity.

D. As treatment has progressed, family members have displayed better follow-through on daily responsibilities and are taking care of financial concerns.

### 9. Shame and Humiliation for Family Members (9)

A. Family members described feelings of shame and humiliation because of the family member's compulsive behavior.

B. Family members often make excuses for the family member's compulsive behavior in order to save face.

C. As treatment has progressed, family members have obtained perspective on the compulsive family member's responsibility for the compulsive behavior.

D. As a result of communicating family members' experience of shame and humiliation, the family member with the compulsive behaviors has been able to reduce the frequency of these types of behaviors.


## INTERVENTIONS IMPLEMENTED

### 1. Determine Degree of Compulsivity (1)*

A. Interviewing techniques were used to determine the degree of compulsivity or excessive engagement in activities.

B. Specific inventories were administered to determine the degree of compulsivity or excessive engagement in activities.

C. The daily activities chart from *Cognitive Therapy: Basics and Beyond* (Beck) was used to access the degree of compulsivity and excessive engagement in activities.

D. *Measuring Non-Pathological Anxiety and Compulsiveness* (Kagen and Squires) was used to determine the degree of compulsivity or excessive engagement in activities.

E. A significant level of compulsivity and excessive engagement in activities was identified.

F. A rather limited level of compulsivity or excessive engagement in activities was identified.

### 2. Solicit Family Member Input (2)

A. Family members were asked to identify why they believe the activity is excessive or compulsive.

B. All family members were encouraged to provide their opinion about the excessiveness or compulsiveness of the family member's behavior.

---

*The numbers in parentheses correlate to the number of the Therapeutic Intervention statement in the companion chapter with the same title in *The Family Therapy Treatment Planner*, Second Ed. (Dattilio, Jongsma, and Davis) by John Wiley & Sons, 2010.

C. It was reflected to the family that family members consistently see the activity as excessive or compulsive.

D. It was reflected to the family members that there is some variance between family members' opinions of the excessive and compulsive types of behaviors.

### 3. Review Effects on Family (3)

A. Family members' perspectives were obtained regarding the negative effects that the compulsive behavior has had on all family members and the family dynamics.

B. The perceived effects of the compulsive behavior on family members' self-esteem, employment, health, social relations, personal finances, and family life were assessed.

C. A special emphasis was placed on the impact that denial has played on the family dynamics.

D. Family members' perspectives about the negative effects of the compulsive behavior were summarized and reflected to the family.

### 4. Assign Reading Material (4)

A. Reading material was assigned regarding the compulsive behavior and its effects, controlled behavior, and the family dynamics of addiction.

B. *Sex, Drugs, Gambling and Chocolate: A Workbook for Overcoming Addictions* (Horvath and Hester) was recommended to family members.

C. Family members were directed to read *Compulsive Gamblers and Their Families* (McEnvoy).

D. *Caught in the Net* (Young) was recommended to family members.

E. *Consuming Passions: Help for Compulsive Shoppers* (Catalan and Sonenberg) was recommended to family members.

F. Family members have read the assigned reading material, and key points were reviewed.

G. Family members have not read the assigned reading material and were redirected to do so.

### 5. Review Reading Material (5)

A. A discussion session was held with family members to process the material that they have read about compulsive behavior.

B. Family members were asked to identify new insights that they have gained through the reading of material about the compulsive behavior.

C. Family members have read the assigned material about compulsive behavior, and key points were reviewed.

D. Family members have not read the assigned material about compulsive behavior and were redirected to do so.

### 6. Contract for Sessions (6)

A. A joint family contract was developed for all members to sign, agreeing to attend all sessions and to be completely open about any compulsive behaviors that they may engage in themselves.

B. Family members were reinforced for signing the contract regarding sessions.

C. Family members have not signed the contract regarding sessions, and the reasons for this failure were processed.

### 7. Request Agreement for Abstinence and Support Group (7)

A. Since the session attendance contract was broken, the compulsive family member was asked to sign an agreement of abstinence from all excessive behaviors.

B. Since the session attendance contract was broken, the compulsive family member was asked to sign an agreement to attend a support group related to the compulsive behavior.

C. The abstinence and support group agreement was completed, and positive feedback was provided.

D. The compulsive family member has not agreed to abstinence and attending a support group, and greater focus was provided in this area.

### 8. Refer for Psychiatric Intervention (8)

A. The compulsive family member was referred to a psychiatrist specializing in obsessive-compulsive behavior.

B. The compulsive family member has followed through on the referral to a physician and has been assessed for a prescription of psychotropic medication, but none was prescribed.

C. Psychotropic medications have been prescribed for the compulsive family member.

D. The psychotropic medications were monitored for side effects and are being appropriately titrated.

E. The compulsive family member has refused a prescription for psychotropic medication provided by the physician, and this opposition was processed.

### 9. Contract Regarding Aggression (9)

A. A written contract was developed stipulating that no member of the family will engage in aggressive or assaultive threats on any other family member.

B. Positive feedback was provided for family members regarding the agreement not to engage in aggressive or assaultive threats.

C. Family members have not agreed to refrain from aggressive or assaultive threats, and the focus of treatment was changed to this area.

### 10. Develop Refuge Plan (10)

A. The need for safety if violence does erupt was emphasized.

B. A specific refuge plan was developed should violence erupt when compulsive behavior is challenged.

C. Family members have been periodically reminded about the refuge plan.

### 11. Refer for Anger Treatment (11)

A. The acting-out family member was referred to another provider for individual or group treatment of the explosive disorder.

B. The acting-out family member has completed treatment regarding the explosive disorder and is able to be more functional in the family therapy sessions.

C. The acting-out family member has refused to attend individual or group treatment for anger control and was reminded about the need for this helpful resource.

### 12. Contract for Control of Excessive Behavior (12)

A. The family member engaging in compulsive behavior was assigned to follow a structured format for controlling the excessive behavior.

B. The family member with the compulsive behavior was directed to use a stipulated, written activity schedule.

C. The family member with the compulsive behavior was directed to attend a 12-step program.

D. An agreement was made that if the contract for controlling the excessive behavior was broken a designated number of times (e.g., twice), a complete abstinence contract will be instituted.

E. Positive feedback was provided as the compulsive family member openly agreed to the structured format for controlling excessive behavior.

F. The family member with the compulsive behavior has not agreed to follow a structured format for controlling the excessive behavior and was redirected to this important need.

### 13. Contract Regarding Frequency of Behavior (13)

A. The compulsive member was asked to sign a written contract that stipulates the moderate frequency of behavior to be engaged in on a daily and weekly basis.

B. Positive feedback was provided as the compulsive family member has agreed on the frequency of the behavior to be engaged in.

C. The compulsive family member has declined to sign a written contract that stipulated the frequency of behavior to be engaged in and was redirected toward this important concept.

### 14. Use Daily Record Form (14)

A. A daily record form was developed to help track the frequency and intensity of the compulsive behaviors.

B. The record form was reviewed in order to determine the family member's ability to consistently control the behavior.

C. It was reflected to the family member that the daily record form shows the ability to consistently control the behavior.

D. It was reflected to the family member that the daily record form shows an inability to consistently control the behavior.

### 15. Teach Cognitive-Behavioral Strategies (15)

A. Cognitive-behavioral strategies were taught for use in anger and stress control.

B. Controlled breathing and thought-stopping techniques were taught for anger and stress control.

C. Family members have read the assigned material and key points were reviewed.

D. Family members have not read the assigned material and were redirected to do so.

### 16. Explore Perceived Benefits (16)

A. The compulsive family member was assisted in clarifying the benefits that are obtained by engaging in the excessive behavior.

B. The compulsive family member was assisted in identifying needs that were being met by the excessive behavior.

C. The compulsive family member was provided with tentative examples about the perceived benefits of engaging in the excessive behaviors (acceptance by friends/peers, reduction of social or other anxiety, escape from family tensions).

## 17. Replace Compulsive Behaviors (17)

A. Specific strategies were developed that can replace compulsive behaviors, while still obtaining the benefits sought.

B. The compulsive family member was reminded about the concept that the benefits obtained from the compulsive behavior could be found through healthier behaviors, but may take a longer period of time to achieve.

C. The compulsive family member was reinforced for identifying several behaviors to be used in place of the compulsive behavior.

D. The compulsive family member has not used behavioral strategies to replace the compulsive behavior and was redirected in this area.

## 18. Teach Stress Management Techniques (18)

A. The compulsive family member was taught relaxation techniques such as progressive relaxation, guided imagery, and biofeedback.

B. The compulsive family member was assigned to relax twice a day for 10 to 20 minutes.

C. The compulsive family member has reported regular use of the prescribed relaxation techniques, which has led to decreased anxiety and decreased compulsive behaviors.

D. The compulsive family member has not implemented the identified relaxation techniques and continues to feel quite stressed in anxiety-producing situations.

## 19. Model Assertiveness and Social Skills Training (19)

A. Modeling and role-playing techniques were used to teach assertiveness and social skills.

B. The compulsive family member was reinforced for use of assertiveness and other social skills.

C. The compulsive family member was assisted in weighing the pros and cons of using assertiveness and other social skills as an alternative to the excessive behavior.

## 20. Teach about "Caring Days" (20)

A. Family members were taught about the concept of "caring days."

B. Family members were encouraged to set aside time to do something kind for another family member, without expecting anything in return.

C. Family members have performed caring activities for each other, and the benefits of this pattern were reviewed.

D. Family members have not participated in "caring days" and were reminded about this helpful technique.

## 21. Develop Plan for Social Activities (21)

A. Family members were encouraged to formulate a plan for social activities with other couples or families that did not include the compulsive activity.

B. Family members were assisted in developing their plan for social activities that do not include the compulsive activity.

C. Tentative suggestions were provided to family members, such as church, hobby, work associates, and recreational groups as possible network opportunities for outreach.

D. Positive feedback was provided as family members have developed several alternative social engagements.

E. Family members have not developed a plan for social activities that does not include the compulsive behavior and were redirected about this important need.

## 22. Schedule Roles for Specific Activity (22)

A. The family was assisted in scheduling a specific recreational activity.

B. Each family member was assigned a specific role in making the activity happen.

C. Family members have developed specific activities and responsibilities that do not include the compulsive behavior and were provided with specific feedback in this area.

D. Family members have not developed specific roles and activities and were redirected to do so.

## 23. Identify Relapse Triggers (23)

A. The family was assisted in identifying triggers of relapse for the compulsive behavior.

B. The family was provided with tentative examples of triggers that might cause a relapse of the compulsive behavior.

C. The compulsive family member was assisted in developing ways to avoid future relapse.

## 24. Develop Coping Strategy Reminders (24)

A. The family was directed to develop index cards that list alternative coping strategies for compulsive behaviors.

B. The compulsive family member was directed to regularly review the alternative coping strategies.

C. The compulsive family member was reminded to use the alternative coping strategies in the face of stimuli that trigger relapse.

D. The family was provided with tentative examples of alternative coping behaviors (e.g., connecting with sponsors at the support groups or using stress inoculation techniques).

## 25. Address Subtle Enabling (25)

A. The subtle ways in which family members may enable each other regarding compulsive behaviors were reviewed and processed.

B. The subtle cover-up behaviors that may be used to avoid confrontation regarding compulsive behaviors were reviewed and processed.

C. Family members acknowledged the subtle enabling and cover-up behaviors that have been used and were supported and encouraged for this honesty.

D. Family members were educated about possible cover-up or enabling behaviors.

### 26. Role-Play Family Scenarios (26)

A. Possible family scenarios were role-played, with an emphasis on the noncompulsive family member not taking responsibility for the compulsive family member's behavior.

B. Support and feedback were provided to family members without the compulsive behaviors when they were able to decline to take responsibility for the compulsive family member's behavior.

C. Family members were reminded about ways in which they can enable each other, and these were role played within the session.

### 27. Review Successful Avoidance of Enabling Behaviors (27)

A. Instances of family interaction at home in which family members have avoided enabling behaviors were emphasized.

B. Positive feedback was provided to family members for examples of situations in which they have avoided enabling behaviors.

C. Family members indicated no situations in which they have avoided enabling behaviors and were assisted in identifying situations in which they could have done so; identification of these situations was reinforced.

### 28. Brainstorm Constructive Response to High-Risk Situations (28)

A. The family was assisted in brainstorming ideas on how to more constructively respond to situations that previously precipitated enabling behaviors.

B. Family members were helped to narrow down and identify alternative responses to situations that previously precipitated enabling behaviors.

### 29. Teach about Roles (29)

A. Family members were taught about the roles usually adopted by children of addictive parents.

B. Family members were provided with feedback about roles such as "the family hero," "the scapegoat," "the lost child," and "the mascot."

C. The children were assisted in identifying the roles each has adopted.

### 30. Encourage Changing Roles (30)

A. The children were encouraged to give up their unhealthy role assumptions.

B. The children were encouraged to express their needs, feelings and desires directly and assertively.

C. When children participated in an unhealthy role, they were gently confronted and redirected.

D. The children were reinforced for situations in which they have expressed their needs, feelings, and desires directly and assertively.

### 31. Recommend Apology (31)

A. It was recommended that the compulsive family member formally apologize for the pain caused to other family members as a result of the excessive behavior and the time taken away from the family.

B. The compulsive family member was assisted in formulating an apology to other family members.

C. The compulsive family member has completed the apology to other family members, and this experience was processed.

D. The compulsive family member has declined to do any type of formal apology to other family members and was provided with additional feedback in this area.

# DEATH OF A CHILD

## CLIENT PRESENTATION

### 1. Accidental Sudden Death (1)*

A. A child from the family has recently, suddenly, accidentally died.

B. The family history includes the accidental, sudden death of a child.

C. The surviving family members experience significant grief related to the accidental, sudden death of the child within the family.

D. Family members have begun to process their grief.

### 2. Loss of Pregnancy (2)

A. Expecting parents have lost the child *in utero* (stillborn).

B. A child died at birth.

C. The expecting parents and family members grieve over the loss of the expected child.

D. As treatment has progressed, the parents have moved through the stages of grief.

### 3. Death Due to a Long, Terminal Illness (3)

A. The family has lost a child following a long, terminal illness.

B. Despite extensive medical treatment, the child succumbed to a terminal illness.

C. Family members have expressed pain and grief related to the long illness and eventual death of the child.

D. As treatment has progressed, the family has begun to grieve the loss of the child and found a sense of meaning in the illness and death.

### 4. Death Due to an Acute Illness (4)

A. The family has lost a child due to an acute illness.

B. The family expressed shock at the quickness with which the illness took their child.

C. As treatment has progressed, the family has begun to cope with the loss of their child due to an acute illness.

### 5. Guilt and Trauma Due to Death of a Child (5)

A. Family members witnessed the accidental death of a child.

B. Family members participated in the accidental death of a child (e.g., auto accident).

C. Family members experience high levels of guilt and trauma due to the accidental death of the child.

D. Family members appeared to be overwhelmed by guilt and trauma.

E. As treatment has progressed, the family members appear to be less overwhelmed by the guilt and trauma related to the accidental death of the child.

*The numbers in parentheses correlate to the number of the Behavioral Definition statement in the companion chapter with the same title in *The Family Therapy Treatment Planner*, Second Ed. (Dattilio, Jongsma, and Davis) by John Wiley & Sons, 2010.

### 6. Changing Family Dynamics (6)

A. The child's death has had an impact on family dynamics.

B. The siblings have reordered their lives with one another to cope with the loss.

C. The changes in family dynamics due to the child's death have presented new problems for the family.

D. Family dynamics have been sent into a state of disequilibrium due to the loss of the child.

E. The family has begun to function again in a more stable manner after the loss of child.

### 7. Overprotectiveness of Survivors (7)

A. The parents have a fear of future loss of the surviving children.

B. The parents display overprotectiveness of their surviving children.

C. The parents' pattern of overprotectiveness has led to conflict with the surviving children.

D. As treatment has progressed, the parents have demonstrated a healthy level of protection and concern for the surviving children.

### 8. Stuck in Grief Process (8)

A. One or more family members have become "stuck" at an earlier stage of grief than would be expected.

B. Family members frequently overfunction for the family member stuck in the grief process.

C. Compensation for another family members lack of progress in the grief process has diminished.

D. All family members are seen as making adequate progress in the grief process.

## INTERVENTIONS IMPLEMENTED

### 1. Allow Venting of Grief (1)*

A. The family was allowed to vent their grief together.

B. The family was supported and encouraged as they shared feelings of grief and pain associated with their loss.

C. The family tends to talk about the losses experienced, but the feelings associated with these losses were not shared; this discrepancy was reflected to them.

### 2. Promote Unity (2)

A. A sense of unity among the surviving family members was promoted and encouraged.

B. Family members were assisted in developing cohesiveness as a changing family unit.

C. Comments or behaviors that displayed a sense of unity and cohesiveness among the surviving family members were consistently reinforced.

D. It was reflected to the family members that they do not display a great deal of family cohesiveness or mutual support, and they were encouraged to increase this pattern.

*The numbers in parentheses correlate to the number of the Therapeutic Intervention statement in the companion chapter with the same title in *The Family Therapy Treatment Planner*, Second Ed. (Dattilio, Jongsma, and Davis) by John Wiley & Sons, 2010.

### 3. Facilitate Individual Review of Grief (3)

A. Each family member was encouraged to express the personal effects of the loss.

B. Each family member was provided with ample time to express the personal effects of the loss.

C. The differences and similarities between family members' grief were highlighted and defined.

### 4. Educate about Stages of Grief (4)

A. The family was educated about the stages of grief.

B. Adults in the family were encouraged to read *How to Survive the Loss of a Child* (Sanders).

C. Children within the family were encouraged to read *The Fall of Freddie the Leaf* (Buscaglia).

D. Family members have read the assigned material on the stages of grief, and key points were processed.

E. Family members have not read the assigned material on the stages of grief and were reminded to do so.

### 5. Discuss Family Coping Methods (5)

A. A discussion was held with the family regarding the methods of coping with the loss of the child/sibling.

B. The use of various rituals to express or preserve memories was explored.

C. The family was supported as they identified specific rituals to use to help cope with the loss of the child/sibling.

D. Family members were provided with tentative examples to use to cope with their loss (e.g., wearing certain clothing that belonged to the deceased or constructing a shrine).

### 6. Teach Cognitive-Behavioral Coping Strategies (6)

A. Family members were taught cognitive-behavioral coping strategies for grief.

B. Family members were encouraged and guided in imagery tasks that suggest how the deceased would want the survivors to go on.

C. Family members were urged to review how the deceased would be dealing with the reverse situation if the circumstances had been different.

### 7. Explore Religious Beliefs (7)

A. Family members' religious beliefs were explored.

B. Family members' certainty about life after death was reviewed.

C. Family members were reinforced regarding the notion that the deceased is safe and free from pain.

D. Family members were encouraged to read *The Grieving Garden: Living with the Death of a Child* (Redfern and Gilbert).

E. Family members have read the assigned material, and key concepts were processed.

F. Family members have not read the recommended material and were redirected to do so.

### 8. Explore Use of Memorial Service (8)

A. Family members were asked about the use of a memorial service to honor the deceased and reaffirm their religious faith.

B. Family members were assisted in making arrangements for a memorial service to honor the deceased and reaffirm their religious faith.

C. A memorial service was held and the benefits of this ritual were reviewed.

D. Family members have not held a memorial service and were reminded about this helpful technique.

### 9. Hold Family Session at Graveside (9)

A. A family session was held at graveside to allow family members to express their thoughts and feelings to each other and the deceased.

B. Family members were encouraged to express their emotions during the graveside session.

C. Family members declined to use a graveside session for fear of the emotions that might occur and were reminded that this is an option for the future.

### 10. Share Images (10)

A. Each family member was encouraged to share an image or photo of the deceased family member.

B. Family members were supported as they shared photos, images, and memories of the deceased.

C. An emphasis was placed on the sharing of memories of the deceased to keep that person "alive in spirit."

### 11. Emphasize Deceased "Living Within" (11)

A. The concept of the deceased "living within" was emphasized.

B. Family members were encouraged to express how they experience the deceased living within themselves.

C. Family members were encouraged to recognize the characteristics of the deceased within each other.

### 12. Discuss Circumstances of Death (12)

A. The details regarding the actual circumstances of the child's death were discussed in the session.

B. Family members were helped to differentiate between survivor guilt and guilt for not being able to do more to save the child from pain, suffering, and death.

C. Family members were supported as they expressed the specific details of the child's death.

### 13. Educate about Survivor Guilt (13)

A. Family members were educated about the concept of survivor guilt.

B. Survivor guilt was emphasized as a natural stage of the grief process.

C. The adults within the family were encouraged to read *Survivor Guilt* (Matsakis).

D. Key concepts learned from the assigned reading material were reviewed.

E. Family members have not read information about survivor guilt and were redirected to do so.

14. **Identify Overprotective Behaviors (14)**

A. Family members were encouraged to recognize their excessive, overprotective behaviors.

B. Family members were helped to differentiate between healthy protection and excessive overprotective behaviors.

C. Family members were assisted in reorganizing how over-protection is both a natural reaction and a means of assigning guilt.

D. Family members were encouraged to look for alternative ways of seeking self-reassurance other than being overprotective.

E. The need to be able to let go by giving up overprotective behaviors was emphasized.

15. **Review Negative Effects of Overprotection (15)**

A. Family members were assisted in identifying how overprotection may result in negative side effects (e.g., anxious attachment, social anxiety, separation anxiety).

B. Family members were encouraged to consider the negative side effects of overprotection when deciding how protective to be of the surviving children.

C. Family members were reluctant to endorse the negative side effects of being overprotective of the surviving children and were provided with tentative examples.

16. **Assess Preexisting Psychopathology (16)**

A. An assessment was conducted regarding any preexisting psychopathology that has been brought to the surface by the death of the child.

B. It was reflected to the family members that preexisting psychopathology was identified.

C. No preexisting psychopathology was identified in family members.

D. Appropriate referral or refocusing of treatment was discussed as a way to treat the preexisting psychopathology.

17. **Refer regarding Preexisting Emotional Disorder (17)**

A. Individual family members were referred to a psychotherapist for treatment of a preexisting emotional disorder.

B. Individual family members have been treated for preexisting emotional disorders, which has helped the family to work through the death of the child.

C. Family members have not sought out recommended individual treatment and were reminded to do so.

18. **Explore for Irrational Sibling Guilt (18)**

A. The siblings of the deceased child were assessed regarding irrational sibling guilt.

B. The younger siblings were assessed for irrational guilt regarding the death of the child.

C. No irrational guilt was identified in the siblings.

D. Irrational guilt was found in siblings and was made a focus of treatment.

E. Family members were directed to read *Overcoming Loss Activities and Stories to Help Transform Children's Grief and Loss* (Sorenson).

F. Family members have read the assigned material and key concepts were reviewed.

G. Family members have not read the assigned materials and were reminded to do so.

### 19. Expose Hidden Blame (19)

A. The concept of hidden blame for the child's death was introduced to family members.

B. The pattern of hidden blame for the child's death was reviewed and processed.

C. The hidden blame for the child's death was exposed.

D. No pattern of hidden blame was found.

# DEATH OF A PARENT

## CLIENT PRESENTATION

### 1. Accidental Sudden Death (1)*
A. A parent has recently, suddenly, accidentally died.
B. The family history includes the accidental, sudden death of a parent.
C. Surviving family members experience significant grief related to the accidental, sudden death of the parent.
D. Family members have begun to process their grief.

### 2. Death Due to a Long, Terminal Illness (2)
A. The family has lost a parent subsequent to a long, terminal illness.
B. Despite extensive medical treatment, the parent succumbed to a terminal illness.
C. Family members have expressed pain and grief related to the long illness and eventual death of the parent.
D. As treatment has progressed, the family has begun to grieve the loss of the parent and found a sense of meaning in the illness and death.

### 3. Death Due to an Acute Illness (3)
A. The family has lost a parent due to an acute illness.
B. The family expressed shock at the quickness with which the illness took their parent.
C. As treatment has progressed, the family has begun to cope with the loss of their parent due to an acute illness.

### 4. Guilt and Trauma Due to Death of a Parent (4)
A. Family members witnessed the accidental death of a parent.
B. Family members were involved in the accident that caused the death of a parent (e.g., auto accident).
C. Family members experience high levels of guilt and trauma due to witnessing the accidental death of the parent.
D. Family members appeared to be overwhelmed by guilt and trauma.
E. As treatment has progressed, family members appear to be less overwhelmed by the guilt and trauma related to the accidental death of a parent.

### 5. Changing Family Dynamics (5)
A. The parent's death has had an impact on family dynamics.
B. The children have reordered their lives with one another to cope with the loss of a parent.

---

*The numbers in parentheses correlate to the number of the Behavioral Definition statement in the companion chapter with the same title in *The Family Therapy Treatment Planner*, Second Ed. (Dattilio, Jongsma, and Davis) by John Wiley & Sons, 2010.

C. The changes in family dynamics due to the parent's death have presented new problems for the family.

D. Family dynamics have been sent into a state of disequilibrium due to the loss of the parent.

E. The family has begun to function again in a more stable manner after the loss of the parent.

### 6. Fixation on the Loss of the Parent (6)

A. Family members are fixated on the loss of the deceased.

B. Family members are not adjusting to new increased demands of home life due to fixation on the deceased loved one.

C. As treatment has progressed, the level of function on the loss of the deceased has diminished and a functional flexibility has been developed.

### 7. Overprotectiveness of Survivors (7)

A. Family members have a fear of the future loss of surviving family members.

B. Family members display overprotectiveness of the surviving family members.

C. The family members' pattern of overprotectiveness has led to conflict in the family.

D. As treatment has progressed, the family members have gained a healthy level of protection and concern for the surviving family members.

### 8. Financial Hardships (8)

A. The family has experienced financial hardships since the death of the parent.

B. The stress due to the financial hardships has exacerbated the grief of losing a parent.

C. The family has begun to adjust to the financial changes subsequent to the loss of the parent.

## INTERVENTIONS IMPLEMENTED

### 1. Allow Venting of Grief (1)*

A. The family was allowed to vent their grief together.

B. The family was encouraged to express their feelings about the loss as a whole.

C. The family was supported and encouraged as they shared feelings of grief and pain associated with their loss.

D. The family tends to talk about the losses experienced, but the feelings associated with these losses were not shared; this discrepancy was reflected to them.

### 2. Promote Unity (2)

A. A sense of unity among the surviving family members was promoted and encouraged.

B. Family members were assisted in developing cohesiveness as a changing family unit.

C. Comments or behaviors that displayed a sense of unity and cohesiveness among the surviving family members were consistently reinforced.

---

*The numbers in parentheses correlate to the number of the Therapeutic Intervention statement in the companion chapter with the same title in *The Family Therapy Treatment Planner*, Second Ed. (Dattilio, Jongsma, and Davis) by John Wiley & Sons, 2010.

D. It was reflected to the family members that they do not display a great deal of family cohesiveness, and they were encouraged to increase this pattern.

E. The focus of the session was on how the caretaking role will be fulfilled.

### 3. Facilitate Individual Review of Grief (3)

A. Each family member was encouraged to express the personal effects of the loss.

B. Each family member was provided with ample time to express the personal effects of the loss of the parent.

C. The differences and similarities between family members' grief were highlighted and defined.

D. Adults and teens were urged to use journaling, poetry, and other age-appropriate techniques for expressing their grief.

E. Children were directed to use music, drawings, and other age-appropriate techniques for expressing their grief.

### 4. Educate about Stages of Grief (4)

A. The family was taught about the stages of grief.

B. Adults in the family were encouraged to read *On Grief and Grieving* (Kubler-Ross).

C. Children within the family were encouraged to read *The Fall of Freddie the Leaf* (Buscaglia).

D. Family members have read the assigned material on the stages of grief, and key points were processed.

E. Family members have not read the assigned material on the stages of grief and were reminded to do so.

### 5. Discuss Family Coping Methods (5)

A. A discussion was held with the family regarding the methods of coping with the loss of the parent/spouse.

B. The use of various grieving rituals was explored.

C. The family was supported as they identified specific grieving rituals to use to help cope with the loss of the parent/spouse.

D. Family members were provided with tentative examples to use to cope with their loss (e.g., wearing certain clothing that belonged to the deceased or constructing a shrine).

### 6. Teach Cognitive-Behavioral Coping Strategies (6)

A. Family members were taught cognitive-behavioral coping strategies for grief.

B. Family members were encouraged and guided in imagery tasks that suggest how the deceased would want the survivors to go on.

C. Family members were urged to review how the deceased would be dealing with the reverse situation if the circumstances had been different.

D. The family was encouraged to read *Grief: Climb toward Understanding* (Davies).

E. Family members have read the assigned material on grief, and key points were processed.

F. Family members have not read the assigned material on grief and were reminded to do so.

### 7. Explore Religious Beliefs (7)

A. Family members' religious beliefs were explored.

B. Family members' certainty about life after death was reviewed.

C. Family members were reinforced regarding the notion that the deceased is safe and free from pain.

D. Family members were encouraged to meet with their clergyperson.

E. Family members have read the assigned material on dying, and key concepts were processed.

F. Family members have not read the recommended material on dying and were redirected to do so.

### 8. Explore Use of Memorial Service (8)

A. Family members were asked about the use of a memorial service to honor the deceased and reaffirm their faith.

B. Family members were assisted in making arrangements for a memorial service to honor the deceased and reaffirm their faith.

C. A memorial service was held and the benefits of this technique were reviewed.

D. Family members have not held a memorial service to honor the deceased and were reminded about this helpful technique.

### 9. Discuss Circumstances of Death (9)

A. The details regarding the actual circumstances of the parent's death were discussed within the session.

B. Family members were helped to differentiate between survivor guilt and guilt for not being able to do more to save the parent from pain, suffering, and death.

C. Family members were supported as they expressed the specific details of the parent's death.

### 10. Educate about Survivor Guilt (10)

A. Family members were taught about the concept of survivor guilt.

B. Survivor guilt was emphasized as a natural stage of the grief process.

C. Adults within the family were encouraged to read *Survivor Guilt* (Matsatis).

D. Children within the family were encouraged to read *Overcoming Loss: Activities and Stories to Help Transform Children's Grief and Loss* (Sorenson).

E. Key concepts regarding the assigned reading material were reviewed.

F. Family members have not read information about survivor guilt and were redirected to do so.

### 11. Hold Family Session at Graveside (11)

A. A family session was held at graveside to allow family members to express their thoughts and feelings to each other and the deceased.

B. Family members were encouraged to express their emotions during the graveside session.

C. Family members declined to use a graveside session for fear of the emotions that might occur and were reminded that this is an option for the future.

### 12. Share Images (12)

A. Each family member was encouraged to share an image or photo of the deceased parent.

B. Family members were supported as they shared photos, images, and memories of the deceased.

C. An emphasis was placed on the sharing of memories of the deceased to keep that person "alive in spirit."

### 13. Emphasize Deceased "Living Within" (13)

A. The concept of the deceased "living within" was emphasized.

B. Family members were encouraged to express how they experience the deceased living within themselves.

C. Family members were encouraged to recognize the characteristics of the deceased within each other as they appear.

### 14. Identify Overprotective Behaviors (14)

A. Family members were encouraged to recognize their excessive, overprotective behaviors.

B. Family members were helped to differentiate between healthy protection and excessive overprotective behaviors.

C. Family members were encouraged to look for alternative ways of self-reassurance.

D. The need to let go by giving up overprotective behaviors was emphasized.

### 15. Review Negative Effects of Overprotection (15)

A. Family members were assisted in identifying how overprotection of the other surviving family members may result in negative side effects (e.g., separation anxiety, agoraphobia).

B. Family members were encouraged to consider the negative side effects of overprotection when deciding how protective to be of other surviving family members.

C. Family members could not identify the negative side effects of being overprotective of the other surviving family members and were provided with tentative examples.

### 16. Assess Preexisting Psychopathology (16)

A. An assessment was conducted regarding any preexisting psychopathology that may have been brought to the surface by the death of the parent.

B. It was reflected to family members that preexisting psychopathology was identified.

C. No preexisting psychopathology was identified in family members.

D. Appropriate referral or refocusing of treatment was discussed as a way to treat the preexisting psychopathology.

### 17. Refer Regarding Preexisting Emotional Disorder (17)

A. Individual family members were referred to a psychotherapist for treatment of a preexisting emotional disorder.

B. Individual family members have been treated for preexisting emotional disorders, which has helped the family to work through the death of the parent.

C. Family members have not sought out recommended individual psychotherapy treatment and were reminded to do so.

### 18. Explore for Irrational Guilt in Children (18)

A. The children of the deceased parent were assessed regarding irrational sibling guilt.

B. The younger children were closely assessed for irrational guilt regarding the death of the parent.

C. No irrational guilt was identified in the children.

D. Children within the family were encouraged to read *Overcoming Loss: Activities and Stories to Help Transform Children's Grief and Loss* (Sorenson).

E. Key concepts regarding the assigned reading material were reviewed.

F. Family members have not read information about survivor guilt and were redirected to do so.

### 19. Expose Hidden Blame (19)

A. The concept of hidden blame for the parent's death was introduced to family members.

B. Any pattern of hidden blame for the parent's death was reviewed and processed.

C. The hidden blame for the parent's death was exposed.

D. No pattern of hidden blame was found.

### 20. Facilitate Extended Family Bonding (20)

A. The family was assisted in identifying how extended family members can bond with the children as a substitute for the deceased parent.

B. The children were reminded that the family member cannot replace the deceased but can only follow in the deceased family member's footsteps.

C. The children were allowed to express their concerns, reluctance, and fears about bonding with another adult.

### 21. Recommend Talking and Writing about the Missing Parent (21)

A. The children of the deceased parent were urged to talk about the missing parent as often as they feel the need to do so.

B. The children were encouraged to keep a journal of thoughts about the lost loved one.

C. The children were encouraged to write letters to the lost loved one on a regular basis.

D. The family has not used writing or talking about the deceased parent on a regular basis, and they were encouraged to use this helpful process.

### 22. Search for Financial Alternatives (22)

A. The family was focused on how to seek out alternative financial resources.

B. The family was helped to discuss how to cope with financial changes brought on by the death of a parent.

C. The anger and resentment felt by family members regarding the financial changes were facilitated.

# DEPENDENCY ISSUES

## CLIENT PRESENTATION

### 1. Extreme Need to be Cared for by Others (1)*
A. One family member displays an extreme need to be taken care of by other family members.
B. The dependent family member often displays clinging types of behaviors.
C. The dependent family member is unusually submissive to other family members.
D. As treatment has progressed, the dependent family member has become less reliant on others.

### 2. Abandonment Fears (2)
A. The dependent family member described a history of being very anxious whenever there is any hint of abandonment in an established relationship.
B. The dependent family member's hypersensitivity to abandonment has caused a pattern of desperate clinging to relationships.
C. The dependent family member has begun to acknowledge fears of abandonment as excessive and irrational.
D. Conflicts within the relationship have been reported by the dependent family member, but there is no longer the automatic assumption that abandonment will result.
E. The dependent family member's fear of abandonment has been resolved and more self-confidence has been displayed.

### 3. Friction in the Home (3)
A. The dependent pattern of one family member causes increased responsibility for other family members.
B. Other family members experience tension and anxiety due to their increased need to take over responsibilities from the dependent family member.
C. Friction within the home has often developed into arguments over dependency issues.
D. As the dependent family member has become more independent, tension in the home has decreased.

### 4. Seeks Approval (4)
A. The dependent family member seeks excessive advice, support, and reassurance from others.
B. The dependent family member's dependency on others is reflected in the seeking out of their approval at any cost.
C. The dependent family member has decreased seeking approval from others.

*The numbers in parentheses correlate to the number of the Behavioral Definition statement in the companion chapter with the same title in *The Family Therapy Treatment Planner*, Second Ed. (Dattilio, Jongsma, and Davis) by John Wiley & Sons, 2010.

### 5. Avoids Disagreements (4)

A. The dependent family member has been unable to make decisions or initiate actions due to the desire to avoid disagreement or conflict.

B. The family member's dependency on others is reflected in the avoidance of any conflict.

C. The dependent family member has shown the ability to make decisions on a small scale without regard for the possibility of disagreement or conflict.

D. The dependent family member has shown confidence in implementing decision-making skills regardless of the possible conflict.

### 6. Guilt (5)

A. The dependent family member often experiences guilt.

B. The dependent family member has low self-esteem due to the experience of guilty feelings.

C. As treatment has progressed, the family member's sense of guilt and low self-esteem has been resolved.

### 7. Reluctance to Make Decisions (6)

A. The dependent family member has been unable to make decisions or initiate actions without excessive advice, support, and reassurance from others.

B. The family member's dependency on others is reflected in seeking out their approval before taking any action.

C. The dependent family member has shown the ability to make decisions on a small scale without seeking approval from others.

D. The dependent family member has shown confidence in implementing problem-solving techniques to enhance decision-making skills.

### 8. Enabling (7)

A. Nondependent family members enable the dependent family member by giving in to frequent demands for contact and reassurance.

B. Passive-aggressive or manipulative behaviors are often reinforced by the nondependent family members.

C. Tension has risen within the family as the nondependent family member has refused to enable the dependent family member.

D. The dependent family member has become more direct and assertive.

### 9. Anxiety and Depression (8)

A. The dependent family member acknowledged strong feelings of panic, fear, helplessness, and depression when faced with situations in which the other family members are not available for support or encouragement.

B. The dependent family member described a pattern of avoidance of situations in which the other family members are not available for support or encouragement.

C. The dependent family member has begun to overcome feelings of anxiety and depression associated with situations in which other family members are absent.

### 10. Loss of Purpose (9)

A. The dependent family member described a loss of purpose and meaning in life when insufficient support is perceived from other family members.

B. The dependent family member experiences a loss of self when not sufficiently supported by other family members.

C. The dependent family member has begun establishing personal boundaries.

D. The dependent family member has developed personal interests and is not as dependent on others for a sense of purpose and meaning.

## INTERVENTIONS IMPLEMENTED

### 1. Develop Dependency Issue (1)*

A. Each family member was asked to describe the evidence for excessive dependency in one family member.

B. Support and encouragement were provided to the dependent family member as others expressed their concern about the level of dependency.

C. Family members were encouraged to be open and honest about their view on the dependent family member's pattern of behavior.

D. Family members were very cautious and tended to minimize the dependent family member's patterns of behavior and were encouraged to be open and honest in this area.

### 2. Develop Definitions and Metaphor (2)

A. The family was assisted in developing operational definitions to help identify specific dependent behaviors and dynamics.

B. Family members were assisted in developing accurate metaphors for describing the pattern of dependent behaviors and dynamics.

C. Family members were supported and encouraged as they clearly defined the client's dependent behavior and dynamics

D. Remedial assistance was provided to family members to more clearly define the pattern of dependent behaviors and dynamics.

### 3. Personalize Dependency Issues (3)

A. Each family member was asked to clearly identify the personal ways in which the depeency issues have had an effect.

B. Family members were assisted in identifying their own behaviors and family dynamics that have changed due to the dependency issues.

C. Family members were provided with encouragement to be open about how the dependent family member's patterns have had a personal effect.

*The numbers in parentheses correlate to the number of the Therapeutic Intervention statement in the companion chapter with the same title in *The Family Therapy Treatment Planner*, Second Ed. (Dattilio, Jongsma, and Davis) by John Wiley & Sons, 2010.

### 4. Develop Acceptance and Etiology of Problems (4)

A. Family members were urged to clearly endorse that the dependency problem truly exists.

B. Family members were helped to explore the dynamics of how the dependency pattern has developed.

C. Family members were reinforced for endorsing the existence and etiology of the dependency problems.

D. Family members were uncertain about the existence of the dependency problems and were assisted in seeing this problem more clearly.

E. Family members were assisted in developing the etiology of the dependency problems.

### 5. Develop Genograms (5)

A. The parents' families of origin were explored to help make connections to other dependent people in the family.

B. A genogram was used to review the existence of dependent relationships within extended family members.

C. Family members were supported for their insight as they have reviewed the pattern of dependency within the extended family.

### 6. Educate about Unhealthy Dependency (6)

A. Family members were educated about the dynamics of unhealthy dependency (e.g., enabling, exploitation of power).

B. Family members were provided with reading material about unhealthy dependency.

C. Family members were reinforced when showing a clear understanding of the dynamics of dependency.

### 7. Assign Reading in Codependency (7)

A. Specific readings on codependency were suggested to the family.

B. The family was encouraged to read *Codependent No More* (Beattie) and *Beyond Codependency* (Beattie).

C. Family members have read the assigned material on codependency, and key concepts were reviewed.

### 8. Explore Fears of Abandonment (8)

A. The dependent family member's fear of abandonment was explored.

B. The dependent family member was asked to explore what it means to be alone.

C. Reframing techniques were used to help the dependent family member perceive being alone in a different manner.

### 9. Contrast Beliefs about Being Alone (9)

A. Family members were asked to express their beliefs and feelings about being alone.

B. The family members' beliefs about being alone were compared and contrasted with the beliefs of the dependent family member.

C. The dependent family member was reinforced for insights into beliefs and emotions about being alone.

D. The dependent family member was defensive about being alone and was helped to process these feelings.

## 10. Encourage Brainstorming to Overcome Irrational Thoughts (10)

A. Family members were encouraged to brainstorm techniques that can be used to overcome irrational thoughts about abandonment.

B. Family members were reinforced for identifying helpful techniques to overcome irrational thoughts about abandonment.

C. Family members struggled to identify helpful techniques for overcoming irrational thoughts about abandonment and were provided with tentative examples in this area (e.g., utilize rational self-talk, fill free time with constructive activity, implement thought-stopping).

## 11. Use Family-Sculpting Techniques (11)

A. Since family members seem to have difficulty verbally expressing themselves, family-sculpting techniques were used to help express these thoughts and feelings.

B. Reverse role-playing techniques were used to help express feelings and thoughts.

C. Family members were reinforced for their use of family-sculpting and reverse role-playing techniques.

D. Family members continued to be guarded despite the use of family-sculpting and reverse role-playing techniques and were urged to be more open with their feelings.

## 12. Encourage Acceptance of Responsibility (12)

A. Individual family members were encouraged to accept responsibility for their own contributions to the overall tension in the family.

B. Family members were reinforced when they took responsibility for the overall tension within the family.

C. Family members were reminded about the need to take responsibility for the tension in the family when they tended to dismiss this responsibility.

## 13. Discuss Avoidance of Conflict (13)

A. The issue of avoiding conflict was discussed within the family therapy session.

B. Family members were urged to express their feelings about dealing with the dependency issue in a direct manner.

C. Family members were supported as they identified both positive and negative emotions regarding dealing directly with the dependency issue.

## 14. Identify Irrational Thoughts about Conflict (14)

A. Family members were probed for irrational thoughts about conflict.

B. Family members identified some of their irrational thoughts about conflict and were assisted in remediating these patterns.

C. Family members denied any irrational thoughts about conflict and were provided with tentative examples in this area (e.g., one will be totally rejected by other family members if disagreement arises).

## 15. Review Conflict Resolution Styles (15)

A. The styles of disagreement of each family member were reviewed.

B. The methods of conflict resolution were reviewed for each family member.

C. The notion that all families experience conflict and that conflict is necessary for family growth and development was reinforced.

D. Feedback was provided to family members regarding their patterns of disagreement and conflict resolution.

## 16. Role-Play Thoughts Regarding Guilt (16)

A. Family members were directed to role-play the expression of thoughts that they have regarding guilt issues.

B. Family members' thoughts regarding guilt were reflected and processed.

C. Family members were encouraged to describe more directly their thoughts and feelings of guilt.

## 17. Contrast Beliefs about Guilt (17)

A. Family members were asked to express their beliefs and feelings about guilt.

B. Family members' beliefs about guilt were compared to and contrasted with the beliefs of the dependent family member.

C. The dependent family member was reinforced for insights into beliefs and emotions about guilt.

D. The dependent family member was defensive about guilt feelings and was helped to process these feelings.

## 18. Teach about Guilt (18)

A. Family members were taught about common experiences related to feeling guilt.

B. Family members were reminded that most guilt feelings are self-inflicted.

C. Family members were reinforced for a more clear understanding of the issues related to guilt.

D. Family members continued to have a poor understanding of concerns related to feelings of guilt and were provided with remedial assistance in this area.

## 19. Recommend Ten Days to Self-Esteem! (19)

A. Homework assignments from *Ten Days to Self-Esteem!* (Burns) were recommended to help teach cognitive restructuring techniques.

B. Family members have completed the homework assignments from *Ten Days to Self-Esteem!* and these were processed.

C. Family members were reinforced for using the techniques learned in the homework assignments to reduce guilt and build self-esteem.

D. Family members have not completed the homework assignments and were redirected to do so.

### 20. Discuss Decision Making (20)

A. A family discussion was facilitated regarding decision making.

B. Fears of making bad decisions or failing were discussed within the family therapy session.

C. Family members were encouraged and validated as they described their own beliefs and comfort levels in making decisions.

### 21. Decrease Perfectionism (21)

A. Family members were encouraged to decrease their pattern of perfectionism.

B. Family members were encouraged to be more accepting of making bad decisions or failing.

C. Family members who were accepting of the dependent family member's failed attempts at decision making were reinforced for their accepting attitude.

D. Family members were confronted when they were not accepting of attempts to make decisions.

### 22. Teach Decision-Making Techniques (22)

A. The family was taught about decision-making techniques.

B. The family was taught about how to make decision trees.

C. The family members were taught about how to weigh pros and cons to help make decisions.

D. All family members were encouraged to learn decision-making techniques.

### 23. Encourage Reinforcing Independent Decisions (23)

A. Family members were encouraged to use positive reinforcement when the dependent family member makes independent decisions.

B. Family members were encouraged to validate and reinforce the dependent family member when a decreased need to rely on the other family members was shown.

C. Family members were reinforced when they used reinforcement techniques on the dependent family member.

D. Family members have not reinforced the dependent family member for some independent decisions and were redirected in this area.

### 24. Review Successful Decisions (24)

A. Incidences in which the dependent family member has successfully made independent decisions were reviewed.

B. Family members were assisted in developing rituals that would reinforce the dependent family member's independent decision making.

### 25. Encourage Admission of Enabling (25)

A. Family members were encouraged to admit situations in which they have enabled the dependent family member to remain dependent.

B. Family members were helped to discuss the etiology of their decision to enable the dependent family member.

C. Family members were reinforced for their insightful identification of situations in which they have enabled the dependent family member.

D. Enabling family members were unable to identify specific situations in which the enabling had occurred and were provided with tentative examples of this dynamic.

## 26. Explore Guilt (26)

A. The concept of guilt feelings as an underlying motivating factor for enabling dependent behavior was reviewed.

B. Family members were assisted in identifying their own guilt feelings and how this may lead to enabling dependent behaviors due to feelings of guilt.

C. Family members were reinforced for their open acknowledgment of enabling of the dependent behaviors.

D. Family members were guarded regarding their own guilt feelings and how this contributes to enabling dependent behaviors and were provided with additional encouragement and feedback in this area.

## 27. Assess Underlying Reinforcers for Family (27)

A. The hidden reinforcers for keeping the dependent family member in a dependent state were reviewed.

B. Family members were able to openly acknowledge some of the hidden motivators for keeping the dependent family member in a dependent state. These motivators were processed.

C. Tentative examples of the underlying motivators for keeping the dependent family member in a dependent state were provided (e.g., for their own self-esteem, because of power issues, fears).

## 28. Develop Alternative Behaviors (28)

A. The family was assisted in identifying alternative behaviors on the part of the nondependent family members that will contribute to overall family change.

B. Family members were reinforced for identification of alternative behaviors for nondependent family members.

C. Family members were uncertain about alternative behaviors and were provided with tentative examples (e.g., refusal to respond to the dependent family member's call for reassurance of being loved or being capable, reinforcing independent behaviors).

## 29. Define Assertiveness vs. Aggressiveness (29)

A. The differences between assertive and aggressive expressions of emotions were highlighted.

B. Role-playing and modeling techniques were used to teach assertive expression of thoughts and feelings.

C. Family members were reinforced for situations in which they have appropriately used assertive communication to express their thoughts and feelings.

D. Family members were redirected when using aggressive techniques to express their thoughts and feelings.

## 30. Refer for Assertiveness Training (30)

A. The dependent family member was referred to an assertiveness training class.

B. The dependent family member has attended the assertiveness training class, and key concepts were reviewed and processed.

C. The dependent family member has not attended the assertiveness training class and was redirected to do so.

### 31. Reverse Roles (31)

A. The family was encouraged to use role-reversal exercises to foster support for role changes among family members.

B. The more dominant decision maker was urged to function in a more passive manner.

C. The quiet family member was urged to become more expressive.

D. The passive family member was urged to become more assertive.

E. Changes in roles were reviewed with the family members and the benefits of these changes were processed.

F. Family members were asked to discuss how they felt when they reversed roles or tried out new roles in the family.

G. Family members were supported and validated as they expressed their feelings about changing roles within the family.

# DEPRESSION IN FAMILY MEMBERS

## CLIENT PRESENTATION

### 1. Sadness and Hopelessness (1)*

A. One or more family members reported feeling deeply sad and having periods of tearfulness almost on a daily basis.

B. A family member's depressed affect was clearly evident as tears were shed within the session.

C. The depressed family member has reported feelings of hopelessness and worthlessness that began as the depression deepened.

D. The depressed family member has begun to feel less sad and can experience periods of joy.

E. The depressed family member appeared to be happier within the session, and there was no evidence of tearfulness.

F. The depressed family member reported no feelings of depression.

G. The depressed family member expressed hope for the future and affirmation of self-worth.

### 2. Disinterest in Activities (2)

A. The family member with depression symptoms displays a disinterest in normally enjoyable activities (e.g., visiting relatives or dining out).

B. The depressed family member displays disengagement with normally enjoyable activities.

C. The depressed family member turns down family activities that have previously been enjoyable.

D. The depressed family member is gradually increasing his/her interest in normally enjoyable activities.

E. The depressed family member is regularly involved in family activities.

### 3. Lack of Concentration (3)

A. The depressed family member reported an inability to maintain concentration and is easily distracted.

B. The depressed family member reported an inability to read material with good comprehension because of being easily distracted.

C. The depressed family member reported an increased ability to concentrate as the depression lifted.

### 4. Sleeplessness/Hypersomnia (4)

A. The depressed family member reported periods of being unable to sleep and other periods of sleeping for many hours without the desire to get out of bed.

B. The depressed family member's problem with sleep disturbance has diminished as the depression has lifted.

---

*The numbers in parentheses correlate to the number of the Behavioral Definition statement in the companion chapter with the same title in *The Family Therapy Treatment Planner*, Second Ed. (Dattilio, Jongsma, and Davis) by John Wiley & Sons, 2010.

C. Medication has improved the depressed family member's problems with sleep disturbance.

D. The depressed family member reported a normal sleep routine resulting in feeling rested.

### 5. Low Self-Worth (5)

A. The depressed family member described a very negative self-perception.

B. The depressed family member's low self-esteem was evident within the session when self-disparaging remarks were made and very little eye contact was maintained.

C. The depressed family member's self-esteem has increased as demonstrated by affirmations of self-worth.

D. The depressed family member verbalized positive self-worth.

### 6. Lack of Social Involvement (6)

A. The depressed family member reported a diminished interest in or enjoyment of social activities that were previously pleasurable.

B. Family members reported that the depressed family member is less involved in social activities.

C. The depressed family member has begun to be more involved with social activities that were previously pleasurable.

D. The depressed family member has returned to an active interest in, and enjoyment of, activities.

### 7. Movement Retardation (7)

A. The depressed family member displayed a pattern of movement retardation.

B. The depressed family member presents as having little energy and slow patterns of movement.

C. As the depressed family member has begun to recover from the depression, activity levels have returned to normal.

### 8. Agitation (7)

A. The depressed family member displayed an abnormally increased movement pattern.

B. The depressed family member displays pacing or other agitated patterns of movement.

C. The depressed family member's agitation has begun to diminish.

D. As the depressed family member has begun to recover from the depression, activity levels have returned to normal.

### 9. Guilt (8)

A. The depressed family member described feelings of pervasive, irrational guilt.

B. The depressed family member identified feelings of guilt about how the marital relationship has been affected by the depression.

C. The depressed family member's feelings of guilt have caused a lack of desire to go on living.

D. Although the depressed family member verbalized an understanding that the guilt was irrational, it continues to be prominent.

E. The irrational guilt has lifted as the depression has subsided.

F. The depressed family member no longer expresses feelings of irrational guilt.

### 10. Suicidal Ideation (9)

A. The depressed family member reported experiencing suicidal thoughts but has not initiated any action on these thoughts.

B. The depressed family member reported strong suicidal thoughts that have resulted in suicidal gestures or attempts.

C. Diminished suicidal urges have been reported as the depression has lifted.

D. The depressed family member denied any suicidal thoughts or gestures and is more hopeful about the future.

### 11. Poor Treatment Response (10)

A. The depressed family member has attempted the use of antidepressant medication but has not displayed a therapeutic response.

B. The depressed family member declines any use of antidepressant medication for the depression symptoms.

C. The depressed family member has displayed a poor response to therapy interventions.

D. With family involvement, the depressed family member is gaining a more significant benefit from therapeutic interventions.

### 12. Decreased Energy Level (11)

A. The depressed family member reported feeling a very low energy level.

B. It was evident within the session that the depressed family member has low energy levels as demonstrated by slowness of walking, minimal movement, lack of animation, and slow responses.

C. The depressed family member's energy level has increased as the depression has lifted.

D. It was evident within the session that the depressed family member is demonstrating normal levels of energy.

### 13. Irritable and Frustrated (12)

A. The depressed family member often displays irritability.

B. The depressed family member displays a low frustration tolerance.

C. Arguments between family members often occur due to the high level of irritability and low frustration tolerance evidenced by the depressed family member.

D. As treatment has progressed, the depressed family member displays a greater frustration tolerance and reduced irritability.

### 14. Children React to Emotionally Unavailable Parent (13)

A. The children have experienced the depressed parent as emotionally unavailable.

B. The children have reacted to the emotionally unavailable parent by acting out behaviorally.

C. The children display depression symptoms similar to the emotionally unavailable parent.

D. As treatment has progressed, the effects of the parent's depression has been minimized.

## INTERVENTIONS IMPLEMENTED

### 1. Review Depression Symptoms (1)*

A. Each family member was asked to describe the evidence for depression symptoms in a family member.

B. Support and encouragement were provided to the depressed family member as others expressed their concern about the level of depression.

C. The family members were encouraged to be open and honest about their view on the depressed family member's pattern of symptoms.

D. Family members were very cautious and tended to minimize the depressed family member's patterns of behavior and were encouraged to be more open and honest in this area.

### 2. Identify Etiology (2)

A. The family members were assisted in trying to identify any specific events that may have triggered the depressive symptomology.

B. Family members were helped to process a possible etiology of the depression symptoms.

C. Family members were uncertain about etiological factors for developing the depression and were provided with tentative examples in this area.

### 3. Administer Depression Inventories (3)

A. The depressed family member was assessed with a standardized depression inventory.

B. The depressed family member was assessed using the *Beck Hopelessness Scale* (Beck).

C. The depressed family member was assessed using the *Children's Depression Inventory* (Kovacs).

D. The results of the depression inventory were reviewed with family members.

### 4. Review Assessments (4)

A. The assessments for depression, hopelessness, and suicidality were reviewed with the family.

B. The results of the depression assessment were explained to family members.

C. Questions regarding the assessment of the depressed family member's level of depression were answered.

### 5. Personalize Depression Symptoms (5)

A. Each family member was asked to clearly identify the personal ways in which the depression symptoms have had an effect.

B. Family members were assisted in identifying their own behaviors that have changed due to the depression symptoms.

C. Family members were encouraged to be open about how the depressed family member's depression symptoms have had a personal effect.

*The numbers in parentheses correlate to the number of the Therapeutic Intervention statement in the companion chapter with the same title in *The Family Therapy Treatment Planner*, Second Ed. (Dattilio, Jongsma, and Davis) by John Wiley & Sons, 2010.

### 6. Allow Emotional Expression (6)

A. The expression of negative emotions regarding the depressed family member's effect on the family was allowed and encouraged.

B. It was noted that family members often experience negative emotions, such as resentment, in reaction to the pall that is cast over the family by the depressed family member.

C. Family members were cautious about expressing their emotion for fear of creating more depressed feelings in the depressed family member and were encouraged to be open, but not unkind, in this area.

### 7. Inquire about Manipulation (7)

A. Family members were asked to identify any thoughts or beliefs that the depression is not real but is a means of manipulation.

B. Family members were supported as they described their thoughts and beliefs about the genuineness of the depression symptoms.

C. None of the family members seemed to indicate any belief that the depression is just a way for that family member to manipulate others, and this was reflected to the family.

### 8. Assess Social Involvement (8)

A. The depressed family member's level of involvement in social situations was assessed.

B. Family members were asked to provide feedback about the level of social involvement for the depressed family member.

C. The depressed family member's level of social disengagement and disinterest was rated as quite significant.

D. The depressed family member's level of social engagement and interest was rated as appropriate.

### 9. Contract for Social Involvement (9)

A. A behavioral contract was developed regarding a specified number of activities for the depressed family member to engage in with friends and family.

B. A weekly schedule of social activities was developed.

C. Positive feedback was provided for the increased involvement in social activities by the depressed family member.

D. The depressed family member continues to have very limited involvement in social activities and was urged to become more socially active.

### 10. Remediate Behavioral Deficits (10)

A. Techniques to reduce behavioral deficits that contribute to the depression were taught.

B. Assertiveness skills were taught to the depressed family member.

C. The depressed family member was taught social skills.

D. The depressed family member was reinforced for applying new social and assertiveness skills to daily life situations.

## 11. Recognize Cognitive Distortions (11)

A. The depressed family member was taught how to recognize and identify distorted, negative cognitive messages that support depressed feelings and low self-esteem.

B. The family was taught how to recognize and identify distorted, negative cognitive messages that support depressed feelings and low self-esteem.

C. The family was recommended to read *The Feeling Good Handbook* (Burns) or *Mind over Mood* (Greenberger and Padesky).

D. Family members have read the information on identifying distorted cognitive messages, and key points were processed.

E. Family members were reinforced for their identification of cognitive distortions.

F. Family members have not read the assigned material on cognitive distortions and were redirected to do so.

## 12. Teach Realistic Self-Talk (12)

A. The family was taught about the use of positive, reality-based self-talk that can replace distorted cognitive messages.

B. Nondepressed family members were encouraged to remind the depressed family member to think positively and realistically.

C. The depressed family member's use of positive, reality-based self-talk was consistently reinforced.

D. The depressed family member was assisted in identifying situations in which self-talk could become more positive and reality-based.

## 13. Develop Genograms (13)

A. The parents' families-of-origin were explored to help identify other depressed people in the extended family.

B. A genogram was used to review the existence of depression symptoms within extended family members.

C. Family members were supported for their insight when they reviewed the pattern of depression symptoms within the extended family.

## 14. Suggest Mind Exercises (14)

A. Techniques for maintaining the level of concentration and avoidance of daydreaming were presented.

B. The depressed family member was encouraged to stay active, engage in brief reading activities, and practice recall exercises.

C. The family members' use of mind exercises was reviewed and reinforced.

D. The depressed family member reported difficulty in using mind exercises to maintain the level of concentration and avoid daydreaming and was redirected toward these helpful techniques.

### 15. Encourage Healthy Sleeping and Eating (15)

A. The depressed family member was encouraged to gain healthy eating and sleeping patterns.

B. The depressed family member was encouraged to be involved in family activities.

C. Nondepressed family members were supported in their encouragement of the depressed family member's increased participation in activities.

D. The depressed family member continues to have limited activity levels and was redirected in this area.

### 16. Recommend Self-Esteem Exercise (16)

A. It was recommended to the family that they implement self-esteem-building exercises.

B. Specific self-esteem-enhancing exercises were assigned (e.g., practicing assertiveness, praising others, positive affirmations).

C. The family has regularly used self-esteem-building exercises and was reinforced for these helpful techniques.

D. The family has not regularly used the self-esteem-building exercises, and the reasons for this failure were processed and remediated.

### 17. Explore/Remediate Avoidant Behaviors (17)

A. The depressed family member was assessed for a pattern of avoidant behaviors.

B. Avoidant behaviors were identified, and graduated exposure techniques were used to reduce the avoidant behavior.

C. Coping skills training was used to reduce an identified pattern of avoidant behavior.

D. Although the depressed family member was assessed for a pattern of avoidant behaviors, no such pattern was identified.

### 18. Assess for Anger Issues (18)

A. The family was assessed for how they deal with anger.

B. The family was noted to have significant concerns related to suppressed anger.

C. Family members were taught how suppressed anger can lead to avoidance behavior and depression symptoms.

D. The family was assessed for anger concerns, but none were identified.

### 19. Teach about Assertiveness (19)

A. Family members were taught about assertion, passivity, passive-aggressiveness, and aggressiveness.

B. Family members were taught how to use assertive techniques to express their anger.

C. Family members were reinforced for implementing assertiveness in their daily life.

D. Family members were redirected when they did not use assertiveness skills.

### 20. Incorporate Alternative Forms of Expression (20)

A. Family members were taught about alternative forms of expressing anger and depression feelings.

B. Family members were taught how to use journaling as a way to express anger feelings.

C. Family members were taught to use artwork as a way to express emotions.

D. The processing of journaling, artwork, or other ways of expressing feelings of anger and depression was facilitated, with a specific focus on avoiding unnecessary attacks among family members.

E. Family members have not used alternative means to express their emotions and were redirected to do so.

### 21. Assess for Suicide Risk (21)

A. An assessment to determine the level of risk for suicide was completed.

B. Since the level of risk for suicide was identified as significant, a plan for the support and safety of the depressed family member was initiated.

C. The depressed family member was assessed for suicide but was noted to have very low risk.

### 22. Develop Response for High Suicide Risk (22)

A. Methods were identified and reinforced for the family to stay in contact with each other during a period of high suicide risk.

B. The use of a crisis hotline during periods of high suicide risk was encouraged.

C. Family members have regularly used methods to stay in touch during a high suicide risk and were reinforced for this crucial communication.

D. Family members have not responded well to the suicide risk situations and were redirected in this area.

### 23. Develop No-Self-Harm Contract (23)

A. A no-self-harm contract was developed and signed by all members of the family.

B. The family was encouraged to remind the depressed family member about the no-self-harm contract during times of increased suicide risk.

C. The depressed family member declined to sign the no-self-harm contract; therefore, more specific steps for assuring safety were developed.

D. An agreement was developed regarding the immediate use of hospitalization should any gestures or attempts at suicide occur.

E. Family members were reminded to implement the hospitalization agreement should the depressed family member's hopelessness increase to gestures or attempts at suicide.

### 24. Assess Family Depression and Refer to Psychiatrist (24)

A. The extended family was assessed for depression symptoms.

B. A referral was made to a physician to evaluate the need for psychotropic medication.

C. The family member has followed through on the referral to a physician and has been assessed for a prescription of psychotropic medication, but none was prescribed.

D. Psychotropic medication has been prescribed for the depressed family member.

E. The family member's psychotropic medication was monitored for side effects and is being appropriately titrated.

F. The depressed family member has refused a prescription for psychotropic medication provided by the physician, and this opposition was processed.

G. The family was encouraged to maintain close communication with the physician.

### 25. Monitor Medication Compliance (25)

A. As the depressed family member has taken the antidepressant medication prescribed by his/her physician, the effectiveness and side effects of the medication were monitored.

B. The depressed family member reported that the antidepressant medication has been beneficial in reducing sleep interference and in stabilizing mood; the benefits of this progress were reviewed.

C. The depressed family member reported that the antidepressant medication has not been beneficial; this was relayed to the prescribing clinician.

D. The depressed family member was assessed for side effects from his/her medication.

E. The depressed family member has not consistently taken the prescribed antidepressant medication and was redirected to do so.

### 26. Review Alternative Treatments (26)

A. The family was assisted in brainstorming and developing a list of alternative treatments.

B. Family members' list of alternative treatments that may meet the depressed family member's needs was reviewed.

C. Family members were provided with several alternative means of treatment, including hospitalization, day treatment programs, intensive individual, and/or group psychotherapy.

### 27. Identify Effective Reinforcers (27)

A. Family members were assisted in identifying the reinforcers that were most effective for the depressed family member's progress.

B. Family members were assisted in identifying new ways to implement the effective reinforcers for the depressed family member.

C. It was noted that the depressed family member has made increased progress due to the use of regular reinforcement.

### 28. Facilitate Unsolicited Contact (28)

A. An agreement was developed for nondepressed family members to make unsolicited contact with the depressed family member.

B. Family members were encouraged to make unsolicited contact through e-mails and phone calls.

C. Family members were reinforced for their regular use of unsolicited contact with the depressed family member.

D. Family members have not used unsolicited contacts with the depressed family member as a way to provide support and were redirected to do so.

### 29. Encourage Physical Activities (29)

A. A plan was developed that involves all family members interacting in physical activities.

B. Family members were helped to identify several physical activities that could be used to involve all family members.

C. Family members were provided with examples of physical activities that can include all family members (e.g., swimming, going to the fitness center, playing badminton or winter sports, or ice skating).

D. Family members were reinforced for their regular use of physical activities.

### 30. Teach about Monitoring Progress (30)

A. Family members were taught how to monitor progress after depression symptoms have subsided.

B. Family members were taught about the recurring nature of depression.

C. Family members were taught the markers of potential relapse (e.g., an increase in social withdrawal, engaging in denial).

### 31. Explore Early Trauma (31)

A. The possibility of early trauma and how this might be contributing to the depression was explored.

B. Specific trauma such as sexual, physical, or psychological abuse was reviewed.

C. The depressed family member was supported while the experience of early trauma was described.

D. Although early trauma was explored, no specific early traumas were identified.

### 32. Assess Dynamics of Guilt (32)

A. The family dynamics were assessed regarding indicators that guilt may be subtly induced by other family members.

B. It was reflected to family members that guilt appears to be a significant dynamic within the family communication style.

C. Family members were encouraged to discuss and consider alternatives to guilt-inflicting behaviors.

D. Family members were assisted in developing other means of communication rather than using guilt-inflicting behaviors.

E. Family members were confronted when they used guilt-inflicting behaviors.

F. Family members were reinforced for using alternatives to guilt-inflicting behaviors.

G. It was noted that guilt does not appear to be a significant indicator in the family dynamics.

### 33. Address Enabling (33)

A. Family members were identified as engaging in many enabling behaviors that support the depressed family member's pattern of depression.

B. The desire for others to overpower or enhance control by enabling the depressed family member's pattern of depression was discussed.

C. Family members were urged to reduce enabling behaviors.

D. Whenever family members reported or displayed enabling behaviors, they were confronted and redirected.

# DISENGAGEMENT/LOSS OF FAMILY COHESION

## CLIENT PRESENTATION

### 1. Disengagement/Disillusionment (1)*
A. Family members appear to be quite disengaged from each other.
B. Family members report disillusionment with the state of the family's connectedness.
C. Family members report feeling that they are out of touch with each other.
D. As treatment has progressed, family members have become more connected with each other.

### 2. Lack of Enjoyment Together (2)
A. Family members rarely laugh or have fun with each other.
B. Family members found it difficult to identify any recent interactions in which they enjoyed each other's company.
C. Family members do not have many family jokes.
D. As the family has become more cohesive, they have identified that they enjoy each other's company.

### 3. Alienation from the Family Unit (3)
A. A family member has identified feelings of alienation from the family unit.
B. Family members acknowledge that one family member is estranged from the family unit.
C. Although the family displays a pattern of cohesion, this does not include all family members.
D. All family members report feeling a place within the family.

### 4. Activities Outside of the Family Unit (4)
A. Family members have developed individual activities outside of the family unit.
B. As the family has attempted to develop cohesion, the family members' activities outside of the family unit have made it difficult for family members to bond together.
C. Family members have developed a healthy balance between individual activities and family relationships.

### 5. Tension and Conflict (5)
A. Family members report a pattern of quick escalation to tension and conflict when family members do interact.
B. Crisis situations are very difficult for the family, since past conflicts are not set aside during periods of family crisis.
C. Family members have developed a healthier pattern of interaction, with less tension and conflict.

---

*The numbers in parentheses correlate to the number of the Behavioral Definition statement in the companion chapter with the same title in *The Family Therapy Treatment Planner*, Second Ed. (Dattilio, Jongsma, and Davis) by John Wiley & Sons, 2010.

### 6. External Parties React Negatively (6)

A. External parties have identified a lack of communication, cohesion, and harmony in the family.

B. External parties have often commented about the disengagement and loss of family cohesion.

C. External parties have begun to see the family as more cohesive and engaged.

### 7. Behavioral Health Side Effects (7)

A. Negative behavioral side effects have been identified due to the family's level of disengagement.

B. Mental illness concerns appear to be directly related to the family's pattern of disengagement.

C. A pattern of physical illness problems has resulted from the family's pattern of disengagement.

D. Family members have engaged in substance abuse in reaction to the pattern of family disengagement.

E. Family members have engaged in criminal activities, prompted, in part, by the lack of family cohesion.

F. As family cohesion has increased, the negative behavioral side effects have decreased.

### 8. Lack of Shared Activities (8)

A. Family members report that they rarely share activities with each other.

B. Celebrations rarely occur within the family.

C. Family members do not celebrate birthdays, anniversaries, or other important holidays.

D. As the family members have developed greater cohesion, they have increased their use of mutual celebrations and shared activities.

### 9. Lost Sense of Self (9)

A. Family members report that they have a lost sense of self due to the family's pattern of disengagement.

B. Family members demonstrate a poor understanding of their family history.

C. As the family has become more cohesive, information about the family has been shared, helping to develop a better sense of self for each family member.

### 10. Loss of Family Rituals/Identity (10)

A. The family described a loss of previous family rituals.

B. As inquiries were made, the family identified a lack of family rituals (i.e., dinner together, birthday celebrations, holiday events).

C. Family members described a loss of family identity when describing the loss of family rituals.

D. Family members report an increase in family rituals, leading to a sense of increased family identity and affiliation.

## INTERVENTIONS IMPLEMENTED

### 1. Discuss Family Functioning (1)*

A. A discussion was facilitated about each family member's perception of the family and how it functions.

B. Family members were encouraged to provide their opinion about how engaged and cohesive the family has been.

C. Family members were supported as they provided their opinions about the level of engagement and family cohesion.

D. It was sensed that the family members were minimizing concerns related to disengagement and loss of family cohesion, and they were encouraged to be more open about these issues.

### 2. Explore Effects of Disengagement (2)

A. The emotional responses that family members have displayed as a result of the pattern of disengagement were explored.

B. Family members were asked about how their behavior has been affected as a result of the family's disengagement.

C. Family members were supported as they identified personal effects of the family's pattern of disengagement.

D. Family members were cautious about describing the effects of the pattern of disengagement and were encouraged to participate in this discussion.

### 3. Define Contributors to Disengagement (3)

A. Family members were encouraged to define what is contributing to the disengagement in behavioral terms.

B. *The Family-of-Origin Inventory* (Stuart) was administered to aid in determining how disengagement may have been learned in childhood experiences.

C. Family members were supported for their insights on how the pattern of disengagement has occurred.

D. Family members were assisted in developing behavioral terms for describing the pattern of disengagement.

### 4. Identify Missing Components (4)

A. Each family member was encouraged to list what is desirable but missing within the family.

B. Each family member's list of desirable family components was processed within the session.

C. Family members were encouraged to read *Seven Habits of Highly Effective Families* (Covey).

D. Family members have read the assigned material, and the key points in this area were reviewed.

E. Family members have not read the assigned material and were redirected to do so.

---

*The numbers in parentheses correlate to the number of the Therapeutic Intervention statement in the companion chapter with the same title in *The Family Therapy Treatment Planner*, Second Ed. (Dattilio, Jongsma, and Davis) by John Wiley & Sons, 2010.

### 5. Assess Family Cohesion (5)

A. The family's cohesion was assessed through specific testing instruments.

B. *The Family Adaptability and Cohesion Scales* (Olsen) were administered to assess the family's cohesion.

C. *The Family's Sense of Coherence and Family Adaptation Scales* (Antonovsky and Sourani) were administered to assess the family's cohesion.

D. Family members were provided with feedback regarding the results of the test instruments used to assess the family cohesion.

### 6. Ask for Video Example of Family (6)

A. Family members were asked to select a movie that best exemplifies their sense of disengagement.

B. Family members were supported when they identified a movie that has exemplified their sense of disengagement.

C. Family members were provided with examples of a video representation of disengaged families (e.g., *Ordinary People*).

### 7. Encourage Creativity to Express Alienation (7)

A. Family members were encouraged to express how alienation and loss of closeness is experienced within the family.

B. Family members were encouraged to use creative techniques such as poems, artwork, songs, or drama to express how they experience the alienation and loss of closeness within the family.

C. Family members were supported for their attempts to describe how they have experienced alienation.

### 8. Discuss Outside Activities (8)

A. Family members' gravitation to outside activities and relationships was discussed.

B. Family members' gravitation to outside activities and relationships was normalized, given their current situation.

C. Family members were supported as they acknowledged their own use of outside activities as a way to cope with the family pattern of alienation.

D. Family members were encouraged to consider reinvesting in family relationships.

### 9. Identify Individual Patterns of Outside Relationships (9)

A. Each family member was asked to acknowledge how they have personally sought out relationships with others outside of the family.

B. Family members were assisted in identifying how this has helped them to fill the void left by the family pattern of alienation.

C. Family members were cautious to admit to developing outside relationships to help fill the void in their own family and were encouraged to express themselves in this area.

### 10. Encourage Acceptance of Responsibility (10)

A. Each family member was encouraged to take responsibility for contributions to the family's gravitating toward disengagement.

B. Family members were supported as they took responsibility for their own contributions to the family's disengagement.

C. Family members were guarded and defensive about identifying their own responsibility for disengagement within the family and were encouraged to take responsibility for this problem.

### 11. Encourage "I" Messages (11)

A. Family members were encouraged to use "I" messages.

B. Family members were urged to reduce the pattern of blame within the family.

C. Family members were provided with feedback about the difference between "I" and "you" messages.

D. Family members were reinforced whenever they changed from "you" to "I" messages.

### 12. Discuss Fear of Redeveloping Family Relationships (12)

A. A discussion was held about the fear and difficulties inherent in gravitating back to the family unit.

B. Each family member was urged to discuss how decreasing disengagement and increasing cohesion would affect them personally.

C. The need to adjust to the new pattern within the family was normalized.

### 13. Brainstorm Reinvestment in the Family (13)

A. Methods for coping with the reinvestment within the family were brainstormed.

B. Family members were urged to identify how they would respond to fears and resistance to changes within the family.

C. Family members were provided with tentative examples about how to cope with changes within the family (e.g., taking one step at a time, discussing the risk involved with trusting each other, considering how to start spending time with each other, and what to expect).

### 14. Encourage Risk Taking (14)

A. Family members were encouraged to take risks to reinvest in their own family.

B. Family members were encouraged to reinvest in their own family by taking a leap of faith.

C. Family members were reinforced for faithfully trusting in the family and reinvesting in the family relationships.

D. Family members have not taken a risk and reinvested in their own family and were encouraged to do so.

### 15. Discuss Conflicts during Required Interactions (15)

A. Family members were directed to identify situations in which they must interact with each other.

B. Family members were encouraged to describe the conflicts that arise when they must interact with one another.

C. Family members were supported as they discussed the conflicts that occur during their unavoidable interactions with each other.

### 16. Normalize Tension and Conflict (16)

A. Family members were prepared for the tension and conflict as a natural part of the rehabilitation process for the family.

B. A discussion was held about ways to inoculate against tension and conflict.

C. Family members were urged to use progressive muscle relaxation, identification of likely areas of conflict, and how to anticipate and resolve the conflicts.

D. Family members were encouraged to weigh alternative responses to the typical patterns of tension and conflicts.

### 17. Teach Coping Strategies (17)

A. Conflict-resolution strategies were taught to the family.

B. Tension-reducing techniques were taught to the family.

C. The family was taught how to use time-out procedures, ventilation sessions, third-party mediators, and other tension-reducing skills.

D. Family members were encouraged to use the coping skills to deal with tension and conflict.

E. Family members have not used the coping skills to deal with tension and conflict and were redirected to do so.

### 18. Brainstorm Better Ways to Interact during a Family Crisis (18)

A. Family members were assisted in brainstorming ways to prepare for interactions during family crises.

B. Role-play techniques were used to help the family develop better ways to interact during crises.

C. Positive feedback was provided for the family's identification of better ways to interact during crises.

### 19. Teach Communication Skills (19)

A. The family was taught principles of healthy communication.

B. The family was taught how to use healthy problem-solving skills.

C. Speaker/listener techniques were taught to the family.

D. Pro versus con problem-solving strategies were taught to the family.

E. The family was reinforced for their understanding of the ways in which they can use communication skills.

F. The family has not used healthy communication skills and was redirected to do so.

### 20. Role-Play Conflictual Communication (20)

A. The family was asked to identify an actual situation of conflictual communication.

B. Role-playing techniques were used to enact the actual situation of conflictual communication.

C. The family was coached to use the communication and problem-solving skills within daily life situations.

D. Family members were provided with positive feedback about their use of communication and problem-solving skills.

E. The family was provided with redirection when they had not used healthy communication and problem-solving skills.

### 21. Assess for Behavioral Health Disturbances (21)

A. Family members were assessed for any signs of mental illness.

B. Family members were assessed for any signs of physical health problems.

C. Family members were assessed for substance abuse problems.

D. Family members were assessed for the presence of criminal behavior patterns.

E. The results of the assessments for behavioral health problems were reflected to the family.

### 22. Discuss Etiology of Behavioral Health Problems (22)

A. The behavioral health problems identified within the family were reviewed for their connection to the pattern of disengagement within the family.

B. Family members were assisted in identifying a direct connection between the behavioral health problems within the family and the family's pattern of disengagement.

C. Family members did not develop any connection between the behavioral health problems within the family and the pattern of disengagement and were provided with tentative examples of how this may be occurring.

### 23. Facilitate Emotions Regarding Behavioral Health Problems (23)

A. Family members were assisted in expressing their emotions related to the psychological or behavioral health problems of a family member.

B. Family members were supported as they expressed their feelings about the behavioral health problems identified within the family.

C. Family members were guarded about their emotions related to the behavioral health problems within the family and were urged to be more open.

### 24. Assess for Adjunctive Therapy (24)

A. Family members were assessed regarding their need for adjunctive therapeutic intervention.

B. Family members were referred to their family physician.

C. Family members were referred to a psychiatrist.

D. Family members were assessed regarding their need for adjunctive therapy, but no needs were identified.

### 25. Confront Acting Out (25)

A. The troubled family member was confronted for acting out as a way to blame or manipulate others.

B. The troubled family member was assisted in identifying other ways to communicate his/her concerns.

## 26. Generate List of Activities (26)

A. Family members were assisted in generating a list of enjoyable family activities in which they would like to engage.

B. Family members have developed a list of family activities that they would like to engage in and were provided with positive feedback in this area.

C. Family members have not developed a list of enjoyable family activities and were redirected to do so.

## 27. Process Expectations for Family Activities (27)

A. Each family member was asked to fantasize about how the proposed family activities would unfold.

B. A discussion was held regarding the fear of failure and disappointment that family members may experience related to the proposed family activities.

C. Family members were supported as they expressed their emotions regarding the proposed family activities.

## 28. Brainstorm Ways to Avoid Failures (28)

A. The family was assisted in brainstorming ways to avoid failures on the proposed family activities.

B. Family members were assisted in identifying ways to facilitate the more successful enjoyment of family activities.

C. Family members were reinforced for their identification of healthy ways to facilitate greater success and avoid failure in family activities.

D. Tentative examples were provided to the family members about how to best facilitate the enjoyable family activities.

## 29. Review Lost Identity (29)

A. Family members were assisted in identifying ways in which each family member has experienced a weakened or lost sense of self due to the disengagement within the family.

B. Family members were assisted in comparing their experiences regarding a lost sense of self.

C. Family members were provided with feedback about ways in which they are similar and dissimilar in regard to their lost sense of identity.

## 30. Generate Activities for Developing Connection (30)

A. The family was assisted in generating a list of family activities that may help to restore a sense of self and connection between family members.

B. Family members were supported as they identified several ways in which they could restore a sense of self and connection between family members.

C. Family members were provided with tentative examples of ways in which they could restore a sense of self and connection between family members (e.g., volunteering time together to aid the less fortunate; activities focused on survival and working together, such as a rafting trip).

D. The family members were directed to read portions of *The Intentional Family* (Doherty).

E. Family members have read portions of the assigned reading and key points were reviewed and processed.

F. The assigned reading has not been completed and the family members were redirected to do so.

### 31. Include Family-of-Origin Members within Session (31)

A. A family session was coordinated to include family-of-origin members to address the lack of personal identity and allow for a process of ventilation of the emotion attached to it.

B. Family members participated in an intergenerational session to address the lack of personal identity.

C. The process was begun for family members to gain a greater sense of identity.

# EATING DISORDERS

## CLIENT PRESENTATION

### 1. Body Image Disturbance (1)*

A. A family member has a history of preoccupation with body image and a self-perception of being overweight, even when thin.

B. The family member is beginning to acknowledge that body image thoughts are grossly inaccurate and that some weight gain is necessary.

C. As the family member has begun to gain some weight, anxiety levels have increased and the fear of obesity has returned.

D. The family member has been able to gain weight to normal levels without being overwhelmed by a distorted fear of becoming overweight.

### 2. Denial of Effects of Weight Loss (2)

A. The eating-disordered family member has a poor understanding of the physical effects of the weight loss.

B. The eating-disordered family member is in denial about being emaciated and its negative medical effects.

C. As treatment has progressed, the eating-disordered family member has become more realistic about the negative physical effects of severe weight loss.

### 3. Extreme Weight Loss (3)

A. The family member's eating disorder has resulted in extreme weight loss and a refusal to consume enough calories to increase the weight to more normal levels.

B. The extreme weight loss has resulted in amenorrhea in the family member.

C. The family member's weight loss has plateaued.

D. The eating-disordered family member is beginning to acknowledge the need for a gain in weight.

E. The family member has begun to gain weight gradually and endure the anxious feelings associated with that experience.

F. The family member is now at the lower end of a normal weight level and has been able to maintain it.

### 4. Limited Food Intake (4)

A. The eating-disordered family member has greatly restricted the intake of food.

B. The eating-disordered family member's restrictive eating pattern has resulted in extreme weight loss.

---

*The numbers in parentheses correlate to the number of the Behavioral Definition statement in the companion chapter with the same title in *The Family Therapy Treatment Planner*, Second Ed. (Dattilio, Jongsma, and Davis) by John Wiley & Sons, 2010.

C. The eating-disordered family member has refused to consume enough calories to increase the weight to normal levels.

D. The family member's weight loss has plateaued, and there is an acknowledgement of the need for weight gain.

E. The eating-disordered family member has begun to eat at more normal levels and is gaining weight gradually.

F. The eating-disordered family member is now at the lower end of normal in terms of weight and has been able to maintain it.

### 5. Amenorrhea (5)

A. The eating-disordered family member has obtained such a low weight that she no longer menstruates.

B. As treatment has progressed, the eating-disordered family member has begun to gain weight and menstruate again.

### 6. Bingeing/Purging (6)

A. The eating-disordered family member periodically consumes large quantities of high-calorie foods.

B. The eating-disordered family member compensates for high-calorie food intake, including vomiting or inappropriate use of laxatives to avoid gaining weight.

C. As treatment has progressed, the eating-disordered family member has decreased the frequency and intensity of the binge/purge pattern.

### 7. Irrational Feeling of Becoming Overweight (7)

A. The eating-disordered family member has developed a predominating, intense fear of becoming overweight.

B. The eating-disordered family member's fear of becoming overweight has caused a limiting of food intake to an extreme level.

C. The eating-disordered family member has used purging methods to control weight levels.

D. The eating-disordered family member's fear of becoming overweight has diminished.

E. The eating-disordered family member has not reported any fear of becoming overweight.

### 8. Potassium/Chloride Reduction (8)

A. The eating-disordered family member has been identified as having a reduction of potassium levels in the body due to excessive vomiting and/or elimination.

B. The eating-disordered family member has been identified as having a decreased chlorine level due to the excessive vomiting and/or elimination.

C. As the eating-disordered family member has gained a more appropriate and healthy pattern of eating, potassium and chloride levels have become more typical.

### 9. Electrolyte Imbalance (9)

A. An electrolyte imbalance resulting from the family member's eating disorder is causing a compromised health status.

B. The family member has accepted that the eating disorder has resulted in a fluid and electrolyte imbalance.

C. The eating-disordered family member has agreed to terminate the bingeing/purging behavior that has resulted in the electrolyte imbalance.

D. The eating-disordered family member has agreed to modify the level of nutritious food intake and terminate purging behaviors to correct a fluid and electrolyte imbalance.

E. The eating-disordered family member's fluid and electrolyte imbalance have been corrected as the food intake and purging behavior have been modified.

### 10. Avoidance of Sexual Contact (10)

A. The eating-disordered family member described a desire to avoid sexual contact.

B. The eating-disordered family member's partner described that the family member persistently avoids sexual contact.

C. As the eating disorder has improved, the family member identified an increased desire to share sexual contact with the partner.

D. The eating-disordered family member has become comfortable in having increasingly sexual contact with the partner.

### 11. Avoidance of Affection (10)

A. The eating-disordered family member described a desire to avoid expressive affection with other family members.

B. Other family members described that the eating-disordered family member persistently avoids expressions of affection.

### 12. Flat Affect (11)

A. The eating-disordered family member presents with a recurrent pattern of depression.

B. The eating-disordered family member displays current symptoms of depression, including sleep and appetite changes, irritability, sadness, lack of energy and feelings of worthlessness, hopelessness, and helplessness.

C. As treatment has progressed, the eating-disordered family member's pattern of depression symptoms has been significantly decreased.

D. As the family member's eating disorder has improved, there has been an increased desire to share affection with other family members.

E. The eating-disordered family member has become appropriately comfortable in expressing affection toward other family members.

### 13. Defensiveness about Dieting, Bingeing, and Purging (12)

A. Family members have had arguments related to eating disorder problems.

B. Family members report persistent arguments over the adaptations that the eating disorder has forced family members to make.

C. Family members have frequently been at odds with each other over issues related to the eating disorder.

D. As the family member's eating disorder symptoms have been eliminated, the arguments between the family members have decreased.

### 14. Tension about Eating Habits (13)

A. The family experiences significant tension around the topic of the eating-disordered family member's eating habits.

B. Family meals are often characterized by anxiety and tension.

C. Family members have begun to make family eating time less tense and more enjoyable.

D. As treatment has progressed, family members have described less feelings of tension surrounding the eating-disordered family member's eating habits.

### 15. Excessive Exercise (14)

A. The eating-disordered family member often uses excessive exercise to compensate for food intake.

B. The eating-disordered family member uses several hours of strenuous exercise to keep weight levels down.

C. As treatment has progressed, the eating-disordered family member has decreased the use of exercise as a compensatory behavior.

## INTERVENTIONS IMPLEMENTED

### 1. Review Criteria for Eating Disorder (1)*

A. The *DSM* criteria for an eating disorder were reviewed with all family members.

B. Specific diagnostic criteria for an eating disorder that were relevant to the family member's symptomology were highlighted.

C. Family members endorsed evidence of an eating disorder within the family, and this was reflected to them.

### 2. Discuss Healthy and Unhealthy Eating Patterns (2)

A. Eating patterns were discussed with all family members.

B. Family members were helped to identify what eating behaviors were healthy or unhealthy.

C. Family members were provided with feedback for their identification of healthy and unhealthy eating behaviors.

D. Family members were encouraged to read literature about eating disorders.

### 3. Use Assessment Instruments (3)

A. Objective assessment instruments were used to make a clearer diagnosis of the eating disorder.

B. The family member was administered the *Eating Disorder's Inventory-2* (Garner).

C. The family member was assessed using the *Family-of-Origin Scale* (Hovestadt).

D. Results of the assessment tools were reflected to the family members.

*The numbers in parentheses correlate to the number of the Therapeutic Intervention statement in the companion chapter with the same title in *The Family Therapy Treatment Planner*, Second Ed. (Dattilio, Jongsma, and Davis) by John Wiley & Sons, 2010.

### 4. Review Beliefs about Eating Disorder Development (4)

A. Family members were asked to express their beliefs about how the eating patterns have developed.

B. The dynamics between the specific family members were focused on as the family described their beliefs about the development of the eating patterns.

C. Feedback was provided to the family about their beliefs on the development of the eating disorder.

### 5. Explore Contributors to Eating Disturbance (5)

A. Patterns within the family behavior were reviewed to help identify factors that may contribute to the eating disturbance in the family.

B. Family members were supported as they identified factors that contribute to eating disturbances in the family.

C. Family members were unable to identify patterns of behavior that may contribute to the eating disturbance in the family and were provided with tentative examples (e.g., criticism during mealtime, overemphasis on weight and body image).

### 6. Encourage Sharing about Behavior and Cues (6)

A. The eating-disordered family member was encouraged to share the bingeing and purging pattern with the family.

B. The eating-disordered family member was supported while disclosing about eating behaviors and cues.

C. Family members were reinforced as they provided positive feedback to the family member with the eating disorder for the disclosures about behavior patterns and cues.

D. The eating-disordered family member was quite guarded about discussing the pattern of bingeing and purging and was urged to be more open in this area.

### 7. Discuss Contributors to Cues (7)

A. Family members were assisted in identifying their own role in the specific interactions that are identified as cues for the eating-disorder behavior.

B. Family members were supported and encouraged as they took responsibility for their own involvement in the cues related to the eating-disorder behavior.

C. Family members were guarded and tended to deny their own contributions to the cues for the eating-disorder behavior and were urged to take greater responsibility for these interactions.

### 8. Review Knowledge about Eating Disorders (8)

A. Family members were encouraged to provide information about eating disorders as they have identified it through various media, reading, or from other people.

B. Family members were redirected about misperceptions of eating disorders.

C. Family members were reinforced as they identified accurate information regarding eating disorders.

### 9. Assign Reading Material (9)

A. Family members were assigned reading materials on eating disorders to broaden their knowledge base.

B. Family members were directed to read *Reviving Ophelia* (Pipher).

C. Family members were encouraged to read *Secret Language of Eating Disorders* (Claude-Pierre).

D. Family members were directed to read *Eating Disorders* (National Institute of Mental Health).

E. Family members have read the assigned material on eating disorders and the key concepts were reviewed.

F. Family members have not read the assigned material on eating disorders and were redirected to do so.

### 10. Assign Self-Monitoring of Food Intake (10)

A. The family member with the eating disorder was assigned to self-monitor food intake, thoughts and feelings.

B. "A Reality Journal: Food, Weight, Thoughts and Feelings" from the *Adult Psychotherapy Homework Planner*, 2nd ed. (Jongsma) was assigned to the client.

C. "Daily Record of Dysfunctional Thoughts" from *Cognitive Therapy for Depression* (Beck et al.) was assigned to the client.

D. Journal material was processed with the family to allow them to challenge maladaptive patterns of thinking and behaving.

E. Family members were encouraged to replace dysfunctional thoughts with adaptive alternatives.

F. The family member with the eating disorder was supported and reinforced for his/her completion and sharing of the journal.

G. The family member has not been willing to complete and share a record of eating patterns, weight, and thoughts/feelings, and was redirected to do so.

### 11. Develop Awareness of Automatic Thoughts (11)

A. The family was assisted in developing an awareness of automatic thoughts, underlying assumptions, associated feelings, and actions that are consistent with maladaptive eating patterns and weight control practices.

B. The family was provided with examples of dysfunctional automatic thoughts (i.e., poor self-image, distorted body image, fear of failure/rejections, and fear of sexuality).

C. The family was assisted in identifying how automatic thoughts may lead to dysfunctional patterns.

D. The family was supported for making the connection between automatic thoughts and dysfunctional patterns.

E. The family struggled to connect automatic thoughts to dysfunctional patterns and was provided with remedial feedback in this area.

12. **Identify Negative Cognitive Messages (12)**

A. The family was assisted in the identification of negative cognitive messages (e.g., catastrophizing, exaggerating) that mediate dysfunctional eating behavior.

B. The family was trained to establish realistic cognitive messages regarding food intake and body size.

C. The family was assigned "Fears Beneath the Eating Disorder" from the *Adolescent Psychotherapy Homework Planner*, 2nd ed. (Jongsma, Peterson, and McInnis).

D. The family has completed the assignments and the results were processed.

E. The family has not completed the assignments regarding negative cognitive messages and was redirected to do so.

13. **Assess/Refer for Additional Treatment (13)**

A. The eating-disordered family member was assessed for the need for treatment outside of the family therapy.

B. The eating-disordered family member was referred to an individual therapist for additional treatment.

C. The eating-disordered family member was referred to a psychiatrist for additional treatment.

D. The eating-disordered family member was assessed for additional treatment, but no additional treatment seems necessary.

14. **Solicit Support for Hospitalization (14)**

A. Family members were reviewed regarding support for hospitalizing the eating-disordered family member if this condition becomes severe enough.

B. Family members were noted to be in support of hospitalizing the eating-disordered family member.

C. Involuntary commitment procedures were instituted as the eating-disordered family member has refused inpatient care.

D. Hospitalization for the eating-disordered family member was identified as inappropriate at this time.

15. **Encourage Open Discussion of Medical Treatment Needs (15)**

A. All family members were encouraged to talk openly about the necessity of medical treatment.

B. Family members were supported as they discussed the need for medical or psychiatric hospitalization.

C. Family members were reinforced as they talked about the need for psychotropic medication for the eating-disordered family member.

D. The eating-disordered family member was supported as the family gave feedback about the need for medical treatment.

E. Family members have been cautious about providing any opinion related to the need for medical treatment and were encouraged to give more specific feedback in this area.

### 16. Solicit Positive Traits (16)

A. Each family member was asked to list positive traits and talents for the eating-disordered family member.

B. Family members were reinforced as they identified ways in which they value the eating-disordered family member.

C. Family members had minimal positive feedback about the eating-disordered family member's traits and were urged to develop greater attentiveness to this area.

### 17. Facilitate Expression of Anger (17)

A. Family members were assisted in identifying and expressing their anger and resentment regarding the behavior of the eating-disordered family member.

B. Family members were assisted in identifying appropriate ways to express angry, resentful feelings.

C. Family members were redirected when their expression of anger or resentment became destructive or demeaning.

### 18. Identify Cues for Anger (18)

A. Family members were taught about using an anger rating scale from 0 to 10, with 10 being the most severe anger.

B. Family members were assisted in identifying behavioral cues and the level of anger associated with each cue.

C. Family members were assisted in identifying cognitive cues and the level of anger associated with each cue.

D. Family members were assisted in identifying effective cues and the level of anger associated with each cue.

E. Family members were assisted in identifying the level of unhealthiness as anger increases.

### 19. Teach Time-Out Techniques (19)

A. Family members were taught about the six components of time-out techniques: *self-monitoring* for escalating feelings of anger and hurt; *signaling* to the other family member that verbal engagement should end; *acknowledging* the need of the family member to disengage; *separating* to disengage; *cooling down* to regain control of anger; and *returning* to controlled verbal engagement.

B. Positive feedback was provided as the family members displayed understanding of the time-out technique.

C. Family members were advised about the potential for misuse of the time-out technique if implemented to avoid arguments, or manipulate other family members.

D. Family members have misused the time-out technique and were redirected in this area.

E. Family members were reinforced for their reports of successful use of the time-out technique.

### 20. Focus on Ownership of Family Dynamics (20)

A. Each family member was urged to take ownership for the specific behaviors that contribute to the family dynamics.

B. Family members were encouraged to use "I" statements instead of "you" statements.

C. Family members were taught about the tendency to externalize blame as a means of defense and denial over the eating disorder.

D. Family members were provided with positive feedback as they took greater ownership for specific behaviors that contribute to the family dynamics.

E. Family members were redirected when they tended to externalize, blame, deny, or defend themselves about family dynamics and eating disorder concerns.

21. **Refer to Dietician (21)**

A. Family members were referred to a dietician to review meal planning.

B. The eating-disordered family member was assisted in developing specific meal plans.

C. Family members were assisted in developing meal plans, with a focus on how this will help the eating-disordered family member.

D. The family has not met with the dietician and was redirected to do so.

22. **Encourage Support of Gradual Progress (22)**

A. Family members were reminded that the eating-disordered family member's move toward a balanced diet and increased food intake would be a gradual pattern.

B. Family members were encouraged to support the gradual movement toward a more balanced diet.

C. Family members were reinforced for their support of the eating-disordered family member's gradual movement toward a more balanced diet.

D. Family members have not been supportive of the gradual movement toward a more balanced diet and were reminded that progress will not be instantaneous.

23. **Educate about Hidden Meanings (23)**

A. Family members were taught how the compulsive-eating behavior may be a means of expressing anger or compensating for feelings of low self-esteem.

B. Family members were supported as they displayed a better understanding of the hidden meaning of the compulsive behaviors.

C. When family members did not look underneath the compulsive behavior for the hidden meaning, they were redirected to do so.

24. **Suggest Coping Skills for Perfectionism (24)**

A. Family members were identified as struggling with perfectionism and control issues.

B. Family members were directed to deliberately expose themselves to situations in which they would experience failure and have to live with it.

C. Family members were directed to place themselves in situations where they might feel out of control (e.g., an amusement park ride).

D. Family members were supported as they have begun to deal with perfectionism and control issues, and these types of concerns have decreased.

E. Family members have denied any problems with perfectionism or control issues and were redirected to consider how they may need to work on these issues.

### 25. Focus on Criticism (25)

A. The family was asked to focus on the ways in which criticism is expressed in the family.

B. Family members were assessed for the identification of ways in which criticism can be expressed to cause compulsivity and perfectionism.

C. Family members were assisted in identifying alternative, nonthreatening ways to express criticism.

### 26. Discuss Changes in Family Dynamics (26)

A. Changes in family behavior patterns that will affect the family dynamics were emphasized.

B. Family members were encouraged to focus on improved communication and problem-solving skills.

C. Family members were taught about assertive, rather than passive-aggressive, communication and the use of "I" statements.

D. Family members were reinforced for clearly identifying how family dynamics can be changed.

E. Family members failed to identify ways in which family dynamics may change and were provided with tentative examples in this area.

### 27. Teach Communication and Conflict-Resolution Skills (27)

A. Family members were taught the use of communication skills.

B. Family members were taught techniques for conflict resolution.

C. Family members were reinforced for their increased communication and conflict-resolution techniques.

D. Family members were redirected when they used poor communication skills or failed to use conflict-resolution techniques.

### 28. Address Boundary Issues (28)

A. Family members were encouraged to focus on personal boundary issues.

B. Enactment and unbalancing techniques were used for the purpose of restructuring personal boundaries within the family.

C. As family members have been assisted in developing better boundaries, they have identified feeling a loss of control. Family members were provided with alternatives for dealing with feelings of loss of control and direction of power.

### 29. Explore Issue of Control (29)

A. Family members were assisted in exploring whether control has been an issue for the family in the past.

B. The role that control has played in development of the eating disorder was identified.

C. It was reflected to the family that control issues have been very prominent in the family.

D. It was reflected to the family that control issues do not appear to be very prominent in the family.

**30. Review Effects of Perfectionism (30)**

A. Family members were asked to identify how perfectionism may interfere with various aspects of their relationship.

B. Family members were asked about how perfectionism affects their communication.

C. Family members were asked about how perfectionism affects their sexual functioning.

D. Family members identified a variety of ways in which perfectionism affects their relationship, and these were processed in the session.

E. Family members did not identify significant effects of perfectionism on their relationship and were provided with additional feedback.

**31. Discuss Role of Perfectionism (31)**

A. The role that high standards and perfectionism play in the life of the eating-disordered family member was discussed.

B. Family members were reinforced for their identifying and understanding of the roles that high standards and perfectionism play in continuing an eating disorder.

C. Family members could not identify ways in which high standards and perfectionism have played a role in the development of the eating disorder and were given tentative feedback in this area.

**32. Brainstorm Alternatives to Perfectionism (32)**

A. Alternatives to the perfectionist schemas were brainstormed.

B. Family members identified healthier behaviors to use besides perfectionist schemas.

C. Family members struggled to identify alternatives for perfectionism and were provided with tentative examples (e.g., accentuating positive qualities, providing each other with room for failure, changing family schemas about making mistakes).

**33. Identify Specific Feedback Desired (33)**

A. The eating-disordered family member was asked to describe in detail the specific positive feedback that is most desired from the other family members.

B. The eating-disordered family member was reinforced for identifying specific positive feedback that is desired to help build self-esteem and efforts to overcome the eating disorder.

# EXTRAFAMILIAL SEXUAL ABUSE

## CLIENT PRESENTATION

### 1. Verbal Demands for Sexual Interaction (1)*

A. A verbal demand has been made to accede to sexual interaction by someone outside of the immediate and extended family.

B. The family member who has been directed to accede to sexual interaction was guarded and evasive about the sexual abuse.

C. A family member has previously reported to others making demands to accede to sexual interaction, but has since recanted these earlier statements.

D. The family member has verbally denied being directed to accede to sexual interaction.

### 2. Physical Threats/Coercion (2)

A. Physical threats have been made toward a family member to fulfill sexual demands.

B. Psychological coercion has been used on a family member in order to cause submission to ongoing sexual abuse.

C. A family member identified experiencing threats or coercion and has therefore submitted to sexual abuse.

D. Although threats and attempts to coerce a family member into sexual abuse have been made, the family member did not submit to the abuse.

### 3. Reluctance to Share Trauma (3)

A. The sexually abused family member has been reluctant to share the trauma of the abuse with anyone, including other family members.

B. The sexually abused family member has experienced fear of rejection, retaliation, or other responses to sharing the trauma of the abuse.

C. As treatment has progressed, the sexually abused family member has become more open and willing to express the trauma of the abuse.

### 4. Feelings of Guilt and Shame (4)

A. The sexually abused family member expressed strong feelings of guilt, shame, anger, resentment, and depression as a result of the abuse.

B. The sexually abused family member has continued to experience strong feelings of guilt, shame, anger, resentment, and depression despite reassurances about not being responsible for the sexual abuse.

---

*The numbers in parentheses correlate to the number of the Behavioral Definition statement in the companion chapter with the same title in *The Family Therapy Treatment Planner*, Second Ed. (Dattilio, Jongsma, and Davis) by John Wiley & Sons, 2010.

C. The sexually abused family member's guilt and shame regarding the abuse have started to decrease due to the recognition that the perpetrator is responsible for the sexual abuse.

D. The sexually abused family member has successfully worked through and resolved the feelings of guilt, shame, anger, resentment, and depression.

### 5. Confusion about Changes Prompt Suspicion of Abuse (5)

A. Family members are confused by the changes in emotions and behaviors in a specific family member.

B. The family member displays significant symptoms of agitation, avoidance, depression, and withdrawal.

C. Family members have suspected that sexual abuse may have occurred.

D. As treatment has progressed, the sexually abused family member has been able to connect the agitation, avoidance, depression, and withdrawal to the history of being abused.

### 6. Emotional Responses to Learning of the Abuse (6)

A. Family members have displayed a range of emotions in reaction to learning of the sexual abuse.

B. Family members have become enraged in reaction to learning of the sexual abuse.

C. Family members express guilt and sorrow in reaction to learning of the sexual abuse.

D. Family members express feelings of depression and sadness in reaction to learning of the sexual abuse.

E. As family members have worked through their feelings, these emotions have become less volatile.

### 7. Sexual Acting Out (7)

A. A family member has a history of engaging in inappropriate sexual behavior with younger children.

B. The abused family member acknowledged that sexual behavior with younger children is inappropriate.

C. The sexually abused family member has displayed increased sexual involvement at a level greater than would be expected based on that family member's age.

D. The abused family member reported no recent initiation of inappropriate sexual behavior.

E. The abused family member's risk for engaging in inappropriate sexual behavior appears to be greatly reduced because of the successful resolution of issues related to the past sexual victimization.

### 8. Family Denial of Abuse (8)

A. Family members deny that any sexual abuse occurred to the victim.

B. Family members minimize the extent and effect of the sexual abuse against the victim.

C. The victim of the sexual abuse has expressed feelings of shame, anger, betrayal, and embarrassment as the family members have not believed and supported him/her about the abuse.

D. As treatment has progressed, the family members have come to believe and support the victim of the abuse, resulting in a sense of support for the victim.

### 9. Pressure to Report Abuse (9)

A. Family members were pressuring the victim of the sexual abuse to report the abuse to the authorities.

B. The sexually abused person has pressed charges and entered the due process of the court system.

C. The victim of the sexual abuse has experienced additional stress due to the pressure of pressing charges.

D. The victim of sexual abuse feels empowered to seek due process through the court system.

### 10. Pregnancy (10)

A. The victim of sexual abuse is pregnant as a result of the rape.

B. The victim of sexual abuse was pregnant, but her pregnancy was aborted.

C. The victim of sexual abuse is pregnant, and she has elected to deliver and keep this child.

### 11. Premature Expectation of Recounting of the Abuse (11)

A. The family has expected the victim of the abuse to recount the abuse when he/she is not yet ready to do so.

B. Family members pressure the victim to disclose about the abuse on a more frequent basis than he/she feels comfortable with.

C. The victim reports a sense of being retraumatized by the pressure exerted from the family to disclose about the abuse.

D. The family members have gained a healthier perspective about the expectations of when, how, and how often the victim may be able to recount his/her experience of the abuse.

## INTERVENTIONS IMPLEMENTED

### 1. Display Warmth (1)*

A. As the victim expressed feelings associated with the sexual abuse, a nonjudgmental, warm, accepting manner was displayed.

B. Good eye contact was maintained as the victim expressed feelings associated with the sexual abuse.

C. Family members were encouraged to be nonjudgmental, warm, accepting, and in good eye contact as the victim expressed feelings associated with the sexual abuse.

D. Family members were reinforced as they presented a nonjudgmental, accepting attitude toward the sexual abuse victim.

E. It was emphasized to the victim that he/she is not responsible for the abuser's actions.

F. Family members have not been very accepting toward the sexual abuse victim and were redirected in this area.

---

*The numbers in parentheses correlate to the number of the Therapeutic Intervention statement in the companion chapter with the same title in *The Family Therapy Treatment Planner*, Second Ed. (Dattilio, Jongsma, and Davis) by John Wiley & Sons, 2010.

## 2. Use Indirect Methods to Facilitate Talking about the Abuse (2)

A. Indirect methods were used to facilitate expression of the effects of the sexual abuse.

B. Play therapy, artwork, psychodrama, and other expressive techniques were used to help the sexual abuse victim talk about the effects of the abuse.

C. *The Modified Posttraumatic Symptoms Scale* (Resick et al.) was used to help assess the effects of the sexual abuse.

D. *The Sexual Assault Symptom Scale* (Ruch et al.) was used to help assess the effects of the sexual abuse.

E. The sexually abused family member has failed to process the abuse and its effects and was encouraged to do this when able.

## 3. Refer to Victims' Abuse Group (3)

A. The sexually abused family member was referred to a group for victims of abuse.

B. Family members were encouraged to support the victim's attendance at a victim support group.

C. The sexually abused family member has attended a group for victims of abuse and the benefits of this program were reviewed.

D. The sexually abused family member has not attended the recommended group for victims of abuse and was redirected to this helpful resource.

## 4. Facilitate Emotional Expression (4)

A. The victim of sexual abuse was assisted in identifying different modes of emotional expression.

B. The victim of sexual abuse was directed to use journaling or artwork to express emotions.

C. The victim of sexual abuse was assisted in identifying which modes of expression seem to be more comforting and which are more anxiety producing.

## 5. Assign Written Material (5)

A. Family members were assigned information about sexual abuse and how it affects the victim.

B. Family members were assigned to read *Hush* (Bromley).

C. Family members have read the assigned material on sexual abuse and how it affects the victim and key points were processed.

D. Family members have not read the assigned material on sexual abuse and were redirected to do so.

## 6. Educate about Post Traumatic Stress Disorder (PTSD) Effect (6)

A. The family and victim were educated about the posttraumatic effects of sexual abuse.

B. Family members were taught how effects can be quite subtle in some sexual abuse victims and very blatant in others.

C. Family members were taught specific effects of sexual abuse, including withdrawal and acting out behaviors.

### 7. Brainstorm Support Regarding Perpetrator (7)

A. The need for the family to provide support for the victim's feelings regarding the perpetrator was emphasized.

B. The family was assisted in brainstorming ways in which they can support the victim's feelings regarding the perpetrator.

C. Family members were reinforced as they identified a variety of ways to support the victim's feelings regarding the perpetrator.

D. Family members did not identify ways to support the victim's feelings regarding the perpetrator and were provided with tentative examples of how to do this (e.g., avoiding anything to do with the perpetrator or the perpetrator's family).

### 8. Address Distortions (8)

A. Distortions that often occur on the part of the sexual abuse victim were reviewed, including the fear that submitting the perpetrator to the authorities may cause harm to the victim.

B. It was acknowledged that sexual abuse perpetrators often make direct or indirect threats to the victim contingent on whether the perpetrator is submitted to the authorities.

C. Family members were assisted in supporting the sexual abuse victim and addressing the distortions that the victim may have about submitting the perpetrator to the authorities.

D. It was noted that the sexual abuse victim has very few concerns related to submitting the perpetrator to the authorities.

### 9. Direct Family to Provide Reassurance of Safety (9)

A. As the sexual abuse victim has displayed fear of retaliation by the perpetrator, the family was directed to provide reassurances of safety and support.

B. The sexual abuse victim has decided to report the perpetrator to the authorities, and the family was redirected to provide regular safety and support through this process.

C. It was emphasized to the sexual abuse victim that the family is ready to provide safety and support.

D. Family members were reinforced for their provision of safety and support to the sexual abuse victim.

E. Family members were redirected when they failed to provide safety and support to the sexual abuse victim.

### 10. Educate about Sexual Abuse (10)

A. Family members were educated about the harmful effects that sexual abuse has on victims.

B. Family members were educated about perpetrators of sexual abuse and the dynamics of this kind of behavior.

### 11. Brainstorm Techniques for Coping with Symptoms (11)

A. Individual techniques were brainstormed to help deal with the symptoms in the sexual abuse victim as they appear.

B. The family was provided with specific examples of individual techniques to use to deal with the symptoms in the sexual abuse victim as they appear (e.g., rewriting a new rendition of the abusive event).

C. Family techniques were brainstormed to assist in dealing with symptoms in the sexual abuse victim as they appear.

D. The family was provided with examples of ways to provide comfort to the sexual abuse victim when the symptoms are experienced (e.g., providing hugs).

## 12. Caution about Overanticipating Symptoms (12)

A. The nonabused family members were cautioned about the tendency to overanticipate symptoms in the sexual abuse victim to the point of seeing what is not there, and/or inducing it.

B. Family members were provided with examples of how overanticipating a symptom can actually cause the symptom to appear.

C. Family members were helped to dispel the myths and inaccuracies regarding the symptoms that they should anticipate.

D. Family members were redirected when they displayed inappropriate anticipation of symptoms in the sexual abuse victim.

## 13. Focus on Family Members' Reactions to the Abuse (13)

A. The focus of treatment was redirected to the behaviors and emotions of other family members that have developed in reaction to the sexual abuse experience.

B. Family members were assisted in expressing their emotions in reaction to the sexual abuse experience.

C. Family members' behaviors in reaction to the sexual abuse experience were reviewed.

D. Family members were supported as they learned how to share their own emotional and behavioral reactions to the sexual abuse.

E. Family members tended to avoid focus onto their own feelings and behaviors in response to the sexual abuse and were redirected in this area.

## 14. Brainstorm Coping Skills (14)

A. Family members were assisted in brainstorming coping skills to deal with emotions (e.g., anger, guilt, despair).

B. Specific coping skills were suggested to the family (e.g., cognitive restructuring of negative self-talk).

C. Family members were reinforced for their regular use of healthy coping skills to deal with emotions (e.g., anger, guilt, despair) in reaction to the sexual abuse.

D. Family members have not used healthy coping skills and were redirected to using these helpful techniques.

## 15. Encourage Victim to Help Others Heal (15)

A. The sexual abuse victim was assisted in becoming part of the healing process for other family members.

B. The sexual abuse victim was supported for expressing anger about feeling vulnerable.

## 16. Explore Conflicts (16)

A. Conflicts that have emerged among family members over the sexual abuse were explored.

B. Family members were noted to often blame each other for not protecting the sexual abuse victim better.

C. Siblings were noted to resent that the victim is getting so much attention due to the sexual abuse.

D. Family members were supported as they worked through the conflict that has emerged due to the sexual abuse.

### 17. Use Conflict-Reduction Strategies (17)

A. The family was taught about conflict-reduction strategies.

B. The family was taught about the use of behavioral contracts to reduce conflict.

C. The family was taught cognitive restructuring techniques to assist in reducing conflict among family members.

D. The family has regularly used conflict-reduction strategies and was provided with positive feedback about these helpful techniques.

E. The family has not used conflict-reduction strategies and was reminded about these helpful techniques.

### 18. Develop Referred Support Method (18)

A. Family members were helped to identify a variety of methods for supporting the sexual abuse victim in dealing with feelings of vulnerability.

B. Family members were taught to use supportive listening to assist the sexual abuse victim in dealing with feelings of vulnerability.

C. Family members were taught empathetic listening skills to assist the sexual abuse victim in dealing with feelings of vulnerability.

D. Family members were taught about determination of comfort zones to assist the sexual abuse victim in dealing with the vulnerability.

E. Family members were assisted in identifying the best method of supporting the victim.

### 19. Develop Coping Skills for Anxiety and Depression (19)

A. The family was assisted in developing strategies for dealing with the sexual abuse victim's anxiety and depression.

B. The family was taught about using relaxation methods to assist with dealing with the sexual abuse victim's anxiety and depression.

C. The family was taught about using cognitive behavioral techniques to address the victim's anxiety and depression.

D. Family members were assisted in identifying the most helpful and supportive techniques for coping with the victim's depression symptoms.

### 20. Support Direct, Legal Response to Perpetrator (20)

A. Family members were encouraged to have a direct, legal response to the sexual abuse perpetrator.

B. Family members were discouraged from using illegal means to respond to the sexual abuse perpetrator as this may rob the victim of necessary family members (who may land in jail).

C. Family members were encouraged to help validate and empower the sexual abuse victim through dealing with the sexual abuse perpetrator in a legal, direct manner.

D. Family members were reinforced for their assistance to the sexual abuse victim in dealing with the sexual abuse perpetrator in a legal, direct manner.

E. Family members have not dealt with the sexual abuse perpetrator in a legal, direct manner and were reminded to only respond in this manner.

### 21. Process Thoughts and Feelings Regarding Prosecution (21)

A. The family was helped to process their thoughts and feelings about reporting the sexual abuse perpetrator to legal authorities.

B. The family was encouraged to express their thoughts and feelings about proceeding with prosecution.

C. The sexual abuse victim's feelings and comfort level were identified as being of paramount importance.

D. The family was supported regarding their decision about whether to prosecute the sexual abuse perpetrator.

### 22. Refer to Victim's Rights Advocate (22)

A. The family was referred to a victim's rights advocate with the legal system.

B. The local district attorney or police station was contacted for resources for victim's rights advocates.

C. The family has connected with an advocate for victim's rights, and their experiences in this area were processed.

D. The family has not connected with a victim's rights advocate and was redirected to do so.

### 23. Refer to Local Authorities (23)

A. The family was referred to the local authorities to report the sexual abuse perpetrator.

B. The family was directed to contact the local prosecuting attorney's office to report the sexual abuse perpetrator.

C. The family was directed to contact the local police unit to report the sexual abuse perpetrator.

D. The family has contacted the proper authorities to report the sexual abuse perpetrator, and their experience in this area was processed.

E. The family has not contacted the proper authorities to report the sexual abuse perpetrator and was redirected to do so.

### 24. Develop Sensitivity to the Victim's Pace (24)

A. The nonabused family members were urged to see their own emotions as secondary to those of the sexually abused family member.

B. The nonabused family members were urged to focus on the sexual abuse victim's needs for setting the pace for working through these issues.

C. Family members were advised about how doing too much too quickly can have a negative affect on the sexual abuse victim.

D.  Family members were advised about how intimidating testifying can be for a sexual abuse victim.

E.  Family members were reinforced for giving top priority to the sexual abuse victim's feelings.

F.  When the family members did not seem to be giving top priority to the sexual abuse victim's feelings, they were redirected to do so.

## 25. Allow for Ventilation of Emotions (25)

A.  The nonabused family members were encouraged to ventilate their emotions and frustrations.

B.  The nonabused family members were specifically focused onto their emotions about how slowly the prosecution of the sexual abuse perpetrator has been conducted.

C.  Family members emotions related to the slowness of the prosecution of the perpetrator were normalized.

## 26. Discuss Best Approaches to Outbursts from the Abuse (26)

A.  A discussion was held regarding how each of the nonabused family members can best aid the victim in dealing with behavioral and emotional outbursts from the abuse.

B.  Family members were assisted in differentiating between how a parent and a sibling can comfort a sexual abuse victim and how each of these can be interpreted differently by the victim.

C.  Family members were provided with examples of alternatives for aiding the sexual abuse victim (e.g., using humor as opposed to physical embracing).

## 27. Brainstorm about Moving Forward (27)

A.  Family members were assisted in brainstorming how to move forward and heal from the effects of the sexual abuse.

B.  Family members were encouraged to use specific rituals to help in the process of healing from the sexual abuse.

C.  Family members were referred to community support programs.

D.  Family members have moved forward in healing from the effects of the sexual abuse, and the benefits of this progress were reviewed and processed.

E.  Family members have not used specific techniques to help move forward and heal from the effects of the sexual abuse and were reminded about these helpful techniques.

## 28. Reinforce Agreement Not to Revisit, Blame, or Excuse (28)

A.  The family was facilitated in agreeing not to revisit the sexual abuse trauma too often, use the event to blame family members, or as an excuse for other nonrelated behaviors in the future.

B.  Family members were reminded about their commitment not to excuse, blame, or revisit.

C.  Family members were reinforced for their willingness to move on from these issues.

D.  Family members continued to revisit the trauma and use the incident to blame or excuse unrelated behavior, and they were reminded about why this pattern was unhealthy.

## 29. Identify Factors Related to Sexual Acting Out (29)

A. Family members were assisted in identifying the different factors that may be contributing to the sexually abused family member's pattern of sexual acting out.

B. Family members were assisted in identifying how preexisting individual or family issues might contribute to the sexual abuse victim's current pattern of sexual acting out.

C. Family members were reinforced as they identified preexisting individual or family issues that may lead to the sexual abuse victim's sexual acting out.

D. Family members were unable to identify any preexisting individual or family issues that may be contributing to the sexual abuse victim's sexual acting out and were provided with tentative examples in this area (e.g., lack of attention, low self-esteem, need for additional comfort, anger toward men/women).

## 30. Assess How to Approach Sexual Acting Out (30)

A. The family was assisted in accessing the specific aspects of the sexual abuse victim's sexual acting out that can be dealt with within the family.

B. The family was assisted in assessing specific aspects of the sexual abuse victim's sexual acting out that may need to be addressed in individual or group therapy.

## 31. Explore Relocation (31)

A. Due to the intense effects of the sexual abuse on the victim, the family was urged to consider relocating geographically.

B. The pros and cons of relocating the family were reviewed and processed.

C. The family was reinforced for their decision to relocate geographically in order to decrease the effects on the sexual abuse victim.

D. The family was supported for their decision not to relocate geographically.

# FAMILY ACTIVITY DISPUTES

## CLIENT PRESENTATION

### 1. Disagreements about Activities (1)*

A. The family described disagreements over the activities in which the family engages.

B. The family described that arguments about the family activities have become quite heated at times.

C. Disengagement has occurred due to the pattern of disagreement over family activities.

D. The family has begun to be more open to sharing activities.

E. The family has developed better techniques for resolving activity disputes.

### 2. Younger Children Complaints (2)

A. Younger children in the family often complain about not being able to do the same activities as the older children.

B. Younger children in the family often expect that they will have the same level of freedom and activities as the older children in the family.

C. As treatment has progressed, family members have developed a more realistic expectation of what is appropriate for each age range.

### 3. Separate Activities (3)

A. Family members often decline involvement with each other due to the arguments that arise over family activity disputes.

B. Family members describe a lack of cohesion within the family.

C. As treatment has progressed, family members have begun to be more engaged with each other and participate in activities together.

D. The family reports a greater sense of engagement and cohesion.

### 4. Investment in Other Families (4)

A. Family members often become more invested in other families' activities to compensate for what is missing from their own family.

B. Family members often elect to be involved in other families because of the nurturing that they receive in that setting.

C. As treatment has progressed, family members have identified the missing components that family members seek in other settings.

D. Family members have replaced the missing components to their own family, resulting in greater involvement by all family members.

---

*The numbers in parentheses correlate to the number of the Behavioral Definition statement in the companion chapter with the same title in *The Family Therapy Treatment Planner*, Second Ed. (Dattilio, Jongsma, and Davis) by John Wiley & Sons, 2010.

**5. Disagreements over Financial Resources (5)**

A. Family members described disagreements over how money should be spent for the family.

B. Family members have different priorities regarding the relative amounts of money to be spent on needs, wants, and pleasurable pursuits.

C. Family members have developed a more unified approach to how money should be spent on needs, wants, and pleasurable pursuits.


## INTERVENTIONS IMPLEMENTED

**1. Facilitate Discussion of Dissatisfaction with Activities (1)***

A. Each family member was asked about their level of satisfaction with the family's pattern of activities.

B. Each family member was assisted in describing their level of satisfaction with recreational activities that are done as a family.

C. Family members' level of satisfaction with recreational activities was reflected to them.

**2. Encourage Description of Feelings (2)**

A. Family members were urged to use adjectives to help define how they feel about the family activity pattern.

B. Family members were supported and reinforced as they identified specific descriptors for their feelings related to the family activity pattern.

C. Family members were guarded about their emotions related to the family activities and were encouraged to be more open in this area.

D. Family members were unable to clearly define how they feel and were provided with specific adjectives to assist them in this area (e.g., selfish, cheated, left out, lonely, resentful).

**3. Generate a List of Desired Activities (3)**

A. Family members were asked to generate a list of desired activities in the following categories: (a) activities to do alone, (b) to do with other family members, (c) to do with family members and nonfamily members, and (d) to do with nonfamily members.

B. Family members were asked to complete the *Family Inventory of Life Events and Changes* (McCubbin and Thompson).

C. Family members' lists of desired activities were reviewed in session.

D. Family members have not generated a list of desired activities and were redirected to do so.

**4. Assess Lack of Tolerance (4)**

A. Family members were assessed as to their level of tolerance for different family activities.

B. Family members were assisted in identifying how their pattern of intolerance for each other may have originated.

C. Specific exercises were suggested that would help to build greater tolerance.

---

*The numbers in parentheses correlate to the number of the Therapeutic Intervention statement in the companion chapter with the same title in *The Family Therapy Treatment Planner*, Second Ed. (Dattilio, Jongsma, and Davis) by John Wiley & Sons, 2010.

D. Family members were urged to engage in positive talk about each other.

E. Family members were urged to weigh the value of having to put their own needs on hold as a way to build tolerance.

### 5. Clarify Objections to Family Activities (5)

A. Family members were assisted in understanding that their objections to family activities are "all-or-nothing" versus having objections to certain aspects of the activities.

B. Family members were assisted in constructing a list of specific objections to the family activities.

C. A review was conducted about the specific objections that family members identified regarding family activities.

D. Family members have not identified any specific objections to the pattern of family activities and were encouraged to do so.

### 6. Critique Family Activities (6)

A. After family members participated in several activities of differing lengths as an experiment to see what members like and dislike, the pros and cons of family members' activities were reviewed.

B. Family members were assisted in expressing their opinions about the different family activities.

C. Family members' opinions about the different activities were summarized and reflected to them.

### 7. Emphasize Personal Effect (7)

A. Family members were allowed to talk personally about the effect a particular activity had on them.

B. Family members were assisted in evaluating why they were affected by this particular activity (e.g., personality traits versus dynamics of the activity, or a mixture of both).

### 8. Emphasize an Open Mind and Flexibility (8)

A. Family members were encouraged to maintain an open mind and remain flexible about activities suggested by other family members.

B. Family members were reinforced when they displayed an open mind and flexibility about activities suggested by other family members.

C. Family members were redirected when they displayed a closed mind and inflexibility about activities suggested by other family members.

### 9. Request Trial Activity (9)

A. Family members were asked to agree to try one of the other family members' activity suggestions.

B. After family members attempted another family member's activity, the experience was reviewed within the session.

C. Family members have not tried one of the other family members' activity suggestions and were redirected to do so.

## 10. Schedule Activity for a Minimal Amount of Time (10)

A. Based on the list of each family member's favorite activities, a specific activity was selected.

B. The activity selected was emphasized to be tried for a minimal amount of time.

C. Family members' experience of a small amount of time engaged in a variety of activities was processed.

D. Family members have not participated in the scheduled activity and were redirected to do so.

## 11. Rate Degree of Enjoyment (11)

A. Family members were directed to rate the degree of enjoyment of an activity on a scale from 0 to 10.

B. Family members were administered the *Family Times and Routines Index* (McCubbin and Thompson).

C. Family members were allowed to express discontent about certain activities, but only if they were able to list positives along with the negatives.

D. Family members' ratings of enjoyment of the activity were processed within the session.

## 12. Brainstorm Mutually Enjoyable Activities (12)

A. Brainstorming techniques were used to develop a list of mutually enjoyable activities for the family.

B. Assessments of the family's previous activities were used to help develop a list of mutually enjoyable activities.

C. Family members were supported as they identified a list of mutually enjoyable activities.

D. Family members have not developed a list of mutually enjoyable activities and were asked to reemphasize this area.

## 13. Encourage Investment (13)

A. Family members were encouraged to invest effort and cooperation into an activity, even though it may not appeal to them initially.

B. Family members were reinforced when they invested effort and cooperation into an activity, even though it did not appeal to them initially.

C. Some family members have not invested effort or cooperation into family activities and were redirected to do so.

## 14. Emphasize Sacrifice as a Way to Show Love (14)

A. Family members were taught about the concept of family members' sacrificing personal interest for the pleasure of another family member.

B. Family members were taught that sacrificing for another family member is a way to show love, respect, and unity.

C. Family members were reinforced whenever they sacrificed personal interest for the pleasure of another family member.

## 15. Request Commitment to Sacrifice (15)

A. Family members were requested to consider committing to sacrificing by displaying interest in an activity that they might not be pleased with.

B. Family members were reinforced for their commitment to sacrifice for the consideration of others.

C. Family members were assisted in identifying some of the potential rewards of sacrificing for others (e.g., giving a gift of self, making other family members happy, learning a new activity).

D. Family members declined to commit to sacrifice for others and were redirected in this area.

16. **Emphasize Balancing the Scales (16)**

A. The family was taught about "balancing the scales" by mixing one family member's enjoyable activity with another family member's enjoyable activity.

B. An agreement was solicited that after engaging in one family member's enjoyable activity, the family will eat at another family member's favorite restaurant to balance the scales.

C. Family members were reinforced for identifying ways in which one family member's enjoyable activity can be connected with another family member's enjoyable activity.

17. **Discuss Ways to Increase Attractiveness of Activities (17)**

A. A discussion was held about the ways to increase the attractiveness of certain activities for certain family members.

B. Family members were urged to pair together activities that are enjoyed by different members.

C. The family was reinforced for their own ideas about how to increase the attractiveness of different activities.

18. **Brainstorm about Underlying Factors (18)**

A. Family members were assisted in brainstorming about what underlying factors might be affecting the disputes regarding family activities.

B. Family members were supported as they identified specific factors that may be underlying the family activity disputes.

C. Family members struggled to identify any underlying factors that may be affecting the family activity disputes and were provided with tentative examples in this area (e.g., jealousy, insecurity, favoritism).

19. **Review Other Issues (19)**

A. A review was conducted about other issues that may be influencing the conflict over family activities.

B. Family members were supported as they identified other issues that may be influencing the conflict over the family activities.

C. The family activities dispute was characterized as the "tip of the iceberg," acknowledging that the real conflict was over other issues.

D. Family members struggled to identify any other issues that may be influencing the conflict over family activities and were provided with tentative examples in this area (e.g., the need to avoid social contact or the need for power and control).

## 20. Develop Alternative Coping Mechanism (20)

A. The family was assisted in developing alternative ways to compensate for personality traits or underlying conflicts other than by disagreeing over activities.

B. Family members were reinforced when they identified other ways to cope with underlying conflicts or personality trait differences.

C. Family members have not used alternative ways to cope with underlying conflicts and personality trait differences and were provided with redirection regarding situations in which they can use these alternatives.

## 21. Assess Need for Individual Counseling (21)

A. Family members were assessed regarding the need for referral to individual counseling to address more ingrained issues (e.g., self-centeredness, depression, narcissism).

B. Family members were referred for individual therapy.

C. Family members were assessed, but no individual therapy needs were identified.

D. Family members have followed through on the referral for individual therapy, which has been noted to assist in the increased functioning of the family.

E. Family members were referred for individual therapy, but have not followed through on this; they were reminded about this helpful resource.

## 22. Propose Lottery (22)

A. A proposal was made to the family about using a lottery or some random drawing to rotate family activities.

B. The family was assisted in identifying the positive aspects of using a random drawing or lottery to rotate family activities.

C. Family members have declined the use of a lottery or random drawing to rotate family activities and were reminded about these helpful techniques.

## 23. Emphasize Need for Courtesy and Tolerance (23)

A. The need for mutual courtesy surrounding family activities was emphasized.

B. The need for tolerance or a "give-and-take" attitude was emphasized.

C. Family members were reinforced for tolerance and courtesy while engaging in activities.

D. Family members were redirected when it was noted that they have not been tolerant or courteous.

## 24. Normalize Inability to Please Everyone (24)

A. The family was presented with the idea that not everyone will always be pleased.

B. Family members were urged to "inoculate" themselves against disagreement by expecting that not everyone will always be pleased by the family activity pattern.

C. Family members were reinforced for acceptance of the idea that not everyone will be pleased by every activity.

# FAMILY BUSINESS CONFLICTS

## CLIENT PRESENTATION

### 1. Jealousy Due to Time Commitments (1)*

A. The children are angry and jealous because of the time and energy required by the family business.

B. The spouse is angry and jealous because of the time and energy required by the family business.

C. Family members often display their anger and jealousy related to the time and energy devoted to the family business.

D. Family members report a better balance between the family and the amount of time required by the family business.

### 2. Resentful about Own Time Dedicated to the Family Business (2)

A. The children are angry and resentful about having to dedicate their own time to the family business.

B. The spouse is angry and resentful about having to dedicate personal time to the family business.

C. A better balance of time devoted to the family business has been developed.

D. Family members are more at peace with the time they dedicate to the family business.

### 3. Conflict for Control (3)

A. A conflict has arisen between two family members vying for control of the family business.

B. Several family members are vying for control of the family business.

C. Family members are sabotaging each other to gain the upper hand in controlling the family business.

D. Family members have resolved issues related to competition for control of the family business.

### 4. Parental Interference (4)

A. The parents continue to interfere with the operation of the family business after handing over the reins to the children.

B. The parents often make decisions related to the family business without knowledge of the full impact of such decisions due to having handed the business over to the children.

C. After they have handed over the business to the children, the parents often comment about the decisions made by the children.

D. The family has developed a better understanding and protocol for parents' involvement in the business after handing over the reins to the children.

---

*The numbers in parentheses correlate to the number of the Behavioral Definition statement in the companion chapter with the same title in *The Family Therapy Treatment Planner*, Second Ed. (Dattilio, Jongsma, and Davis) by John Wiley & Sons, 2010.

### 5. Conflict between Multiple Spouses (5)

A. Spouses of siblings who are involved with the family business often have conflict over control and finances related to the business.

B. Family members have developed better boundaries regarding how to deal with conflict among the spouses of the siblings who are involved with the family business.

### 6. Conflict about New Spouse's Involvement (6)

A. The new spouse of a parent has become involved with the family business.

B. Conflict has arisen among family members about the new spouse's role within the family business.

C. Resentment has arisen regarding the level of involvement of the new spouse in the family business.

D. As communication has increased, the family has become more settled with the new spouse's role in the family business.

### 7. Resentment over Position in the Business (7)

A. Different family members have different levels of power, compensation, or privileges associated with the business.

B. Family members have become resentful over the variations in power, compensation, or privileges associated with the business.

C. Emotional issues related to the family-of-origin have surfaced in feelings of resentment and anger about the position each family member holds within the family business.

D. Family members have become more at peace with the level of power, compensation, and privileges associated with the family business.

### 8. Resentment toward Benefits Enjoyed by Non involved Family Members (8)

A. Some family members are employed in the family business, and other members are not employed in the family business.

B. Family members not employed in the family business continue to derive financial remuneration from the business.

C. Family members employed in the family business feel anger and resentment toward the family members who derive financial remuneration from the business, but are not involved in it.

D. Passive-aggressive comments and actions indicate resentment toward family members who are not employed in the business, but derive financial remuneration from it.

E. Family members have become more at ease with the financial benefits derived by family members who are not employed in the family business.

### 9. Failure to Consult (9)

A. Some family members fail to consult with other family members about important business decisions.

B. Family members sometimes make major business decisions without consulting other family members about these important decisions.

C. Family members have expressed anger about business decisions made without their consultation or consent.

D. As communication has increased, family members report a better pattern of involvement for all those involved in making important business decisions.

### 10. Eroding Family Relationships (10)

A. Hidden anger and resentment about business issues have eroded family relationships.

B. Typical family activities have been negatively affected by anger and resentment about business issues.

C. Family members have a difficult time differentiating business concerns from family relationships and activities.

D. As treatment has progressed, family members have been more open about feelings related to business issues and have disconnected these from the family relationships.

### 11. Blame (11)

A. Family members engage in blaming each other for the lack of financial success of the family business.

B. Family members tend not to take responsibility for the lack of financial success of the family business.

C. As communication has increased, family members have been more direct about their own contribution to the lack of financial success of the family business.

### 12. Family Schisms (12)

A. Family schisms have resulted from conflicts over business issues.

B. Family members have been excluded from holiday celebrations or special events due to the schisms occurring because of business decisions.

C. As family schisms have been healed, the family has developed a new pattern of social relationships.


## INTERVENTIONS IMPLEMENTED

### 1. Explore Thoughts and Feelings about Family Business Issues (1)*

A. Family members were encouraged to describe thoughts and feelings generated by the family business.

B. Family members were supported as they expressed themselves regarding family business issues.

C. An emphasis was placed on all family members being free to express their own thoughts and feelings about the issues of the family business without recrimination.

D. Family members were cautious about expressing their thoughts and feelings related to the family business, and the reasons for this caution were reviewed and processed.

*The numbers in parentheses correlate to the number of the Therapeutic Intervention statement in the companion chapter with the same title in *The Family Therapy Treatment Planner*, Second Ed. (Dattilio, Jongsma, and Davis) by John Wiley & Sons, 2010.

## 2. Review Previous Communication (2)

A. Each family member was polled about how feelings have been expressed.

B. Family members were asked to identify the conflicts that have arisen from the past expression of feelings.

C. Family members were encouraged to identify the conflicts that have occurred due to the nonexpression of feelings.

D. The pattern of communication within the family was reflected to family members

## 3. Facilitate Hierarchy of Goals and Objectives (3)

A. The family was helped to construct a hierarchy of goals and objectives for the family business.

B. The family was assisted in stipulating how the goals and objectives for the family business will be used to achieve the projections set forth for their business each year.

C. Family members were assisted in reviewing and ranking the goals and objectives for the company and comparing this list with the original expectations for the family business.

## 4. Rank and Select Family Members for Directing the Company (4)

A. Family members were assisted in ranking the skills of each family member.

B. Family members were assisted in a discussion regarding the suitability of each family member for directing the company.

C. Family members were asked to vote on who should be in control of the family company.

D. Family members were supported for their open and honest review of each family member's skills and suitability.

## 5. Normalize Difficulty with Letting Go (5)

A. Family members who have legally transferred control of the company were assisted in identifying how it has been difficult for them to let go of the company emotionally.

B. Role-play, empty chair, and cognitive restructuring techniques were used to facilitate the expression of emotions.

C. The emotions felt by family members who have had difficulty letting go of the reins of the company were normalized.

D. Family members' struggles with a sense of loss of power and control or lessened self-esteem were emphasized and normalized.

E. Family members were assisted in planning for a post-leadership role for those who have released control of the business to others.

F. Family members tended to be quite guarded about their emotions regarding letting go of the reins of the company and were provided with tentative examples of what is often experienced in this position.

## 6. Develop Role of Former Leaders (6)

A. A level of understanding was secured from family members regarding the role of former leaders in the family business.

B. Specific rules of disengagement were developed to guide the former leader's level of involvement in the family business.

C. Former leaders' ability to provide support to the current leaders was emphasized.

D. Family members seemed to struggle with the place of former leaders within the business and were provided with remedial feedback in this area.

### 7. Brainstorm about Nonfamily-of-Origin Members (7)

A. A brainstorming session was held about the ways spouses and family members should be treated regarding power in the family business.

B. An agreement was facilitated about the role of nonfamily-of-origin members.

C. Family members were reinforced for developing a healthy role for nonfamily-of-origin members within the business structure.

D. Family members failed to develop expectations for nonfamily-of-origin members and were provided with tentative examples in this area.

### 8. Develop Formal Mechanism Regarding Spouse Conflicts (8)

A. Family members were assisted in developing a formal mechanism for working through the conflict that exists over the role of spouses of family members within the business.

B. Positive feedback was provided as family members have developed a clear expectation about how spouses should be involved in the business.

C. It was noted that conflicts have decreased since the institution of formal mechanisms for dealing with spouses of family members within the business.

### 9. Explore Boundary Issues (9)

A. The boundary issues inherent in the family-of-origin were explored.

B. Feelings related to boundary issues within the family-of-origin were reviewed and processed.

C. Family members were encouraged to express their emotions about the restrictions imposed by boundaries related to the family-of-origin.

D. Family members were guarded about expressing their emotions about the boundary issues, and tentative examples were provided about how other families have handled these concerns.

### 10. Differentiate Rules between Business and Nonbusiness Interaction (10)

A. Family members were assisted in clarifying what interactions are related to the family business and what are nonbusiness-related family interactions.

B. Family members were assisted in developing rules or guidelines that govern interactions within the business.

C. Family members were assisted in developing a set of guidelines that govern interaction in nonbusiness-related family situations.

D. Family members were assisted in reviewing how family business interactions and nonbusiness interactions are dealt with in a different manner.

E. Family members had a difficult time differentiating between how to interact within the business versus nonbusiness family situations and were provided with tentative examples in this area.

### 11. Solicit Agreement about Financial Benefits (11)

A. Family members were asked to agree with the concept that family-of-origin members are all equally eligible for some financial benefit from the family business.

B. The expectation that contributing and noncontributing members will have a different level of financial benefit from the family business was emphasized.

C. Family members were supported for their acceptance of a structure to compensate both contributing and noncontributing members.

D. Family members rejected expectations about how contributing and noncontributing members will be eligible for financial benefits and were provided with remedial assistance in this area.

### 12. Recommend Family Business Consultant (12)

A. It was recommended that family members use a skilled family business consultant to help them with issues of fairness, succession, buy-sell agreements, and so on.

B. Family members were directed to read *Family Wars* (Gordon and Nicholson).

C. Family members were referred to a specific consultant to help with issues of fairness, succession, buy-sell agreements, and so on.

D. Family members have used a skilled business consultant to help resolve important issues, and the benefits of this were reviewed and processed.

E. Family members have not used a skilled family business consultant and were redirected to do so.

### 13. Use Interventions to Reduce Anger (13)

A. Role-playing techniques were used to reduce the anger of family members.

B. Empty-chair techniques were used to reduce the anger of family members.

C. Cognitive-restructuring techniques were used to reduce the anger of family members.

D. Positive feedback was provided as family members were able to reduce their anger related to business issues.

E. Family members have not reduced their anger despite the use of many techniques to help them do so, and they were provided with remedial assistance in this area.

# FAMILY MEMBER SEPARATION

## CLIENT PRESENTATION

### 1. Temporary Separation (1)*

A. Family members have been forced to be temporarily separated from one another.

B. Employment obligations have made it necessary for family members to be temporarily separated.

C. Military duty responsibilities have caused a temporary separation of family members.

D. A family member has been incarcerated and is therefore unable to regularly spend time with other family members.

E. A family member has been separated from other family members due to a chronic illness.

F. The separation of family members has ended, and they are now regularly involved with each other.

### 2. Emotional Effects of Separation (2)

A. Family members report experiencing strong negative emotions due to the separation.

B. Family members feel disengaged from each other due to the separation.

C. Family members report feelings of insecurity due to the separation.

D. Family members are having difficulty coping with the separation.

E. Family members have become more capable of coping with the separation.

F. As the separation of family members has been resolved, the emotions related to the separation have diminished.

### 3. Redistribution of Power (3)

A. The balance of power within the family system has been redistributed due to the separation from a family member.

B. Conflict and turmoil have ensued due to the disequilibrium within the family balance of power.

C. As the balance of power has stabilized, conflict and turmoil have decreased.

### 4. Emotional and Behavioral Regression (4)

A. The children have emotionally regressed due to the separation.

B. The children's behavior has regressed to behavior of an earlier age due to the separation.

C. As the family has begun to cope with the separation, the children's pattern of emotional and behavioral regression has decreased.

D. The children have regained their chronologically appropriate level of emotional and behavioral development.

---

*The numbers in parentheses correlate to the number of the Behavioral Definition statement in the companion chapter with the same title in *The Family Therapy Treatment Planner*, Second Ed. (Dattilio, Jongsma, and Davis) by John Wiley & Sons, 2010.

## 5. Difficulty Adjusting to Reuniting Family (5)

A. A family member has returned to the family after a significant period of absence.

B. The family, which had a significant period of adjustment to the absence of the family member, has been thrown into disequilibrium due to the return of the absent family member.

C. The previously absent family member expects the family to be functioning the same as it did prior to the separation.

D. Family members have begun to readjust to the family being reunited.

E. Family members have displayed resiliency and have developed a healthy readjustment to the family member's return.

## 6. Conflict over Varying Reactions (6)

A. Some family members reacted with grief over the separation.

B. Some family members reacted with relief over the separation.

C. Conflict has arisen among family members who have differing responses to the separation.

D. As treatment has progressed, family members have become more tolerant of how others react to the separation.

## INTERVENTIONS IMPLEMENTED

### 1. Hold Predeparture Family Session (1)*

A. The family member who will be leaving was brought into a predeparture family session to gather perceptions about how the separation will affect the family as a whole.

B. The family member who will be leaving was asked to review how the separation is expected to affect the family as a whole.

C. The expectations regarding how the separation will affect the family were reviewed and processed.

D. The family member who will be leaving had a difficult time identifying how the separation will affect the family as a whole and was provided with tentative examples.

### 2. Review Coping Mechanisms for Departing Family (2)

A. The family member who is departing was asked to talk about ways to cope with the separation.

B. Positive feedback regarding the coping skills for the separation was provided to the family member who was about to depart.

C. The family member who is about to depart had rather vague expectations about how to cope with the separation and was provided with more specific feedback in this area.

### 3. Brainstorm Ways to Stay in Contact (3)

A. Family members were assisted in identifying ways in which they wish to stay in touch with each other.

---

*The numbers in parentheses correlate to the number of the Therapeutic Intervention statement in the companion chapter with the same title in *The Family Therapy Treatment Planner*, Second Ed. (Dattilio, Jongsma, and Davis) by John Wiley & Sons, 2010.

B. Family members had few ideas about how to stay in touch with each other and were provided with tentative examples in this area (e.g., videos, e-mail).

### 4. Explore Impact of the Loss (4)

A. Each family member was asked to explore how the loss is expected to impact the family.

B. Family members were asked how they have been impacted by the loss.

C. Family members were supported as they described how they have been affected by the absence of one of the family members.

D. Family members were quite guarded as they described how they have been affected by the loss and were provided with specific examples.

### 5. Determine Appropriate Coping Skills (5)

A. The family was assessed for whether the absence is likely to be short, long, or permanent.

B. Family members were assisted in developing coping skills depending on the expected length of the separation.

C. Family members struggled to identify coping skills for the separation and were provided with tentative examples in this area.

### 6. Discuss Coping Attempts (6)

A. Family members were encouraged to discuss how each family member is attempting to deal with the loss.

B. Family members were encouraged to share their own ways of coping with the loss.

C. Family members were encouraged to adapt other family members' healthy techniques for dealing with the loss.

### 7. Discuss Variation in Coping Skills (7)

A. The family was noted to have a variety of coping skills.

B. Family members were assisted in identifying ways in which internal coping skills differ among family members.

C. Family members were assisted in identifying the causes for why various internal coping skills differ among family members.

D. The family was provided with positive feedback about their insight into how coping skills differ among family members.

E. Family members failed to identify ways in which internal coping skills differ among family members and were provided with tentative feedback in this area.

### 8. Help Clarify Conflicts (8)

A. Family members were assisted in identifying conflicts over the absence of the family member.

B. Family members were assisted in tracing when conflicts arose.

C. Family members were helped to relate the development of conflicts to the departure of the absent family member.

D. Family members were reinforced for their insight into how conflicts arose.

E. Family members had significant difficulty developing how conflict had arisen and were provided with tentative interpretations in this area.

## 9. Work through Conflicts (9)

A. Family members were assisted in working through conflicts resulting from the family member's absence.

B. Family members were taught to respect each other's perceptions and viewpoints.

C. Family members were assisted in developing compromises regarding the conflicts that result from a family member's absence.

D. Family members were encouraged to be more giving to each other to help the family cope with the family member's absence.

## 10. Help Identify Changes (10)

A. The family was assisted in identifying the changes that have occurred within the family during the absence.

B. Family members were assisted in identifying changes in specific roles within the family.

C. Family members were assisted in identifying how the balance of power within the family has changed.

D. Family members were assisted in identifying how interpersonal alliances have changed during the absence.

E. Family members were assisted in identifying how the caretakers within the family have changed during the absence.

F. The changes within the family were summarized and reflected to family members.

## 11. Normalize Redistribution of Roles (11)

A. Family members were taught the pattern of redistribution of roles within a new situation.

B. The expectation that roles would be redistributed was reviewed with family members.

## 12. Reinforce Role Alterations (12)

A. Family members were assisted in changing their roles, expectations, and perceptions.

B. Cognitive-restructuring techniques were used to help reinforce alteration in the roles, expectations, and perceptions of family members.

C. Family members were assisted in weighing the alternatives among old and new roles, expectations, and perceptions.

D. Family members were encouraged to provide specific evidence to reinforce changes in roles, expectations, and perceptions.

E. The changes in roles, expectations, and perceptions were reflected to the family.

## 13. Teach about Support and Role Redistribution (13)

A. Family members were taught how to support each other in the use of coping skills.

B. Family members were taught about the need to redistribute the roles in the household.

C. Family members were reinforced when they provided support for each other.

D. Family members were reinforced for their healthy redistribution of roles in the household.

E. Family members were redirected when they did not provide support for each other in the use of coping skills.

F. Family members were redirected when they did not appropriately redistribute roles within the household.

### 14. Educate about Regression (14)

A. Family members were taught how regressive behaviors often occur for children during periods of stress, crisis, or loss.

B. Family members were provided examples of how children might regress during periods of stress, crisis, or loss.

C. The family's experience of children's regressive behaviors was normalized.

### 15. Emphasize Positive Response to Regressive Behaviors (15)

A. Family members were instructed not to berate the children for their regressive behaviors.

B. Family members were encouraged to use comfort, nurturance, and role modeling as ways to help children cope with their regressive behaviors.

C. Family members were reinforced for their positive response to the children's regressive behaviors.

D. It was reflected to the family that the children appear to be returning to their chronologically appropriate level of functioning.

### 16. Encourage Reminders for Children (16)

A. The children were encouraged to use a variety of techniques to help remember the absent family member.

B. Children were taught how to use imaging techniques to help remember the absent family member.

C. Children were directed to periodically view videos or photos of the absent family member.

D. Children were provided meaningful mementos or personal items belonging to the absent family member.

E. Family members have not encouraged the use of reminder techniques for the children and were redirected to do so.

### 17. Emphasize Bonding Activities with Remaining Family Members (17)

A. Remaining family members were encouraged to support the grieving children by developing activities that strengthen the bond with the grieving child.

B. Family members were encouraged to read books together, play together, go for a walk or to a movie together, or watch a children's video together as a way to strengthen the bond with the remaining family members.

C. Family members were reinforced for their increased bonding exercises to help the grieving child cope.

D. Family members have not used increased bonding exercises to help the children cope and were provided with tentative examples about how to do this.

### 18. Review Family Cohesiveness Activities (18)

A. Activities that help to promote family cohesiveness and engagement were reviewed.

B. Self-constructed board games were used to promote family cohesiveness and engagement.

C. Sculptural metaphors were used to help promote family cohesiveness and engagement.

D. Family members were encouraged for their use of activities that promote family cohesiveness and engagement.

E. Family members have not used techniques to help develop family cohesiveness and engagement and were redirected to do so.

### 19. Investigate Reasons for Relief (19)

A. The reasons were investigated why certain family members have experienced relief as a result of the other family member's absence.

B. Issues related to jealousy and abuse were reviewed as possible explanations for relief reaction of family members.

C. Family members were supported as they expressed their perceptions regarding the relief experienced as a result of the other family member's absence.

D. Family members were quite guarded about the reasons for their sense of relief and were urged to be open about these concerns when the trust level is commensurate with such disclosures.

### 20. Explore Anger at the Returning Family Member (20)

A. The issue of anger/resentment toward the absent family member for returning to the family unit was reviewed.

B. Constructive methods for venting anger/resentment were reviewed with family members.

C. Family members were encouraged to read *The Dance of Anger* (Lerner).

D. Family members were encouraged to read *When Anger Hurts* (McKay, Rogers, and McKay).

E. Family members were encouraged to read *The Anger and Aggression Workbook* (Liptak, Leutenberg, and Sippola).

F. Family members have read information about anger, reviewed constructive methods for venting anger, and these were processed within the session.

G. Family members have not read the assigned material on anger and resentment and were redirected to do so.

### 21. Discuss the Expected Effects of Reintroducing the Absent Family Member (21)

A. The expected effects of reintroducing the absent member into the family were discussed.

B. The ways in which the family has already changed were contrasted with how reintroduction of the absent family member will cause further changes.

# FAMILY-OF-ORIGIN INTERFERENCE

## CLIENT PRESENTATION

### 1. Attempted Control by Spouse's Parents (1)*

A. One of the spouse's parents has expressed unsolicited opinions and judgments about the behavior or decisions of the couple in an apparent attempt to control the situation.

B. A spouse's parents often make critical comments about decisions that the couple has made.

C. The spouse's parents make many passive-aggressive comments about family decisions.

D. As treatment has progressed, the couple has become more cooperatively assertive with the spouse's parents in order to decrease unsolicited opinions and judgments.

E. The spouse's parents have decreased their pattern of expressing unsolicited opinions and judgments.

### 2. Grandparent Interference (2)

A. The grandparents often attempt to impose their beliefs about how the parents should raise the grandchildren.

B. The grandparents have undermined the authority of the parents by critiquing their parenting skills in front of the children.

C. The grandparents have often disregarded the parents' wishes in regard to raising the grand-children.

D. As treatment has progressed, the parents have been able to develop greater control over the grandparents' level and type of involvement with the children.

### 3. Aunt/Uncle Interference (3)

A. The parents' siblings often interfere with decisions regarding raising the children.

B. The parents' siblings have undermined the authority of the parents by criticizing their parenting skills in front of the children.

C. The parents' siblings have often disregarded the parents' wishes in regards to raising the children.

D. As treatment has progressed, the parents have been able to develop greater control over the parents' siblings' level and type of involvement with the children.

### 4. Arguments about Boundaries (4)

A. The couple frequently argues about the perception that one spouse's family-of-origin is overstepping their boundaries.

B. Resentment and anger have been expressed regarding the perception that one spouse's family-of-origin is overstepping their boundaries.

---

*The numbers in parentheses correlate to the number of the Behavioral Definition statement in the companion chapter with the same title in *The Family Therapy Treatment Planner*, Second Ed. (Dattilio, Jongsma, and Davis) by John Wiley & Sons, 2010.

C. One spouse often blames the other spouse for that spouse's family-of-origin overstepping the boundaries.

D. As the couple has become more of a team, they have set better parameters and boundaries against the family-of-origin interference.

### 5. Children's Acting Out (5)

A. Family interference has resulted in emotional outbursts by the children.

B. Family interference has resulted in behavioral outbursts by the children.

C. The children displayed confusion about the adults' disagreements and family-of-origin interference.

D. As the parents have developed better boundaries and family-of-origin interference has decreased, the children's emotional and behavioral functioning has also improved.

### 6. Family-of-Origin Dissension (6)

A. Family-of-origin members have been confronted over their interference, leading to strained relationships.

B. Dissension has occurred among family members about the family-of-origin interference.

C. Family members appear to be taking sides regarding the level of family-of-origin involvement.

D. As family communication has improved, family-of-origin interference has decreased, and relationships have improved.

## INTERVENTIONS IMPLEMENTED

### 1. Gather Members' Perspectives on Negative Effects of Family-of-Origin Interference (1)*

A. Each family member was asked to provide a perspective on the negative effects that the family-of-origin interference has had on family members and the general family dynamics.

B. Individual sessions were held with family members to provide them with a safe environment in which to explore the negative effects that the family-of-origin interference has had on family members and the general family dynamics.

C. The effects of intimidation and denial were decreased by exploring the negative effects of family-of-origin interference on the family and the relationships.

D. Family members tended to minimize the effects of family-of-origin interference on the relationships within the family and were urged to focus on this in a more realistic manner.

E. Family members were realistic about the effects of family-of-origin interference in the relationships within the family and were supported for their honesty.

### 2. Facilitate Emotional Expression (2)

A. Family members' expression of feelings was facilitated to promote understanding and empathy.

---

*The numbers in parentheses correlate to the number of the Therapeutic Intervention statement in the companion chapter with the same title in *The Family Therapy Treatment Planner*, Second Ed. (Dattilio, Jongsma, and Davis) by John Wiley & Sons, 2010.

B. Family members were supported as they expressed their feelings regarding family-of-origin interference.

C. Family members were guarded about expressing their feelings and were urged to be more open when they feel safe in doing so.

### 3. Reduce Tension Levels (3)

A. Family members were taught to use techniques to help decrease the level of tension among family members over the issue of extended family interference in their lives.

B. Family members were taught thought-stopping techniques to help decrease the level of tension over the issue of extended family interference.

C. Family members were taught cognitive-restructuring techniques to help decrease the level of tension over the issue of extended family interference.

D. Family members were taught anger-management techniques to help decrease the level of tension over the issue of extended family interference.

E. Family members were reinforced for using coping techniques to manage the tension due to extended family interference.

F. Family members have not used coping techniques for managing the tension regarding extended family interference and were redirected to do so.

### 4. Train in Communication Strategies (4)

A. The parents were taught how to deal effectively with interfering family-of-origin members.

B. Family members were taught improved communication techniques.

C. Family members were taught assertiveness skills.

D. Family members were taught problem-solving strategies.

E. Family members were assigned to read information on family conflict such as *Toxic Parents* (Forward).

F. Family members have read information on family-of-origin interference, and the key points were reviewed.

G. The family members have not read the assigned information and were redirected to do so.

### 5. Role-Play Setting Boundaries (5)

A. Role-playing techniques were used to help teach family members how to approach difficult family-of-origin members and set boundaries on their interference.

B. Modeling techniques were used to teach family members how to approach difficult family-of-origin members and set boundaries on their interference.

C. Behavioral-rehearsal techniques were used to teach family members how to approach difficult family-of-origin members and set boundaries on their interference.

D. Family members were reinforced for displaying a clearer understanding of how to set boundaries on the interfering family-of-origin family members.

E. The parents continue to struggle with setting boundaries on the interfering family members, and they were provided with remedial feedback in this area.

## 6. Reinforce Mutual Support (6)

A. An emphasis was placed on the parent's need to take a united position in maintaining a stance with their respective family-of-origin members.

B. The parents were encouraged to support each other in maintaining a stance with their family-of-origin members.

C. Verbal reinforcement was used to highlight the parents' support and for taking a united stance against interference from respective family-of-origin members.

D. Family members were redirected when they failed to support each other regarding their united stand with respect to family-of-origin interference.

## 7. Assign Setting of Boundaries (7)

A. The parents were assigned to work together to set boundaries on interfering family members.

B. The parents' attempts at setting boundaries with interfering family members were reviewed and processed.

C. The parents have not set boundaries on interfering family members, and the reasons for this lapse were processed.

## 8. Hold Session with Family-of-Origin Members (8)

A. The interfering family-of-origin members were invited to participate in a therapy session, but declined to do so.

B. The interfering family-of-origin members agreed to participate in a therapy session, and the issue of their interference was directly addressed.

C. Family-of-origin members were verbally reinforced for acceptance of their pattern of interference, and they agreed to discontinue this pattern.

D. The family-of-origin members vehemently denied any pattern of interference and were provided with specific examples in this area.

## 9. Develop Protocol for Offering Suggestions (9)

A. The parents were assisted in identifying acceptable ways that extended family members can offer suggestions to them when they are invited to do so.

B. The parents were reinforced for identifying ways in which they wish to be advised by extended family members.

C. The parents struggled to identify or agree on how extended family members should provide advice or suggestions; they were provided with specific examples in this area.

## 10. Share Techniques for Decreasing Blame (10)

A. Spouses were taught about techniques for not holding each other responsible for the family-of-origin interference.

B. Spouses were taught about detriangulation as a way to avoid blaming each other for the family-of-origin interference.

C. Spouses were taught about the use of "I" statements as a way to avoid blame for the family-of-origin interference.

D. Spouses were taught about the use of metaphorical objects.

E. The spouses were reinforced for the use of techniques to decrease blame for family-of-origin interference.

F. The spouses have not regularly used the techniques for decreasing blame and were redirected to do so.

## 11. Explore Children's Confusion (11)

A. Any confusion that has occurred in the children as a result of extended family interference was explored.

B. The parents' sense of power and control in the situation was reaffirmed.

C. The children's confusion was identified and processed.

D. No confusion was identified for the children, and the parents were urged to continue to monitor this dynamic.

## 12. Address Individual Issues (12)

A. Each parent was assisted in identifying individual issues that may be perpetuating family interference.

B. Individual issues that may be perpetuating family interference were addressed and processed.

C. Each parent was helped to identify specific individual issues that may be perpetuating family interference.

D. No patterns of perpetuating family interference issues were identified, and the couple was provided with tentative examples of these types of concerns (e.g., unresolved guilt feelings, a history of having always been controlled by or dependent on the family-of-origin).

## 13. Support Assertiveness about Therapy for Extended Family (13)

A. The parents were supported in their assertiveness regarding the need for extended family members to get counseling for themselves.

B. Role-playing techniques were used to help the parents rehearse asserting themselves about the extended family member's need for treatment.

C. Letter-writing techniques were used to help the parents express their belief that the extended family members need treatment.

D. Family members failed to identify issues that make each angry and were provided with tentative suggestions in this area.

## 14. Offer Therapy Alternatives (14)

A. Interfering members of the family-of-origin were offered the option of obtaining sessions with the clinician.

B. Extended family members were provided with options for obtaining individual or family therapy through alternative sources.

C. Extended family members were supported for their acceptance of the need for treatment.

D. Extended family members have declined any offers for treatment and were urged to consider this at a later date.

## 15. Teach Assertiveness to Children (15)

A. Assertiveness-training techniques were taught to the children to enable them to direct interfering people to their parents.

B. Role-playing techniques were used to teach the children how to direct interfering people to their parents.

C. Modeling techniques were used to teach the children how to direct interfering people to their parents.

D. The children were verbally reinforced and validated for redirecting interfering people to their parents.

E. The children have not redirected interfering people to their parents and were reminded about this helpful resource.

## 16. Increase Family Cohesiveness (16)

A. Family communication and group activities were encouraged to increase cohesiveness, tighten the family bond, and close gaps that may be facilitating external interference.

B. The family was reinforced for developing greater closeness and closing the gaps that facilitate interference.

C. Family members have not participated in family-bonding experiences and were redirected to do so.

## 17. Confront Children's Acting Out (17)

A. The children's acting-out behavior was directly confronted.

B. The parents were assisted in setting limits on the children's acting-out behavior.

C. The children's acting-out behavior was interpreted as a reflection of their confusion generated by outside interference in the family dynamics.

## 18. Rebalance Marital Relationship (18)

A. The reasons why interference has had such a significant effect on the marital relationship were explored.

B. The couple was provided with suggestions for methods to rebalance the relationship.

C. The issue of loyalty to parents versus loyalty to a spouse was addressed.

D. Problem-solving techniques were used to help balance the loyalty to parents with the loyalty to the spouse.

## 19. Refer to Conjoint Therapy (19)

A. The couple was referred for conjoint therapy due to the extensive problems within the marriage.

B. The couple has used conjoint therapy to help resolve problems within the relationship, and this was reinforced.

C. The couple has not used conjoint therapy and was reminded about this helpful resource.

# FINANCIAL CHANGES

## CLIENT PRESENTATION

### 1. Income Decrease (1)*

A. The family has experienced a drastic decrease in income.

B. One parent has become unemployed, causing a significant decrease in income for the family.

C. Both parents have become unemployed, causing a significant decrease in income.

D. The family is in a state of financial crisis.

E. As treatment has progressed, the family has become more financially stable.

### 2. Arguments about Spending (2)

A. Family members have experienced significant reductions in the amount of money available for family use.

B. Family members described multiple arguments over the issue of how one family member is spending money.

C. Family members hold different viewpoints about the amount of money spent by one family member and the necessity for these expenditures.

D. Family members have begun to talk constructively about spending and saving guidelines for each family member.

E. There have been no recent disagreements over the amount of money spent.

### 3. Critical Comments about Earnings (3)

A. One family member reports that another family member often makes critical comments about earning capabilities.

B. Family members complained that the family income level is too low, blaming the breadwinner.

C. Family members have agreed not to make critical comments about each other's earning potential.

D. Family members have formed a specific plan to develop greater earning potential.

### 4. Arguments about Saving (4)

A. Family members described a pattern of conflict over savings goals and practices.

B. Family members have begun to talk constructively about savings guidelines.

C. Agreement has been reached among family members regarding a savings goal and practices.

### 5. Arguments over Price Shopping (5)

A. Family members reported frequent arguments over the need to shop for the best possible price on an item.

*The numbers in parentheses correlate to the number of the Behavioral Definition statement in the companion chapter with the same title in *The Family Therapy Treatment Planner*, Second Ed. (Dattilio, Jongsma, and Davis) by John Wiley & Sons, 2010.

B. Family members described how other family members tend to spend a great deal of time shopping for additional savings.

C. Family members described that other family members do not sufficiently comparison shop, often paying a higher price than is needed.

D. Family members have developed a healthy compromise regarding how to price shop, and they no longer argue about this issue.

### 6. Disagreement about Children's Financial Independence (6)

A. The children desire to earn income for themselves.

B. The children are reluctant to provide information to the parents about how they choose to spend their money.

C. Family members often have arguments about control of the children's income.

D. Family members have come to an understanding about the level of control exerted over the children's income.

### 7. Unable to Meet Fixed Expenses (7)

A. The family is unable to pay bills for fixed expenses because income level is too low.

B. The family has had to cancel commitments or services (e.g., phone service).

C. Bill collectors are dunning the family regarding past-due bills.

D. The family has to relocate to lower living expenses.

E. As treatment has progressed, family members have made adjustments to be able to meet fixed expenses.

### 8. Verbal/Physical Abuse

A. Anger and tension have built up for the family over the financial stressors.

B. Family members have lost control and engaged in verbal abuse of each other.

C. Family members have engaged in physical abuse incidents.

D. As treatment has progressed, the family has been free of verbal or physical abuse.

## INTERVENTIONS IMPLEMENTED

### 1. Facilitate an Accepting Atmosphere (1)*

A. Family members were encouraged to express their feelings about their financial situation without fear of reprisals from other family members.

B. Family members were reinforced for expressing their emotions about the family financial situation.

C. Family members were redirected when they attempted to punish others for expressing their feelings.

---

*The numbers in parentheses correlate to the number of the Therapeutic Intervention statement in the companion chapter with the same title in *The Family Therapy Treatment Planner*, Second Ed. (Dattilio, Jongsma, and Davis) by John Wiley & Sons, 2010.

### 2. Focus on Feelings and Beliefs about Financial Situation (2)

A. The focus of the session was turned to the family members' feelings and beliefs about the restrictions caused by the financial situation.

B. Family members were encouraged to express themselves regarding feelings and beliefs that they have about the financial situation.

C. Family members were supported as they described their feelings and beliefs regarding the financial situation.

D. Family members were quite guarded about expressing their thoughts and feelings regarding the financial restrictions the family is experiencing and were provided with additional feedback in this area.

### 3. Explore Anger (3)

A. The nature of family members' expression of anger was explored.

B. An emphasis was placed on how conflicts and arguments tend to exacerbate the stress of the situation.

C. Family members were encouraged to express their anger in a healthy manner.

### 4. Brainstorm Alternatives for Ventilating Frustration (4)

A. Family members were assisted in brainstorming alternative healthy ways to ventilate frustrations.

B. Family members were supported as they identified healthy ways to ventilate their frustration.

C. Family members struggled to identify healthy alternatives to ventilating frustration and were provided with tentative examples in this area (e.g., express aggression via sports, develop an exercise routine, or keep a feelings journal).

### 5. Train in Communication Skills (5)

A. Family members were trained in healthy communication skills.

B. Family members were taught structured techniques for sharing duties regarding speaking and listening.

C. Family members were reinforced for their use of healthy communication techniques.

D. Family members often failed to use healthy communication skills and were redirected in this area.

### 6. Focus Energy onto Problem-Solving (6)

A. The family members were encouraged to separate their feelings of frustration with the financial situation from the people in the situation.

B. The family members were directed to focus their energy onto the problem rather than fighting.

C. The family members were reinforced for focusing on problem resolution rather than infighting.

### 7. Facilitate Confrontation of Exacerbating Behaviors (7)

A. Family members' behavior was explored for issues such as substance abuse, gambling, or compulsive shopping that may be contributing to their financial problems.

B. Family members were assisted in confronting individual family member's issues that may be contributing to or causing financial problems.

C. Family members with problems that may be contributing to or causing financial problems were referred for treatment related to that specific issue.

D. Family members have been cautious about confronting family members who are contributing to or causing the financial problems and were provided with additional support in this area.

### 8. Elaborate on Priorities (8)

A. Family members were assisted in identifying their priorities regarding financial expenditures.

B. Family members were assisted in identifying how they arrived at their values regarding financial expenditures.

C. The similarities in priorities were emphasized.

D. It was noted that family members have very divergent values and priorities.

### 9. Encourage Sharing Expectations (9)

A. Family members were encouraged to share their expectations regarding future income, expenses, and savings.

B. Family members were assisted in more clearly identifying their expectations regarding financial concerns.

C. Family members' expectations regarding future income, expenses, and savings were summarized and reflected to the family.

D. A discussion was held regarding how realistic the family members' expectations of future income, expenses, and savings are.

### 10. Brainstorm Cooperative Financial Planning Avenues (10)

A. The family was assisted in identifying various avenues for financial planning.

B. Family members were encouraged to prioritize financial planning avenues that focus on family cooperation.

C. Family members were urged to use cooperative financial planning options that help to reduce conflict.

D. Family members were assigned "Plan a Budget" from *The Adult Psychotherapy Homework Planner*, 2nd ed. (Jongsma).

E. Family members struggled to identify helpful financial planning options and were provided with tentative examples (e.g., consultation with financial advisors, use of computer software for budgeting income and recording expenditures).

### 11. Encourage Coping Skills for Violated Expectations (11)

A. Family members were encouraged to use communication skills when other family members' ideas or actions seem to violate their expectations.

B. Family members were encouraged to use "I" messages, reflective listening, and time-out techniques.

C. Family members were encouraged to use anger/frustration management skills to help cope with other family members' ideas and actions that violate expectations.

D. Family members were reinforced as they used healthy coping skills for situations when their expectations appear to have been violated.

E. Family members have not used healthy communication and anger/frustration management skills and were redirected to do so.

## 12. Refer to Anger Management Treatment (12)

A. The angry family member was referred to individual anger management treatment to build skills in effectively controlling angry feelings.

B. The angry family member was referred to an anger management group to build skills in effectively controlling angry feelings.

C. The benefits and gains from attending an anger management group were explored and identified.

D. The client followed through on referral to the anger management group and reported positive gains.

E. The client has not followed through on the referral to the anger management group and was redirected to do so.

## 13. Explore Financial Options (13)

A. Family members were helped to identify the need for consolidating loans.

B. Family members were assisted in identifying the need for declaring bankruptcy.

C. Family members were supported as they identified the need for applying for welfare and other entitlement programs.

D. The family was referred to a professional financial planner.

E. Family members were referred to *Consumer Reports*, January 1998, for a review of financial planning services.

F. Family members were referred to *Family Economics Review* (U.S. Department of Agriculture) for information about professional financial planning.

## 14. Assist in Coping Skill Development (14)

A. Family members were assisted in identifying specific coping skills that need to be developed because of the change in their financial situation.

B. Family members were supported as they identified several coping skills to use to help deal with the change in their financial situation.

C. Family members struggled to identify coping skills to help with the changes in their financial situation and were provided with tentative examples (e.g., living with less, spending more wisely, borrowing items, or bartering).

## 15. Reinforce Healthy Money Management Changes (15)

A. Family members were reinforced for adopting money management practices that reflect compromise and cooperation.

B. Family members were reinforced for adopting money management practices that emphasize responsibility and perseverance.

C. Family members were reinforced for adopting money management practices that focus on planning for their financial future.

### 16. Assess for Mental Illness (16)

A. Family members were assessed for the presence of a mental illness that may interfere with responsible financial planning.

B. Family members were assessed for a personality disorder that may contribute to their financial problems.

C. A family member was identified as suffering from a mental disorder that affects financial functioning and was referred for individual treatment.

D. Family members were assessed for mental health concerns but no specific mental health problems were identified.

### 17. Develop Plan for Additional Income Sources (17)

A. Additional income sources were identified, including children's employment, spouse's employment, and other areas.

B. An agreement was developed for how income earned by the children will be spent.

C. A balance was identified regarding the children's contribution to the family income, their personal spending money, and savings.

D. An agreement was developed regarding how the spouse's income will be spent.

### 18. Develop Alternative Income Sources (18)

A. Family members were assisted in identifying how other sources of income can be developed.

B. Family members were supported as they identified realistic expectations for alternative sources of income.

C. Family members were unrealistic about their expectations for alternative sources of income and were provided with redirection in this area.

# GEOGRAPHIC RELOCATION

## CLIENT PRESENTATION

### 1. Relocation for Employment (1)*

A. One of the parents has been forced to relocate due to a transfer to another geographic area to maintain employment.

B. Both parents were forced to relocate due to a transfer to another geographical area to maintain employment.

C. The parent being asked to relocate will experience significant occupational distress if the request to relocate is refused.

### 2. One Parent Seeks a Better Life through Relocation (2)

A. One of the parents believes that a better life awaits the family after relocating.

B. One parent desires to live in a different climate.

C. One parent wishes to relocate due to extended family connections.

D. One parent believes that there are better job opportunities in the new location.

E. There is conflict within the family about the desire to relocate.

### 3. Both Parents Seek a Better Life through Relocation (2)

A. Both parents believe that a better life awaits the family after relocation.

B. Both parents desire to live in a different climate.

C. Both parents wish to relocate due to extended family connections.

D. The family believes there are better job opportunities in the new location.

E. There is conflict within the family about the desire to relocate.

### 4. Differing Opinions about Relocation (3)

A. The spouse does not wish to relocate due to the current level of comfort in the home and community.

B. Family members do not wish to relocate because they are very comfortable in the present home and community.

C. Family members have often disagreed about the necessity for and benefits of relocating.

D. As treatment has progressed, family members have become more cohesive about whether to move.

### 5. Dissension about Relocation (4)

A. Family members often argue about whether the family should relocate.

B. Family members have stated that they refuse to relocate.

---

*The numbers in parentheses correlate to the number of the Behavioral Definition statement in the companion chapter with the same title in *The Family Therapy Treatment Planner*, Second Ed. (Dattilio, Jongsma, and Davis) by John Wiley & Sons, 2010.

C. Family members often blame each other for disagreements about the family relocation.

D. The dissension and opposition about the family relocating has spread to other areas of family life.

E. Family members have been able to develop healthy ways to discuss their varying opinions regarding the relocation.

### 6. Demands to Switch Jobs (5)

A. The spouse has demanded that the breadwinner find another job locally instead of relocating.

B. The children have advocated that the parents find another job locally instead of relocating.

C. Family members often argue about the decision to relocate versus seeking a different job locally.

D. As treatment has progressed, family members have become more unified in the decisions regarding relocating or seeking a new job locally.

### 7. Children Threaten to Act Out (6)

A. The children have made threats about noncompliance and acting out behaviors in reaction to relocation.

B. The children have threatened to run away if the family should attempt to relocate.

C. The children have threatened to assault the parents in an attempt to control the decision about relocating.

D. The children have made false allegations of abuse to manipulate the parents into rescinding their decision to relocate.

E. The children have demanded to be allowed to stay in the current area and live with a friend.

F. The children have made threats to do poorly academically in reaction to the relocation.

G. As treatment has progressed, the children have discontinued inappropriate attempts to control the parents' decision about relocation.

### 8. Inability to Adjust (7)

A. Despite several months in the new area, family members feel they cannot adjust to relocation.

B. Despite an extended period of time in the new area, family members continue to emphasize how life was better in the previous location.

C. As treatment has progressed, family members have begun to understand and accept the benefits of the relocation.

D. The parents have come to admit that the move was a mistake and are debating a return to the original area.

### 9. Emotional Reaction to Relocation (8)

A. Family members often feel grief regarding the issue of relocation

B. Family members become angry when discussing the issue of relocation.

C. Family members feel sad and depressed regarding the issue of relocation.

D. As family members have adjusted, the emotional reaction to the issue of relocation has been decreased.

## INTERVENTIONS IMPLEMENTED

### 1. Explore Opinions (1)*

A. Each family member's thoughts and feelings regarding the possible relocation were explored.

B. Family members were encouraged to voice their opinion about the relocation and why they feel that way.

C. Family members were supported as they expressed their opinions about the relocation.

D. Family members were quite guarded about their thoughts and feelings regarding the possible relocation and were encouraged to be more open in this area.

### 2. Promote Discussion (2)

A. All family members were encouraged to discuss their reluctance to relocate.

B. The issues related to the relocation were reviewed and identified as a marital issue and the focus of treatment was shifted to marital therapy to consider the financial realities and power and control issues.

C. Family members reluctant to relocate were assisted in expressing their opinions.

D. Family members were guarded about expressing their feelings and were urged to do this when they feel safe in doing so.

### 3. Explore Motivation for Moving (3)

A. Family members were asked about the motivations for the suggested move.

B. The possibility that the move is to escape a problem that would be best dealt with without moving was explored.

C. The family was provided with examples of situations in which a move might be due to a problem that would best be dealt with otherwise (e.g., feeling bored or restless rather than a true financial necessity or job relocation).

D. Family members discussed the inappropriate motives for moving, and were directed to develop alternative options for these problems.

E. Family members denied any inappropriate motives for the move, and this was accepted at face value.

### 4. Use Systemic Approach (4)

A. The interfamilial dynamics regarding how conflict is resolved were addressed.

B. The family was assisted in identifying how they normally deal with disagreements and were encouraged to use healthy problem-solving and communication skills.

C. An emphasis was placed on keeping the family from dividing, forming schisms and subgroup alliances.

### 5. Brainstorm Advantages and Disadvantages (5)

A. Family members were assisted in brainstorming possible advantages of relocating.

B. Family members were assisted in brainstorming possible disadvantages of relocating.

*The numbers in parentheses correlate to the number of the Therapeutic Intervention statement in the companion chapter with the same title in *The Family Therapy Treatment Planner*, Second Ed. (Dattilio, Jongsma, and Davis) by John Wiley & Sons, 2010.

C. Family members were helped to compare the advantages and disadvantages of relocating.

D. Family members struggled to identify many of the advantages or disadvantages of relocating and were provided with tentative examples of each.

## 6. Request Three Alternatives (6)

A. Family members were requested to identify three alternatives to relocation.

B. The family was supported as they identified alternatives to relocation.

C. The family was encouraged to strongly consider the possibility of implementing aspects of all three alternatives.

D. Family members immediately rejected the alternative ideas and were urged to consider these for a longer period of time.

## 7. Address Individual Noncompliant Behaviors (7)

A. Individual noncompliant rebellious behaviors were identified.

B. The impact of one family member's rebellious behaviors on other family members was emphasized.

C. Effective ways in which the noncompliant rebellious behaviors can be modified were reviewed.

D. The family was reluctant to focus on the rebellious behaviors, their impact, or alternatives and were provided with tentative examples in this area.

## 8. Address Children's Acting Out (8)

A. The parents were assisted in setting limits for the children's acting-out behaviors.

B. The parents were taught about the use of response cost, grounding, and other limit-setting actions for the children's acting-out behavior.

C. An emphasis was placed on the feelings that are being expressed through the children's acting-out behavior.

D. Tentative examples were offered to help explain the emotions being expressed by the children's acting-out behavior.

## 9. Meet with Parents to Set Behavioral Responses (9)

A. A separate conjoint session was held with the parents to focus on the appropriate behavioral responses to the children's acting-out behavior.

B. The parents were supported as they identified appropriate responses for the children's acting-out behavior.

C. The parents struggled to identify appropriate responses to the children's acting-out behavior and were provided with tentative examples (e.g., loss of privileges, selected chores, community service).

## 10. Discuss Disciplinary Measures (10)

A. A conjoint session was held with parents to review the disciplinary measures to help modify acting-out behavior.

B. The parents were assisted in identifying alternative responses to acting-out behavior.

C. Parents were urged to use removal of privileges due to acting-out behavior.

D. Parents were urged to temporarily remove the child from the home due to the acting-out behavior.

E. Positive feedback was provided to the parents for use of healthy reaction alternatives to the child's acting-out behavior.

## 11. Separate Anger from Criminal Behavior (11)

A. The family was assisted in separating the children's anger from involvement in criminal behavior.

B. Family-sculpting techniques were used to help address the feelings and behavior separately.

C. Reverse role-play techniques were used to help separate the anger feelings and the criminal behavior.

D. An emphasis was placed on how the children's anger and criminal behavior affect the overall functioning of the family.

## 12. Facilitate Expression of Children's Feelings (12)

A. The children were encouraged to express their feelings of powerlessness and/or frustration regarding the issue of relocation.

B. The children were assisted in expressing their emotions regarding the relocation to the parents and to other family members.

C. The children were reinforced for the healthy style of expressing their emotions regarding the relocation.

D. Other family members were urged to accept and validate the children's emotions regarding the issue of relocation.

E. The children had difficulty in expressing their emotions and were provided with additional support and direction in this area.

## 13. Strengthen Parent-Child Relationship (13)

A. The parents were assisted in strengthening the relationship with their children.

B. The parents were encouraged to use parent/child dates, family game nights, and other means to increase connection and reduce acting-out behaviors.

C. The parents were reinforced for the use of relationship-strengthening techniques.

D. The parents have not attempted the relationship-strengthening tasks and were redirected to do so.

## 14. Address Anger Issues (14)

A. The children were identified as having significant anger issues about the expected relocation.

B. The children's anger was normalized.

C. The children were taught anger control and anger expression techniques.

D. The children were reinforced for their healthy use of anger management techniques.

E. The children have not used the anger management techniques and were redirected to do so.

### 15. Offer Alternatives for Anger Expression (15)

A. The children were urged to develop alternative techniques for anger expression.

B. The children were reinforced for their identification and use of alternative techniques for expressing their anger.

C. The children were provided with specific techniques for expressing their anger (e.g., sports, music, use of punching bag).

D. The children were reinforced for their use of alternative techniques for expressing their anger.

E. The children have not used alternative techniques for expressing their anger and were reminded about these techniques.

### 16. Explore Abuse Allegations (16)

A. The children's accusations of physical or sexual abuse were explored in family therapy.

B. The children's accusations of physical or sexual abuse were explored in a session with only the abusing parent.

C. As the allegations of physical or sexual abuse were identified as being potentially truthful, the allegations were reported to the appropriate authorities.

D. The sexual and physical abuse was identified as being used as a way to have the child removed from the home and not have to relocate.

E. Issues of power, control, and resentment were emphasized as the family worked through false accusations of physical or sexual abuse.

### 17. Refer to Protective Services (17)

A. The family was referred to protective services or another social service agency regarding the allegations of physical or sexual abuse.

B. The agency investigating the allegations of physical or sexual abuse was worked with in a collaborative manner.

C. The allegations of physical or sexual abuse were deemed to be true by the child protection agency and the focus of treatment has been modified.

D. The allegations of physical or sexual abuse were accepted as unverified.

### 18. Suggest Temporary Removal of the Children (18)

A. Due to the possibility that physical or sexual abuse has occurred, the temporary removal of the children was suggested.

B. The family was assisted in temporarily removing the children due to the possibility that physical or sexual abuse has occurred.

### 19. Identify Losses (19)

A. Family members were asked to identify the losses they have experienced due to relocation.

B. Family members were supported as they identified and described the losses they have experienced due to relocation.

C. Family members were provided with tentative examples about some of the losses they may have experienced due to relocation.

**20. Facilitate Expression of Grief (20)**

A. Family members were urged to express their feelings of grief about the losses due to the relocation.

B. Family members were supported as they expressed their grieving feelings.

C. All family members were included in the expression of grief to develop family unity on this issue.

D. Family members were encouraged to empathize with each other about the feelings of grief associated with the relocation.

**21. Emphasize New Horizons (21)**

A. Family members' losses were validated.

B. Family members were encouraged to concentrate on the new horizons they will experience due to the relocation.

C. Family members were encouraged to focus on expanding their ideas, friendships, and experiences through the relocation.

**22. Address Alternative Living Options (22)**

A. The option of having a family member remain in the current area and live with a friend or relative was reviewed.

B. The family was urged to identify the pros and cons of alternative living options.

C. The ways that alternative living arrangements would affect the family were reviewed.

**23. Reinforce Family Structure (23)**

A. The concept of the parents as the architects of the family structure was emphasized.

B. The family was compared to an organization in which the parents, as executives, have ultimate authority.

C. The parents were encouraged to be the final decision makers regarding the relocation, taking into account all of the needs of the family.

D. The parents were supported as they exercised their appropriate decision-making authority.

E. When family members attempted to usurp the decision-making authority from the parents, they were redirected.

**24. Devise Ritual for Losses (24)**

A. The family was directed to develop a ritual or ceremony to commemorate the loss of their old home and the future in their new home.

B. The family was offered ideas to commemorate the changes resulting from the move (e.g., compiling a scrapbook of memories of the old home, taking certain mementos from the old home to the new home, etc.).

C. The family has developed rituals and ceremonies to commemorate changes and these were processed.

D. The family did not use rituals to commemorate the changes and were redirected to do so.

# INCEST SURVIVOR

## CLIENT PRESENTATION

### 1. Verbal Demands for Sexual Interaction (1)*

A. A verbal demand has been made to accede to sexual interaction by a fellow family member.

B. The family member who has been asked to accede to sexual interaction was guarded and evasive about the sexual abuse.

C. A family member has previously reported another family member making demands to accede to sexual interaction, but has since recanted these earlier statements.

D. The family member has verbally denied being asked or directed to accede to sexual interaction.

### 2. Physical Threats/Coercion (2)

A. Physical threats have been made toward a family member to fulfill sexual demands.

B. Psychological coercion has been used on a family member to cause submission to ongoing sexual abuse.

C. A family member identified experiencing threats or coercion and therefore submitting to sexual abuse.

D. Although threats and attempts to coerce a family member into being sexually abused have been made, the family member did not submit to the abuse.

### 3. Reluctance to Share Trauma (3)

A. The abused family member has been reluctant to share the trauma of the abuse with anyone, including other family members.

B. The abused family member has experienced fear of rejection, retaliation, or other responses to sharing the trauma of the abuse.

C. As treatment has progressed, the abused family member has become more open and willing to express the trauma of the abuse.

### 4. Feelings of Guilt and Shame (4)

A. The abused family member expressed strong feelings of guilt, shame, anger, resentment, isolation, and depression as a result of the abuse.

B. The abused family member has continued to experience strong feelings of guilt, shame, anger, resentment, isolation, and depression about the past sexual abuse, despite reassurances about not being responsible for the abuse.

---

*The numbers in parentheses correlate to the number of the Behavioral Definition statement in the companion chapter with the same title in *The Family Therapy Treatment Planner*, Second Ed. (Dattilio, Jongsma, and Davis) by John Wiley & Sons, 2010.

C. The abused family member's emotions regarding the abuse have started to decrease due to the recognition that the perpetrator is responsible for the abuse.

D. The abused family member has successfully resolved the feelings of guilt, shame, anger, resentment, isolation, and depression about past abuse.

### 5. Confusion about Changes Prompt Suspicion of Abuse (5)

A. Family members are confused by the changes in emotions and behaviors in a specific family member.

B. A family member displays significant symptoms of agitation, avoidance, depression, and withdrawal.

C. Family members have suspected that abuse may have occurred.

D. As treatment has progressed, the abused family member has connected the agitation, avoidance, depression, and withdrawal to the history of being abused.

### 6. Emotional Responses to Learning of the Abuse (6)

A. Family members have displayed a range of emotions in reaction to learning of the abuse sustained by the victim.

B. Family members have become enraged in reaction to learning of the abuse that the victim has experienced.

C. Family members expressed guilt and sorrow in reaction to learning of the abuse.

D. Family members expressed feelings of depression and sadness in reaction to learning of the abuse done to the victim.

E. As family members have worked through their emotions, their emotions have become less unstable.

### 7. Sexual Acting Out (7)

A. The sexually abused family member has a history of engaging in inappropriate sexual behavior with younger children.

B. The sexually abused family member acknowledged that sexual behavior with younger children is inappropriate.

C. The sexually abused family member has displayed increased sexual involvement at a level greater than would be expected based on that family member's age.

D. The sexually abused family member reported no recent inappropriate sexual behavior.

E. The sexually abused family member's risk for engaging in inappropriate sexual behavior appears to be greatly reduced because of the successful resolution of issues related to past sexual victimization.

### 8. Pressure to Remain Silent (8)

A. Family members have pressured the victim of the sexual abuse not to report the abuse to the authorities.

B. Family members have used emotional threats to pressure the victim not to report the abuse to the authorities.

C. Family members have made overt threats to the victim in order to keep the abuse a secret.

D. As the family has progressed in treatment, they have seen the need for the authorities to be fully advised about the abuse.

### 9. Guilt about Reporting the Abuse (9)

A. Family members have taken responsibility for reporting the sexual abuse to authorities, which has caused significant changes within the family.

B. The victim feels guilty about the responsibility for the changes that have occurred within the family.

C. As treatment has progressed, the victim has taken less responsibility for the changes that occur due to the sexual abuse being reported to the authorities.

D. The victim of the sexual abuse has placed responsibility for family changes solely on the perpetrator.

### 10. Family Denial of Abuse (10)

A. Family members deny that any sexual abuse occurred to the victim.

B. Family members minimize the extent and effect of the sexual abuse against the victim.

C. The victim of the sexual abuse has expressed feelings of shame, anger, betrayal, and embarrassment as the family members have not believed and supported him/her about the abuse.

D. As treatment has progressed, the family members have come to believe and support the victim of the abuse, resulting in a sense of support for the victim.

### 11. Removal from the Home (11)

A. The victim has been temporarily removed from the home by court-appointed authorities.

B. The removal of the victim from the home has caused stress and emotional strain to the family.

C. The victim has remained with the family but the perpetrator has been removed.

D. Treatment has led to the safe reuniting of the family members, including the victim and the perpetrator.

### 12. Threats to Expose the Abuse (12)

A. The victim threatens to expose the abuse to relatives, neighbors, friends, or others.

B. The victim often uses threats to expose the abuse to others as a way to manipulate the family.

C. Family members have become open and honest about the abuse, which has decreased the victim's attempts to manipulate them.

## INTERVENTIONS IMPLEMENTED

### 1. Display Warmth (1)*

A. As the victim expressed feelings associated with the abuse, a nonjudgmental, warm, accepting manner was displayed.

---

*The numbers in parentheses correlate to the number of the Therapeutic Intervention statement in the companion chapter with the same title in *The Family Therapy Treatment Planner*, Second Ed. (Dattilio, Jongsma, and Davis) by John Wiley & Sons, 2010.

B. Good eye contact was maintained as the victim expressed feelings associated with the abuse.

C. Family members were encouraged to be nonjudgmental, warm, accepting, and maintain good eye contact as the victim expressed feelings associated with the abuse.

D. Family members were reinforced as they presented a nonjudgmental, accepting attitude toward the victim.

E. Family members have not been very accepting toward the victim and were redirected in this area.

2. **Encourage Expression of Feelings (2)**

A. The victim was given encouragement and support to tell the entire story of the sexual abuse and to express the feelings experienced during and after the abuse.

B. The victim was assigned the exercise "My Story" in the *Brief Adolescent Homework Planner* (Jongsma, Peterson, and McInnis).

C. Support was provided as the victim described the sequence of events before, during, and after the sexual abuse incidents.

D. Client-centered principles were used to encourage and support the victim in expressing feelings about past sexual abuse.

E. Family members were encouraged to allow the victim the opportunity to express thoughts and feelings about the sexual abuse while at home.

3. **Encourage Support for the Victim (3)**

A. Family members were encouraged to offer verbal support to the sexually abused family member.

B. Family members were encouraged to offer as much physical support to the sexually abused family member as the victim can tolerate.

C. Family members were reinforced for their support of the sexually abused family member.

D. Family members have not provided significant support to the sexually abused family member and were redirected to do so.

4. **Use Indirect Methods to Facilitate Talking about the Abuse (4)**

A. Indirect methods were used to facilitate the expression of the effects of the abuse.

B. Play therapy, artwork, psychodrama, and other expressive techniques were used to help the victim talk about the effects of the abuse.

C. *The Modified Posttraumatic Symptoms Scale* (Resick) was administered to help the victim express the effects of the abuse.

D. *The Sexual Assault Symptom Scale* (Ruch) was administered to help the victim express the effects of the abuse.

E. The victim has failed to process much of the sexual abuse and its effects and was encouraged to do this when able.

5. **Refer to Victims' Abuse Group (5)**

A. The victim was referred to a support group for victims of abuse.

B. The abused family member has attended a support group for victims of abuse, and the benefits of this program were reviewed.

C. The abused family member has not attended the recommended support group for victims of abuse and was redirected to this helpful resource.

### 6. Assign Written Material (6)

A. Family members were assigned to read material about sexual abuse and how it affects the victim.

B. Family members were assigned to read *Repair for Kids* (McKinnish).

C. Family members were assigned to read *Hush* (Bromley).

D. Family members have read the assigned material on sexual abuse and how it affects the victim, and key points were processed.

E. Family members have not read the assigned material on sexual abuse and were redirected to do so.

### 7. Educate about PTSD Effect (7)

A. The family and the victim were educated about the posttraumatic effects of sexual abuse.

B. Family members were taught about how effects can be quite subtle in some victims and very blatant in others.

C. Family members were taught about specific traumatic effects of sexual abuse including flashbacks and external cues.

### 8. Brainstorm Protection (8)

A. The family was helped to discuss ways the family can protect the victim from being alone with or having contact with the perpetrator.

B. The family was assisted in brainstorming ways the victim can be protected from the perpetrator.

C. Family members were assisted in reviewing the usefulness of techniques to keep the victim protected from the perpetrator.

D. Family members have not identified ways to keep the victim protected from the perpetrator and were provided with tentative examples.

### 9. Resolve Fears of Perpetrator's Prosecution (9)

A. The victim was encouraged to express possible fears that the perpetrator would be criminally prosecuted if the abuse is reported.

B. The victim was assisted in processing the concern that the perpetrator will be prosecuted.

C. The tendency for victims to retract their statements was discussed and normalized.

D. The victim was supported when comments were made indicating resolution of the fears of being responsible for the perpetrator being criminally prosecuted.

### 10. Support Family Member through Fear of Retaliation (10)

A. The victim was supported as fears were identified about retaliation by the perpetrator.

B. Family members were encouraged to provide support to the victim during the process of reporting the abuse.

C. Fears about retaliation were normalized.

D. The desire of a victim to recant reports about the abuse were normalized.

### 11. Brainstorm Techniques for Coping with Symptoms (11)

A. Individual techniques were brainstormed to help family members deal with symptoms of abuse as they appear in the victim.

B. The family was provided with specific examples of techniques to use to deal with symptoms as they appear in the victim.

C. Family group techniques were brainstormed to assist in dealing with symptoms as they appear in the victim.

D. The family was provided with examples of ways to provide comfort to the victim when symptoms resulting from abuse are experienced.

### 12. Caution about Overanticipating Symptoms (12)

A. Family members were cautioned about the tendency to overanticipate a symptom in the victim to the point of seeing what is not there and/or inducing it.

B. Family members were provided with examples of how overanticipating a symptom can actually cause the symptom to appear.

C. Family members were helped to dispel the myths and inaccuracies regarding symptoms that they anticipate in the victim.

D. Family members were redirected when they displayed inappropriate anticipation of symptoms in the victim.

### 13. Develop Preferred Support Method (13)

A. The family members were helped to identify a variety of methods for supporting the victim in dealing with feelings of vulnerability.

B. Family members were taught to use supportive listening to assist the victim in dealing with feelings of vulnerability.

C. Family members were taught to use empathetic listening to assist the victim in dealing with the feelings of vulnerability.

D. Family members were taught about determination of comfort zones to assist the victim in dealing with the vulnerability.

E. Family members were assisted in identifying the best method of supporting the victim.

### 14. Explore Effects on Nonabused Family Members (14)

A. Today's session focused on exploring the effects of the abuse on nonabused family members.

B. Family members were encouraged to express their emotions related to the abuse.

C. Family members were assisted in identifying how they have been expressing their feelings about the abuse.

D. Family members have been guarded about their own emotional reactions to the abuse and were encouraged to be more open in expressing their feelings.

### 15. Brainstorm Coping Skills (15)

A. Family members were assisted in brainstorming coping skills to deal with their emotions (e.g., anger, guilt, despair).

B. Specific coping skills were suggested to the family.

C. Family members were reinforced for their regular use of healthy coping skills to deal with emotions such as anger, guilt, and despair in reaction to the sexual abuse.

D. Family members have not used healthy coping skills and were redirected to use these techniques.

### 16. Encourage Victim to Help Others Heal (16)

A. The victim was assisted in becoming part of the healing process for other family members.

B. The victim expressed anger about vulnerability as a way to help the family members work through healing; the family was helped to work through these emotions.

### 17. Explore Conflicts (17)

A. Conflicts that have emerged among family members over the abuse were explored.

B. The family was taught communication techniques for the emergent conflicts.

C. Family members were noted to often blame each other for not protecting the victim better.

D. Resentment by siblings was noted, citing that the victim is getting too much attention due to the sexual abuse.

E. Family members were supported as they worked through the conflict that has emerged due to the abuse.

### 18. Use Conflict-Resolution Strategies (18)

A. The family was taught conflict-resolution strategies.

B. The family was taught about the use of behavioral contracts to resolve conflict among family members.

C. The family was taught about cognitive restructuring techniques to reduce conflict among family members.

D. The family has regularly used conflict reduction strategies and was provided with positive feedback about these techniques.

E. The family has not used conflict-resolution strategies and was reminded about these techniques.

### 19. Teach Deep Muscle Relaxation (19)

A. The incest victim was taught deep muscle relaxation.

B. Family members were taught deep muscle relaxation techniques.

C. Family members were reinforced for their use of relaxation techniques to help cope with feelings of anxiety related to the abuse.

D. Family members have not regularly used relaxation techniques and were reminded about these techniques.

## 20. Identify Dysfunctional Thoughts (20)

A. Family members were assisted in identifying dysfunctional, negative automatic thoughts that generate anxiety.

B. Family members were helped to identify negative automatic thoughts by bringing that thought to a more extreme conclusion.

C. Family members struggled to identify negative automatic thoughts and were provided with tentative examples in this area.

D. An emphasis was placed on how thoughts trigger emotions.

## 21. Replace Negative Thoughts (21)

A. Family members were assisted in identifying positive, realistic messages that promote confidence and calm.

B. Family members were urged to use the positive, calming messages whenever they experience negative automatic, dysfunctional thoughts.

C. Family members were redirected to more positive, calming thoughts when they expressed negative automatic thoughts within the session.

## 22. Develop Sensitivity to the Victim's Pace (22)

A. The nonabused family members were urged to see their own emotional reactions as secondary to those of the victim.

B. The nonabused family members were urged to focus on the victim's needs for setting the pace for working through these issues.

C. Family members were advised about how intimidating testifying can be for a victim.

D. Family members were reinforced for giving top priority to the victim's feelings.

E. When family members did not seem to be giving top priority to the victim's feelings, they were redirected to do so.

## 23. Allow for Ventilation of Emotions (23)

A. The nonabused family members were encouraged to ventilate their emotions and frustrations.

B. The nonabused family members were specifically focused on their emotions about how slowly the prosecution of the perpetrator has been conducted.

C. Family members emotions related to the slow pace of the prosecution of the perpetrator were normalized.

## 24. Assess/Refer to Victim-Centered Treatment (24)

A. The victim was assessed as to the need for individual or group therapy to process the trauma.

B. A referral was made to a group for survivors of incest.

C. A referral was made to an individual therapist with an understanding of sexual abuse issues.

D. The incest survivor has been involved in treatment specific to his/her sexual abuse victimization, and the benefits of his/her therapy were reviewed.

E. The victim of the abuse has not been involved in treatment specific to his/her sexual abuse victimization, and was redirected to these resources.

## 25. Brainstorm about Moving Forward (25)

A. Family members were assisted in brainstorming how to move forward and heal from the effects of the abuse.

B. Family members were encouraged to use specific rituals to help in the process of healing from the abuse.

C. Family members were referred to community support programs.

D. The family was encouraged to use an apology from the perpetrator as a way to begin to move forward.

E. Family members have used techniques to move forward and heal from the effects of the abuse, and the benefits of this progress were reviewed and processed.

F. Family members have not moved forward and healed from the effects of the abuse and were reminded about the need to focus on the future.

## 26. Reinforce Agreement Not to Revisit, Blame, or Excuse (26)

A. The family was facilitated in agreeing not to revisit the trauma too often or use the event to blame family members or as an excuse for other nonrelated behaviors in the future.

B. Family members were reminded about their commitment not to excuse, blame, or constantly revisit the issue.

C. Family members were reinforced for their willingness to move on from these issues.

D. Family members continued to revisit the trauma and use the sexual abuse to blame or excuse unrelated behavior and were reminded about why this pattern was unhealthy.

## 27. Support Direct, Legal Response to Perpetrator (27)

A. The family was encouraged to facilitate a direct, legal response to the perpetrator.

B. Family members were discouraged from using illegal means to respond to the perpetrator, because this may deny the victim of necessary family members (who may land in jail).

C. Family members were encouraged to help validate and empower the victim through dealing with the perpetrator in a legal, direct manner.

D. Family members were reinforced for their assistance to the victim in dealing with the perpetrator in a legal, direct manner.

E. Family members have not dealt with the perpetrator in a legal, direct manner and were reminded to respond only in this manner.

## 28. Refer to Victim's Rights Advocate (28)

A. The family was referred to a victim's rights advocate.

B. The family was referred to a victim's support group.

C. The local district attorney and police station were contacted for resources for victim's rights advocates.

D. The family has connected with an advocate for victim's rights, and their experiences in this area were processed.

E. The family has not connected with a victim's rights advocate and was redirected to do so.

### 29. Refer to Local Authorities (29)

A. The family was referred to the local authorities to report the sexual-abuse perpetrator.

B. The family was directed to contact the local prosecuting attorney's office.

C. The family was directed to contact the local police unit.

D. The family has contacted the proper authorities, and their experience in this area was processed.

E. The family has not contacted the proper authorities and was redirected to do so.

### 30. Refer for Medical Testing (30)

A. The victim was referred for a medical evaluation to screen for sexually transmitted diseases (STDs), pregnancy, and so forth.

B. Testing was arranged for STDs.

C. The client was tested to determine if she is pregnant.

D. Follow-up treatment for the client's STDs was coordinated.

E. The client has tested positive for pregnancy and was assisted in processing this development.

F. The client has tested negatively for STDs, and this information was passed on to him/her.

### 31. Explore for Sexual Acting Out (31)

A. The family was taught that victims sometimes react to the abuse by sexually acting out.

B. The victim was assessed for the presence of sexual acting out as a response to the abuse.

C. It was reflected to family members that the victim has been sexually acting out as a response to the abuse, and appropriate responses were reviewed.

D. It was reflected to family members that the victim has not been sexually acting out as a response to the abuse.

### 32. Teach Connection between Victimization and Sexually Acting Out (32)

A. Family members were taught the connection between sexual acting out by the victim and the sexual abuse.

B. Family members were assisted in understanding the dynamics between the victim's abuse and the sexual acting out that the victim has done.

C. The family was urged to calmly set clear limits on the victim's sexual acting out.

D. Family members were urged not to have an emotional overreaction to the victim's sexual acting out.

### 33. Identify Factors Related to Sexual Acting Out (33)

A. The family was assisted in identifying the different factors that may be contributing to the victim's pattern of sexual acting out.

B. Family members were assisted in identifying how preexisting individual or family issues might contribute to the victim's current pattern of sexual acting out.

C. Family members were reinforced as they identified preexisting individual or family issues that may lead to the victim's sexual acting out.

D. Family members were unable to identify any preexisting individual or family issues that may be contributing to the victim's sexual acting out and were provided with tentative examples in this area (e.g., lack of attention, low self-esteem, need for additional comfort, anger toward men or women).

### 34. Assess How to Approach Sexual Acting Out (34)

A. The family was assisted in assessing the specific aspects of the victim's sexual acting out that can be dealt with within the family.

B. The family was assisted in assessing specific aspects of the victim's sexual acting out that may need to be addressed in individual or group therapy.

### 35. Explore Readiness for Apology (35)

A. The victim's ability to accept an apology from the perpetrator was assessed.

B. The victim was identified as being ready to accept an apology from the perpetrator, and this apology was coordinated.

C. The perpetrator's request to make an apology to the victim was turned down because the victim is not ready for such an apology.

D. Family members were assessed regarding their ability to accept an apology from the perpetrator.

E. Family members were identified as being ready to accept an apology from the perpetrator, and this apology was coordinated.

F. The perpetrator's request to make an apology to the victim was turned down because the family members are not ready for such an apology.

### 36. Outline Change and Support Needs Regarding the Perpetrator (36)

A. The family was assisted in outlining the changes they would like to see in the perpetrator.

B. Family members were surveyed regarding their willingness to support the perpetrator through rehabilitation.

C. Family members were supported as they identified the changes they need to see in the perpetrator, and their willingness to support the perpetrator through rehabilitation.

### 37. Facilitate Confrontation of Perpetrator (37)

A. A family forum was coordinated in which the perpetrator was confronted regarding responsibility for the abuse.

B. The victim was given priority for expressing feelings toward the perpetrator and for assigning responsibility to the perpetrator for the abuse.

C. Any thought distortions that focused on placing the blame on the victim were quickly challenged as the perpetrator was confronted about responsibility for the abuse.

D. The family has declined to allow the perpetrator to have any contact with the victim, and this was accepted.

## 38. Provide Forum for Apology (38)

A. The family was assisted in coordinating a forum for the perpetrator to ask for forgiveness of the victim and the family.

B. Any thought distortions regarding minimizing or justifying the perpetrator's offenses were quickly pointed out.

C. The victim was provided with time to respond to the perpetrator's request for forgiveness.

D. Other family members were provided with the chance to respond to the perpetrator's apology.

E. The victim was provided with the choice to delay responding until a later time.

# INFIDELITY

## CLIENT PRESENTATION

### 1. Explicit Relationship Expectations Violated (1)*

A. One parent has engaged in sexual behavior that violates the explicit expectations of the relationship.

B. One parent has engaged in sexual intercourse with someone outside the relationship.

C. One parent has engaged in kissing or fondling with someone outside the relationship.

D. The sexual behavior outside the relationship has been discontinued.

### 2. Implicit Relationship Expectations Violated (1)

A. One parent has engaged in sexual behavior with someone outside the relationship that violates the implicit expectations of the relationship.

B. The sexual behavior with someone outside the relationship that violates the implicit expectations of the relationship has been discovered by the other parent.

C. An "exchange of intimacy" has occurred by one parent outside the boundaries of the relationship.

D. The sexual behavior with someone outside the relationship that violates the implicit expectations of the relationship has been discontinued.

### 3. Sharing Intimate Feelings with Extramarital Partner (2)

A. Nonsexual behavior that involves sharing intimate feelings with an extramarital partner has occurred.

B. One parent has expressed feeling hurt by the other parent's sharing of intimate feelings with an extramarital partner.

C. The sharing of intimate feelings with an extramarital partner has been discontinued.

### 4. Secrecy (2)

A. The unfaithful parent has displayed a pattern of secrecy that violated the implicit and explicit expectations of the relationship.

B. The unfaithful parent has gone to significant lengths to cover up contact with an extramarital partner.

C. As the affair has been uncovered, the pattern of secrecy has been discontinued.

D. The unfaithful parent is open about contact with the extramarital partner.

### 5. Children's Discovery of Infidelity (3)

A. The children of the family have discovered the extramarital involvement by one parent prior to the other parent's awareness of this infidelity.

---

*The numbers in parentheses correlate to the number of the Behavioral Definition statement in the companion chapter with the same title in *The Family Therapy Treatment Planner*, Second Ed. (Dattilio, Jongsma, and Davis) by John Wiley & Sons, 2010.

B. The offending parent has put pressure for secrecy on the children who have discovered the extramarital involvement in an attempt to keep the other parent from becoming aware of the infidelity.

C. The children attempt to manipulate or blackmail the offending parent with threats to disclose the infidelity.

D. The infidelity issue has been resolved, and the children are no longer in the middle of this conflict.

### 6. Nonoffending Parent Confides in Children (4)

A. The nonoffending parent has become aware of the spouse's involvement with an extramarital partner.

B. The nonoffending parent has confided in the children prior to confronting the spouse.

C. The nonoffending parent has confided in the children subsequent to confronting the spouse about the infidelity.

D. The parents have elected to make the infidelity an issue only between the adults and have discontinued confiding in the children.

### 7. Offending Parent Confides in Children (5)

A. The offending parent has secretly shared feelings for a nonspousal partner with the children.

B. The children have felt conflicting loyalties regarding whether to tell the nonoffending parent about the offending parent's secret feelings.

C. The parents have elected to make the infidelity an issue only between the adults and have discontinued confiding in the children.

## INTERVENTIONS IMPLEMENTED

### 1. Refer for Couple's Therapy (1)*

A. The parents were referred for conjoint couple's therapy without involvement of the children.

B. The parents have followed through on conjoint couple's therapy without involvement of the children, and their progress in this treatment was monitored.

C. The parents have not complied with the referral for conjoint couple's therapy and were redirected to do so.

### 2. Discuss Separation (2)

A. A session was held with the children to discuss their feelings about the option of the parents separating.

B. The impact of a marital separation was reviewed.

C. The coping skills required for maintaining functioning during a separation period were reviewed.

D. Living arrangements for all parties were discussed with specific timelines identified.

---

*The numbers in parentheses correlate to the number of the Therapeutic Intervention statement in the companion chapter with the same title in *The Family Therapy Treatment Planner*, Second Ed. (Dattilio, Jongsma, and Davis) by John Wiley & Sons, 2010.

### 3. Discuss Feelings and Coping Skills (3)

A. An open-ended discussion about the children's feelings of anger, frustration, and betrayal of trust was conducted.

B. The children were assisted in expressing their emotions about the infidelity.

C. Assertiveness and confrontation skills were used to help the children express their emotions.

D. The children were encouraged to write letters and use other means of communication to help the parents understand their emotions.

E. Positive feedback was provided to the children for the healthy communication of their emotions.

F. The children have been quite guarded about expressing their emotions and were redirected in this area.

### 4. Use Exercises for Anger Mediation (4)

A. Exercises were used to help with the expression of anger.

B. Rituals were used to help deal with the lack of trust and feelings of abandonment.

### 5. Solicit Apology (5)

A. The offending parent was urged to provide an apology to the nonoffending parent and/or the children.

B. An emphasis was placed on how forgiveness may take time, but is necessary to move beyond the affair.

C. The family was directed to read *How Can I Forgive You?* (Spring).

D. An apology has occurred, and the family members were helped to process the apology.

E. The offending parent has declined any apology, and was urged to provide this at a later date.

### 6. Address Emotions Regarding Loyalty Conflicts (6)

A. The children identified a loyalty conflict regarding whether to tell the other parent about the infidelity that has been disclosed by the offending parent; they were supported for their insightfulness in this area.

B. Feelings of guilt, anger, frustration, and disappointment regarding the bind of loyalty were normalized.

C. The children were assisted in resolving their decisions regarding whether to tell the other parent of the infidelity.

### 7. Discuss Boundaries (7)

A. The appropriateness of personal boundaries was discussed.

B. The parents were assisted in identifying the appropriateness of their personal boundaries.

C. An emphasis was placed on how breaking role boundaries can result in an enmeshment with and parentification of the child.

D. The parent was assisted in identifying ways in which the role boundaries with the children have been broken.

E. The parents denied any pattern of breaking boundaries with the children and were provided with tentative examples in this area.

F. The parents have read material such as *Boundaries* (Katherine); key points were reviewed.

G. The parents have not read the information on boundaries and were redirected to do so.

## 8. Commit Not to Use Children as Pawns (8)

A. The parents were requested to commit to not using the children as pawns in their marital conflict.

B. Parents were assisted in listing behaviors that all agree would be unfair, retaliatory, and destructive to the children.

C. The parents were provided with suggestions about behavior that would be considered off limits (e.g., denial of visitation, telling children complaints about the spouse, urging the children to not visit the spouse, asking the children to "spy" on the spouse, etc.).

D. The parents were reinforced for not using the children as pawns in their struggles.

E. The parents described situations in which they have used the children as pawns and were reminded that this was unhealthy.

## 9. Emphasize Clear Message that Children Are Not to Blame (9)

A. The parents were asked to give a clear message to the children of the children not being to blame for the parents' relationship failure.

B. The parents were reinforced for giving a clear message to the children of the children not being to blame for the parents' relationship failure.

C. Parents have made some blaming statements to the children about responsibility for the parents' relationship problems and were redirected in this area.

## 10. Remind Children Regarding Parents' Responsibility (10)

A. The children were reminded that the parents are responsible for their own behavior.

B. The children were reminded that they should not be held accountable for the behaviors of their parents, or the loyalty conflicts that the parents have created.

C. The children were reminded that it was not their responsibility to "fix" the situation.

D. The children were reinforced when making comments about how they were not responsible for the parents' decisions and behavior.

E. The children were redirected when they took responsibility for their parents' behavior and problems.

## 11. Address How to Cope with Reactions Outside the Family (11)

A. The expectation that information about the infidelity and family problems would reach extended family members and others in the community was reviewed.

B. Supportive listening was provided regarding how the children will react to extended family members and others gaining information about the infidelity.

C. Coping skills for dealing with the effects of the greater community finding out about the infidelity were emphasized.

D. Family members were encouraged to read *Private Lies* (Pittman).

E. Family members have read the assigned information on coping with others' learning about the infidelity, and key points were reviewed.

F. The family has not read information to assist in coping with how information about the infidelity will impact others and was redirected to do so.

# INHERITANCE DISPUTES BETWEEN SIBLINGS

## CLIENT PRESENTATION

### 1. An Inheritance (1)*

A. The family has inherited a significant sum of money.

B. Assets have been passed on to the family members through an inheritance.

C. Both money and assets have been earmarked in a will for family members.

### 2. Perceptions of Imbalance in Inheritance Allocations (2)

A. Allocations of inheritance funds or assets are perceived by one of the family members to be unfair or imbalanced.

B. Several family members see unfairness and imbalance in the allocation of the inheritance funds.

C. Family members are in conflict due to the belief that the allocation of inheritance funds or assets were done in an unfair or imbalanced manner.

D. Family members have resolved their disputes about the fairness and balance of allocations of inheritance funds.

### 3. Disputes about How to Divide Assets (3)

A. The deceased family member did not leave explicit directions about how to divide money or assets among siblings.

B. Family members have differing opinions about how money or assets should be divided among siblings.

C. Family members have argued about the fairest way to divide money or assets between siblings.

D. As treatment has progressed, family members have come to an agreement about how to divide money or assets among siblings.

### 4. Favoritism Issues (4)

A. Old feelings of resentment have been rekindled due to the conflicts over the inheritance.

B. Family members have brought up feelings of resentment and beliefs about favoritism that have been held in abeyance for an extended period of time.

C. Negative feelings have arisen between the siblings.

D. Negative feelings have been expressed about the deceased and the experience of favoritism.

E. As treatment has progressed, feelings of favoritism have been resolved and no longer affect emotions between the siblings or toward the deceased.

---

*The numbers in parentheses correlate to the number of the Behavioral Definition statement in the companion chapter with the same title in *The Family Therapy Treatment Planner*, Second Ed. (Dattilio, Jongsma, and Davis) by John Wiley & Sons, 2010.

5. **Suspicions of Unfair Influence (5)**

A. Siblings are suspicious of one another with regard to having influenced the deceased to bias the will in their favor.

B. Family members believe the distribution of money and assets to be unfair due to undue influence on the deceased.

C. Family members claim that they are not receiving their fair share, due to changes made in the will when the deceased was unable to understand the effect of these changes.

6. **Inheritance Distribution Based on Relationship (6)**

A. The distribution of the inheritance was based on the quality of the relationship between the offspring and the parent prior to death.

B. Family members that have had a close relationship with the deceased seem to have obtained a larger portion of the inheritance.

C. Family members who did not have a very close relationship with the deceased are upset that their distribution of the inheritance has been diminished.

D. Family members are more at peace with the distribution of the inheritance, and the quality of the relationship with the deceased.

7. **Decreased Communication between Siblings (7)**

A. Siblings refuse to speak with each other.

B. Family gatherings, holidays, and other special events have become more difficult since siblings refuse to speak with each other subsequent to an inheritance dispute.

C. Siblings often talk with each other through other family members, but not directly.

D. As treatment has progressed, relationships have been healed, and the siblings are more capable of socializing and communicating with each other.

## INTERVENTIONS IMPLEMENTED

1. **Collect Facts (1)***

A. Facts regarding the inheritance asset distribution were collected from legal documents.

B. Facts about the inheritance asset distribution were collected from various family members.

C. The information about the inheritance asset distribution from legal documents and family members was synthesized.

D. Inconsistencies in information about the inheritance asset distribution were highlighted and resolved.

E. Significant gaps or inconsistencies were identified regarding the inheritance asset distribution, and family members were requested to obtain additional information to provide a more complete picture.

---

*The numbers in parentheses correlate to the number of the Therapeutic Intervention statement in the companion chapter with the same title in *The Family Therapy Treatment Planner*, Second Ed. (Dattilio, Jongsma, and Davis) by John Wiley & Sons, 2010.

### 2. Brainstorm about Deceased's Decision to Distribute Assets (2)

A. Family members were assisted in brainstorming ideas about why the deceased may have arrived at certain decisions to distribute assets in a specific manner.

B. Family members were supported as they identified reasons why the deceased may have directed assets to be distributed in a certain manner.

C. Family members tended to emphasize only accusations toward others and were encouraged to brainstorm other ideas for why assets have been disbursed in the manner decided by the deceased.

D. Family members were helped to work through the emotional impact of the reasons why the deceased made decisions to distribute assets in a specific manner.

E. Family members struggled to identify reasons why the deceased asked for assets to be dispersed in a certain manner and were provided with tentative examples in this area.

### 3. Discuss Specific Resentments (3)

A. Family members were assisted in discussing the specific resentments that have surfaced between siblings.

B. Face-to-face confrontations were used to bring out the resentments that may have surfaced between siblings.

C. Exercises to help increase communication were used to bring resentments to the surface.

D. Family members needing to confront each other were asked to sit opposite each other, look directly into each other's eyes, and softly, respectfully say what they think and feel.

E. Positive feedback was provided to family members when they have been able to communicate the resentments and concerns that have surfaced due to the inheritance.

F. Family members were redirected when they began communicating their resentments in an unhealthy or negative manner.

### 4. Rewrite Will (4)

A. The siblings were asked to rewrite the deceased's will, as they would have liked it to read.

B. Family members have rewritten the deceased's will in the manner that they would have liked it to read, and these ideas were processed.

C. Obvious negatives in each version of the will were highlighted in a matter-of-fact manner.

D. Family members were asked to discuss the effect of the will-rewriting exercise.

E. Family members were supported as they expressed the emotions that developed through the will-rewriting exercise.

F. Family members were quite guarded about expressing their emotions subsequent to the will-rewriting exercise and were urged to be more open in this area.

### 5. Discuss Accepting or Changing the Conditions of the Will (5)

A. Siblings were asked to discuss what it means to accept the conditions of the will the way that it is written.

B. Siblings were assisted in identifying how accepting the conditions of the will as it is written will affect their relationships.

C. Siblings were helped to identify their emotions about accepting the will as it is written.

D. The option of redistributing the inheritance in a manner different than the way the will was written was explored.

E. The options for accepting or changing the will were reviewed and processed.

6. **Explore the Meaning of the Inheritance (6)**

A. Each family member was asked to explore the personal meaning of the inheritance.

B. Family members were asked to identify how the inheritance fulfills their individual needs financially and emotionally.

C. Active listening was provided as family members explored the deeper meaning of the inheritance.

7. **Examine Emotional Impact of the Will (7)**

A. A discussion was held regarding the need for each sibling to gain the parent's love, attention, and acceptance.

B. A connection was made between how each sibling gains the parent's love, attention, and acceptance, and the meaning of the inheritance.

C. The variety of emotions and meanings for the inheritance for each family member were accepted and contrasted.

8. **Facilitate Sharing about Relationships (8)**

A. Siblings were directed to confide in one another regarding their relationship with the deceased.

B. Siblings were assisted and encouraged to confide in one another during the session about their relationship with the deceased.

C. Family members were urged to connect their relationship with the deceased with their self-esteem.

D. Family members were urged to talk with each other outside of the session about their relationship with the deceased.

E. Family members were noted to have been guarded about sharing their experience and beliefs regarding their relationship with the deceased and were urged to do this when they felt safe to do so.

9. **Recommend Mediational Strategies (9)**

A. Family members were encouraged to consider using mediational strategies to reallocate the inheritance.

B. Family members were urged to use mediational strategies to heal previous wounds.

C. Family members were urged to use strategies that would provide a sense of comfort to one another.

D. Family members were supported for their willingness to release allocations to make a more equitable distribution of the inheritance.

## 10. Negotiate More Equitable Distribution (10)

A. Siblings were assisted in negotiating a more equitable formula for distribution of the inheritance.

B. Siblings were assisted in identifying their individual expectations about a more equitable formula for distributing the inheritance.

C. Siblings were noted to have fairly similar ideas about how to distribute the inheritance.

D. Siblings were noted to be rather divergent in their expectations for an equitable formula for distributing the inheritance and were assisted in reconciling these differences.

## 11. Reevaluate Evidence for Suspicions (11)

A. Siblings who are suspicious were assisted in identifying the perceived evidence that supports their suspicions.

B. Siblings were assisted in reevaluating their beliefs about how one or more siblings may have unfairly influenced the deceased to favor them in the will.

C. The beliefs about how siblings may have unfairly influenced the deceased were challenged with new, contrary information that is uncovered during the family meeting.

## 12. Facilitate Alternative Communication Methods (12)

A. A brainstorming session was held in which siblings were asked to consider alternative methods to deal with their feelings.

B. Family members identified a variety of methods to express their emotions, rather than silence; positive feedback was provided in this area.

C. Family members struggled to identify alternative methods for expressing their feelings and were provided with tentative examples in this area (e.g., assertiveness, "I" messages, active listening).

D. Family members were encouraged to use alternative methods to increase their communication rather than using silence to communicate their feelings.

E. Family members were reinforced for using healthy communication rather than the use of silence to deal with their feelings.

F. Family members have continued to use silence as a way to express their feelings and were urged to be more communicative in this area.

## 13. Role-Play Communication Strategies (13)

A. The family members were encouraged to role-play communication strategies.

B. Family members were assisted in role-playing communication strategies to help express their feelings.

C. Family members were encouraged to implement the communication strategies *in vivo*.

## 14. Assess Psychopathological Reasons for Suspicions (14)

A. Suspicious family members were assessed for any additional psychopathology that may be contributing to the suspicions.

B. Suspicious family members were assessed and identified as suffering from paranoia, depression, or delusions.

C. Suspicious family members were referred for psychological testing.

D. Suspicious family members were referred for a separate clinical evaluation and treatment.

E. Suspicious family members were assessed, but no additional psychopathology was identified.

# INTERFAMILIAL DISPUTES OVER WILLS AND INHERITANCE

## CLIENT PRESENTATION

### 1. An Uneven Inheritance (1)*

A. A parent has died, leaving beneficiaries with an uneven distribution of the inheritance.

B. Some beneficiaries have received a greater portion of the inheritance from the decedent than others.

C. Some beneficiaries have received a portion of the inheritance, and others have received nothing at all.

### 2. Suspicions of Unfair Influence (2)

A. Beneficiaries are suspicious of one another with regard to having influenced the deceased to bias the will in their favor.

B. Family members believe the distribution of money and assets to be unfair due to undue influence on the deceased.

C. Family members claim that they are not receiving their fair share due to changes made in the will when the deceased was unable to understand the effect of these changes.

### 3. Hostility (3)

A. Family members reported that intense hostility and resentments have built toward the family member(s) who received the larger amount of the inheritance.

B. The family members that have received the lesser inheritance described their justification for their hostile behavior toward the larger beneficiary.

C. The family member that received the larger portion of the estate described the unfairness of the hostile behavior from other family members.

D. As treatment has progressed, the family members have decreased their hostile behavior toward their loved ones.

### 4. Demands for Redistribution (4)

A. Family member(s) make demands of the beneficiaries of the larger amounts of the inheritance to share their portion with the others in order to even out the distribution.

B. Family members have made various threats of how they will respond to a failure to redistribute the inheritance (i.e., violence, estrangement, legal suits).

C. As treatment has progressed, family members have decreased their call for a redistribution of the inheritance.

D. As treatment has progressed, a redistribution of the inheritance has been agreed upon.

---

*The numbers in parentheses correlate to the number of the Behavioral Definition statement in the companion chapter with the same title in *The Family Therapy Treatment Planner*, Second Ed. (Dattilio, Jongsma, and Davis) by John Wiley & Sons, 2010.

## 5. Favoritism Conflicts (5)

A. Conflict and fighting has developed between family members who are beneficiaries over the inequitable distribution.

B. The symbolic nature of the favoritism expressed within the decedent's wishes has been emphasized.

C. As treatment has progressed, favoritism conflicts have been substantially resolved.

## 6. Estrangement (6)

A. Conflict and fighting have continued for an extended period of time due to inheritance discrepancies.

B. As a result of the conflict and fighting, family members have entered into major battles with each other.

C. Family dynamics are dominated by the disagreements between family members.

D. Siblings refuse to speak with each other.

E. Siblings often talk with each other through other family members, but not directly.

F. Family members have become estranged from their family-of-origin.

G. As treatment has progressed, the estrangement between family members has eased.

H. Family members have resolved their conflicts.

## 7. Resentment about Keepsakes (7)

A. Family members express resentment about how keepsake items of sentimental value formerly belonging to the deceased have been distributed among family members.

B. Distribution of keepsake items is perceived by one of the family members to be unfair or imbalanced.

C. Family members are in conflict due to the belief that the keepsakes were allocated in an unfair or imbalanced manner.

D. Family members are suspicious of each other for taking items of the deceased quickly after his/her death.

E. Family members have resolved their disputes about the fairness and balance of allocations of keepsake items.


# INTERVENTIONS IMPLEMENTED

## 1. Identify Thoughts and Emotions (1)*

A. The family members were asked to identify their specific thoughts and feelings in regard to the details of the will.

B. Active listening was used as the family members expressed thoughts and feelings about the details of the will.

C. Family members were encouraged to listen and accept the emotions of the other family members in regard to the details of the will.

*The numbers in parentheses correlate to the number of the Therapeutic Intervention statement in the companion chapter with the same title in *The Family Therapy Treatment Planner*, Second Ed. (Dattilio, Jongsma, and Davis) by John Wiley & Sons, 2010.

## 2. Probe for Inferences (2)

A. Family members were asked about inferences that they make about the distribution of the estate and how it affects them personally.

B. Possible inferences were reflected to the family members about the distribution of the estate (i.e., favoritism, manipulation, punishment, justice).

C. Family members were supported as they aired their beliefs about what the inheritance decisions may mean.

## 3. Discuss Personal Hurt (3)

A. Family members were assisted in discussing the specific hurts and resentments that have surfaced due to the estate distribution.

B. Support and active listening were used to bring out resentments that may have surfaced because of the allocation of the inheritance.

C. Exercises to help increase communication were used to bring resentments to the surface.

D. Family members needing to confront each other were asked to sit opposite each other, look directly into each other's eyes and softly, respectfully say what they think and feel.

E. Positive feedback was provided to the family members, as they have been able to communicate the resentments and concerns that have surfaced due to the inheritance.

F. Family members were redirected when they began communicating their resentments in an unhealthy or negative manner.

## 4. Discuss Previous Expectations (4)

A. Family members were asked to discuss what their expectations were prior to the estate being disbursed.

B. Family members were supported and encouraged as they described their expectations that the estate would be dispersed in a certain manner.

C. It was reflected to the family member that the expected disbursement appears to have been reasonable.

D. It was reflected to the family member that the expected disbursement does not appear to have been reasonable or fair to others.

## 5. Discuss Violation of Expectations (5)

A. Family members were asked to discuss where their prior expectations were violated by the actual disbursement of the estate.

B. Family members were supported and encouraged as they described how their expectations were violated.

C. It was reflected to the family members that the sense of having their expectations violated appears to have been reasonable.

D. It was reflected to the family member that the sense of having their expectations violated does not appear to be reasonable or fair to others.

E. The family members were asked about resentment toward the deceased.

### 6. Discuss Suspicions (6)

A. Family members were asked about their suspicions about the possibility of the deceased having been manipulated by others.

B. Family members that are suspicious of pre-death manipulation were assisted in identifying the perceived evidence that supports their suspicions.

C. The family members were assisted in reevaluating their beliefs about how one or more family members may have unfairly influenced the deceased to favor them in the will.

D. The beliefs about how family members may have unfairly influenced the deceased were challenged with new, contrary information that is uncovered during the family meeting.

### 7. Assess Alternative Reasons for Suspicions (7)

A. The suspicious family members were assessed for any other reasons that may be contributing to the suspicions.

B. The suspicious family member was assisted in identifying defense mechanisms that might lead to such suspicions.

C. The suspicious family member was referred for a separate session to deal with his/her denial and reaction to the deceased's actual wishes.

D. The suspicious family members were assessed, but no other reasons for the suspicions were identified.

### 8. Regulate Emotions (8)

A. Family members were assisted in using cognitive restructuring and emotional regulation skills to cope with the sense of rejection by the decedent and self-worth struggles.

B. The family members were helped to reduce maladaptive emotional and/or behavioral responses to rejection issues through the regular use of adaptive behavioral patterns and emotional skills.

C. The family members were assisted in tolerating the self-concept issues stemming from the sense of rejection and in reducing self-blame.

E. The family members have been noted to be successful in using their cognitive restructuring and emotional regulation skills in managing the effects of the rejection.

### 9. Explore Spitefulness (9)

A. The family members were asked to explore their recollections about the spitefulness that the decedent may have displayed when he/she was alive.

B. The family members were supported as they reviewed the decedent's pattern of spitefulness.

C. The family members were assisted in exploring reasons for the decedent's actions in the will.

### 10. Investigate Redistribution (10)

A. The family members were assisted in reviewing the possibility of negotiating a more equitable formula for distribution of the inheritance.

B. The family members were assisted in identifying their individual expectations about whether they should redistribute the inheritance.

C. Family members were supported for their decisions about whether they should redistribute the inheritance.

D. The family members were noted to have fairly similar ideas about distribution of the inheritance.

E. The family members were noted to be rather divergent in their expectations for redistribution of the inheritance, and were assisted in reconciling these differences.

## 11. Negotiate More Equitable Distribution (11)

A. The family members were assisted in negotiating a more equitable formula for distribution of the inheritance.

B. The family members were assisted in identifying their individual expectations about a more equitable formula for distributing the inheritance.

C. The family members were noted to have fairly similar ideas about how to distribute the inheritance.

D. The family members were noted to be rather divergent in their expectations for an equitable formula for distributing the inheritance, and were assisted in reconciling these differences.

## 12. Discuss Redistribution Effects (12)

A. The redistribution of the inheritance was discussed.

B. Possible effects of the redistribution were reviewed.

C. Family members were reminded that the redistribution may create as much resentment as maintaining the original wishes of the decedent.

## 13. Review Family Dynamics (13)

A. The effect of a possible redistribution on family dynamics was reviewed.

B. The family members were provided with possible scenarios for how the redistribution might affect family dynamics.

C. Family members were reinforced for their understanding of the various family dynamic changes that might occur.

## 14. Identify Alternatives for Balancing Inequities (14)

A. The family was asked to identify alternative ways to balance out inequities.

B. The family was reinforced for developing creative ways that the inequities could be resolved.

C. The family was provided with examples of how to balance out feelings of inequity and strengthening family bonds (e.g., sharing memories, healing wounds between family members).

## 15. Emphasize Relationships over Materialism (15)

A. The family was encouraged to deemphasize the importance and symbolism of material goods and emphasize the nature of close relationships and family bonds.

B. The family agreed that the family bonds were more important than disagreements over the inheritance.

C. The family was directed to read *The Settlement Game* (Morris).

D. The family has read the suggested material on how to work with inheritance/settlements, and the key points were processed.

E. The family has not read the recommended material on how to work through the settlement/inheritance issues, and was redirected to do so.

# INTERRACIAL FAMILY PROBLEMS

## CLIENT PRESENTATION

### 1. Children Experience Rejection (1)*

A. The children of an interracial marriage experience conflict in their community and school.

B. The children of an interracial marriage have experienced rejection by their peers.

C. The children of an interracial marriage have experienced rejection within the community.

D. The family has developed healthy supportive responses to the rejection of the children of the interracial marriage.

### 2. Backlash from the Children (2)

A. The children have resented their mixed race status and believe that the parents have exposed them to a difficult life.

B. The children feel the need to punish their parents for having exposed them to problems due to their mixed race.

C. The parents have experienced behavioral problems and emotional backlash from their children, who resent their mixed race and the difficulties that this has prompted.

D. As treatment has progressed, the children and parents have become more unified in working through the problems presented due to their mixed racial status.

### 3. Parents' Racial Prejudices (3)

A. Despite choosing to be in an interracial marriage, the parents display their own hidden prejudices.

B. The parents have experienced marital conflict due to their hidden racial prejudices.

C. The children have experienced the effects of the parents' marital conflict related to the parent's hidden racial prejudices.

D. The parents have begun to resolve their hidden racial prejudices.

E. The family described an increased level of functioning as the parents have resolved their hidden racial prejudices.

### 4. Children Downplay/Deny their Heritage (4)

A. Interracial children have identified their discontent with their mixed heritage.

B. Interracial children who experience discontent with their mixed heritage attempt to downplay or deny their "undesirable" race.

C. Children attempting to downplay their "undesirable" race have made a habit of ignoring important cultural aspects of their heritage.

---

*The numbers in parentheses correlate to the number of the Behavioral Definition statement in the companion chapter with the same title in *The Family Therapy Treatment Planner*, Second Ed. (Dattilio, Jongsma, and Davis) by John Wiley & Sons, 2010.

D. Children who are discontented with their mixed heritage have made superficial appearance changes to downplay their race (e.g., dying the hair).

E. Children have become more content with their mixed heritage and have decreased the ways in which their race is denied.

### 5. Rejection by Extended Family Members (5)

A. Extended family members are opposed to the parent's interracial partnership.

B. Biracial children have been rejected by the extended family members.

C. Extended family members have rejected the spouse of a different race.

D. The family has become more guarded regarding contact with the extended family.

E. The extended family has become more open and accepting of the parents' interracial partnership.

### 6. Tension from Child's Decision (6)

A. An adult child from the family has selected a mate of another race.

B. Tension has developed in the family in regard to the interracial relationship.

C. Family members have made demeaning or racially insensitive remarks about the new family member.

D. As treatment has progressed family members have become more accepting of the new family member.

## INTERVENTIONS IMPLEMENTED

### 1. Explore Rejection (1)*

A. The children were assisted in exploring the rejection that they have experienced due to their biracial heritage.

B. The children were supported as they explored the experiences of rejection due to their biracial heritage.

C. The children were assisted in identifying the feelings generated by having experienced racial prejudice.

D. The children were cautious about identifying the rejection they have experienced due to their biracial heritage and were encouraged to be open about this when they feel comfortable doing so.

### 2. Explore Emotional Reaction to Racial Prejudice (2)

A. The parents and other family members were helped to explore the feelings generated by having experienced racial prejudice.

B. The feelings generated by the experience of racial prejudice were reviewed, processed, and normalized.

---

*The numbers in parentheses correlate to the number of the Therapeutic Intervention statement in the companion chapter with the same title in *The Family Therapy Treatment Planner*, Second Ed. (Dattilio, Jongsma, and Davis) by John Wiley & Sons, 2010.

C. The family was reluctant to express their feelings about the racial prejudice they have experienced and were urged to do this when they feel safe to do so.

### 3. Empathize with Victims of Social Prejudice (3)

A. Empathy was provided to the children who have endured social prejudice.

B. Comments of respect and support were provided for the children who have had to endure social prejudices.

### 4. Ensure Expression of Feelings (4)

A. A session was facilitated whereby interracial children were able to ventilate their feelings.

B. The parents were encouraged to allow the children to express their feelings without recrimination or fear of retaliation.

C. The children were supported as they expressed their feelings about the problems of being biracial.

D. The parents were supported as they accepted, without recrimination or retaliation, the children's expression of emotions.

E. The parents were redirected when they tended to react negatively to their children's feelings.

F. The children were very cautious about expressing their feelings about being biracial and were urged to do this as they feel safe in doing so.

### 5. Role-Play Regarding Anger and Resentment (5)

A. Role-play techniques were used to help the parents connect with their children's sense of anger and resentment.

B. Role-reversal techniques were used to help the parents connect with their children's sense of anger and resentment.

C. As the role-play and role-reversal techniques were used, the parents and children were supported regarding the emotions they have experienced.

### 6. Focus on Parents' Decisions (6)

A. The parents were encouraged to explain their reasons and decisions for marrying and having children in an environment hostile to interracial relationships and children of mixed heritage.

B. The parents were supported as they described their reasons for marrying and having children.

C. The parents were helped to elaborate on the decisions they have made regarding their interracial marriage and having children of mixed heritage.

D. The parents were very cautious about describing their reasons and decisions for marrying and having children in an environment hostile to such decisions and were encouraged to provide this information.

### 7. Direct Parents to Share Experiences of Prejudice (7)

A. The parents were urged to share stories from their own courtship about how they were victims of prejudice.

B. The parents were assisted in expressing their emotions about their experiences of prejudice as a young couple.

C. The parents were encouraged to describe ways they coped with prejudice during their courtship.

### 8. Use Literature to Teach about Successful Mixed-Race Individuals (8)

A. The children were introduced to literature about individuals who have struggled through interracial challenges (e.g., Fredrick Douglass).

B. The children have read information about mixed-race people who have struggled through interracial challenges, and the key points of these stories were reviewed.

C. The children have not read about individuals who have struggled through interracial challenges and were redirected to do so.

### 9. Refer to Mixed-Race Support Group (9)

A. The children were referred to a mixed-race support group, appropriate to their developmental level.

B. The parents were referred to a mixed-race support group within the community.

C. The family has followed up on the referral to attend a mixed-race support group, and their experience was reviewed and processed.

D. Family members have not followed up on the referral to a mixed-race support group and were redirected to do so.

### 10. Explore Parents' Prejudice (10)

A. The parents were assisted in exploring their own prejudices against a particular race.

B. The parents were helped to explore the sources of their prejudice.

C. The parents were assisted in identifying how their prejudice was developed and sustained.

D. The parents were guarded and denied any prejudices against a particular race and were urged to review this in more detail.

### 11. Develop Underlying Needs for Rejection of Race (11)

A. The children were urged to search behind the superficial rejection of their race and to identify the real reason for their desire to be different.

B. The children identified the underlying reasons for their desire to be different and were supported as they expressed these concerns.

C. The children denied any underlying reasons for their rejection of their race, and were provided with tentative examples in this area (e.g., low self-esteem, desire for power and control, fear of prejudicial rejection).

### 12. Explore Positive Identification with Race (12)

A. The children were assisted in identifying ways to positively identify with their particular race.

B. The children were assisted in creating a list of individuals of their race whom they can look up to (e.g., scientists, astronauts, religious leaders, politicians, sports figures, movie stars).

C. The children have developed many ways to identify with their particular race and were provided with positive feedback in this area.

D. The children struggled to identify with their particular race and were provided with tentative examples of how to do this.

### 13. Focus on Fantasies about Race Preference (13)

A. The children were asked to freely express their fantasies of what race they would prefer to be (if they were able to change) and why they would make this choice.

B. The children were directed to make a list of the pros and cons of changing to a specific race.

C. The children's expression of racial preference fantasies and the pros and cons of this change were openly accepted.

D. The children have been cautious about openly expressing their desires regarding race preferences and were encouraged to be more open about this when they feel safe in doing so.

### 14. Develop Avenues of Social Exchange (14)

A. The family was assisted in developing a list of avenues of social exchange and interaction with members of various races.

B. Community activities were identified as a way to develop avenues of social exchange with members of various races.

C. Church activities were suggested as a way to develop avenues of social exchange with members of various races.

D. The family was supported as they used many avenues of social exchange and interaction with members of various races.

E. Family members have not sought out social exchange and interaction with members of various races and were redirected to do so.

### 15. Explore Pain of Family Rejection (15)

A. Today's session focused on the experience of rejection from extended family members.

B. The ways in which rejection from extended family members was prejudice-based was explored.

C. Family members were encouraged to express their feelings that have occurred due to prejudice-based rejection of the children.

D. Family members were guarded about the feelings that resulted from prejudice-based rejection by extended family members and were provided with common experiences and feelings in this area.

### 16. Propose Individual Therapy (16)

A. As some family members have been unable to cope with the rejection expressed by extended family members, individual treatment was proposed.

B. Family members were reinforced for their acceptance of a referral for individual treatment.

C. The course of individual treatment for family members who are struggling with rejection from the extended family was monitored and reinforced.

D. Although individual therapy has been suggested, family members have declined to access this treatment; they were encouraged to reconsider this treatment.

### 17. Explore Underlying Reasons for Rejection (17)

A. The family was led in an exploration of what may lurk behind the grandparents' rejection of their own grandchildren.

B. The children were assisted in gaining a greater understanding of the reasons why grandparents might reject their own grandchildren.

C. The family struggled to identify reasons why the grandparents might reject their own grandchildren and were provided with tentative examples in this area (e.g., jealousy, need to overcontrol).

### 18. Encourage Extended Family Meeting (18)

A. The parent from the rejecting family-of-origin was encouraged to establish a family-of-origin meeting to discuss the issue of inappropriate rejection of the biracial children.

B. The parent of the family that is rejecting the interracial relationship and children was supported for coordinating a meeting to discuss the inappropriate rejection of the biracial children.

C. The family was helped to discuss the inappropriate rejection of the biracial children in an extended family meeting.

D. The family has declined the use of an extended family meeting and was urged to use this helpful resource at a later time.

### 19. Propose a Rebonding Session (19)

A. The formerly rejecting grandparents or extended family members were noted to be more accepting of the biracial children.

B. A rebonding session was proposed in an attempt to heal the wounds of the rejection.

C. A family-of-origin or multigenerational meeting was held to work on rebonding and healing old wounds.

D. The family has declined a rebonding session and was redirected to use this technique when they may need it in the future.

### 20. Teach Coping Strategies for Tolerance (20)

A. The family was taught about the difference between coping with tolerance of the new family member first, then acceptance.

B. The family was assisted in brainstorming ways to display tolerance for the new family member.

C. The family was assisted in developing greater acceptance of the new family member.

D. The reduction in tension within the family was noted.

### 21. Facilitate Familiarity with the Interracial Mate (21)

A. The family was directed to develop familiarity with the new family member in order to ease tension within the family.

B. The family was assisted in brainstorming and implementing ways to gain familiarity with the new family member.

C. The family was reinforced for attempts to gain greater familiarity with the new family member.

D. The family has not developed ways to become more familiar with the family member and was redirected to do so.

## 22. Emphasize New Family Member's Strengths (22)

A. The family was asked to identify the strengths and positive qualities of the family member's choice of a mate.

B. The family was assisted in developing a list of characteristics that they like about the new family member.

C. The family was redirected when they became negative about the new family member's traits.

# INTOLERANCE/DEFENSIVENESS

## CLIENT PRESENTATION

### 1. Rigid Attitudes (1)*

A. Family members display a rigid, consistent attitude that their own behavior, beliefs, feelings, and opinions are right and other family members' are wrong.

B. Family members are much more open to discussion of each other's behaviors, beliefs, feelings, and opinions.

C. Family members have become much more tolerant of each other's behavior, beliefs, feelings, and opinions.

### 2. Closed Mind to Others' Opinions (2)

A. Family members display a refusal to keep an open mind about considering the opinions of other family members.

B. Family members displayed very little desire to entertain or try to understand the beliefs of the other family members.

C. As treatment has progressed, family members have become more open to considering other family members' opinions.

### 3. Irritable Responses toward Others (3)

A. Family members often display irritability toward others' habits or actions.

B. Family members often seem quite irritated with other family members expressing their opinions.

C. Emotional expression is met with negative responses from other family members.

D. As treatment has progressed, family members have become more accepting of other family members' habits, actions, and expression of feelings or opinions.

### 4. Denial of Intolerance (4)

A. Family members have been confronted about their intolerance, but deny any pattern in this area.

B. Family members have shut down and refused to discuss any concerns related to intolerance.

C. Family members have been more open to acknowledging their pattern of intolerance.

### 5. Ultimatums for Change (5)

A. Family members have issued ultimatums that others within the family must make changes.

B. Family members have required each other to choose sides regarding the ultimatums to make changes.

---

*The numbers in parentheses correlate to the number of the Behavioral Definition statement in the companion chapter with the same title in *The Family Therapy Treatment Planner*, Second Ed. (Dattilio, Jongsma, and Davis) by John Wiley & Sons, 2010.

C. Family members report feeling very awkward about having to choose sides regarding the ultimatums.

D. Family members have refused to choose sides regarding the ultimatums, allowing those family members to work out problems without interference or coercion.

E. Family members have discontinued the use of ultimatums to induce change in others.

## INTERVENTIONS IMPLEMENTED

1. **Administer Standardized Assessment (1)\***

A. Each family member was asked to complete a standardized assessment scale of relationship satisfaction.

B. Each family member was requested to complete the *Conflict Tactics Scale* (Strauss and Gelles).

C. Each family member was asked to complete the *Family Awareness Scale* (Kolevzon and Green).

D. Each family member has completed a standardized assessment scale of relationship satisfaction, and the results were reviewed within the session.

E. Family members were interviewed in order to identify relationship satisfaction levels.

F. Family members have not completed the standardized assessment scale of relationship satisfaction, and were redirected to do so.

2. **Summarize Assessment Result (2)**

A. The family was provided feedback about the results of the assessment of the conflict level and relationship satisfaction.

B. Family members were helped to categorize the areas of conflict based on the assessment results.

C. Family members affirmed the areas of conflict as defined by the assessment results.

D. Family members rejected the areas of conflict as defined by the assessment results.

3. **Develop Meaningful Terms (3)**

A. Family members were asked to replace conflict terms that they don't understand with their own terms.

B. Family members identified terms they can relate to and were urged to use these in order to express their concerns about intolerance and defensiveness.

C. Family members were provided with examples of how to change conflict terms into terms they can relate to (e.g., changing "defensive" to "copping an attitude").

4. **Assess Relationship Strengths and Needs (4)**

A. The current strengths and needs of the family relationships were assessed via interviews.

B. Psychological inventories were used to assess the strengths and needs of the relationship.

---

*The numbers in parentheses correlate to the number of the Therapeutic Intervention statement in the companion chapter with the same title in *The Family Therapy Treatment Planner*, Second Ed. (Dattilio, Jongsma, and Davis) by John Wiley & Sons, 2010.

C. The results of the relationship strengths and needs evaluation were shared with the family members.

## 5. Identify Strengths (5)

A. Each family member was asked to describe personal strengths in the current relationships.

B. Family members were provided feedback as they identified their strengths in the current relationships.

C. Each family member was provided feedback by other family members regarding the identified strengths in the current relationships.

D. Family members struggled to identify strengths in their current relationships and were provided with some tentative examples in this area.

## 6. Probe Development of Weaknesses (6)

A. Family members were assisted in identifying their own weaknesses.

B. Family members were assisted in identifying how their weaknesses have developed.

C. Family members were supported as they described how their weaknesses were created and developed.

D. Family members failed to identify their own weaknesses or how they have been developed and were provided tentative examples in this area.

## 7. Assess Family Dynamics (7)

A. The family dynamics and their development were assessed through an interview process.

B. The development of family dynamics was assessed through the use of inventories.

C. The *Family-of-Origin Scale* (Hovestadt et al.) was used to assess the family dynamics.

D. The *Family-of-Origin Questionnaire* (Stewart) was used to assess the family dynamics.

E. The family dynamics assessment results were reviewed, and feedback was provided to the family about how these have developed.

## 8. Request Assessment of How the Family Functions (8)

A. Family members were asked to make an overall assessment of what they do and do not like about how the family functions.

B. Family members were asked to identify the qualities they see as desirable or as undesirable for the family.

C. Family members were asked to identify historical high and low points for the family.

D. Family members were asked to identify what they would change about the family if they could.

E. Family members were open about how the family functions, and their responses were synthesized and reflected to them.

F. Family members were cautious and guarded about their assessment of how the family functions and were urged to be more open in this area.

## 9. Request Honesty about Feelings toward Each Other (9)

A. Family members were encouraged to be honest about their feelings toward other family members.

B. Family members were asked about whether they experience emotions such as jealousy and envy.

C. Family members were reinforced as they were open about the feelings they experience regarding other family members.

D. Family members were guarded and were encouraged to be more open about their feelings regarding the other family members as they feel comfortable doing so.

## 10. Trace Intolerance from Parents' Family-of-Origin (10)

A. The parents' pattern of intolerance, criticism, and judgmental attitudes were traced as to how their family-of-origin may have contributed to these attitudes.

B. It was reflected to the parents that members of their family-of-origin display significant degrees of intolerance, criticism, and judgmental attitudes.

C. The parents' experience of intolerance, criticism, and judgmental attitudes in their family-of-origin was compared to the current family dynamics.

D. The ways in which current family dynamics are reflective of the parents' family-of-origin dynamics were reflected to the parents.

E. It was reflected to the parents that the current family dynamics do not recreate their family-of-origin dynamics.

## 11. Explore Examples of Closed-Mindedness (11)

A. Family members were asked to cite examples of when their ideas were rejected, criticized, or ignored by other family members.

B. The ways in which family members' closed-mindedness led to their rejection of other family members' ideas was reviewed.

C. The feelings related to being rejected by a family member were reviewed.

D. Family members identified anger, frustration, and disappointment due to a family member's closed-mindedness.

## 12. Poll Regarding Open Minds (12)

A. Each family member was asked to identify what it would take to keep an open mind toward others.

B. Family members were supported as they described the preconditions necessary for an open mind toward others.

C. Family members were asked to identify how it would feel to live in an atmosphere of acceptance.

D. Family members' expectations for open-mindedness and acceptance were reviewed and summarized to them.

## 13. Role-Play Regarding Open Minds (13)

A. Role-play techniques were used to teach family members to keep an open mind.

B. One family member was asked to talk to another family member to get them to see a different side of a neutral issue.

C. Role-reversal techniques were used to highlight feelings of hurt and frustration associated with being rejected.

D. Family members were asked to provide feedback about their experience within the role-plays.

E. Family members were reinforced for their more open-minded comments.

### 14. Assign Homework Regarding Realistic Situations (14)

A. Family members were assigned homework to apply role-playing of tolerance and respect to try to get other family members to respect their point of view.

B. Family members have attempted the techniques to get another family member to respect another point of view, and the results of this were reviewed in session.

C. Family members have not attempted the homework assignment for changing a family member's point of view and were redirected to do so.

### 15. Explore Irritability (15)

A. Family members' experience of irritability was explored.

B. Triggers for irritability were identified.

C. How each family member expresses irritability was reviewed.

D. Feedback was provided to family members regarding how they experience and express irritability.

### 16. Explore Impact of Irritability (16)

A. The ways in which expressions of irritability have impacted individual family members was assessed.

B. Family members were encouraged to express how other family members' irritability has had a direct impact on them.

C. The level of manipulation attained through expressions of irritability was assessed.

D. It was reflected to family members that they often use irritability to try to manipulate or control others.

E. It was reflected to family members that irritability does not seem to be used as a way to manipulate or control others.

### 17. Teach Alternatives to Irritability as Manipulation (17)

A. It was reflected to family members that irritability has been used to try to control or manipulate other family members.

B. Family members were taught about how using irritability to control or manipulate others could be destructive.

C. Alternative ways to try to achieve behavior or attitude change in others were reviewed.

D. Family members were taught assertiveness techniques to use to get their needs met.

E. Family members were taught to use positive statements as a way to get others to meet their needs.

### 18. Brainstorm Ways to Express Frustration (18)

A. Family members were assisted in brainstorming more constructive techniques for expressing frustration other than irritability.

B. Family members were taught about the use of "I" messages to express anger and frustration.

C. Family members were encouraged to write letters to express their negative emotions.

D. Family members were encouraged to take a time-out before expressing their feelings.

E. Family members were encouraged to be accepting of alternative modes of expressing anger and frustration.

F. Positive feedback was provided for the use of alternative constructive methods of expressing anger and frustration.

G. Family members have not used alternative constructive methods to express anger and frustration and were redirected to do so.

## 19. Suggest Tension-Reduction Techniques (19)

A. Tension-reduction techniques were suggested to the family.

B. Family members were taught how to use meditation as a way to reduce tension.

C. Family members were taught the use of deep breathing exercises to reduce their tension.

D. Family members were taught the use of journaling to reduce their frequency of irritable responses.

E. Family members were taught thought-restructuring techniques that will help to decrease tension and irritable reactions.

F. Family members were reinforced for their frequent use of techniques to decrease tension and reduce irritable responses.

G. Family members have not used helpful techniques to reduce their experience of tension and frustration and were redirected to do so.

## 20. Work through an Actual Conflict (20)

A. Family members were asked to work through an actual conflict among themselves while in session.

B. The process of working through a family conflict was observed, and ineffective strategies were pointed out.

C. Family members were provided with examples of ineffective strategies or communication techniques (e.g., talking when others are talking, misinterpretation of statements, cutting each other off).

D. Family members were verbally reinforced for being open to the feedback provided to them.

E. Family members were intolerant of the feedback being provided to them in session, and this was reflected to them.

## 21. Propose Alternative Strategy for Conflict Resolution (21)

A. The family's pattern of maladaptive conflict-resolution interaction was confronted, and alternative strategies were introduced.

B. Family members were urged to use techniques such as active listening, clarification, and pursuing closure.

C. Family members were directed to read *The Anatomy of Peace* (Arbinger Institute).

D. Family members were encouraged to read *The Joy of Conflict Resolution* (Harper).

  E. Family members have read the assigned material on conflict resolution, and key points were reviewed.

  F. Family members have not read the assigned material on conflict resolution and were redirected to do so.

## 22. Model and Role-Play Conflict-Resolution Techniques (22)

  A. Modeling techniques were used to teach the family members effective conflict-resolution techniques.

  B. Role-play techniques were used to teach effective conflict-resolution strategies.

  C. An argument was staged within the session, and each family member was coached on how to respond.

  D. Role-play was used to exemplify effective and noneffective ways to interact.

## 23. Teach Problem-Solving Skills (23)

  A. The family was taught problem-solving skills.

  B. The family was taught to define the problem narrowly, brainstorm options for solutions, generate the pros and cons of each option, select one option for implementation, implement the selected option, evaluate the results, and adjust the solution as needed.

  C. The family was directed to apply the problem-solving techniques as a group exercise.

## 24. Review Implementation of Conflict Resolution

  A. The family's use of conflict resolution and problem-solving skills were applied to every day issues.

  B. The family was reinforced for successfully applying the conflict resolution and problem-solving skills.

  C. The family was redirected for situations in which they did not properly use the conflict resolution and problem-solving skills.

## 25. Confront Intolerance (25)

  A. Family members who engage in denial of intolerance were directly confronted.

  B. Confrontation of family members who deny their intolerance was urged and facilitated.

  C. Family members were reinforced for being direct with an intolerant family member.

  D. As denial has decreased for intolerant family members, they were reinforced for being more accepting of how this occurs.

## 26. Describe Denial as a Defense Mechanism (26)

  A. The family was taught that denial can be a primitive form of defense.

  B. The use of denial was suggested as a response to underlying feelings of helplessness or vulnerability.

  C. Family members denying their own intolerance were asked to consider how feelings of helplessness or vulnerability might contribute to their denial.

  D. Family members were reinforced when they made comments that were more accepting and acknowledged their own pattern of intolerance.

### 27. Expression of Vulnerability (27)

A. Encouragement was provided as family members identified feelings that tend to underlie their denial of vulnerability.

B. Verbal support was provided to family members as they openly expressed their feelings of vulnerability.

C. Family members were guarded about expressing their vulnerability and were encouraged to open up about these feelings as they feel safe to do so.

### 28. Assess for Blaming Behaviors (28)

A. Family members were assessed for the presence of blaming behaviors.

B. Blaming behaviors were identified and were connected to the family members' denial of taking personal responsibility.

C. The focus of treatment was shifted toward family members' pattern of blaming.

### 29. Educate about How Ultimatums Stall Problem Resolution (29)

A. The family was educated about how issuing ultimatums as a means of controlling others usually stalls problem solving.

B. Specific examples of how ultimatums decrease the ability to resolve problems were provided to family members.

C. Family members were supported as they described their own examples of how ultimatums have resulted in decreased problem resolution.

### 30. Probe for Frustration That Leads to Ultimatums (30)

A. Family members who tend to issue ultimatums were helped to identify feelings of frustration.

B. Family members were supported and reinforced when they expressed feelings of frustration instead of issuing ultimatums.

C. Despite identifying their own level of frustration, family members continue to issue ultimatums and were provided with additional feedback in this area.

### 31. Contract for Discontinuation of Ultimatums (31)

A. A behavioral contract was developed to stipulate that family members would not issue ultimatums to one another.

B. A contract was developed to specify in concrete terms which ultimatums are to be avoided.

C. Family members were supported as they agreed to discontinue issuing ultimatums.

### 32. Suggest Family Meeting Rather than Ultimatums (32)

A. Family members were urged to hold a family meeting when feeling the need to issue an ultimatum.

B. Family members were urged to use communication during a family meeting to get changes to their satisfaction.

C. Family members have used family meetings rather than issuing ultimatums, and the benefits of this practice were reviewed.

D. Family members have not used family meetings in place of issuing ultimatums and were provided with examples of how this could be beneficial.

### 33. Review Ultimatum as Exerting Power (33)

A. The family was taught how ultimatums may be used as a means of exerting power.

B. The family was taught about how ultimatums may be used as a way to call attention to oneself.

C. A discussion was held about who has power and control in the family, and how this power and control is governed.

D. Patterns of power and control were reviewed with the family.

E. Family members were supported as they acknowledged how ultimatums have been used to exert power or to call attention to themselves.

F. Family members were encouraged to use other options to exert their power or to call attention to themselves.

### 34. Brainstorm Restructuring of Power and Control (34)

A. The family was assisted in brainstorming ways in which power and control can be restructured within the family.

B. The family was assisted in developing a list of tasks or decision areas in which each family member has some strengths.

C. A discussion was held in which family members were asked to develop scenarios where family members could take the lead in areas in which they have strengths.

D. The family has given over leadership in some areas to those who have strengths in those areas, and the benefits and struggles of this were reviewed and processed.

E. The family has not relinquished leadership of strength areas to the capable family members, and was redirected to attempt this technique.

### 35. Use Give-and-Take Exercises (35)

A. Give-and-take exercises were used to help family members share power and control within the family.

B. Family members were encouraged to share taking the lead in planning an activity or directing a major task in the household that needs to be accomplished.

C. Family members were asked to express their feelings about being in command, as well as about being on the receiving end of planning and directing an activity.

D. A discussion was held about how each family member has skills that may dictate when to take a lead role.

### 36. Play the Ungame (36)

A. The Ungame (Zakich) was used to help family members change their patterns of power and control.

B. The family has played the Ungame, and their experience was processed.

C. The family played the Ungame within the session, with breaks from time to time to review their experience.

D. The family has not played the Ungame and was redirected to do so.

### 37. Normalize Expectation of Frustration (37)

A. The family was encouraged to acknowledge the common occurrence of being frustrated with each other.

B. Family members were encouraged to see frustration with each other as a common situation for all families.

C. Family members were encouraged to use acceptance when they become frustrated rather than lashing out in intolerance.

### 38. Propose Acceptance of Irritating Behaviors (38)

A. Family members were taught about the concept of simply accepting the other family member's irritating behaviors since they are unlikely to change.

B. Acceptance of irritating behaviors was emphasized as a means of coping with that irritating behavior.

C. Family members were provided with examples of how accepting an irritating behavior can reduce tension.

D. Family members were provided with positive feedback as they worked on accepting other family members' irritating behaviors.

E. Family members rejected the idea of accepting irritating behaviors and were urged to consider this in the future.

### 39. Discuss Coping Strategies (39)

A. A discussion was held regarding the use of coping strategies for building family members' tolerance levels.

B. Family members were encouraged to engage in self-talk that would facilitate acceptance of other family members' shortcomings.

C. Family members were encouraged to read the book *Simple Courtesies* (Gallant).

D. Family members have read the assigned material on accepting others, and key points were reviewed.

E. Family members have not read the assigned material on accepting others and were redirected to do so.

# JEALOUSY/INSECURITY

## CLIENT PRESENTATION

### 1. Tension and Conflict (1)*

A. Family members have displayed a pattern of jealousy and insecurity toward each other.

B. The behavior resulting from jealousy and insecurity has created feelings of tension within the family.

C. Family members are often in conflict with each other due to the feelings and behaviors related to jealousy and insecurity.

D. As family members have become less jealous and more secure, tension and conflict have been reduced.

### 2. Arguments about Time Spent with Each Other (2)

A. Family members report limited time spent with each other on social and recreational activities.

B. Family members state that they prefer being involved in social and recreational activities with others rather than with family members.

C. The family often argues about how much time family members spend with each other.

D. As the family has grown closer, their pattern of social and recreational activities with each other has increased.

### 3. Accusations of Favoritism (3)

A. Family members have perceived a pattern of parental favoritism.

B. Family members believe that the parents display a lack of interest and concern for certain family members.

C. Family members often accuse the parents of displaying favoritism toward some children and showing a lack of interest for other children.

D. Family members have become more balanced and accepting of the interests and concern for all family members.

### 4. Control over Other's Activities (4)

A. The jealous family member often attempts to control the actions of other family members.

B. The jealous family member often demands that other family members stay at home, limits family members' access to important resources, or does other controlling actions to restrict the other family members' activity.

C. The controlling family member is fearful of losing the attention of the other family members.

D. Attempts to control family members have resulted in a backlash of resentment.

---

*The numbers in parentheses correlate to the number of the Behavioral Definition statement in the companion chapter with the same title in *The Family Therapy Treatment Planner*, Second Ed. (Dattilio, Jongsma, and Davis) by John Wiley & Sons, 2010.

E. As the family has made progress, the jealous family member has shown a decreased pattern of attempting to control the other family members' freedom.

F. The level of resentment has been decreased as the jealous family member has decreased attempts at overcontrol.

### 5. Need for Attention (5)

A. The insecure family member appears to need a high level of attention.

B. The insecure family member often displays dependent behaviors in order to obtain attention from others.

C. The insecure family member is often reluctant to make decisions, avoids disagreements, or becomes a "doormat" due to feelings of insecurity.

D. As the insecure family member has become more secure, the level of dependent behaviors has decreased.

### 6. Children's Acting-Out (6)

A. The children appear to be experiencing emotional struggles related to jealousy and insecurity.

B. The children tend to act out their emotions in their behavior.

C. The children have engaged in delinquent or incorrigible behaviors, which appear to be due to their feelings of jealousy and insecurity.

D. As the emotional needs have been resolved for the children, the level of acting-out has decreased.

### 7. Rageful Jealousy (7)

A. A family member has expressed an insatiable pattern of jealousy that is pathological.

B. The jealous family member often becomes rageful toward other family members.

C. The jealous family member has physically destroyed property of other family members.

D. The jealous family member has become assaultive toward other family members.

E. Family members have taken steps to create safety in spite of the jealous family member's rages.

F. The jealous family member has decreased the pattern of rageful outbursts.

### 8. Mistrust (8)

A. One family member displays a severe degree of mistrust over another family member's actions, motives, and time spent away from family.

B. Family members display strong reactions and responses to the actions of another family member.

C. As treatment has progressed, the family members have decreased their mistrust of each other.

## INTERVENTIONS IMPLEMENTED

### 1. Focus on Emotions Regarding Jealousy (1)*

A. Family members were asked to identify specific situations during which jealousy has arisen.

B. The family member identified as experiencing jealousy was asked to identify the emotions that were experienced during the situations noted by family members.

C. Family members were asked to identify the feelings they experienced when seeing another family member display jealousy.

D. The emotions experienced were synthesized and reflected to the family members.

### 2. Compare Perceptions (2)

A. The interpretations of jealous and nonjealous family members regarding a jealousy-inducing event were contrasted.

B. Comparisons were made between the jealous and nonjealous family members' perceptions.

C. Family members were supported for being able to identify how interpretations varied among family members.

### 3. Identify Specific Conflicts (3)

A. The jealousy and insecurity patterns were identified by having family members describe specific conflicts.

B. Family members were asked to role-play a situation that induced jealousy or insecurity.

C. Family members were supported as they described specific conflicts that created jealousy and insecurity.

D. Family members were rather guarded about identifying any pattern of jealousy or insecurity and were probed with more specific questions and examples of how this sometimes occurs.

### 4. Assess for Children's Modeling (4)

A. The children were assessed for jealousy or insecurity feelings and behaviors.

B. The children's jealousy and insecurity were assessed as to how they related to jealousy and insecurity in older family members.

C. The family was supported as they identified connections between the children's feeling of jealousy and insecurity and those types of behaviors modeled by older family members.

D. It was reflected to the family that the children do not display a significant degree of jealousy or insecurity.

### 5. Focus on Effects of Jealousy and Insecurity (5)

A. Family members were urged to express how they have been affected by the dynamics of jealousy and insecurity within the family.

B. Verbal support and encouragement was provided as family members described the ways in which they have experienced the effects of jealousy and insecurity.

*The numbers in parentheses correlate to the number of the Therapeutic Intervention statement in the companion chapter with the same title in *The Family Therapy Treatment Planner*, Second Ed. (Dattilio, Jongsma, and Davis) by John Wiley & Sons, 2010.

C. Family members were guarded about expressing how jealousy and insecurity has affected them and were urged to be more open in this area.

### 6. Educate about Irrational Thoughts (6)

A. Family members experiencing jealousy were explored for irrational thoughts.
B. The family was educated about how jealousy is often related to insecurity and possessiveness.
C. Family members were referred to reading material about jealousy and insecurity.
D. Family members were asked to read *The Psychology of Jealousy and Envy* (Salovey).
E. Family members were directed to read *Overcoming Jealousy* (Dryden).
F. Key topics from the reading about jealousy and insecurity were processed.
G. Family members have not obtained further education through reading about jealousy and envy and were redirected to do so.

### 7. Brainstorm Rational Self-Talk (7)

A. Family members were asked to brainstorm more rational self-talk, that can replace irrational thoughts that trigger jealousy.
B. Family members were supported as they identified a variety of different interpretations or more rational self-talk.
C. Family members were urged to be creative about alternative ways to view an event.
D. Family members have not identified many rational self-talk statements that can replace irrational thoughts and were provided with tentative examples in this area.

### 8. Teach REBT (8)

A. The family was educated about Rational Emotive Behavior Therapy (REBT), and how to restructure thoughts.
B. The family was assisted in applying Rational Emotive Behavior Therapy (REBT) theory to feelings of jealousy.
C. Family members were taught about REBT's concepts of Antecedent adversities, Beliefs about those adversities, the emotional and behavioral Consequences of those beliefs, and Disputing the irrational beliefs which leads to realistic thinking (ABCD).
D. The family members were provided with positive feedback as they showed how to apply the ABCD method to reduce jealousy and insecurity.
E. Family members failed to use the ABCD method to reduce jealousy and insecurity, and were provided with tentative examples of how to do this.

### 9. List Jealous/Insecure Behaviors (9)

A. Family members were asked to develop a list of jealous and insecure behaviors noted within the family members.
B. Each family member was assisted in creating a list of jealous or insecure behaviors at their own developmental level.
C. Lists of jealous and insecure behaviors were reviewed within the session.
D. Family members have not worked diligently to develop lists of jealous or insecure behaviors displayed within the family and were redirected to do so.

### 10. Develop Alternative Behaviors (10)

A. The family was asked to develop alternative, healthy behaviors to be used instead of the jealous or insecure behaviors.

B. Family members were supported and reinforced as they identified healthy, alternative behaviors instead of the jealous and insecure behaviors.

C. The family struggled to identify healthy alternative behaviors to jealousy and was guided with tentative examples in this area.

### 11. Connect Insecure Thoughts to Destructive Behavior (11)

A. Family members were taught how insecure thoughts lead to jealousy, which leads to emotional deterioration and destructive behavior.

B. Specific examples of how insecure thoughts have lead to destructive behaviors were identified with the family members.

C. Family members were provided with specific examples of how insecure thoughts have led to jealousy, emotional deterioration, and destructive behavior.

### 12. Recommend Interventions for Jealous Rage (12)

A. Family members were provided with a variety of alternatives when they experience jealous rage.

B. Family members were taught to use time-out procedures when they feel jealous rage.

C. Family members were taught deep-breathing techniques for behavioral control of anger.

D. Nonjealous family members were directed to prompt the rageful, jealous individual to use alternative coping behaviors.

E. Family members' use of alternative coping behaviors when experiencing feelings of rage were reviewed and processed.

F. Family members have not used alternative coping behaviors when feeling rage and were reminded about this helpful technique.

### 13. Search for Coalitions/Favoritism (13)

A. Family dynamics were searched for patterns of favoritism displayed by one family member toward another.

B. Family dynamics were consistently assessed for the presence of coalitions between or against family members.

C. Patterns of favoritism or coalitions were reflected to the family.

D. No family patterns of favoritism or coalitions were identified.

### 14. Confront Favoritism (14)

A. Favoritism was identified in family interaction patterns and was immediately confronted.

B. The reasons for the pattern of favoritism were assessed and reviewed.

C. The family was assisted in developing insight into why favoritism occurs.

### 15. Emphasize Unhealthy, Devastating Effects of Favoritism (15)

A. Family members were taught how favoritism can be unhealthy within a family.

B. The potentially devastating effects of a pattern of favoritism were emphasized.

C. Family members were reinforced as they identified how favoritism can have a very negative effect on family members.

D. Family members tended to downplay any negative effect of favoritism and were provided with additional feedback and examples in this area.

## 16. Use Role-Reversal Techniques (16)

A. Role-reversal techniques were used to teach how it feels to be on the receiving end of exclusion and favoritism.

B. Family members were directed to change roles and act out how favoritism occurs.

C. Family members were asked to provide their emotional response to the role-reversal experience.

D. Family members were supported as they expressed emotions of rejection, resentment, and guilt.

## 17. Define and Review Overcontrol (17)

A. The concept of overcontrol of others was presented to the family.

B. Overcontrol was defined as when one family member wants to dictate other family members' personal choices.

C. The family was asked to provide examples of overcontrol of others.

D. Support and encouragement were provided to family members as they described situations in which family members have attempted to overcontrol others.

E. Family members were provided with tentative examples of overcontrol of others.

## 18. Review Etiology and Effects of Overcontrol (18)

A. The family was assisted in identifying how overcontrol of others began.

B. Overcontrol of others was connected to feelings of insecurity or jealousy.

C. Family members were assisted in identifying how overcontrol of others only provides a false sense of security.

## 19. Process Fears about Being Less Controlling (19)

A. Family members were asked about their emotional reaction to giving up overcontrol of others.

B. Family members were supported as they identified how giving up overcontrol of others would be fearful and uncertain for them.

C. Family members were assisted in working through their emotions regarding giving up overcontrol of others.

## 20. Solicit Nonaggression Agreement (20)

A. All family members were asked to agree to discontinue any aggressive or assaultive behavior.

B. The family was assisted in developing a policy of refusing to tolerate aggressive or assaultive behavior.

C. A behavioral contract was developed with clear ramifications for the response should the nonaggression agreement be broken.

D. Family members have become aggressive, and the family was directed to implement the behavioral consequences for such aggression.

E. Family members have not responded to aggression by other family members with the behavioral consequences and were redirected to do so.

F. Family members were supported for their significant decrease in aggressive or assaultive types of behaviors.

## 21. Brainstorm Alternatives to Aggression (21)

A. The family was assisted in identifying alternative ways to express jealousy and insecurity, without becoming aggressive.

B. The family was reinforced for identifying many ways of expressing feelings without becoming aggressive.

C. It was reflected to the family that they have selected helpful responses to feelings of jealousy or insecurity.

D. Family members were provided with tentative examples of how to deal with jealousy and insecurity.

## 22. Refer for Adjunctive Treatment (22)

A. Family members who cannot control their aggression or anger were referred for adjunctive treatment.

B. A referral was made for individual therapy for anger control.

C. A referral was made for group treatment of anger control.

D. A referral was made to a psychiatrist for medication to assist the family member in attaining anger control.

E. Family members referred for adjunctive treatment have followed up on this treatment, and the benefits were processed.

F. Family members have not followed up on the adjunctive treatment and were redirected to do so.

## 23. Encourage Support for Outside Treatment (23)

A. Family members were encouraged to be supportive and encouraging to the family member requiring outside treatment.

B. Family members were reinforced for providing support and encouragement to the family member requiring outside treatment.

C. Family members have not been supportive of the family member requiring outside treatment and were redirected to do so.

## 24. Trace Etiology of Dependent, Insecure Behaviors (24)

A. The family was assisted in identifying the origin of dependent, insecure behaviors.

B. The history and pattern of dependent, insecure behaviors were reviewed within the family.

C. The pattern of dependent, insecure behaviors within the family was synthesized and reflected to the family members.

D. The family members had little insight into how dependent or insecure behaviors have been created and supported and were provided with tentative examples of how this occurs.

### 25. Explore Enabling (25)

A. The ways in which family members may be enabling dependent behaviors were explored.

B. Specific patterns of enabling of dependent behavior were identified and reflected to the family members.

C. Family members were supported as they acknowledged their pattern of enabling of dependent behavior.

D. Family members denied any pattern of enabling of dependent behavior and were encouraged to continue to monitor this dynamic.

### 26. Teach about Effects of Dependent Behavior (26)

A. The family was taught about how dependent behaviors often interfere with the family functioning.

B. Family members were provided with tentative examples of how dependent behaviors affect the family (e.g., one family member constantly needing to rely on other family members, restricting their mobility, independence, and thwarting their personal growth).

C. The family was supported as they identified how dependent behaviors have interfered with the family functioning.

### 27. Encourage Independent Behaviors (27)

A. The dependent family member was encouraged to practice independent behaviors.

B. The dependent family member was encouraged to use assertiveness, "I" messages, and self-affirmation.

C. The dependent family member was verbally reinforced for more independent behaviors.

D. The dependent family member has not used more independent communication and was encouraged to do so.

### 28. Reinforce Family Support for Independence (28)

A. The family was encouraged to provide support to the family member attempting to acquire more independent behaviors.

B. Family members encouraging the dependent family member in the quest for independence were verbally reinforced.

C. Family members have not been able to identify any examples of their support for the dependent family member's independent behavior and were redirected to provide this support.

### 29. Explore for Delinquent Behavior (29)

A. The family was explored for delinquent or incorrigible behavior.

B. The family was supported as they identified delinquent and incorrigible types of behaviors.

C. A discussion was held with the family about how delinquent or incorrigible behavior may be a means for children to act out the fairness imbalance within the family.

D. The family denied any pattern of delinquent or incorrigible behaviors, and this was accepted.

### 30. Encourage Parents' Unity (30)

A. The parents were directed to pull together to confront the child's incorrigible behavior.

B. The parents were urged to work together as a team in dealing with the child's incorrigible behavior.

C. The parents were urged to reinforce more appropriate, desirable behaviors in the incorrigible child.

D. Differences between the parents' approach to the delinquent child were reviewed, processed, and either synthesized or accepted.

E. The parents have failed to work together as a team to confront the child's incorrigible behavior and reinforce desirable behaviors; they were provided with additional assistance in overcoming this barrier.

## 31. Develop Behavioral Contract (31)

A. The parents were assisted in devising a behavioral contract against delinquent or incorrigible behavior.

B. The consequences for specific behaviors was clearly defined.

C. The rewards for replacing delinquent behavior with healthy behavior were clearly delineated.

D. The parents were reinforced for using behavioral contracts.

E. The parents have not used the behavioral contract on a regular basis and were redirected to do so.

## 32. Facilitate Open Expression of Perception of the Family (32)

A. The delinquent child was encouraged to provide feedback regarding the difficulties perceived within the family.

B. The delinquent child was supported for the honest expression of perceptions and reactions to the difficulties in the family.

C. When family members attempted to restrict the delinquent child in expressing perceptions about the family, this restriction was redirected.

## 33. Refer Delinquent Child for Treatment (33)

A. The delinquent child was referred for individual treatment as the delinquent behaviors have continued.

B. The family has followed up on individual treatment for the delinquent child, and the benefits of this treatment were reviewed.

C. The family has not followed up on individual treatment for the delinquent child and was redirected to do so.

## 34. Explore Alternative Living Arrangements (34)

A. Alternative living arrangements for the delinquent child were explored.

B. Group homes, residential treatment, or foster homes were considered as alternative living arrangements for the delinquent child.

C. Family members have been overwhelmed by the child's delinquent behaviors, and plans have been made to move the delinquent child to a different setting.

D. Although alternative living arrangements have been reviewed, none has been selected.

### 35. Educate about Mental Illness (35)

A. The family members were educated about mental illness (e.g., paranoia, major depression, bipolar disorder).

B. Family members were taught about the difference between jealous/insecure behaviors and mental illness.

C. It was reflected to the family members that other family members are jealous/insecure, but not mentally ill.

D. The family members' questions about mental illness symptoms were answered.

### 36. Use Objective Assessment Techniques (36)

A. The family members were referred for an objective psychological assessment of an emotional, personality, or cognitive disorder.

B. A psychological assessment has been completed regarding an emotional, personality, or cognitive disorder, and the results of this assessment were reviewed and processed.

C. The family has not followed up on the referral for objective assessment, and was redirected to do so.

### 37. Refer to Psychologist or Psychiatrist (37)

A. The jealous, insecure family member was referred for an individual consultation with a clinical psychologist.

B. The jealous, insecure family member was referred for an individual consultation with a psychiatrist.

C. The jealous, insecure family member has followed up on the referral for a consultation, and the outcome was reviewed.

D. The jealous, insecure family member has not followed up on the referral for individual treatment and was redirected to do so.

### 38. Devise Follow-Up Plan (38)

A. A follow-up plan was devised for working with the family while the mentally ill family member is either hospitalized or in outpatient follow-up.

B. The family was assisted in identifying some concerns that they would work on while the mentally ill family member is receiving concurrent treatment.

C. The family treatment focus was switched to providing support and encouragement to the mentally ill family member.

### 39. Encourage Support to Mentally Ill Family Member (39)

A. The family was assisted in finding ways that they could provide encouragement to the mentally ill family member.

B. The family was directed to provide specific support to the mentally ill family member.

C. The family was reinforced for their support to the mentally ill family member.

D. The family has not provided significant support the mentally ill family member and was redirected to use this integral portion of the treatment.

# LIFE-THREATENING/CHRONIC ILLNESS

## CLIENT PRESENTATION

### 1. Life-Threatening Illness (1)*

A. A family member has been diagnosed with a life-threatening illness.

B. A family member is experiencing serious medical problems that are having a negative impact on the daily functioning of the family.

C. The family has pursued treatment for the seriously ill family member.

D. The family has not sought treatment for a family member's medical condition.

E. The seriously ill family member has been under treatment and is showing signs of improvement.

### 2. Chronic Illness (1)

A. A family member has been diagnosed with a chronic physical illness.

B. A family member has been diagnosed with a chronic mental illness and has displayed a long-term pattern of symptoms in this area.

C. The family member's chronic illness has continued, resulting in less adaptive behavior, more withdrawal and significant decreases in family functioning.

D. The family has learned effective coping skills for adapting to the family member's chronic illness.

### 3. Progressive Deterioration (2)

A. A family member has displayed progressive deterioration throughout the course of an illness.

B. As the family member's health has progressively deteriorated, the family has become more consumed by the illness.

C. As the family member's medical condition has deteriorated, there has been a decreased connection to the daily functioning of the family.

D. The family has found a healthy balance between being consumed by and decreasing involvement with the ill family member.

### 4. Increased Time and Attention (3)

A. A great deal of time and attention has been devoted to the ill family member.

B. Other members of the family have had to give up time and attention due to the needs of the ill family member.

C. Family members have complained that the time and attention devoted to the ill family member has detracted from the time that they need from the family.

D. The family has taken steps to provide appropriate amounts of time to the ill family member, as well as to other family members.

---

*The numbers in parentheses correlate to the number of the Behavioral Definition statement in the companion chapter with the same title in *The Family Therapy Treatment Planner*, Second Ed. (Dattilio, Jongsma, and Davis) by John Wiley & Sons, 2010.

### 5. Guilt (4)

A. The healthy family members feel guilty over their own good health.

B. The ill family member often makes guilt-inducing comments to the other family members.

C. The healthy family members feel responsible for the other family member's illness.

D. Family members have resolved their sense of guilt over their own good health, and the other family member's illness.

### 6. Tension and Strain (5)

A. The family is uncertain about the course of the illness and impending death.

B. Family members are withholding information about the course of the illness and possible death from younger family members.

C. Arguments have erupted within the family regarding how to cope with the family member's illness and possible death.

D. Family members are beginning to develop a healthier approach to the illness and possible death.

### 7. Denial (6)

A. Family members act as though there were nothing wrong with the acutely ill family member, despite evidence to the contrary.

B. The family has refused to disclose or acknowledge that a family member has any medical problem.

C. Family members reported that they did not agree with the seriousness of the other family member's condition as diagnosed by the physicians.

D. The family members seemed to vacillate between accepting and denying the other family member's diagnosed medical condition.

E. The family's denial has started to lessen, and they are beginning to talk about the family member's illness in a realistic manner.

### 8. Emotional Reaction (7)

A. Significant emotional effects resulting from the ill family member's condition have been displayed by the healthy family members.

B. Family members displayed anxious feelings related to the other family member's serious medical condition.

C. Family members appeared very angry about the other family member's serious medical condition.

D. Family members seem to be resentful of the ill family member's condition.

E. As the family has been able to communicate their emotions, they have begun to resolve some of these emotions.

### 9. Financial Stress (8)

A. The family has failed to access or follow through with the financial arrangements for a family member's treatment.

B. Income changes and treatment expenses have placed significant financial stress on the family.

C. The family has experienced a significant decrease in financial resources due to expenses related to the medical condition.

D. The family has obtained financial resources to assist with the cost of the medical treatment.

E. The ill family member's medical problems have improved due to gaining access to affordable medical treatment.

**10. Social Isolation (9)**

A. Recently, the ill family member has discontinued contact with most friends.

B. The ill family member has been spending a significant amount of time alone.

C. The ill family member has been avoiding the other family members since learning of the medical condition.

D. Due to the specific medical condition, the family member who is ill has seen no reason to interact or have relationships with others.

E. Family members have decreased their social interaction with others due to the effects of the family member's serious illness.

F. As the family has become more accepting of the medical condition, the ill family member has begun to reconnect with others and receive their support.

G. Family members have reconnected with others, and they enjoy the support these friendships can give.

**11. Imbalance between Family Needs and Medical Treatment Decisions (10)**

A. Family members are often in conflict over decisions about what is medically best for the ill family member versus what is best for the family.

B. Family members strongly pursue every available medical option, regardless of the effects that this has on the rest of the family.

C. Family members tend to resist pursuing some medical treatments, in order to tend to the needs of the other family members.

D. The family members often argue about which approach to treatment is best when considering the needs of the family and the ill family member.

E. Family members have developed an agreement regarding how to approach the balance between medical treatment and family needs.

## INTERVENTIONS IMPLEMENTED

**1. Refer for Information about Illness and Treatment (1)\***

A. Family members were referred to written material to learn more about the symptoms, treatment, and course of the family member's illness.

B. Family members were encouraged to attend support groups to learn more about the family member's illness.

---

\*The numbers in parentheses correlate to the number of the Therapeutic Intervention statement in the companion chapter with the same title in *The Family Therapy Treatment Planner*, Second Ed. (Dattilio, Jongsma, and Davis) by John Wiley & Sons, 2010.

C.  Family members were encouraged to talk with the treating physician about the symptoms, treatment, and course of the family member's illness.

D.  Family members have sought out additional information about the family member's illness, and this information was processed and summarized.

E.  Family members have not sought out additional information about the family member's illness and were redirected to do so.

## 2. Suggest Sharing of Medical Information (2)

A.  Family members were encouraged to share new medical information with each other during family meetings.

B.  Family members were supported as they reported sharing information with each other during family meetings.

C.  Family members have not shared information with each other during family meetings and were redirected to do so.

## 3. Encourage Networking (3)

A.  Family members were encouraged to become involved with other families who have endured a similar illness.

B.  Family members were referred to a support group to help find others who have endured a similar illness.

C.  Family members have sought out others who have endured a similar illness, and the benefits of this connection were processed.

D.  Family members have not sought out others who have endured a similar illness and were redirected to do so.

## 4. Facilitate Discussion about Illness (4)

A.  Family members were encouraged to share their thoughts associated with the illness.

B.  Family members were encouraged to express their feelings regarding the family member's illness.

C.  An intentional focus was placed on including the ill family member in the discussion of the thoughts and feelings associated with the illness.

D.  Family members were reinforced as they openly expressed their thoughts and feelings regarding the ill family member's condition.

E.  Family members were very guarded about their thoughts and feelings regarding the ill family member's condition and were encouraged to be more open about this.

## 5. Allow for Ventilation of Emotions (5)

A.  Family members were allowed to ventilate their emotions.

B.  Family members were supported as they expressed feelings of anger, guilt, blame, fear, and frustration.

C.  Family members were helped to explore how their feelings affect their relationship with the ill family member.

D.  Family members were guarded about expressing their feelings, and were provided with typical emotions that family members will experience in this setting.

### 6. Explore Isolation (6)

A. It was reflected to the family that the ill family member has been significantly isolated from the rest of the family.

B. The ill family member's sense of isolation was explored.

C. The family was helped to identify the factors that are contributing to the feeling of isolation.

D. It was reflected to family members that the ill family member does not seem to experience isolation.

### 7. Brainstorm Ways to Reduce Sense of Exclusion (7)

A. The family was asked to brainstorm ways to reduce the ill family member's sense of being excluded from the rest of the family.

B. Family members were supported and reinforced as they developed a variety of ways to decrease the ill family member's sense of exclusion from the rest of the family.

C. Family members struggled to develop ways to decrease the ill family member's sense of exclusion and were provided with tentative examples (e.g., finding things that the ill family member can do for healthy family members).

### 8. Educate about Progressive Stages of Grief (8)

A. The family was educated about how they will progress through various stages (e.g., shock, denial, sadness).

B. Family members were assisted in identifying the stage that they are presently in.

C. The family was assisted in expressing the impact of the illness on the stage of family development.

D. Family members were encouraged to read *Beliefs: The Heart of Healing in Families and Illness* (Wright, Watson, and Bell).

E. Family members have read the recommended material and key points were reviewed.

F. Family members have not read the recommended book regarding how healing occurs in families and were redirected to do so.

### 9. Explore Effects of Parent's Illness (9)

A. The changes that have occurred in the caretaking of the family since the beginning of the parent's illness were reviewed.

B. The family was assisted in identifying how leadership of the family has changed during the course of the parent's illness.

C. The changes that have occurred due to the parent's illness were reflected to family members.

D. Family members were uncertain about how the family has changed due to the parent's illness and were provided with tentative examples of how this sometimes occurs.

### 10. Reassign Leadership in the Family (10)

A. The family was helped to reassign leadership within the family.

B. All family members were asked for input about how leadership duties within the family should be changed.

C. A family vote was held in order to reassign leadership positions within the family, in order to take pressure off the ill family member.

D. The family was reinforced as it is making changes in the leadership of the family in order to take pressure off the ill family member.

## 11. Discuss Illness-Related Chores (11)

A. The family was assisted in listing the chores that must be assumed by other family members due to the illness.

B. Family members were assisted in discussing the assignment of chores related to the illness.

C. The benefits of hiring outside help to lessen the amount of the time absorbed by the illness were discussed.

D. Family members were directed to options for enlisting outside help to lessen the amount of time absorbed by the illness.

E. Family members were supported as they have decided to enlist outside help to lessen the amount of time absorbed by the illness.

F. The family members were supported as they decided to maintain the chores related to the illness within the family.

## 12. Educate about Boundaries (12)

A. The family was educated about the importance of boundaries in human relationships.

B. Family members were taught about how families can become polarized in a conflict.

C. Family members were taught about how families can become enmeshed when faced with a crisis.

D. Family members were assisted in disengaging and setting better boundaries.

E. Family members were assisted in the process of depolarization and reducing unhealthy boundaries.

## 13. Recognize Beliefs (13)

A. The family was assisted in recognizing their beliefs about the effects of the illness on the family.

B. Family members were assisted in finding resources that may help them to prevent the illness from dominating their lives.

C. Family members were recommended to read *Beliefs: The Heart of Healing Families in Illness* (Wright, Watson, and Bell).

D. Family members have read the assigned material to help keep the illness from dominating their lives, and the salient issues from the reading were reviewed.

E. Family members have not read the assigned material and were redirected to do so.

## 14. Emphasize Strengths (14)

A. Family members were encouraged to identify and build on their strengths.

B. Family members were provided with examples of how families can build on their strengths (e.g., playing table games together; developing a family hobby such as coin collecting).

C. Family members were discouraged from bemoaning the family deficits or being over-whelmed by the problems.

D. Family members were provided with examples of how families can contribute to feeling overwhelmed by the problems (e.g., complaining of not having enough money; criticizing each other for not doing a fair share of work).

E. Family members were reinforced as they have emphasized their strengths, rather than their deficits.

F. Family members have continued to emphasize their deficits, rather than focusing on their strengths, and were redirected in this area.

15. **Emphasize Responsibilities over Guilt/Blame (15)**

A. Family members were encouraged to move their focus off guilt and blame, and toward acknowledging their individual and joint responsibilities to deal with the crisis brought on by the illness.

B. Family members were reinforced whenever they identified ways that they can acknowledge their own individual and joint responsibilities to deal with the crisis brought on by the illness.

C. Family members were redirected as they continued to focus on guilt and blame.

16. **Teach Negotiation and Problem-Solving Strategies (16)**

A. Family members were taught techniques to help them cope with the illness.

B. Family members were taught negotiation skills (e.g., family forum meetings, empathy enhancement) to help increase their coping with the illness.

C. Family members were taught problem-solving strategies (e.g., "I" message communication, role reversal) to help increase their coping with the illness.

D. Family members were reinforced whenever they used helpful coping techniques to create a better response to the illness.

E. Family members have not used coping techniques to improve how the family copes with the illness and were redirected to do so.

17. **Teach Decision-Making Method (17)**

A. Family members were provided with examples of methods for making decisions.

B. Family members were taught how to weigh the pros and cons on alternate options.

C. The family was taught to identify the problem, brainstorm possible solutions, weigh the pros and cons, select an option for action, and review the results.

D. "Problem-Solving: An Alternative to Impulsive Action" from the *Adult Psychotherapy Therapy Planner,* 2nd ed. (Jongsma) was assigned to the family.

E. Role-play techniques were used to practice decision-making techniques.

F. Family members were directed to use the decision-making techniques on their own.

18. **Identify Outside Sources of Social Support (18)**

A. The family was assisted in identifying outside sources of social support.

B. Family members have identified outside sources of social support, and were encouraged to seek these out.

C. Family members were uncertain about how to develop outside sources of social support and were provided with specific examples (e.g., hospice, church, extended family, friends).

D. Family members were reinforced for their engagement of outside sources of social support.

### 19. Ask about Contribution to Conflict and Harmony (19)

A. Each family member was asked to assess personal contributions to the family conflict.

B. Family members were supported as they identified their own contribution to the family conflict.

C. Family members were quite guarded about how they may have contributed to the family conflict and were provided with tentative examples of how these occur.

D. Family members were encouraged to identify what they could do differently to contribute to harmony within the family.

E. Family members were reinforced for identifying ways to develop better harmony within the family.

F. Family members were uncertain about how to develop better harmony; they were provided with tentative examples and were asked to commit to using these.

### 20. Focus on Effect of Conflict on Illness (20)

A. The family was asked to identify how tensions due to negative reactions or conflicts have exacerbated the condition of the ill family member.

B. Family members were assisted in identifying how the conflicts have inhibited the improvement of the ill family member's condition.

C. Family members were supported as they acknowledged the obstacles that they have created for the improvement of the ill family member.

D. Family members were guarded about accepting how their conflicts have inhibited the ill family member's recovery and were provided with tentative examples in these areas.

### 21. Teach Stress Reduction and Conflict-Resolution Techniques (21)

A. Measures were suggested to the family to reduce stress (e.g., relaxation training, respite care, exercise, programmed family recreation).

B. Family members were taught conflict resolution-techniques (e.g., family forum meetings, "I" message communication, role reversal, empathy enhancement).

C. Family members were encouraged for their use of stress-reduction techniques and conflict-resolution techniques, and the benefits of these approaches were reviewed.

D. Family members have not used stress-reduction techniques and were redirected to do so.

E. Family members have not used conflict-resolution techniques and were redirected to do so.

### 22. Teach about Overprotectiveness (22)

A. Family members were taught that overprotectiveness is not unusual when one family member is seriously ill.

B. Family members were assisted in identifying how they have displayed overprotectiveness with each other.

C. Family members were reminded that they will each need to exercise some independence to promote less intensity and conflict.

D. Family members were assisted in processing the emotions that lead to overprotectiveness.

E. Family members were reinforced as they have decreased their pattern of overprotectiveness of each other.

F. Family members continued to be quite overprotective of each other and were redirected in this area.

## 23. Teach Attentiveness in Place of Overprotectiveness (23)

A. Family members were taught to use attentive behaviors in place of overprotectiveness.

B. Family members were taught about how to use verbal expression of needs for support.

C. The family members were supported for identifying when they need support, and using it to replace overprotectiveness.

D. Family members have not used attentive behaviors to replace overprotectiveness and were provided with remedial feedback in this area.

# MULTIPLE BIRTH DILEMMAS

## CLIENT PRESENTATION

### 1. Multiple Births (1)*

A. The parents have experienced a pregnancy that yields multiple newborns.

B. Family members have become emotionally overwhelmed by the changes caused by the multiple births.

C. The family has become physically overwhelmed by the responsibilities necessary due to the multiple births.

D. Family members are beginning to develop coping skills for dealing with the responsibilities associated with the multiple births.

E. The family has become emotionally and physically capable of meeting the challenges of multiple births.

### 2. Increased Responsibility (2)

A. The amount of work necessary for sustaining the family since the multiple births has radically increased.

B. Food and supply expenses have significantly increased due to the multiple births.

C. The parents are experiencing many sleepless nights due to the responsibility of caring for multiple newborns.

D. The family has obtained additional support to help with the many responsibilities for caring for the newborns.

E. The family is adjusting to the changes that have been caused by the multiple births.

### 3. Physical/Developmental Concerns (3)

A. The parents are concerned about the possible death of one of the newborns.

B. There are concerns about neurological deficits, physical health disorders, and developmental abnormalities for the newborn children.

C. There are significant medical complications for the newborns, including neurological and developmental difficulties.

D. The birth defects caused by the multiple births have resulted in the death of one of the multiple birth infants.

E. The children have been assessed to be less at risk for birth-related medical complications.

### 4. Parent's Depression (4)

A. As a result of the added burden of multiple birth children, one of the parents has experienced problems with clinical depression.

---

*The numbers in parentheses correlate to the number of the Behavioral Definition statement in the companion chapter with the same title in *The Family Therapy Treatment Planner*, Second Ed. (Dattilio, Jongsma, and Davis) by John Wiley & Sons, 2010.

B. One of the parents describes feeling burned out, overwhelmed, and out of energy due to providing care for the newborns.

C. Postpartum depression has been exacerbated by the many increased responsibilities subsequent to a multiple birth.

D. As treatment has progressed, the parent's experience of depression symptoms has been alleviated.

## 5. Need for Larger Living Quarters (5)

A. The family has too little space for the new arrivals.

B. The family has identified the need for a larger place to live, but has limited resources to obtain such a place.

C. The family has experienced increased stress due to the limited living space, and the multiple children that need to be cared for.

D. The family has obtained adequate living space for the increased number of children.


## INTERVENTIONS IMPLEMENTED

### 1. Provide for Venting (1)*

A. Family members were encouraged to vent their fears that they will not be able to handle the extra burden subsequent to the multiple births.

B. Family members were supported as they expressed their shock at the changes that have happened subsequent to the multiple births.

C. Family members were encouraged to take advantage of resources that will help them cope with their emotions relative to the multiple births.

D. Family members were cautious about expressing their emotions and were urged to be open in this safe setting.

### 2. Brainstorm about Resources (2)

A. Family members were encouraged to brainstorm about resources for childcare and emotional support.

B. Family members were assisted in reviewing the pros and cons of all options relative to childcare and emotional support needs.

C. Family members were helped to select the resources that they would like to seek out to assist in childcare and emotional support needs.

### 3. Replace Negative Self-Talk (3)

A. The parents were assisted in identifying the negative self-talk associated with the responsibility of multiple birth children.

B. Positive reinforcement was provided to the parents as they showed insight into the ways in which they experience negative self-talk.

*The numbers in parentheses correlate to the number of the Therapeutic Intervention statement in the companion chapter with the same title in *The Family Therapy Treatment Planner*, Second Ed. (Dattilio, Jongsma, and Davis) by John Wiley & Sons, 2010.

C. The parents were assisted in replacing the negative self-talk with positive, realistic automatic thoughts.

D. The parents were verbally reinforced whenever they used more positive, realistic self-talk.

E. When parents slipped back into negative self-talk regarding the responsibility of multiple birth children, it was actively confronted and redirected.

### 4. Support through Infant Death (4)

A. Family members were supported as they have gone through the process of grieving the loss of an infant.

B. Bereavement counseling techniques were used to assist family members in coming to grips with the death of an infant.

C. The parents were assigned to read information such as *Necessary Losses* (Viorst).

D. Children were encouraged to read *The Fall of Freddy the Leaf* (Buscaglia).

E. Family members have read the assigned grief material, and the key points were processed.

F. Family members have not read the assigned grief material and were redirected to do so.

### 5. Suggest Grieving Rituals (5)

A. Rituals were suggested for the family to follow to grieve for the lost infant.

B. Rituals were suggested that would help the family focus on seeing the surviving infants as a blessing.

C. Family members were encouraged to develop their own rituals for grieving over the loss and to focus on their remaining blessings.

### 6. Teach Learned Optimism (6)

A. The family was taught methods of learned optimism.

B. The family was encouraged to use the learned-optimism techniques to deal with the stress of the medical problems.

C. The use of learned-optimism techniques was role-played within the session.

D. Family members were verbally reinforced for their use of learned optimism.

E. The family has not used learned-optimism techniques and was given further instruction.

### 7. Develop Schedule for Medical Necessities (7)

A. The family was assisted in developing a schedule for all members to share in attending to the medical necessities of the infants.

B. Tasks such as feeding, changing diapers, assisting in-home nurses, attending to appointments, and giving medications were scheduled among all family members.

C. All family members have been assigned responsibilities associated with the care of the infants, and this was reinforced.

D. Family members continued to have an uneven pattern of care of the infants and were redirected to share this by scheduling it among all family members.

### 8. Allow for Children to Vent (8)

A. The children of the family were allowed to vent their feelings and concerns about the instant addition of new offspring.

B. The children were asked to identify their feelings and concerns related to the instant addition of new offspring.

C. The older children were asked about their fears about being ignored and neglected.

D. The emotions and concerns from the older children were processed with the family.

### 9. Elicit Reassurance (9)

A. The parents were asked to reassure the older children that they would not be ignored.

B. Parents were instructed to schedule structured individual attention for each child.

C. The parents were encouraged to monitor the feelings and concerns of the older children.

### 10. Brainstorm Financial Concerns (10)

A. Family members were asked to brainstorm how they can increase financial income to the family.

B. Family members were assisted in listing ways that they can reduce or contain overhead costs to improve the family's financial situation.

C. The ideas to help create a better financial situation were reviewed and processed.

### 11. Reinforce Family Bonds (11)

A. The family was challenged to find ways to reemphasize the bond that exists between family members.

B. It was emphasized that all of the family members need to work together in a cohesive fashion to contend with the financial concerns and changes in responsibility.

C. Family members were reinforced for comments that emphasize the family's bond.

### 12. Identify Emotional Supports Needed (12)

A. The family was asked to identify what type of emotional support they need to survive the current situation.

B. Ways for the family to obtain the needed emotional support were brainstormed and processed.

C. Family members struggled to identify what type of emotional support they may need and were given tentative examples in this area (i.e., someone to talk to, time away from the stress of family needs, crisis intervention).

### 13. Identify Emotional Supports (13)

A. Family members were asked to identify specific extended family members and friends on whom the family can rely for emotional support.

B. A consensus was built among family members regarding people who can be used for emotional support.

C. Family members were provided with additional ideas for obtaining emotional support, including church involvement, support groups, and other organizations.

### 14. Stress Management Techniques (14)

A. Family members were taught techniques for managing or inoculating against their stress.

B. Family members were taught cognitive-restructuring techniques to manage stress.

C. Family members were taught progressive muscle relaxation techniques to manage stress.

D. Light-hearted recreational activities were recommended to the family to reduce stress levels.

E. The family was encouraged to use exercise to help decrease stress.

F. Family members were reinforced for their report of regularly using stress-reduction techniques.

G. Family members have not regularly used stress-reduction techniques and were reminded about these helpful techniques.

## 15. Treat Depression (15)

A. Cognitive therapy techniques were used to help treat the parent's depression.

B. Medication was used to help treat the parent's depression.

C. It was noted that the parent's depression has decreased due to the treatment provided.

## 16. Refer for Depression Treatment (16)

A. The depressed parent was referred for outpatient treatment.

B. The depressed parent was referred for inpatient psychiatric treatment.

C. The extremely depressed parent was involuntarily hospitalized to treat the depression.

D. It was noted that the depressed parent has responded well to treatment and is meeting the needs of this newly structured family.

## 17. Provide Supportive Family Therapy (17)

A. The nondepressed family members were provided with supportive family therapy.

B. Supportive family therapy has focused on assisting the nondepressed family members in coping with the significant changes and inoculating them against the stress.

C. Family members were assigned to read *Feeling Good* and *Feeling Good Handbook* (Burns).

D. Family members have read the assigned materials, and the key points were processed.

E. Family members have not read the assigned materials and were redirected to do so.

## 18. Teach Decision-Making Paradigms (18)

A. Family members were taught about how to use decision-making paradigms to review their living space options.

B. Family members were assisted in making decisions about the best living space options to suit their new needs.

C. Family members were encouraged to implement their decisions regarding their living space options.

# PHYSICAL/VERBAL/PSYCHOLOGICAL ABUSE

## CLIENT PRESENTATION

### 1. Intentional Pain or Injury (1)*

A. A family member has intentionally inflicted physical pain or injury on other family members.

B. A family member's actions were perceived by other family members as having the intent of inflicting physical pain or injury.

C. A family member has been throwing objects at other family members, pushing, hitting, grabbing, choking, or using extreme verbal coercion.

D. As treatment has progressed, the abusing family member has discontinued the pattern of abuse.

### 2. Insults (2)

A. The abusive family member insults other family members when they are alone.

B. The abusive family member insults other family members in front of others.

C. The abusive family member makes veiled insults to other family members.

D. As treatment has progressed, the frequency and intensity of the insulting behavior has decreased.

E. There have been no reports of insults to family members recently.

### 3. Threats to Harm (3)

A. The psychologically abusive family member makes vague threats about harming other family members.

B. The psychologically abusive family member makes specific threats about harming other family members.

C. As treatment has progressed, threats to do physical harm to other family members have decreased.

D. The psychologically abusive family member has discontinued the pattern of threatening other family members with physical harm.

### 4. Critical about Family Member's Mental Health (4)

A. The abusive family member often makes critical comments about another family member's mental health (e.g., "You are crazy," "You need a psychiatrist," "You are paranoid.").

B. The psychologically abusive family member often belittles other family members for seeking mental health treatment.

C. The abusive family member has terminated critical comments about other family member's mental health.

*The numbers in parentheses correlate to the number of the Behavioral Definition statement in the companion chapter with the same title in *The Family Therapy Treatment Planner*, Second Ed. (Dattilio, Jongsma, and Davis) by John Wiley & Sons, 2010.

### 5. Fear of Abuse (5)

A. Family members have a fear of physical injury from another family member.

B. Family members have a fear of emotional abuse resulting from threats, intimidation, or berating by the abusive family member.

C. As treatment has progressed, family members report less feelings of fear.

### 6. Silent Treatment (6)

A. The psychologically abusive family member often uses the "silent treatment" toward others when angry with them.

B. The psychologically abusive family member does not engage in regular conversation for an extended period of time due to some perceived slight.

C. As treatment has progressed, family members have agreed to discuss issues rather than use manipulative tactics (e.g., the silent treatment).

### 7. Failure to Warn (7)

A. Family members have been reluctant to warn other family members of situations, incidents, or events in which they have knowledge of potential physical harm.

B. Family members have kept silent when they knew that another family member was going to be harmed (e.g., knowing of a planned physical assault against a sibling by another sibling, or an individual outside of the immediate family).

C. Conflict has arisen within the family regarding the effects of a family member failing to warn others about potential risks or physical threats.

D. Family members have become more supportive of each other in maintaining safety, and freely provide information to each other about possible threats.

### 8. Ordering Around (8)

A. The psychologically abusive family member often orders other family members around in a dominating, controlling, and belittling manner.

B. Family members being victimized often feel as though there is no other option but to comply with the psychologically abusive family member's pattern of domination, control, and belittling.

C. As treatment has progressed, the victimized family member has become less willing to acquiesce to the other family member's domination.

D. The psychologically abusive family member has become less dominating, controlling, and belittling toward other family members.

## INTERVENTIONS IMPLEMENTED

### 1. Define Abuse (1)*

A. A family session has defined the issues of the abuse within the family.

B. Individual therapy sessions have been used to focus on the issues related to the abuse within the family.

C. Abusive comments and behaviors have been operationally defined for all family members.

D. Definitions of abusive behavior and comments have been consistent among all family members, and this was reflected to them.

E. It was noted that family members have a variety of opinions regarding the nature, extent, and severity of the abuse; this information was reflected to them and synthesized.

### 2. Explore Dynamics and Plan for Safety (2)

A. The dynamics that facilitate the abusive behavior within the family were explored.

B. The ways in which nonabusive family members have been victimized was addressed.

C. An immediate plan for family safety was developed.

D. Family members were assisted in developing a plan for how to respond to future escalation of the abusive behavior (i.e., where the family can immediately go to obtain safety).

### 3. Recommend Individual Therapy (3)

A. Individual therapy was recommended for the abusive family member.

B. The abusive family member was referred to another clinician to obtain anger management treatment.

C. The treatment was shifted to individual sessions for the abusive family member, focusing on anger issues and impulse control.

D. As a result of individual treatment, the abusive family member has gained significant anger and impulse control, and the focus of treatment has returned to the family issues.

E. The family member referred for individual anger treatment has not complied with this referral and was reminded about this necessity.

### 4. Develop Family Safety Plan (4)

A. Family members were assisted in developing a plan that assures the safety of abused members.

B. Family members were reinforced as they identified several steps that they would take to create family safety if the abuse continued to be a threat.

C. Family members developed a plan to assure the safety of the abused family members and were provided with possible alternatives (e.g., calling the police, escaping to a safe environment).

D. Family members were reinforced for using the identified safety plan when the abuse appeared to be escalating.

*The numbers in parentheses correlate to the number of the Therapeutic Intervention statement in the companion chapter with the same title in *The Family Therapy Treatment Planner*, Second Ed. (Dattilio, Jongsma, and Davis) by John Wiley & Sons, 2010.

E. Family members have not identified a plan for ensuring safety when the abuse become more threatening and were redirected to do so.

## 5. List Community Resources (5)

A. Family members were assisted in developing a list of resources in the community to assist in the escape from abuse.

B. Family members have identified a variety of resources in the community to help them escape from the abuse, and they were encouraged to use these as is necessary.

C. Family members were provided with a list of community resources such as shelters, friends, extended family members.

D. Family members were reinforced for agreeing to use the resources in the community to escape from the abuse.

E. Family members have not agreed to use the resources in the community to escape from the ongoing abuse; they were reminded about these helpful resources.

## 6. Fulfill Legal Mandates (6)

A. Legal mandates regarding the reporting of abuse of a minor were fulfilled.

B. The appropriate protective agency was contacted regarding the abuse of a minor.

C. Even though abuse was only suspected, the appropriate protective service agency has been contacted.

D. Appropriate consultation has been obtained regarding the duty to report the abuse of a minor.

## 7. Contract Regarding Confrontation of Abusive Behavior (7)

A. Family members were assisted in constructing a written contract that assures that no abusive behavior will be tolerated.

B. Family members were reinforced for their agreement to refuse to tolerate abuse and point it out immediately.

C. Family members have followed through on their agreement to immediately point out abuse, and this was reinforced.

D. Family members have not followed through on immediately pointing out abuse, and the reasons for this were reviewed, processed, and problem-solved.

E. Family members have enforced the expectation that the abuser will be involved in therapy.

## 8. Define Contract Violation and Response (8)

A. Family members were assisted in defining what constitutes violation of the nonabuse contract.

B. Family members were assisted in identifying the steps that will be taken to ensure safety (e.g., abuser vacates the situation, victim seeks alternative shelter, call police).

C. Family members were assisted in synthesizing their opinions about what constitutes a violation of the nonabuse contract and what steps are to be implemented to resolve this problem.

## 9. Educate about Effects of Physical Abuse (9)

A. All family members were taught about the emotional destructiveness of physical abuse.

B. Family members were taught about how even the slightest incidences of physical abuse are destructive and illegal.

C. The family was urged to adopt a zero tolerance policy regarding physical abuse.

D. The family was reinforced for their clear understanding of the effects and illegality of the physical abuse.

E. The family continues to minimize and rationalize the effects of the abuse and was redirected in this area.

## 10. Define Psychological/Verbal Abuse (10)

A. The family was assisted in defining what constitutes psychological and verbal abuse.

B. Specific behavioral terms were used to help clearly define what constitutes psychological or verbal abuse.

C. A focus was placed on the subtle, or tacitly implied, verbal and psychological abuse, and the vulnerability of the victims.

D. The family was reinforced for a clear understanding of the meaning of psychological and verbal abuse.

E. The family has displayed a poor understanding of the definition of psychological and verbal abuse and was provided with remedial information in this area.

## 11. Refer for Support and Treatment (11)

A. The victims of the abuse were referred to a support group.

B. The referral to an abuse victim's support group has been accepted, and the benefits of this program were reviewed.

C. The abusive offender has been referred to a treatment program.

D. The abusive offender's involvement in a treatment program was reviewed and processed.

E. Family members have not accepted referrals to a support group and were reminded about this helpful resource.

F. The abusive offender has not accepted the referral to a treatment program, and the focus of therapy was redirected to this area.

## 12. Identify Early Cues of Potential Violence (12)

A. Family members were assisted in identifying the early cues for potential violence.

B. Family members were reinforced as they identified the early cues for potential violence within their specific setting.

C. Family members were uncertain about early cues for potential violence and were provided with examples in this area.

## 13. Teach Anger Cues (13)

A. Family members were taught about how to identify the cognitive, affective, behavioral, and physiological cues of anger.

B. Family members were taught about how to differentiate low, moderate, and high ranges of anger.

C. Family members were directed to read the book *Angry All the Time* (Potter-Efron).

D. Family members have read the assigned material on anger cues and levels, and the information was processed.

E. Family members have not read the assigned material on anger and were redirected to do so.

F. Family members were reinforced for the clear understanding of anger cues and levels.

G. Family members have a poor understanding of anger cues and levels, and were provided with remedial information in this area.

## 14. Differentiate between Styles of Communication (14)

A. Family members were taught about the various styles of communication (assertive, aggressive, and passive-aggressive).

B. Role-plays were used to teach the difference between assertive, aggressive, and passive-aggressive communication.

C. The family was encouraged to use assertive communication as a vehicle for expressing heated emotions.

## 15. Role-Play to Identify Cues (15)

A. Role-play exercises were used to review heated situations and identify the cues that indicate that the situation may spiral out of control.

B. Family members were encouraged to respectfully role-play how other family members give cues that the situation is spiraling out of control.

C. Family members were helped to identify their own cues that a heated situation might spiral out of control.

D. Family members were provided with examples of the cues that indicate pending loss of control (e.g., family members becoming quiet or seething, voices being raised).

E. Positive feedback was provided to family members for their identification of cues that an anger situation is becoming out of control.

## 16. Emphasize Safety to Express in Session (16)

A. An agreement was solicited between family members not to use in-session material against each other when outside of the treatment session.

B. The need for open and honest communication within the therapy session was emphasized.

C. Family members were confronted for using in-session material against each other outside of the treatment session.

## 17. Teach Time-Out (17)

A. Family members were taught time-out procedures to reduce the level of anger in a potentially violent situation.

B. Family members were encouraged to use time-out procedures to reduce the intensity of anger.

C. Family members were taught about the five steps of anger control via time-out, including self-monitoring, signaling, acknowledgment, separation, and returning.

D. Family members were referred to *The Anger and Aggression Workbook* (Liptak, Leutenberg, and Sippola).

E. Family members were reinforced for their use of time-out procedures to reduce the intensity of anger.

F. Family members have not used time-out procedures when anger needed to be reduced and were redirected to do so.

### 18. Emphasize Structure and Boundaries (18)

A. Family members were taught the importance of maintaining structure and boundaries, particularly during emotionally charged discussions.

B. Family members were assisted in operationally defining structure and boundaries for emotionally charged discussions.

C. The connection between verbal or psychological and physical abuse was emphasized.

### 19. Use Role-Reversal Techniques (19)

A. Role-reversal techniques were used to help the abusive family member learn the emotional impact of abuse.

B. The abusive family member was directed to assume the role of the victim to understand the emotional impact of the abuse.

C. The emotional experience for the victim and the abuser were processed.

### 20. List Negative Effects of Abuse (20)

A. The abusive family member was requested to list 10 negative effects of the abuse on the victim and the family.

B. Positive feedback was provided as the abusive family member displayed significant empathy by reviewing the effects of the abuse on the victim and the family.

C. Examples were provided about how the abuse may have affected the victim and the family, including modeling disrespect and violence for children, lowering the self-esteem of the victim, loss of own self-respect, and conflict with other family members over abusive practices.

### 21. Assess for Substance Abuse (21)

A. Family members were assessed for the presence of substance abuse.

B. No substance abuse concerns were identified.

C. Substance abuse concerns were identified, and family members were assisted in identifying how it may be contributing to the dysfunction within the family.

### 22. Refer for Chemical Dependence Treatment (22)

A. Substance abusing family members were referred to Alcoholics Anonymous.

B. Substance abusing family members were referred for chemical dependence treatment.

C. Substance abusing family members were requested to pledge to terminate the substance abuse.

D. The substance abusing family members were supported for participation in an appropriate treatment for chemical dependence.

E. Substance abusing family members have not begun appropriate treatment and were redirected to use these helpful resources.

### 23. Explore Cognitive and Behavioral Precursors (23)

A. Thought patterns that may be encouraging each family member in an abusive exchange were explored.

B. Family members were assisted in identifying behaviors that may be precipitating abusive exchanges.

C. Family members were provided with examples of cognitive precursors to abusive exchanges (e.g., jealousy, prejudices).

D. Family members were reinforced for identifying precursors to abusive exchanges.

### 24. Examine Cycle of Abuse (24)

A. Family-of-origin abuse issues were reviewed with the parents to identify the effects of any verbal/physical abuse sustained by them during their own childhood.

B. The parents described their experience of verbal and physical abuse during childhood and were supported and assisted as they identified how this contributes to their current abusive behavior.

C. Enabling behaviors that were learned by the nonabusive female member during childhood experiences were explored and processed.

D. The repeating nature of the cycle of abuse was emphasized.

### 25. Review Family-of-Origin Reinforcers (25)

A. The aggressive family member was assisted in identifying how family-of-origin experiences have reinforced physical and verbal abuse as an acceptable way of expressing anger/ frustration.

B. Positive feedback was provided as the aggressive family member was able to identify how the family-of-origin experiences have validated the use of abuse as a way to express anger/ frustration.

C. The aggressive family member denied any connection between family-of-origin experiences of abuse and current abuse and was encouraged to reexamine this connection.

### 26. Support Confrontation (26)

A. Family members were encouraged to confront the abuser without excusing the behavior or allowing the abuser to project blame.

B. When the abuser attempted to excuse the abusive behavior or externalize the blame within the session, confrontation was provided.

C. Family members were supported when they reported appropriately confronting the abuser.

D. It was reflected to family members that their confrontation of the abuser allowed excuses for the behavior and projection of the blame, and this pattern was processed to resolution.

### 27. Model Acceptance of Responsibility (27)

A. Within the family therapy sessions, the therapist modeled the process of accepting the responsibility for individual behavior.

B. An emphasis was placed on modeling responsibility for individual behavior without excuses or externalizing blame.

C. Family members were asked to comment on and discuss the ways in which the family therapist accepted responsibility for individual behavior without excuses or externalizing blame.

D. The abusive family member was asked to take responsibility for the abuse.

### 28. Ask for Apology (28)

A. The abusive family member was asked to apologize for the abuse without externalizing blame.

B. The abusive family member has apologized for the abuse, but was redirected in the areas that he/she has placed blame for his/her behavior.

C. The apologizing family member was reinforced for his/her acceptance of blame and willingness to apologize.

D. Today's family session was focused on hearing and processing the abusive family member's apology.

E. The abusive family member has declined to apologize and the ramifications of this refusal were processed.

### 29. Confront Failure to Take Responsibility and Express Remorse (29)

A. The abusive family member was confronted for not taking responsibility for the abuse.

B. The abusive family member was confronted for a lack of remorse for the abuse.

C. The abusive family member was confronted for a lack of sensitivity.

D. Positive feedback was provided as the abusive family member accepted confrontation and rectified problems regarding responsibility, remorse, and sensitivity.

E. The abusive family member reacted in a characteristically volatile manner to the confrontation about taking responsibility and expressing remorse and sensitivity.

### 30. Confront Enabling (30)

A. The victim's pattern of taking responsibility for the abusive family member's behavior was confronted.

B. The victim was provided with examples of how the abusive family member's behavior is enabled.

C. The victim's decision to hold the abusive family member responsible was reinforced.

D. The victim was encouraged to continue to hold the abusive family member responsible for the abusive behavior.

### 31. Review Function of Abuse (31)

A. The abusive family member was assisted in establishing the function of the abuse.

B. Family members were encouraged to provide feedback regarding the function of the aggressive family member's abuse.

C. The aggressive family member was assisted in identifying nonabusive means to accomplish the goals of the abuse.

D. The family had difficulty identifying the function of the abuse and was provided with tentative examples of these types of functions.

### 32. Process Outburst (32)

A. The abusive family member's angry outbursts were reviewed, and an analysis of the contributors to this outburst was conducted.

B. The abusive family member was assisted in identifying the feelings that are associated with the angry outburst.

C. A review was conducted of available alternatives to angry outbursts.

D. The abusive family member was reinforced for an open and honest review of the anger outbursts.

E. The abusive family member was rather guarded about acknowledging angry feelings and was urged to be more open about these feelings and behaviors.

### 33. List Alternative Behaviors (33)

A. The abusive family member was encouraged to write a list of alternative behaviors for processing and controlling anger when it is experienced.

B. The abusive family member was reinforced for identifying healthy alternatives to abusive behavior when anger is experienced.

C. Examples were provided to the abusive family member of healthy alternative behaviors when anger is experienced (e.g., taking a time-out, contacting a support system, taking a walk, writing out feelings, reviewing a list of the negative consequences of violence).

### 34. Assign Readings (34)

A. The abusive family member was assigned to read material about anger.

B. The abusive family member was directed to read *The Anger Trap* (Carter).

C. The abusive family member was encouraged to read *The Angry Book* (Rubin).

D. The abusive family member was directed to read *The Anger and Aggression Workbook* (Liptak et al.).

E. The abusive family member was directed to read *The Verbally Abusive Relationship* (Evans).

F. The abusive family member has read the material regarding anger, and key points were reviewed.

G. The abusive family member has not read the assigned material on anger and was redirected to do so.

### 35. Reinforce Assertiveness (35)

A. Assertive behaviors displayed within the session were reinforced.

B. The family reports of assertive behaviors were highlighted and reinforced.

C. Family members denied any recent pattern of assertiveness; they were reinforced for identifying assertive responses that they could have used during the week.

### 36. Review Modeling of Abuse as Acceptable (36)

A. The victims of the abuse were asked about how they learned to be accepting of a pattern of abusive behavior.

B. The victims of the abuse were focused onto previous experiences that modeled physical or verbal abuse as behavior that is to be expected, excused, and tolerated.

C. Family members that have been victimized by the abuse were supported as they identified incidents that have modeled abuse as expected, excused, and tolerated.

D. Family members denied any pattern of expecting, excusing, or tolerating abuse and were provided with tentative examples about how this dynamic sometimes occurs.

### 37. Teach Responsibility Instead of Blame (37)

A. Family members were taught that everyone is personally responsible for their own behavior.

B. The victims of the abuse were assisted in identifying any patterns of self-blame for another family member's abusive behavior.

C. Abused family members were supported as they shifted the blame from themselves to the abusive family member.

D. Family members were redirected whenever comments were made that focused on the victim as responsible for the abuse.

### 38. Review Healthy Responses to Abusive Behavior (38)

A. Family members who have been victimized by the abuse were asked to cite incidences in which abusive behavior occurred and they did not take responsibility for it.

B. Family members were reinforced for correctly placing the blame on the abusive family member.

C. Emotional support was provided to the family members as they sought to correctly place the blame for the abusive behavior on the perpetrator.

### 39. Review Abuser's History (39)

A. The abusive family member was asked to identify hurtful life experiences that have led to the decision to act out aggressively.

B. Emotional support was provided to the abusive family member as past hurtful life experiences were reviewed and the emotions were processed.

C. The abusive family member was reinforced for identifying the hurtful life experiences that have contributed to the decision to act out aggressively.

D. The abusive family member was quite guarded about past hurtful life experiences and was encouraged to disclose about these as trust levels rise.

### 40. Empathize Feelings Regarding Past Traumas (40)

A. The abusive family member was assisted in identifying and clarifying feelings of hurt and anger tied to past traumas.

B. Empathy skills were used to help normalize the abusive family member's feeling of hurt and anger tied to past traumas.

C. Support was provided for sharing the feelings of helplessness, pain, and rage that past traumas have incurred.

D. Positive feedback was provided to the abusive family member for the willingness to acknowledge hurt or anger related to the past trauma.

E. As the abuse has been contained, the family was helped to see the damage that the abuse did to the perpetrator's self-esteem.

F. The abusive family member appeared to be guarded about feelings related to past trauma and was directed to be more open about this as trust levels increase.

### 41. Connect Past Rage to Current Control (41)

A. The abusive family member was assisted in making the connection between past feelings of rage when abused, and current anger leading to the abuse of others.

B. The abusive family member was reinforced for acknowledging the connection between past abuse and current abuse of others.

C. The abuser denied any connection between the experience of past abuse and current abuse of others and was provided with remedial feedback in this area.

### 42. Discuss Forgiveness (42)

A. The abusive family member was encouraged to consider the need for forgiveness in order to let go of the anger and resentment associated with the past abuse.

B. It was emphasized to the abusive family member that feelings of anger and rage about past abuse must be resolved to decrease the likelihood of further abuse of others.

C. Positive feedback was provided as the abusive family member acknowledged the need to forgive others for past abuse.

D. The abusive family member reacted negatively to the idea that a previous abuser should be forgiven for that abuse and was urged to consider this option in the future.

### 43. Assign Readings on Forgiveness (43)

A. The abusive family member was requested to read material on forgiveness.

B. *Forgiveness is a Choice* (Enright) was assigned to the abusive family member.

C. The abusive family member was assigned to read *How Can I Forgive You?* (Abrams-Spring).

D. The assigned material on forgiveness has been read, and key points were reviewed.

E. The assigned material on forgiveness has not been read, and the abusive family member was redirected to do so.

### 44. Teach Family about Dysfunctional Communication (44)

A. The family was taught about dysfunctional communication patterns that co-occur with an increased likelihood of physical abuse.

B. The family was taught about the dynamics that may contribute to the likelihood of abuse (e.g., vocalizing attribution of family members' blame for problems; fast reciprocation of family members' anger; lack of empathy; contempt for or lack of respect for family members; defensiveness; withdrawal; coerciveness; or entitlement).

C. Family members were encouraged to read *Controlling People* (Evans).

D. Family members identified ways in which their interactions with the abuser were dysfunctional and may have contributed to the likelihood for abuse to occur; this was accepted, but the responsibility for the abuse was maintained as being the abuser's.

E. Family members have read the assigned material about verbal abuse survivors, and key points were reviewed.

F. Family members have not read about the verbal abuse survivors and were redirected to do so.

## 45. Teach Positive Communication Skills (45)

A. Role-playing and behavior rehearsal techniques were used to teach positive communication skills.

B. Family members were taught about clear problem identification, listening skills, problem-solving skills, and behavioral contracting.

C. As a result of the role-play and behavior rehearsal, family members have displayed an increased pattern of communication.

D. Despite the use of role-play and behavior rehearsal techniques, family members continue to struggle with communication, and remedial feedback was provided in this area.

## 46. Teach Displacement Techniques (46)

A. Family members were taught about the use of anger-displacement techniques (e.g., punching bag, jogging, bowling, kickboxing).

B. Family members were urged to use anger-displacement techniques to help work off energy and reduce tension.

C. Family members were warned about using anger-displacement techniques as practice for aggressive behavior.

D. Family members have used anger-displacement techniques, and their experience in this area was reviewed and processed.

E. Family members have not used anger-displacement techniques and were redirected to do so.

# RELIGIOUS/SPIRITUAL CONFLICTS

## CLIENT PRESENTATION

### 1. Disagreements about Religious Faith and Practices (1)*

A. Family members described frequent, upsetting verbal disagreements over religious faith issues (e.g., core beliefs about life and after-life).

B. Family members reported verbal disagreements about religious practices (e.g., communal worship, prayer).

C. Family members described some progress in resolving disagreements about core issues related to religious faith and practice.

D. As treatment has progressed, family members report a resolution of conflict over religious faith and practices.

### 2. Conflicts about Children's Religious Training (2)

A. Family members described frequent arguments about the children's religious training and expected attendance at worship services.

B. One parent supports the children's religious training and attendance at worship services, while the other parent does not support such religious involvement.

C. One parent disparages the other parent's involvement of the children in religious training and worship services.

D. As treatment has progressed, the parents have developed a mutually acceptable level of involvement for the children in religious training and worship services.

### 3. Rejection of Parent's Beliefs (3)

A. An adolescent child has decided to reject the parent's religious faith and beliefs.

B. A child has refused to attend religious services or other spiritual-based activities.

C. The adolescent child has developed religious faith beliefs that are different from the beliefs of the parents.

D. Family members have begun to reconcile the differences in their religious faith and spiritual belief concerns.

### 4. Conflicts about Child Discipline Due to Religious Beliefs (4)

A. The parents report frequent arguments about proper child-discipline strategies.

B. The parents identified that they have divergent child-discipline strategies due (in part) to differing religious and spiritual beliefs about parenting.

C. The children displayed a pattern of confusion due to the differing child-discipline strategies used by the parents.

---

*The numbers in parentheses correlate to the number of the Behavioral Definition statement in the companion chapter with the same title in *The Family Therapy Treatment Planner*, Second Ed. (Dattilio, Jongsma, and Davis) by John Wiley & Sons, 2010.

D. As treatment has progressed, the parents have developed a more cohesive, unified approach to child-discipline strategies.

### 5. Lapsing of Faith Practices (5)

A. The family has become lax in their faith practices.

B. The family has discontinued any type of structured involvement in their faith practices.

C. Family members describe a loss of spirituality in their lives.

D. The family has become involved in meaningful faith practices and reports feeling spiritually revitalized.

### 6. Parents Push Children Away from Faith (6)

A. Parents' attempts to instill their religious/spiritual beliefs in their children have had the effect of pushing the children away from the parents' faith.

B. The parents' use of physical abuse to instill religious/spiritual beliefs pushes the children away from the faith.

C. Shaming messages have been directed toward the children in an effort to instill religious values, but have had the effect of moving the children away from the faith.

D. The parents have modified their approach to the children's training in religious/spiritual issues, resulting in greater acceptance by the children.

## INTERVENTIONS IMPLEMENTED

### 1. Describe History of Religious Experiences (1)*

A. Each parent was asked to identify the role that religion and spirituality played in their childhood home and family experiences through to current involvement.

B. Each spouse was asked to explain how his/her childhood experiences influence present practice and beliefs.

C. The parents were noted to have had very similar family religious and spirituality practices through their lifespan.

D. The parents were noted to have had significantly divergent experiences in their spirituality and religious practices over their lifespan.

### 2. Request Articulation of Faith (2)

A. Each parent was asked to articulate his/her meaningful spiritual faith and belief practices.

B. The parents were supported as they identified faith beliefs and practices that are important to them.

C. Each of the parent's spiritual beliefs and faith practices were compared and contrasted.

D. The parents were identified as having rather similar faith beliefs and practices.

E. It was reflected to the parents that they have very divergent spiritual beliefs and faith practices.

---

*The numbers in parentheses correlate to the number of the Therapeutic Intervention statement in the companion chapter with the same title in *The Family Therapy Treatment Planner*, Second Ed. (Dattilio, Jongsma, and Davis) by John Wiley & Sons, 2010.

### 3. Discuss Previous Expectations (3)

A. The parents were asked to discuss what their expectations were once they had decided to enter into an interdenominational marriage.

B. The agreements regarding religious practices that were clearly understood or explicit at the time that the relationship began were reviewed and explored.

C. The agreements regarding religious practices that were understood or explicit were reflected to the parents.

D. The parents were noted to have had divergent understanding of their explicit or understood agreements at the start of the relationship.

### 4. Explore Changes from Initial Agreement (4)

A. The parents were asked to explore how their preexisting agreements regarding religious practices and/or children's training have fallen by the wayside.

B. The parents were asked to identify how changing agreements and practices have led to the present conflict.

C. The parents were encouraged to discuss with the children how they have abandoned earlier agreements about religious training and practice, leading to the present conflicts.

### 5. Explore Verbalized Misgivings about Religious Training (5)

A. The parents were asked to identify any previously unverbalized misgivings about religious training of the children.

B. Common conflicts regarding the children's religious training were reviewed as they apply to the family.

C. A safe environment for the expression of previously unverbalized misgivings about the religious training of the children was emphasized.

### 6. Identify the Effect of Religious Beliefs and Practices on Relationship (6)

A. The parents were asked to identify how their different spiritual beliefs and practices have impacted the children.

B. The parents were asked to identify how their different spiritual beliefs and practices have had an impact on the marital relationship.

C. Positive feedback was provided as the parents displayed keen insight into the effects of their different spiritual beliefs and practices on their relationship and on the children.

D. The parents tended to downplay or minimize the effect of their different spiritual beliefs and practices on their relationship and on the children; they were provided with additional feedback about how these differences can impact family life.

### 7. Explore Conflicts with In-Laws (7)

A. Family members were surveyed regarding possible conflicts between a spouse and the respective in-laws regarding the issue of religious belief and practice.

B. It was reflected to the family that there are significant conflicts between one of the parents and the respective in-laws regarding religious beliefs and practices.

C. It was reflected to the family that there appears to be very little conflict between the parents and the respective in-laws regarding religious beliefs and practices.

### 8. Clarify Religious Conflicts (8)

A. The partners were assisted in identifying the specific conflicts that exist between them regarding religious beliefs and practices.

B. Each spouse was asked to view their religious belief system from the point of view of the other spouse's belief system.

C. The parents were directed to read books about differing belief systems.

D. The parents were directed to read *Peacemakers in Action* (Little).

E. The parents have read information regarding resolving belief system conflict, and the key points were reviewed.

F. The parents have not read information about resolving belief system conflict and were redirected to do so.

### 9. Brainstorm Pros and Cons of Two Religions in the Family (9)

A. Each family member was asked to construct a list of pros and cons of the impact of two religions in the family.

B. Family members were assisted in brainstorming the positive and negative sides of having two religions in the family.

C. The list of pros and cons of having two religions in the family was summarized and reviewed.

### 10. Develop Reasons for Respecting Religious Practices (10)

A. Family members were directed to develop a list of reasons to respect each parent's religious beliefs and practices.

B. Family members were assisted in developing the reasons behind both parents' religious beliefs and practices.

C. A contract was developed regarding the need for all family members to display respect for the freedom to exercise choice of belief.

### 11. Discuss Emotional Conflicts (11)

A. A discussion was held regarding the family members' emotional reaction to conflicts over religious beliefs and practices.

B. An emphasis was placed on the children's experience of confusion, frustration, and loyalty conflicts resulting from the parents' religious conflicts.

C. Family members were supported as they expressed their emotions regarding the conflicts that occur due to differences in religious beliefs and practices.

D. Family members were encouraged for being more open about the feelings that they experience due to the conflicts regarding religious beliefs and practices.

E. Family members were guarded in regard to their feelings resulting from the family members' conflicts over religious beliefs and practices and were urged to be more open about these emotions as the trust level increases.

### 12. Highlight Areas of Conflict (12)

A. The specific areas where family members may experience religious conflict were highlighted.

B. Family members were asked to identify how conforming to one religion may affect expectations regarding the other religion.

C. Disappointment of the extended family regarding children's failure to reach certain milestones was highlighted.

### 13. Explore Lifestyle Restrictions (13)

A. The lifestyle restrictions that each parent's religious beliefs would impose on the children were explored.

B. Conflicts over lifestyle restrictions were reviewed, processed, and resolved.

### 14. Review Children's Thoughts about Religious Practices (14)

A. The children were asked to state their thoughts about desirable and undesirable characteristics of the parents' religious beliefs and practices.

B. The parents were guided not to intervene with the children as they were describing the desirable and undesirable characteristics of the parents' religious beliefs and practices.

C. The children's viewpoint of the parents' religious beliefs and practices was summarized and reflected to the entire family.

### 15. Review Religious Education Expectations (15)

A. The parents were asked to identify their desires and expectations regarding religious education for the children.

B. Parents were asked to identify what aspects of both religious beliefs and practices they would like to see adopted by the children.

C. An agreement was solicited regarding the children's education and practices.

D. Family members were reinforced for their ability to develop an agreement regarding the children's religious education and practices.

E. Family members continue to be in conflict over the children's religious education and practices and were provided with remedial support in this area.

### 16. Explore Participation and Flexibility (16)

A. Ways in which family members could participate in practices of both parents' religions were explored.

B. Family members were encouraged to use flexibility to develop conflict resolution.

C. Family members were reinforced for developing innovative ways in which family members could participate in practices of both parents' religions.

D. Family members have been inflexible about how participation in both religions can occur and were encouraged to develop more flexibility.

### 17. Emphasize Core Beliefs (17)

A. The core beliefs for each parent were highlighted and points of commonality were noted.

B. Respect for each parent's core beliefs was emphasized.

C. Family members were encouraged to share the core beliefs of each parent.

### 18. Discuss Support of Religious Training Agreements (18)

A. Family members were encouraged to discuss the ways in which they can support the agreements reached over religious training issues.

B. Family members were reinforced as they came up with innovative ways to support the agreements reached over religious training.

C. Family members struggled to identify ways in which they could support the agreements reached over religious training issues and were provided with tentative examples in this area.

### 19. Search for Interdenominational Teen Programs (19)

A. Family members were encouraged to search through both parents' denominations to locate teen groups addressing the issue of interdenominational families.

B. Family members have identified teen programs addressing the issue of interdenominational families and were urged to use these programs.

C. Family members have used the support groups for teens with interdenominational families, and the benefits of this resource were reviewed.

D. Family members have sought out others struggling with interdenominational issues and are using this for support and encouragement.

E. Family members have not sought out formal or informal resources to help those who struggle with interdenominational families and were encouraged to do so.

### 20. Develop Agreement about Independent Decisions Regarding Religion (20)

A. The parents were encouraged to discuss when the children should be able to make independent decisions regarding their participation in religious practices.

B. The parents were helped to discuss and synthesize their views regarding when the children should be able to make independent decisions about their religious practices.

C. The parents were reinforced for healthy decisions regarding when the children should be able to make their own decisions about religious practices.

D. The parents continue to be in conflict about when the children should be able to make their own decisions about religious practices and were assisted in negotiating this impasse.

### 21. Solicit Acceptance of Parents' Decision (21)

A. A discussion was held about the time when children will be able to make their own decisions about participation in religious practices.

B. The parents' expectations about how, when, and to what degree the children should make their own faith practice decisions were delineated and discussed.

C. The children were asked to agree to accept the parents' decision regarding when the children may make an independent decision about participation in religious practice.

D. The children were reinforced for their agreement as to when the parents should allow and expect them to have freedom to make their own decisions about religious practices.

E. The children have not accepted the parents' decisions about when to allow them to make their own decisions about faith practices, and the ramifications of this were discussed.

### 22. Brainstorm Denomination-Related Activities (22)

A. The family was assisted in brainstorming about denomination-related activities that the family could become involved in to help them avoid drifting away from their religion.

B. The family was reinforced for identifying a variety of denomination-related activities in which the family could become involved.

C. The family has become more involved in denomination-related activities, and the benefits of this were reviewed.

D. The family has not yet become involved in denomination-related activities and was encouraged to use this helpful resource.

### 23. Encourage Recommitment Exercises (23)

A. Family members were encouraged to be engaged in religious recommitment exercises.

B. Family members were encouraged to meet with their religious leader privately.

C. Family members were encouraged to read meditation literature together.

D. The benefits of recommitment exercises for promoting adherence to and practice of their religious beliefs was reviewed.

E. Family members have not engaged in religious recommitment exercises and were redirected to do so.

### 24. Encourage Examination of Faith Teaching Methods (24)

A. The parents were asked to describe their practices in regard to how they have worked to instill faith beliefs in their children.

B. The parents were supported as they described the successes and failures at attempting to instill faith beliefs in their children.

C. The parents were asked to examine whether their methods of instilling their religious values in their children are congruent with the value they are trying to instill.

D. The parents were provided with examples of incongruence in instilling faith practices (e.g., yelling when trying to teach peaceful conflict resolution).

E. The parents were reinforced for their honest appraisal of their pattern of instilling faith practices in their children.

### 25. List Changes to Align Beliefs and Actions (25)

A. Values clarification was done to help family members identify their faith values and behaviors.

B. Family members were asked to identify where their behavior was incongruent with their faith values.

C. Each family member was asked to list changes he/she can work on to align their behavior with their religious belief system.

D. Family members were reinforced for their honesty about their level of congruency between faith values and behaviors and their attempts to reconcile incongruence.

E. Family members were redirected for failure to honestly appraise their level of congruency between their behavior and faith values.

# REUNITING ESTRANGED FAMILY MEMBERS

## CLIENT PRESENTATION

### 1. Estrangement (1)*

A. Parents and offspring are estranged and not communicating with each other due to a specific dispute or altercation.

B. Siblings are estranged and not communicating with each other due to a specific dispute or altercation.

C. Family members are intransigent in their estrangement.

D. As treatment has progressed, the family members have become willing to engage with each other.

E. Family members have reunited.

### 2. Coalitions (2)

A. Offspring have formed coalitions with other family members against the estranged family member(s).

B. Siblings have formed coalitions with other family members against the estranged family member(s).

C. The family members often engage in behind the scenes commenting about the estranged family member(s).

D. As treatment has progressed, the family members have been less likely to engage in ganging up against the estranged family member(s).

### 3. Growing Resentment (3)

A. As time has passed, the estranged parties have had increased alienation.

B. Negative sentiments toward each other have increased as time has passed.

C. Estranged parties have been apart for years.

D. As the estranged parties have reunited, resentment of each other has decreased.

### 4. Conflict as Changes Occur (4)

A. As new information is received from third parties about changes for the estranged family member, conflict arises.

B. Conflicting family members are at a crossroads due to recent changes reported about the estranged family member.

C. A crisis situation has led to estranged family members rethinking the nature of their relationships.

*The numbers in parentheses correlate to the number of the Behavioral Definition statement in the companion chapter with the same title in *The Family Therapy Treatment Planner*, Second Ed. (Dattilio, Jongsma, and Davis) by John Wiley & Sons, 2010.

D. As the crisis has passed, estrangement has returned to the warring family members.

E. The formerly estranged family members remain more united even after the family crisis has passed.

### 5. Blame (5)

A. Certain family members blame each other for the ongoing family conflictual estrangement.

B. Family members expect other members of the family to assign blame to one side or the other.

C. Family members tend to see the issue of blame in a dichotomous or "black and white" manner.

D. As treatment has progressed, the issue of blame has been set aside.

E. Family members understand that the issue of blame is a multifaceted one and that it "takes two to tango."

### 6. Holiday Struggles (6)

A. Family member estrangement has caused some family members to struggle during the holidays.

B. Special occasions tend to highlight the fracturing of the family and ultimate loss of cohesiveness.

C. Treatment has helped family members to cope with holidays and special occasions despite ongoing estrangement.

D. As estranged parties have reunited, holidays and special occasions have become even more meaningful.

### 7. Anger and Resentment (7)

A. Family members wrestle with the pent up anger and resentment over the conflict and estrangement.

B. Family members have allowed anger and resentment from the estranged relationships to spill over into other areas in their life.

C. Despite ongoing estrangement, family members have learned to decrease their sense of anger and resentment.

D. As relationships have improved, anger and resentment have decreased.

### 8. Pressure to Serve as Go-Between (8)

A. Certain family members feel pressure by serving as the "go-between" for the estranged parties.

B. The estranged parties have consistently tried to cause others to communicate information and opinions between each other.

C. Family members have placed themselves in the position of a "go-between" in an effort to bring the estranged family members together.

D. Communication has improved within the family, with each party talking for themselves.

## INTERVENTIONS IMPLEMENTED

### 1. Explore Thoughts and Feeling (1)*

A. Active listening with warm, empathic support was used to help family members express thoughts and feelings about the estrangement.

B. Family members were urged to express their thoughts and feelings about the estrangement.

C. The different family members' thoughts and feeling were compared and contrasted.

D. A synopsis of where the different family members are at was reflected back to the family members.

### 2. Collect Information about the Conflict (2)

A. Each family member's perceptions and recollections about the specific areas of conflict were gathered.

B. Each family member was queried as to the responsibility he/she took for his/her own actions in the conflict.

C. Family members not directly involved in the conflict were asked about their recollection of the etiology and maintenance of the conflict.

D. Various observations and opinions were synthesized and reflected to the family members.

### 3. List Emotions (3)

A. Each family member was asked to list the specific emotions (e.g., anger, resentment) they experience and how they change from day to day.

B. Family members were encouraged to speak openly about their emotions and to honor the differing points of view.

C. Family members were reinforced for assertively expressing their emotions.

D. Family members remain cautious about openly asserting themselves about their emotions in regard to the conflict, and were reminded to improve communication in this manner.

### 4. Use a Timeline (4)

A. A timeline was used to clarify and define the specifics of the conflict.

B. Family members helped to develop a timeline that describes how the conflict has unfolded.

### 5. Identify Salient Factors (5)

A. Family members were asked about what factors may have contributed to the actual estrangement over the conflict.

B. Family members were assisted and supported as they developed greater information about the important aspects of how the estrangement and conflict grew.

C. The salient factors in developing the conflict were identified.

### 6. Discuss Changes (6)

A. The family was assisted in identifying specific instances in which family dynamics have changed since the conflict began.

*The numbers in parentheses correlate to the number of the Therapeutic Intervention statement in the companion chapter with the same title in *The Family Therapy Treatment Planner*, Second Ed. (Dattilio, Jongsma, and Davis) by John Wiley & Sons, 2010.

B. Several aspects of family life were reviewed in regard to how the conflict has changed the pattern of family life.

C. The family was supported as they openly discussed changes in family life routine due to the conflict.

### 7. Demonstrate Emotional Factors as Roadblocks (7)

A. The family was assisted in identifying the emotional factors that have been associated with the conflict.

B. The family was directed to identify how emotional factors might be serving as a roadblock to conflict resolution.

C. It was reflected to the family that the emotions may be more of a roadblock to recovery than the actual conflicts themselves.

### 8. List Pros of Reunification (8)

A. The family members were asked to make a list of the positive outcomes (pros) of reunification of the family.

B. Family members were assisted in developing a list of pros for the reunification

C. The family members were assisted in processing the reasons for reunification.

### 9. List Consequences of Reunification Failure (9)

A. The family members were assigned to generate a list of the negative outcomes (cons) if reunification fails.

B. Family members have developed a list of consequences should the reunification be attempted and fail, and these were processed within the session.

C. The list of consequences for attempting reunification and failure has been difficult for the family to develop, so they were given some basic examples of how this might have an effect on others (i.e., greater rift between estranged parties, new resentment for not following through on expected attempts).

D. Family members have not developed a list of consequences for trying reunification and failing, and were redirect to do so.

### 10. List Roadblocks to Reunification (10)

A. Family members were asked to make a list of the potential roadblocks to the reunification process.

B. Family members have struggled to develop a list of potential roadblocks to the reunification process, and were provided with some specific examples (i.e., emotional, geographic distance, financial, health, etc.).

C. The family was reinforced for showing insight into the potential roadblocks to reunification.

D. The family has not done much thinking about the roadblocks to reunification, and was reminded to develop a list of potential problems.

### 11. Consider Initial Contact (11)

A. Various mediums of initial contact (e.g., written correspondence via e-mail, telephone contact, video, etc.) were considered.

B. The pros and cons of each option for how to develop initial contact with the estranged family members were considered.

C. A preferred option for how to contact the estranged family members was selected.

## 12. Write Plan for Reunification Process (12)

A. The family was directed to write out a plan of action for initiating reunification of the family (i.e., how it will unfold, who will execute it and where).

B. The family has developed a plan for how the reunification process should unfold, and it was reviewed and tweaked in the session.

C. The family has had difficulty determining how to proceed with the reunification process, so the plan was developed within the session.

D. The family has not followed through on a written plan for how to proceed with reunification, and was reminded to do so.

## 13. Develop Follow-Up Steps (13)

A. The family was asked to assume a positive reaction to the initial overture to the estranged family members, and then to list any subsequent steps to take as follow-up.

B. Family members have developed a sound plan for continued follow-up with the reunification process, and this was highlighted within the session.

C. The family has not thought through what to do after an initial positive response to the reunification process, and was redirected to do so.

## 14. Make Commitment (14)

A. The family members were asked to state their commitment to the process of reunification.

B. Family members displayed some hesitancy, so this was focused on until they were more completely ready for the process to unfold.

C. Some key family members are still resistant to the option of this reunification, and the session focused on bringing them on board.

D. It was reflected that the family has a significant commitment to make the process of reunification work.

E. It was reflected to the family that there is not a significant enough consensus from the family to recommend proceeding with the reunification process.

## 15. Develop Back-Up Plan for Reunification (15)

A. The family was asked to assume a negative reaction to the initial overture to the estranged family members, and then to list any subsequent steps to take as follow-up.

B. Family members have developed a sound plan for continuing to pursue the reunification process, and this was highlighted within the session.

C. As the initial steps have failed, the family was asked to brainstorm potential remedies (e.g., waiting for a period of time before making a second attempt, a different person making the overture).

D. The family has not thought through what to do after an initial negative response to the reunification process, and was redirected to do so.

## 16. Discuss Motivation for a Second Attempt (16)

A. The family members were asked to list the reasons that would warrant a second attempt at reunification.

B. The family members were assisted in identifying the reasons that would warrant a second attempt at reunification.

C. The reasons for a second attempt at reunification were processed within the session.

D. It was reflected to the family that there is significant motivation and reasoning for the second attempt at reunification.

E. It was reflected to the family that there is not significant motivation and reasoning for the second attempt at reunification.

## 17. Discuss Further Attempts (17)

A. A discussion was held about further attempts at reunification.

B. Each family member was specifically asked about how he/she feels about further attempts at reunification.

C. It was reflected to the family that there is significant commitment for further attempts at reunification.

D. It was reflected to the family that there is not significant commitment for the second attempt at reunification.

## 18. Discuss the Second Attempt Interventions (18)

A. The interventions to use for the second attempt at bringing the estranged family members together were discussed.

B. The family was assisted in developing different ways of approaching the same problem.

C. The family was assisted in taking the reasons why the first attempt failed into consideration when deciding how to approach this second attempt.

## 19. Anticipate and Resolve Roadblocks (19)

A. The family was assisted in anticipating potential objections and roadblocks to the process of reunification.

B. The family was assisted in brainstorming constructive responses to the roadblocks and objections to the reunification process.

C. The family was reinforced for pre-empting possible roadblocks and objections.

## 20. Decide on Family Messenger (20)

A. The family was led in a discussion about who would be the best option for making the overture to the estranged family member.

B. The family was asked to determine what family member would be less threatening and most affective at making the overture to the estranged family member.

C. Volunteers were solicited to make the overture to the estranged family member.

D. A family member has been selected and instructed about how to approach the estranged family member.

### 21. Brainstorm Potential Locations (21)

A. The family was asked to brainstorm locations for approaching the estranged family member.

B. Family members were asked to consider what location would hold a higher level of potential success.

C. Family members were asked to consider a variety of concerns when reviewing the options for where to intervene with the estranged member, including issues such as a public versus private area, or at the estranged family member's home versus a neutral spot.

D. The family has decided on a place for the intervention and this choice was supported.

### 22. Open the Dialogue (22)

A. Today's session was a meeting with the estranged family member.

B. The session focused on the estranged family member meeting with the rest of the family members to open the dialogue.

C. All family members were encouraged to use "I" messages and listening skills (e.g., eye contact, facial expression, empathic or reflective listening.).

D. All family members were given the opportunity for the expression of individual perceptions and feelings.

### 23. Keep Communication Going (23)

A. Each family member was asked to commit to keeping lines of respectful communication open.

B. Although disagreements persist, family members were encouraged to keep lines of respectful communication open.

C. Family members were supported for their willingness to keep lines of communication open.

D. Family members were redirected when they have closed down lines of communication with the estranged family member.

# SEPARATION/DIVORCE

## CLIENT PRESENTATION

### 1. Erosion of Relationships (1)*

A. Marital difficulties have led to disagreements and arguments.

B. An ongoing erosion of marital and family relationships has occurred due to ongoing disagreements and arguments.

C. Despite attempts to decrease conflict in the relationship, marital dissatisfaction has continued to grow.

D. As treatment has progressed, the marital difficulties, disagreements, and arguments have decreased and family relationships are improving.

### 2. Alienation (2)

A. The partners identified increased feelings of being alienated from each other.

B. The partners have identified a sense of distance in the relationship.

C. The family unit has experienced tension due to the alienation between the partners.

D. As treatment has progressed, the partners have developed a closer bond.

E. The partners are sharing time, thoughts, and feelings with each other.

### 3. Fear of Separation (3)

A. Talk about separation and divorce has sparked fear and concern among various family members.

B. Family members have tended to overcompensate, including parentification and overindulgence, due to the fear and concern about separation.

C. As treatment has progressed, talk about separation has decreased.

D. The family has become more at ease with the possibility of separation.

### 4. Separation (4)

A. The parents have made a decision to separate.

B. Family members are uncertain about which family members will remain in the home, and which family members will leave.

C. Children display loyalty conflicts regarding which parent they should be living with.

D. As the family has adjusted to the process of separation, decisions have been finalized regarding where family members will live.

### 5. Loyalty Conflicts (5)

A. The children experience loyalty conflicts due to being separated from one parent.

B. The children display loyalty conflicts due to being separated from other siblings.

---

*The numbers in parentheses correlate to the number of the Behavioral Definition statement in the companion chapter with the same title in *The Family Therapy Treatment Planner*, Second Ed. (Dattilio, Jongsma, and Davis) by John Wiley & Sons, 2010.

C. The parents often make comments that exacerbate the children's loyalty conflicts.

D. The parents have emphasized that children living with one parent versus another does not mean a lack of loyalty to either parent.

E. The children have appeared to have resolved their loyalty conflicts.

### 6. Separated/Divorced within the Same Home (6)

A. The parents have made a decision to separate, but remain under the same roof.

B. The parents have divorced, but remain living in the same home.

C. The estranged parents living within the same home display coldness toward each other.

D. The parents have developed a plan to make the separation more complete, including living in separate homes.

E. The parents have now become physically separated as well as emotionally separated.

### 7. Financial Difficulties (7)

A. Due to the parents' separation, two separate households must be maintained.

B. Financial concerns have developed for the custodial parent.

C. Financial concerns have developed for the noncustodial parent.

D. Both parents experience financial hardship due to needing to maintain two separate homes.

E. Financial resources and amenities for the family members have decreased due to the need to maintain two separate households.

F. Family members have adjusted to the financial changes subsequent to establishing two separate households.

### 8. Emotional/Behavioral Reactions (8)

A. Family members described feelings of anxiety and depression due to the changes that have occurred within the family.

B. Family members have displayed acting-out behaviors due to the changes that have occurred within the family (e.g., substance use, poor school performance).

C. The underlying extramarital emotional conflicts prompting anxiety, depression, and acting-out behaviors were processed and resolved.

D. Family members' symptoms of depression, anxiety, and acting-out behaviors have been decreased.

### 9. Accommodation of New Family Members (9)

A. New relationships have been developed due to remarriage.

B. The stepparent and stepchildren relationships have developed due to the parent's new relationship.

C. New relationships have been developed with stepsiblings.

D. Conflict has arisen due to the changes in relationships between new stepparents, stepchildren, and stepsiblings.

### 10. Child-Management Problems (10)

A. Child-management problems have developed due to the new single-parent status.

B. Child-management problems have been exacerbated by a lack of support from the ex-spouse.

C. Separate families have developed unique rules and guidelines for child behavior that has resulted in uncertainty for the children caught between the two families.

D. The family has adjusted to the single-parent status and has been able to develop healthy child-management techniques.

### 11. Children Assume Blame for Marital Failure (11)

A. Children often make comments about how they feel they were a partial cause for the marital failure.

B. The parents' comments support the children's assumption that they are to blame for the marital failure.

C. Although the parents have made clear statements about the children not being the cause of the marriage failing, other statements and behavior send a contrary message.

D. Both parents have made clear statements that the children are not to blame for the marital failure and back this up on a regular basis.

E. Children no longer take the blame for the marital failure.

## INTERVENTIONS IMPLEMENTED

### 1. Explore Marriage Conflicts (1)*

A. The parents' relationship was explored for conflicts that may be leading to separation and divorce.

B. As the conflicts were assessed, the intensity of these conflicts was noted to be quite severe.

C. The marriage conflicts were assessed and the intensity was judged to be minimal.

D. The nature and severity of the marital conflicts were reflected to the couple.

### 2. Assess Motivation for Resolution (2)

A. Each spouse was assessed regarding the motivation to resolve the conflicts.

B. As both spouses were motivated to resolve the conflicts, the primary focus has been on the marriage relationship.

C. The spouses show ambivalence in their desire to resolve the marital relationship, and the focus was on defining and strengthening this resolve.

D. The spouses have little desire to resolve the marital conflicts, and the focus on treatment has been to facilitate the next steps in the dissolution of the marriage.

*The numbers in parentheses correlate to the number of the Therapeutic Intervention statement in the companion chapter with the same title in *The Family Therapy Treatment Planner*, Second Ed. (Dattilio, Jongsma, and Davis) by John Wiley & Sons, 2010.

### 3. Refer for Couple's Treatment (3)

A. The partners were referred for couple's psychotherapy.

B. The couple was referred to a marriage enrichment group.

C. The couple was requested to read *Cognitive Therapy with Couples* (Dattilio and Padesky).

D. The couple has followed up on the assigned resources for couple's psychotherapy, and the benefits of this treatment were reviewed.

E. The couple has not followed up on the assigned treatment and was reminded about these helpful resources.

### 4. Recommend Conflict Resolution Readings (4)

A. The couple was provided with resources on conflict resolution.

B. The couple was directed to read *Fighting for Your Marriage* (Markman, Stanley, and Blumberg).

C. The couple was directed to read *The Seven Principles for Making Marriage Work* (Gottman and Silver).

D. The couple has read material about conflict resolution, and key concepts were reviewed and processed.

E. The couple has not read material about conflict resolution and was redirected to do so.

### 5. Obtain Other Family Members' Perspective on Marriage (5)

A. Other family members were polled to assess their perceptions of the marital difficulties.

B. The children were assessed for the accuracy of their understanding of the marital difficulties.

C. Because the children are older, direct dialogue was used to assess their understanding of the marital difficulties.

D. Because the children are younger, the *Thinking, Feeling, and Doing Game* (Gardener) was used to assess their understanding of the marital difficulties.

E. Because the children are very young, drawing and play activities were used to assess their understanding of the marital difficulties.

### 6. Facilitate Children's Expression of Emotions (6)

A. The children were encouraged to express their feelings about the marriage conflict.

B. The children were encouraged to write a story about the family and the marriage conflicts.

C. The children were encouraged to depict the family dynamics through the use of drawings.

D. The children were supported as they expressed their feelings about the family dynamics.

E. The children were guarded about their feelings about the marriage difficulties, and were encouraged to express their emotions when they feel able to do so.

### 7. Suggest Parents Disengage from Battle (7)

A. The parents' marital struggle was characterized as a battle with "ugliness" such as arguments and disagreements.

B. The parents were directed to disengage from their battle in order to stay engaged with their children.

C. It was emphasized to the parents that any time spent focusing on the fighting in the marriage is time taken away from the children.

D. The parents were taught about the adverse effects of children seeing the parents battling with constant arguments and disagreements.

E. The parents were reinforced for reporting a decrease in their pattern of displaying marital problems in front of the children.

F. The parents have continued to display the ugliness of their marital problems to the children and were redirected in this area.

## 8. Encourage Structured Family Meetings (8)

A. The use of structured family meetings was encouraged to focus on the children's needs, instead of on the parents' issues.

B. The family was assisted in setting guidelines for structuring family meetings to focus on the children's needs rather than on the parents' issues.

C. The family has used structured family meetings to help discuss the children's needs, and the benefits of these meetings were processed.

D. The family has not used structured family meetings and was redirected to do so.

## 9. Discuss Fears regarding Marital Breakup (9)

A. A forum regarding their fears and concerns about the marital breakup was opened among family members.

B. Family members were assisted in processing the most dreaded outcome as if it were actually to occur.

C. Reading material was provided to the family members to help express their feelings regarding the marital breakup.

D. Family members were directed to read *Mom's House, Dad's House* (Ricci).

E. Family members were directed to read *Dinosaur's Divorce* (Brown and Brown).

F. Family members' feelings were processed after they read the assigned material and expressed emotions regarding the marital breakup.

G. Family members have not read the assigned material on marital breakup and were redirected to do so.

## 10. Suggest Coping Mechanisms (10)

A. The children were assisted in defining their fears and concerns related to the family break-up (e.g., having to live with one parent and visiting the other on weekends, having less money to live on).

B. Specific coping skills were identified to help the children deal with their fears and concerns subsequent to a break-up.

C. The parents were encouraged to have open communication regarding the children.

D. Family members were encouraged to pledge to sacrifice together financially.

E. Periodic family meetings were suggested as a way to exchange views.

F. The children have used the coping mechanisms for dealing with specific fears and concerns, and the benefits of these techniques were reviewed.

G. The children have not used specific coping mechanisms for dealing with fears and concerns and were redirected to do so.

## 11. Develop Community Support Systems (11)

A. Family members were asked to identify support systems in the community that can be used for coping with the problems associated with the marital break-up.

B. Family members were encouraged to use community support services.

C. Family members were provided with examples of community support systems (e.g., extended family members, church groups, school services).

D. Family members have not used the support systems in the community and were reminded about these helpful resources.

## 12. Facilitate Role Description (12)

A. Family members were asked to describe their roles in the family in light of the marital difficulties.

B. Family members were assisted in describing their roles in the family and how they have changed due to the marital difficulties.

C. Analogies and family sculpting techniques were used to accentuate the roles and discuss how each family member's role impacts other family members.

D. Family members were reinforced for their insight into how family roles have changed.

E. Family members were uncertain about how family roles have changed and were provided with tentative examples about how this often occurs.

## 13. Assess for Overcompensation (13)

A. Family members were assessed for overcompensation strategies.

B. Family members were taught about overcompensation strategies, and how these are likely to cause additional problems (e.g., a child taking the role of caretaker, a parent overindulging a child with material items).

C. Family members who have used overcompensating strategies were provided with feedback on this pattern.

D. Family members were supported for no longer using overcompensating strategies to cope with family problems and this was reflected to them.

## 14. Explore Changes in Power within the Family (14)

A. Issues regarding the balance of power that have emerged in the wake of the separation/ divorce were explored.

B. Family members were assisted in identifying how different alliances have developed due to the separation and divorce.

C. Family members were assisted in identifying how different family members have emerged as caretakers for the family due to the separation.

### 15. Suggest Role Change Exercises (15)

A. Family members were directed to role-play how the different family member's roles might be experienced.

B. Family members were asked to express their feelings about taking on different roles.

C. Family members were reinforced for their insight into how other family members may be experiencing their roles within the family.

### 16. Reinforce Role Alteration (16)

A. Family members were reinforced for being open to alteration in roles, expectations, and perceptions.

B. Cognitive restructuring techniques were used to help change the way the family thinks about roles, expectations, and perceptions.

C. The evidence for the acceptance of specific roles, expectations, and perceptions was challenged to help the family restructure their beliefs in this area.

### 17. Suggest Parents Reading on Divorce Issues (17)

A. The parents were directed to read information regarding divorce and its effect on the family.

B. The parents were directed to read *How It Feels When Parents Divorce* (Krementz).

C. The parents were directed to read *Why Are We Getting Divorced?* (Mayle and Robbins).

D. The parents have read appropriate information on divorce and the effects on the family, and the key points of this information were reviewed.

E. The parents have not read information about divorce and its effect on the family and were redirected to do so.

### 18. Brainstorm about Not Moving the Children (18)

A. The parents were asked to brainstorm ways in which the separation can occur without having to move the children.

B. It was suggested that the parents rent an apartment outside of the home that each can use when not spending time with the children, and that the parents rotate in and out of the house while the children remain.

C. One parent was directed to rent a home very near the children to allow easy access and frequent visits by the children.

D. The parents came up with helpful ideas to avoid moving the children and were encouraged to investigate these more fully.

### 19. Reinforce the Need for Working Together (19)

A. The parents were reinforced for working together in order to avoid placing the children in a position of having to choose which parent to live with.

B. The parents were directed to read *The Good Divorce* (Aprons).

C. The parents have read the assigned material on how to have a healthy divorce, and key points were reviewed.

D. The parents have not read the assigned material on having a healthy divorce and were redirected to do so.

E. The parents were reinforced for avoiding placing the children in the middle of the parental conflict.

F. The parents have continued to place the children in the middle of the parental conflict and were confronted about this pattern.

### 20. Facilitate Expression about Loyalty (20)

A. The children were encouraged to express how they feel about loyalty issues.

B. The children were assisted in identifying situations in which they have had to choose between two parents and were helped to process these conflicting feelings.

C. Structured games (e.g., The Ungame) were used to help the children express their feelings about having to choose between parents.

D. The children were reinforced, as they have been open about expressing the emotions that they experience when they have to choose between two parents.

E. The children have been quite defensive about expressing the emotions they experience when having to choose between parents and were encouraged to be open about this as they feel safe in doing so.

### 21. Use Creative Exercises (21)

A. The family was directed to use creative exercises to better understand the feelings about the parents' separation and divorce.

B. *Teens Are Non-Divorceable* (Bonkowski) was used to help adolescents better understand their feelings about their parents' separation and divorce.

C. *Children Are Non-Divorceable* (Bonkowski) was used to help the children better understand their feelings about their parents' separation and divorce.

D. The children's experience of expressing their emotions about the parents' separation and divorce was reviewed.

### 22. Emphasize Boundaries (22)

A. It was emphasized to the family that they need to maintain personal and family role boundaries within the family and between family members.

B. Specific examples of situations in which children have attempted to become caretakers were reflected to the family.

C. Specific situations in which the parents have shared intimate details with the children, or leaned on them for emotional support were reviewed and discouraged from being repeated.

D. Family members were reinforced for maintaining healthy boundaries.

### 23. Recommend Reading on Boundaries (23)

A. The parents were recommended to read information about maintaining personal and family role boundaries.

B. The parents were recommended to read *Boundaries: Where You End and I Begin* (Katherine).

C. The parents have read the material on maintaining personal and family role boundaries, and key points were reviewed.

D. The parents have not read the material on maintaining personal and family role boundaries and were redirected to do so.

### 24. Focus on Financial Losses (24)

A. The family was asked to focus on specific amenities that will be lost due to needing to maintain two households.

B. Family members were encouraged to allow for the release of anger and resentment feelings.

C. Family members were encouraged as they expressed their feelings regarding anger and resentment at the loss of certain amenities to the family members.

D. Family members have been guarded about their emotions regarding losses that will occur due to the separation/divorce and were encouraged to be more open in this area.

### 25. Highlight Coping Skills Needed Due to Financial Changes (25)

A. Family members were assisted in identifying specific coping skills that need to be developed because of the change in the financial situation.

B. Family members were supported as they identified several coping skills to use to help deal with the change in the financial situation.

C. Family members struggled to identify coping skills to help with the changes in the financial situation and were provided with tentative examples (e.g., living with less, spending more wisely, borrowing items, bartering).

### 26. Identify Acting-Out Behaviors (26)

A. Family members were asked to outline the problematic behavior of children who are acting out in reaction to this family crisis.

B. Family members were supported as they openly identified acting-out behaviors that have been occurring within the family.

C. Family members were helped to clearly define the problematic behavior without minimizing or excusing the children's behavior.

### 27. Refer for Adjunctive Therapy (27)

A. The children's specific behavior problems appear to be more than what can be addressed in family therapy, and they were referred for individual therapy.

B. The children were referred for group therapy to assist in resolving their behavior problems.

C. The family has followed up on the referral for adjunctive therapy for the children's behavior problems, and the benefits of this treatment were reviewed.

D. The family has not followed up on the adjunctive treatment for the children's therapy and was redirected to do so.

### 28. Allow for Venting Regarding Blended Family (28)

A. The children were asked to express their feelings regarding having to meet and share with the parent's new mate and new stepsiblings.

B. The children were allowed to vent anger about being a part of a new blended family.

C. The children were supported as they described their resentment about the changes that have happened as the blended family has been created.

D. When the parents tried to defuse or deny the children's feelings about the new blended family they were urged to allow this type of venting.

E. The children were quite guarded about describing their feelings regarding the parent's new mate and the new stepsiblings and were provided with tentative examples of emotions that children may feel in this situation.

## 29. Establish a Neutral Zone (29)

A. The family session was structured to allow the children to express themselves without fear of retaliation.

B. The family session was designated as a neutral zone, in which feelings can be freely and respectfully expressed.

C. Family members were reminded not to retaliate against each other for honest identification of emotions.

## 30. Define Conflict Regarding Blending of Families (30)

A. Family members were asked to specifically define the conflict that occurs as a result of the blending of two family systems.

B. Metaphor techniques were used to help the family clearly define the conflicts resulting from the blending of families.

C. Family-sculpting techniques were used to help facilitate the expression of feelings regarding the blended family status.

D. Family members were reinforced for their willingness to clearly define and express themselves regarding the problems that arise due to the blending of families.

## 31. Plan Blended Family Activities (31)

A. The family was directed to plan group activities involving children from both partners in an attempt to strengthen this bond.

B. The family was assisted in planning specific activities that will involve the children from both partners.

C. Family members' experience of the blended family activities was reviewed and processed.

D. Family members have not engaged in activities that include all of the blended family members and were reminded about how this can be helpful.

## 32. Hold Conjoint Session Regarding Parenting (32)

A. The biological parent/ex-spouse was invited into a conjoint session to discuss differences in parenting philosophies, strategies, and misperceptions.

B. The biological parents were encouraged to identify ways in which their parenting philosophies and strategies are similar.

C. The parents were encouraged to use a unified parenting program.

D. The parents were encouraged to use principles and techniques described in *Parent Effectiveness Training* (Gordon) as a basis for consistent parenting.

E. The parents were encouraged to use the principals of *1-2-3 Magic* (Phelan) as a way to provide consistent parenting.

F. The biological parents were strongly reinforced for reporting the use of similar parenting techniques.

G. The parents do not use similar parenting techniques and were urged to do this immediately.

### 33. Process Resentments (33)

A. A conjoint meeting was held with the biological parents to address and process any resentment or other feelings that may be feeding the children's acting-out behaviors.

B. The parents were reminded about how their resentment can often be directly or indirectly perceived by the children, and lead to acting-out behaviors.

C. The parents were reinforced as they expressed and processed their leftover feelings and resentment.

D. The parents were urged to set aside these old hurts and move on to provide their children with emotional support.

### 34. Address Insecurity, Power, and Favoritism Issues (34)

A. A separate conjoint session was held to address the blended family parents' personal insecurities, feelings of loss of power, and demonstrations of favoritism.

B. The blended family parents were assisted in developing alternative methods for dealing with personal insecurities and fears of loss of power.

C. Conjoint treatment was used to resolve parental insecurity and power issues.

### 35. Address Manipulation (35)

A. The parent's manipulation of the children against the other parent was addressed and processed.

B. The manipulation of one parent against the other by the children was addressed and processed.

C. Family members were confronted when manipulation was evident.

D. Family members were reinforced when they reported a decline in manipulation of other family members.

E. Family members resisting manipulation were reinforced and supported.

### 36. Process Role Options (36)

A. Parents were assisted in identifying the role that each plays in their parenting conflicts.

B. Role exchange techniques were used to help parents see alternatives regarding parenting conflicts.

C. Alternative roles to be used in parenting conflicts were delineated.

D. Parents were encouraged to consider the advantages and disadvantages of behavior changes.

E. Parents were reminded about the fear that accompanies change.

### 37. Emphasize Parents' Responsibility (37)

A. The parents were encouraged to actively take responsibility for the demise of their marriage.

B. The children were reinforced for stating that the failure of the marriage is not their responsibility.

C. The parents were reinforced when they took full responsibility for their separation and divorce.

### 38. Engage Children in Guilt-Reducing Exercises (38)

A. The children were encouraged to engage in guilt-reducing exercises.

B. The children were encouraged to self-monitor statements of self-blame for the failure of the marriage.

C. The children were encouraged to use self-talk techniques to emphasize that they should not assume responsibility for the divorce.

### 39. Discourage Parents Blaming Each Other (39)

A. The parents were encouraged to stop blaming each other for the divorce.

B. The parents were encouraged to take responsibility for their own actions and contributions to the divorce.

C. The parents were reinforced for emphasizing that they are responsible for their own behavior.

### 40. Role-Play Questions about Separation/Divorce (40)

A. The children were asked to role-play social situations in which they may be asked questions about the separation and divorce.

B. The children were provided with examples of how to respond to questions about the separation and divorce.

C. The children were reinforced for providing appropriate, straightforward responses to questions about the parents' divorce.

D. The children were directed to defer questions about the separation and divorce to the parents.

### 41. Refer to Support Group (41)

A. The children were referred to a support group for children of divorce.

B. The children have attended a support group for children from a divorced family, and the benefits of this support group were reviewed and highlighted.

C. The children have not attended a divorce support group and were reminded about this helpful resource.

### 42. Process Support Group Experience (42)

A. The children have been involved in a support group and this experience was processed.

B. The children were asked to identify three things they have learned while in the Children of Divorce Support Group.

C. The children have not been involved in a support group, and the parents were directed to coordinate this.

# SEXUAL ORIENTATION CONFLICTS

## CLIENT PRESENTATION

### 1. Disclosure of Homosexuality/Bisexuality/Transgenderism (1)*

A. A family member has divulged having a homosexual/bisexual/transgendered orientation.

B. The family is struggling with the family member's disclosure of homosexuality/bisexuality/transgenderism.

C. The homosexual/bisexual/transgendered family member has been crushed by the parental rejection received on disclosing the homosexual/bisexual/transgendered orientation.

D. The homosexual/bisexual/transgendered family member was surprised and shocked by the acceptance that has been displayed by the parents after the disclosure of homosexuality/bisexuality/transgenderism.

### 2. Family Reaction (2)

A. Family members expressed mixed emotions regarding the family member's disclosure regarding his or her sexual orientation.

B. Family members seem to have rejected the homosexual/bisexual/transgendered family member due to the disclosure regarding sexual orientation.

C. Family members are experiencing conflict due to the mixed emotions and varied reactions to the disclosure about homosexuality/bisexuality/transgenderism.

D. The family has become more at ease and accepting of the disclosure about a family member's homosexual/bisexual/transgendered orientation.

### 3. Alienation (3)

A. The homosexual/bisexual/transgendered family member has been ostracized by other family members, who refuse to have significant contact.

B. The homosexual/bisexual/transgendered family member feels alienated from other family members.

C. Family members have made unkind remarks, threats, or otherwise mistreated the homosexual/bisexual/transgendered family member.

D. As treatment has progressed, the family has become more capable of supporting and accepting each other.

### 4. Parents' Feelings of Failure (4)

A. The homosexual/bisexual/transgendered family member reported that the parents are feeling responsible and to blame for the homosexual/bisexual/transgendered orientation.

*The numbers in parentheses correlate to the number of the Behavioral Definition statement in the companion chapter with the same title in *The Family Therapy Treatment Planner*, Second Ed. (Dattilio, Jongsma, and Davis) by John Wiley & Sons, 2010.

B. The parents expressed feelings of failure in regard to their child's homosexuality/bisexuality/transgenderism.

C. The parents denied any feelings of responsibility or failure due to their child's homosexuality/bisexuality/transgenderism.

D. The parents have begun to work through their feelings of failure in regard to their child's homosexuality/bisexuality/transgenderism.

### 5. Parents Blame Each Other (5)

A. The parents tend to project the blame for their child's sexual preferences on each other.

B. The parents often have heated arguments because of the projected blame for their child's sexual preferences.

C. The parents have become more realistic in regard to the reasons for their child's sexual orientation and have decreased blaming each other.

### 6. Homophobia (6)

A. Family members revealed homophobic fears that they will be negatively affected by the other family member's sexual orientation.

B. Family members have made unsubstantiated comments about the family member's sexual orientation (e.g., homosexuality will cause the family member to molest children).

C. Family members have become more realistic in their understanding of the family member's sexual orientation.

D. Family members have resolved their homophobic fears.

### 7. Social Reprisal (7)

A. Fears of social reprisal or rejection from people outside the family have been identified by family members.

B. Family members avoid discussing the issue of homosexuality/bisexuality/transgenderism for fear of social reprisal or rejection.

C. The homosexual/bisexual/transgendered family member has declined to make public the homosexual orientation.

D. Family members have been more supportive of each other, and less concerned about social reprisal or rejection.

E. Family members are open about the family member's sexual orientation.

### 8. Family Schisms (8)

A. Family members have different views regarding homosexuality/bisexuality/transgenderism, which have caused major family schisms.

B. Family members often have strong arguments about homosexuality/bisexuality/transgenderism.

C. The homosexual/bisexual/transgendered family member feels caught in the middle of the family members' arguments regarding homosexuality/bisexuality/transgenderism.

D. Family members have agreed to put their arguments about homosexuality/bisexuality/transgenderism aside and emphasize family love and support.

### 9. Rejection of Homosexual/Bisexual/Transgendered Friends/Partner (9)

A. Family members are accepting of the homosexual/bisexual/transgendered family member, but tend to reject that family member's homosexual/bisexual/transgendered friends or partner.

B. Family members have declined to invite the homosexual/bisexual/transgendered family member's partner to family gatherings.

C. The homosexual/bisexual/transgendered family member has been told not to bring homosexual/bisexual/transgendered friends or partners to the home.

D. As family members have become more open and accepting, the homosexual/bisexual/transgendered family member's friends and partner have been more readily accepted.

## INTERVENTIONS IMPLEMENTED

### 1. Discuss Homosexual Preference Revelation (1)*

A. The family was encouraged to discuss how the homosexual/bisexual/transgendered preference of a family member became known.

B. The homosexual/bisexual/transgendered family member was asked to identify whether the disclosure about the homosexual/bisexual/transgendered preference was purposeful or accidental.

### 2. Encourage Expression of Emotions (2)

A. Family members were encouraged to express their feelings regarding how the family member's sexual orientation is affecting everyone in the immediate family.

B. Family members were supported as they expressed their feelings regarding the family member's sexual orientation.

C. Family members were guarded about expressing their feelings about the family member's sexual orientation and were provided with tentative examples about how these revelations affect family members.

### 3. Discuss Heredity versus Choice (3)

A. An open discussion was held regarding the family members' views surrounding the issue of heredity versus choice in determining a person's sexual orientation.

B. Family members were noted to be focused on heredity and genetics as the determining factors for a person's sexual orientation.

C. Family members were noted to be focused on choice as the determining factor in a person's sexual orientation.

D. Family members displayed a balanced focus of heredity and choice as the determining factors for a person's sexual orientation.

---

*The numbers in parentheses correlate to the number of the Therapeutic Intervention statement in the companion chapter with the same title in *The Family Therapy Treatment Planner*, Second Ed. (Dattilio, Jongsma, and Davis) by John Wiley & Sons, 2010.

E. Family members were reinforced for their open discussion about the issues related to sexual orientation.

F. Family members were quite controlling and closed as they talked about the reasons for a person's sexual orientation and were encouraged to be more open to others' opinions.

### 4. Talk about Influences on Sexuality (4)

A. Today's session focused on how each individual is influenced by family members, peers, and the media during their upbringing, and how this affects sexuality.

B. Family members were encouraged to provide their beliefs and ideas regarding how different influences can affect a person's sexuality.

C. Family members were encouraged as they provided specific examples about how family members, peers, and the media have affected their sexuality.

D. Family members were guarded about their beliefs regarding sexuality and were encouraged to be more open in discussing these areas.

### 5. Discuss Research on Sexuality (5)

A. Today's session focused on heredity and sexuality, and how sexual preference may be genetically influenced.

B. Family members were provided with specific information regarding genetic influences on sexuality.

C. An open discussion was held regarding the available information on sexual preference, genetics, and heredity.

D. Family members were opposed to accepting information about heredity, genetic influences, and sexuality; they were encouraged to continue investigating this concept.

### 6. Discuss Moral Values (6)

A. Today's session focused on the moral values that family members have regarding sexual orientation.

B. Family members were asked to identify their moral values regarding sexuality, and how they have arrived at these moral values.

C. Family members were asked to comment on how their individual values may differ from those held by others in the family.

D. It was reflected to the family members that they have a very consistent pattern of moral values regarding sexual orientation.

E. It was reflected to the family that there is a wide divergence of moral values between the family members.

### 7. Develop Understanding of Etiology of Values (7)

A. Family members were asked to describe how they arrived at their moral values regarding sexual orientation.

B. Family members were assisted in understanding the many influences that have helped them to arrive at their moral values regarding sexual orientation.

C. It was noted that family members' values regarding sexual orientation have been based primarily on tradition.

D. It was noted that the family's values regarding sexual orientation have been based primarily on religious beliefs.

E. It was noted that popular culture has influenced much of the family members' beliefs regarding sexual orientation.

## 8. Clarify Religious and Moral Beliefs (8)

A. The family was assisted in clarifying their religious and moral beliefs about whether homosexual/bisexual/transgendered behavior violates their moral expectations.

B. It was noted that family members described no religious or moral prohibitions regarding homosexual/bisexual/transgendered behavior.

C. Family members were uncertain about their religious or moral beliefs regarding homosexual/bisexual/transgendered behavior and were encouraged to develop a greater understanding in this area through such avenues as reading or talking with a clergy.

D. Family members clearly identified that religious and moral beliefs prohibit homosexual/bisexual/transgendered behavior and this was accepted.

## 9. Assess Conflict Regarding Moral Beliefs (9)

A. Family members were assessed regarding conflict due to their differing moral beliefs about sexual orientation.

B. Family members were assessed for their openness regarding others' religious and moral beliefs for homosexual/bisexual/transgendered behavior.

C. It was reflected to the family that there was a great deal of conflict between family members due to their differing religious and moral beliefs.

D. It was reflected to the family that there is very little conflict regarding their differing moral beliefs about sexual orientation.

## 10. Brainstorm Ways to Resolve Religious/Moral Conflicts (10)

A. Family members were assisted in brainstorming ways to address concerns about the violation of their religious beliefs by a family member's homosexual/bisexual/transgendered orientation.

B. Family members were urged to speak with their clergy regarding how the family member's homosexual/bisexual/transgendered orientation violates their religious beliefs.

C. Family members were encouraged to read literature with different religious viewpoints to help resolve the conflicts between their religious beliefs and a family member's homosexual/bisexual/transgendered orientation.

D. Family members were encouraged to speak to a clergy member who is more accepting of homosexual/bisexual/transgendered behavior and to consider these viewpoints, as well.

## 11. Discuss Freedom to Choose Sexual Practices (11)

A. Today's session focused on the discussion of the individual freedom to choose sexual practices.

B. Family members were asked to talk about the need for accountability for one's own actions, without being subject to judgment from others.

C. Family members were reinforced for affirming that each family member must make personal choices and take responsibility for those choices.

## 12. Encourage Respectful Expression of Feelings (12)

A. Family members were encouraged to express their feelings in a manner that promotes release, but is respectful to the homosexual/bisexual/transgendered family member.

B. Role-playing techniques were used to help encourage family members to express their feelings in a respectful manner.

C. Modeling techniques were used to demonstrate to the family how to express feelings in a respectful manner.

D. Assertiveness techniques were taught to the family to help them express their feelings in a manner that promotes release, but is respectful to the homosexual/bisexual/transgendered family member.

E. Family members were reinforced for expressing their feelings in a respectful manner.

F. As family members expressed their feelings in a disrespectful manner, they were redirected.

## 13. Explore for Homophobia/Insecurity (14)

A. Family members' emotions were reviewed for the presence of homophobic fears.

B. Family members' emotions were reviewed for feelings of insecurity that prompt their negative reaction to the family member's sexual orientation.

C. Family members were assisted in processing through their homophobic fears and insecurities.

D. Family members' were assessed for homophobic fears and insecurities, but none were identified.

## 14. Assess Rationality of Beliefs (14)

A. Family members' emotions were assessed as to whether they are based on rational or irrational beliefs.

B. Family members were noted to have incorrect information and were provided with more realistic evidence in this area.

C. Family members' were reviewed for the rationality of their beliefs and it was reflected that their beliefs appear to be rational and based on accurate information.

D. Family members were assisted in developing alternative thoughts and beliefs based on accurate information.

## 15. Use Role-Reversal Techniques (15)

A. Role-reversal techniques were used to encourage the family members to articulate and support others' opinions.

B. Family members were encouraged to consider some of the opposing views of other family members.

C. Family members were asked to describe other family members' opinions from that family member's point of view.

D. Family members were supported as they identified wisdom within opposing points of view.

E. Family members were strongly defended against considering an opposing point of view and were encouraged to consider these as they feel capable of doing so.

## 16. Reinforce Family Cohesiveness (16)

A. Family members were asked to review activities that the family can engage in that might reinforce family cohesiveness.

B. Family members were reinforced for participating in activities that increase family cohesion.

C. Family members have not engaged in family cohesiveness activities and were redirected to do so.

## 17. Review Family Experience of Social Alienation (17)

A. Family members were assisted in determining whether they are experiencing social alienation from others because a family member is homosexual/bisexual/transgendered, and how to cope with this.

B. Family members were supported as they identified situations in which they have experienced social alienation from others because a family member is homosexual/bisexual/transgendered.

C. Coping skills for experiences of social alienation were brainstormed.

D. It was noted that family members do not appear to be experiencing social alienation because another family member is homosexual/bisexual/transgendered, and this was reflected to them.

## 18. Review Fears about Societal Reaction (18)

A. Family members were asked to review their specific fears regarding societal reaction to homosexual/bisexual/transgendered orientation.

B. Family members were supported as they expressed their fears about societal reactions to homosexual/bisexual/transgendered orientation.

C. Family members were asked to rank their fears relative to how realistic these fears may be.

D. Family members were quite guarded and cautious about expressing their fears about societal responses to homosexual/bisexual/transgendered orientation and were encouraged to be more open as they feel that this setting is safe to do so.

## 19. Role-Play Social Situations (19)

A. Family members were directed to role-play social events that deal with responding to questions about family members' marital status, sexual orientation, and so on.

B. Family members were provided with feedback as they role-played less emotionally charged social situations, such as responding to questions about a family member's marital status.

C. Family members were provided with support as they role-played more difficult social situations, such as responding to outside questions about the family member's sexual orientation.

D. Family members were provided with alternative, nondefensive responses to awkward social situations.

## 20. Direct Critiques of Role-Plays (20)

A. Family members were encouraged to provide each other with feedback on the role-plays about difficult social situations.

B. Family members were supported as they suggested alternative, nondefensive responses to social situations regarding sexual orientation questions.

### 21. Suggest Alternative Modes of Expressing Emotions (21)

A. Family members were encouraged to use alternative modes of expressing their emotions, instead of blunt verbalization.

B. Family members were encouraged to use journal writing to express their emotions.

C. Family members were encouraged to use artwork to express their emotions.

### 22. Suggest Literature on Human Sexuality (22)

A. Family members were directed to read literature in the area of human sexuality.

B. Family members were directed to read *The Family Guide to Sex and Relationships* (Walker).

C. Family members were directed to read *A Place at the Table* (Bawer).

D. Family members have not read the assigned information on human sexuality and were directed to do so.

### 23. Discuss Information on Sexuality (23)

A. Family members were asked to review and discuss the information that they have read on human sexuality.

B. Family members were asked how the information about human sexuality has affected their thoughts and beliefs.

C. Family members were assisted in summarizing the information that they have read, and how this changes their thoughts, feelings, and beliefs.

D. Family members were asked to identify how the changes in their thoughts, feelings, and belief will change their actions.

### 24. Examine Blame (24)

A. The parents were asked to elaborate on why they blame themselves for their child's sexual orientation.

B. The parents were assessed for guilt issues related to their child's sexual orientation.

C. The parents were assessed for fears about their own sexuality.

D. The parents were supported as they expressed their feelings of blame, guilt, or fear.

### 25. Suggest Individual Therapy (25)

A. Since unresolvable, significant personal issues of guilt, anxiety, anger, rejection, or depression have been displayed during the family session, individual therapy was suggested.

B. A referral was made for individual therapy for a family member struggling with personal emotional issues.

C. The family therapist will provide individual therapy to a family member due to strong emotional issues.

D. Individual therapy has been used to help resolve issues of guilt, anxiety, anger, rejection, or depression and the benefits of this treatment were reviewed.

E. Individual therapy has not been used as suggested, and family members were redirected to consider this option.

### 26. Interpret Blame (26)

A. The parents were noted to often blame each other for their child's homosexual/bisexual/transgendered orientation.

B. Blaming each other was interpreted as a defense of one's own irrational guilt, fear, disappointment, or worry.

C. The parents displayed insight into how their externalization of the blame has been used as a defense mechanism; this progress was reinforced.

D. The parents denied any use of blame as a defense mechanism and were encouraged to consider this dynamic in the future.

### 27. Explore Family Members' Fears about Own Orientation (27)

A. Family members were asked about their own fears regarding their sexual orientation.

B. Family members were supported as they expressed their own sexual orientation concerns.

C. Family members were referred to educational materials regarding their own sexual orientation.

D. Family members were encouraged to read *Loving Someone Gay* (Clark).

E. Family members were directed to lectures on sexual orientation issues within the community.

F. Family members have utilized resources for education, and the key points were reviewed.

G. Educational resources on sexual orientation issues have not been utilized by the family members and they were reminded about these helpful options.

### 28. Prompt Venting about Social Rejection (28)

A. Family members were encouraged to ventilate their feelings about societal rejection of homosexual/bisexual/transgendered individuals.

B. Family members were asked about any sense of rejection by God.

C. The importance of social acceptance for everyone was emphasized.

D. The homosexual/bisexual/transgendered family member was encouraged to provide feedback regarding societal rejection.

E. The heterosexual family members were asked to express their feelings about societal rejection.

### 29. Recommend Support Group (29)

A. Family members were encouraged to attend a support group (e.g., Parents, Family, and Friends of Lesbians and Gays [PFLAG]).

B. Family members have attended a support group for family, friends, and parents of people with a homosexual/bisexual/transgendered orientation, and the benefits of this support group were reviewed.

C. Family members have not attended a support group for families and friends of homosexual/bisexual/transgendered and they were redirected to do so.

### 30. Review Commonalties and Differences in Beliefs (30)

A. The family was asked to compare and contrast the different family members' beliefs regarding homosexuality/bisexuality/transgenderism.

B. It was reflected to the family that they have many common beliefs regarding homosexuality/bisexuality/transgenderism.

C. It was reflected to the family that there were many points at which the family members' beliefs are quite different.

**31. Encourage Family Cohesiveness (31)**

A. Family members were encouraged to develop cohesiveness within the family.

B. Family members were encouraged to weigh the costs of remaining divided versus forming more of a bond based on tolerance and acceptance.

C. Family members were reinforced for their identification of situations in which they have developed more cohesiveness.

D. When family members displayed increased divisiveness, they were encouraged to form more of a bond based on tolerance and acceptance.

**32. Review Ways to Support Each Other (32)**

A. Family members were encouraged to review the ways that they could be more supportive of each other.

B. Family members were focused on increasing respectful communication as a way to provide more support for each other.

C. Family members were reinforced for the idea that despite differences in sexual orientation, they are still family.

D. Verbal reinforcement was given as family members provided support to each other.

**33. Explore Acceptable Involvement with Same-Sex Partner (33)**

A. Family members were assisted in exploring what is tolerable and what is not, regarding a family member bringing home a same-sex partner.

B. Family members were noted to be intolerant of any contact of the family member's same-sex partner.

C. Limited involvement with a same-sex partner in the home was noted to be acceptable (i.e., for a visit).

D. More acceptance of bringing home a same-sex partner was identified (i.e., for an overnight stay, sleeping together at the home).

**34. Discuss Ways to Build Tolerance for Same-Sex Partner (34)**

A. Family members were encouraged to discuss ways to build tolerance for a same-sex partner of a family member.

B. Family members were encouraged to look beyond superficial issues (e.g., disregard clothing or mannerisms).

C. Family members were encouraged to appreciate the positive character traits of the same-sex partner.

D. Family members were reinforced for developing a greater appreciation of the same-sex partner of the family member.

E. Family members continued to be intolerant of the same-sex partner of a family member and were encouraged to develop a greater tolerance.

### 35. Review Positive and Negative Aspects of Same-Sex Partner (35)

A. Family members were encouraged to list the positive aspects of the family member's same-sex partner.

B. Family members were encouraged to list the negative aspects of the family member's same-sex partner.

C. Family members were asked to list the assets that the same-sex partner brings to the family.

D. Family members were encouraged to emphasize the positive assets that the same-sex partner brings to the family.

# TRAUMATIC LIFE EVENTS

## CLIENT PRESENTATION

### 1. Disruption and Instability (1)*

A. A traumatic event has occurred which has caused disruption and instability in the family.

B. Typical family patterns of activity have been changed due to the traumatic life event.

C. The family has displayed poor coping skills for the disruption and instability caused by the traumatic life event.

D. As the family has adjusted to the traumatic life event, disruption and instability within the family has decreased.

### 2. Role Changes (2)

A. A traumatic life event has caused such disruption within the family dynamics that family members' roles have been changed.

B. Family roles have become imbalanced (e.g., one of the children has become parentified).

C. As family members have been unable to meet their role within the family, other family members have been required to take on added responsibilities.

D. As the family has begun to cope with the experience of the traumatic life event, a greater balance has developed for the family members.

### 3. Disengagement/Disillusionment (3)

A. Family members appear to be quite disengaged from each other.

B. Family members are alienated from each other due to the traumatic life event.

C. Family members report disillusionment with the state of the family's connectedness.

D. Family members report feeling that they are "out of touch" with each other.

E. As treatment has progressed, family members have become more connected with each other.

### 4. Helplessness and Hopelessness (4)

A. A family member has developed feelings of helplessness and hopelessness subsequent to the traumatic life event.

B. Several members of the family have described feelings of helplessness and hopelessness after the traumatic life event has occurred.

C. Family members display learned helplessness, giving up in areas unrelated to the traumatic event.

D. As treatment has progressed, the sense of helplessness and hopelessness has decreased in family members.

*The numbers in parentheses correlate to the number of the Behavioral Definition statement in the companion chapter with the same title in *The Family Therapy Treatment Planner*, Second Ed. (Dattilio, Jongsma, and Davis) by John Wiley & Sons, 2010.

### 5. Disruption of Familiar Family Routines/Rituals (5)

A. The traumatic event has caused a disruption in familiar family routines and rituals.

B. Family unity is struggling as the family no longer gathers for familiar routines and rituals.

C. Family members complain of missing how family life used to be prior to the traumatic event.

D. As treatment has progressed, the family members have reported an increase in intentional use of familiar routines and rituals.

## INTERVENTIONS IMPLEMENTED

### 1. Request Description of the Traumatic Event (1)*

A. Each family member was asked to explain the traumatic event.

B. Family members were directed to allow each family member to make a complete description of the traumatic event.

C. Support and encouragement were provided to the family members when they became emotional as they were describing the traumatic event.

D. Family members were helped to summarize their experience of the traumatic event.

### 2. Assess Coping (2)

A. Structured instruments were used to assess the family's ability to cope with the traumatic life event.

B. The *Adolescent-Family Inventories of Life Events and Changes* were used to objectively assess the family's ability to cope with the traumatic life event.

C. The *Family Inventories of Life Events and Changes* were used to assess the family's ability to cope with the traumatic life event.

D. Picture stories, drawings, and play assessment techniques were used to assess how the smaller children within the family are coping with the traumatic event.

### 3. Identify Changes (3)

A. Each family member was prompted to describe any emotional changes that have resulted from the traumatic event.

B. Each family member was asked to identify any cognitive changes that have happened as a result of the traumatic event.

C. Each family member was asked to identify any behavioral changes that have resulted from the traumatic event.

D. Family members' experience of changes that have resulted from the traumatic event were reviewed and processed.

---

*The numbers in parentheses correlate to the number of the Therapeutic Intervention statement in the companion chapter with the same title in *The Family Therapy Treatment Planner*, Second Ed. (Dattilio, Jongsma, and Davis) by John Wiley & Sons, 2010.

### 4. Use Posttraumatic Paradigm (4)

A. The event was characterized as a major catastrophe.

B. Family members' reactions to the incident were addressed within the framework of a posttraumatic stress reaction.

C. Family members were assessed for symptoms consistent with posttraumatic stress reaction, or any acute stress reaction.

D. The emphasis of treatment has been placed on the posttraumatic stress disorder symptoms.

### 5. Refer for Individual Therapy (5)

A. Since the stress reactions are severe, a referral was made for individual treatment.

B. Family members have attended individual therapy for the stress reaction symptoms, and the benefits of this treatment were reviewed.

C. A collateral involvement was maintained with the professional providing the individual treatment.

D. Family members have not followed up on individual treatment for the stress reaction symptoms and were redirected to the necessary resources.

### 6. Discuss Feelings and Effect (6)

A. A discussion was facilitated regarding family members' feelings related to the traumatic event.

B. The differences in perception of the traumatic event between family members were reviewed.

C. A discussion was held regarding how family members have been affected differently by the traumatic event.

D. Alternative ways to express family members' feelings were suggested (e.g., construct lists of changes, make a drawing, or write journals or poems).

E. Family members were supported as they expressed their feelings and discussed the perceptions and effects of the traumatic event.

F. Family members were rather defensive about their feelings related to the traumatic life event and were encouraged to be more open in this area as they feel capable of doing so.

### 7. Assign Exercises for Reframing (7)

A. Exercises were suggested to the family that may help them to facilitate viewing the trauma in a different manner.

B. Family members were encouraged to identify how they could have adjusted to the traumatic event more adaptively.

C. Family members were assigned to rewrite the story of the traumatic event, describing how they could cope with the situation in a more adaptive fashion.

D. It was noted that family members' use of exercises have helped them to reframe their response to the traumatic event.

### 8. Role-Play/Model New Coping Techniques (8)

A. Role-play techniques were used to help teach the family new ways to react to an unexpected, traumatic event.

B.  Modeling techniques were used to help the family learn new ways to react to an unexpected, traumatic event.

C.  Family members were urged to view the traumatic event as a challenge versus a defeat.

D.  Family members were encouraged to focus on working together to overcome obstacles.

E.  Family members were encouraged to rely on spiritual resources.

### 9.  Teach Conflict Resolution Techniques (9)

A.  Family members were taught conflict resolution techniques in modeling and role-play.

B.  Family members were taught assertiveness techniques such as "I" statements and complaining without blaming.

C.  Family members were taught solution brainstorming techniques to help resolve conflicts and reduce tension in the family.

### 10.  Use Cohesion-Building Strategies (10)

A.  The family was directed to use cohesion-building strategies.

B.  The family was directed to engage in family activities to promote working together on a particular task.

C.  Family members have completed the cohesion-building task, and the benefits of this experience were processed.

D.  The family has not completed the cohesion-building task and was redirected to do so.

### 11.  Reinforce Use of Rewarding Activities (11)

A.  The family was reinforced for accepting the idea that engaging in more rewarding family activities will improve the quality of the overall interaction and the sense of cohesiveness.

B.  Family members were reinforced whenever they focused on developing more rewarding family activities.

C.  The use of rewarding family activities to develop a greater sense of cohesiveness was emphasized as a way to resolve the problems generated by the traumatic event.

### 12.  Address Underlying Fears (12)

A.  Family members were assessed for any underlying fears that may exist regarding intimacy or cohesiveness.

B.  Family members were supported as they identified the fears that they have regarding intimacy or cohesiveness (e.g., "If I get too close to you, you will try to control me or I will lose my autonomy").

C.  The family was taught about how underlying fears can have an effect on intimacy and cohesiveness.

D.  The family denied any pattern of underlying fears that may affect the feeling of intimacy or cohesiveness and were urged to monitor this dynamic.

### 13.  Decrease Fear of Cohesiveness (13)

A.  Family members were urged to directly face the fears that they have regarding cohesiveness.

B.  Family members were encouraged to consider alternative behaviors when experiencing fears of cohesiveness (e.g., "I can still be part of the family unit and maintain my autonomy and personal uniqueness").

C. Family members were supported as they resolved their fears about cohesiveness and closeness with other family members.

D. Family members appeared to have continued fears related to cohesiveness and additional focus was provided in this area.

### 14. Brainstorm about Conflict Resolution and Crisis Coping (14)

A. Family members were assisted in brainstorming behaviors that will facilitate conflict resolution and crisis coping.

B. Family members were asked to brainstorm a list of behaviors that will hinder conflict resolution and crisis coping.

C. Family members were redirected to implement the behaviors that will facilitate conflict resolution and crisis coping, and decrease those that hinder progress.

### 15. Teach Stress-Inoculation Techniques (15)

A. Family members were taught stress-inoculation techniques.

B. Deep breathing techniques were taught to the family members.

C. Family members were taught progressive muscle relaxation techniques.

D. Cognitive-restructuring techniques were taught to the family members.

E. Family members have used the stress-inoculation techniques, and report better ability to cope with the crisis.

F. Family members have not implemented the stress-inoculation techniques and were reminded about these helpful techniques.

### 16. Identify External Support Systems (16)

A. Family members were asked to identify external support systems within the community.

B. Family members were directed to use external support systems in the community.

C. Family members have regularly used external support systems, and the benefits of these supports in developing a cohesive response to the crisis were highlighted.

D. The family has not used external supports to help respond to the crisis and was redirected to do so.

### 17. Emphasize Support (17)

A. Since the family is dealing with a problem outside of their direct control, they were instructed to avoid wasting energy trying to solve the external problem.

B. Family members dealing with a problem outside of their control were encouraged to support each other and decide how they can best react to the unchangeable problem.

C. Family members were reinforced for their increased support of each other.

D. Family members have not focused on support but, continued to try to solve the "unsolvable" problem; they were redirected toward supporting each other.

### 18. Imagine Successful Coping (18)

A. Family members were encouraged to imagine themselves in the near future coping successfully.

B. Family members were encouraged to share their thoughts about how they will handle the transition regarding the traumatic event.

C. Family members were encouraged to utilize the imagined techniques to cope successfully with the traumatic event.

### 19. Teach about Various Coping Capabilities (19)

A. The family was enlightened about how various families cope differently in the face of crisis.

B. Family members were provided with specific examples of the different ways in which families cope when they experience crisis.

C. Family members were taught how the preexisting condition of the family predisposes them to deal with traumatic events in a particular way.

### 20. Discuss Needed Changes in Coping (20)

A. A discussion was facilitated around what may need to change in the family's coping response to the traumatic event.

B. Family members were supported as they identified ways in which their coping with the traumatic event needs to change.

C. Family members were unable to identify ways in which their coping with the traumatic event may need to change and were provided with tentative examples in this area.

### 21. Brainstorm Changes in Coping Behavior (21)

A. Family members were assisted in brainstorming how they might begin to introduce changes in coping behavior in the face of the current event.

B. Family members were helped to evaluate their brainstormed ideas regarding how to change their coping behavior due to the traumatic life event.

C. Family members were reinforced for identifying, evaluating, and selecting ways in which they want to change their coping behavior in the face of the current event.

### 22. Individualize Coping (22)

A. Family members were assisted in adjusting to a personalized style of coping that fits best with their strengths and weaknesses.

B. Individual strengths were emphasized as an important portion of individual and family coping.

C. Each individual was encouraged to balance the preferred style of coping with what best supports the family as a whole.

### 23. Focus on Denial (23)

A. Family members were assisted in admitting their own denial as a defense coping strategy.

B. Confrontative techniques were used to help family members admit to their own denial associated with the traumatic event.

C. Metaphors were used to help facilitate family members' discussion about their denial associated with the traumatic event.

D. Family members were reinforced for their more realistic understanding and decreased denial of the traumatic event.

E. Family members continued to display a great deal of denial of the traumatic event and were provided with remedial feedback in this area.

## 24. Identify Alternatives to Denial (24)

A. Each family member was asked to identify alternative behaviors to counteract denial of the traumatic event.

B. Family members were asked to critique the list of alternative behaviors to help counteract denial of the traumatic event.

C. Feedback was provided to family members about the ways in which they can counteract denial of the traumatic event.

## 25. Encourage Support and Reinforcement (25)

A. Family members were encouraged to support and reinforce each other in overcoming denial of the traumatic event and facing reality in an adaptive manner.

B. Family members were verbally reinforced for the ways in which they have been able to support each other.

C. Family members have not done very much to support and reinforce each other and were redirected to provide this to each other.

## 26. Assess Adaptive Functioning (26)

A. The level of adaptive functioning that exists with the family members was assessed through interviews.

B. An objective inventory was used to assess the family members' level of adaptive functioning.

C. The *Stages of Change Questionnaire* was used to assess the family members' level of adaptive functioning.

## 27. Review Assessment Results (27)

A. The results of the assessment of the family's level of adaptive functioning were reviewed.

B. Feedback was provided to the family about their level of adaptive functioning.

C. It was reported to the family that their level of adaptive functioning has been quite high.

D. It was reported to the family that there are significant deficiencies in their level of adaptive functioning.

E. A discussion was held regarding the family's responses to the results of the assessment of adaptive functioning.

## 28. Explain Stage of Development (28)

A. The family was assisted in a description of how their family differs from others.

B. The family was provided with feedback about how they cope and survive traumatic events.

C. A connection was made between the family's level of development, and their skills at surviving traumatic events.

## 29. Describe Conflicts (29)

A. Family members were asked to describe conflicts that exist within the family as a result of the crisis.

B. Family members were asked to identify the perceptions that have contributed to the current conflicts.

C. It was noted that the family members had very similar perceptions regarding the crisis, and how they have led to current conflicts.

D. Family members were noted to have rather divergent views about the crisis, and the conflicts that have stemmed from these problems.

E. Feedback was provided to the family about the conflicts that they experienced subsequent to the crisis, and the underlying perceptions that contribute to these conflicts.

## 30. Look for Underlying Dynamics (30)

A. The family was assessed for underlying dynamics that may be contributing to the conflicts subsequent to the crisis.

B. The family was assisted in identifying the underlying dynamics that have been contributing to the conflicts.

C. Underlying dynamics such as jealousy and favoritism were identified to the family.

## 31. Resolve Underlying Dynamics (31)

A. The underlying dynamics that may be contributing to conflict were brought to the attention of the family members.

B. Family members were urged to work through their underlying dynamics to resolve them and decrease conflict.

C. Family members' discussion about the underlying dynamics was facilitated and monitored.

D. Family members were reinforced for working through the underlying dynamics that contribute to conflicts.

E. Family members have not worked through the underlying dynamics that lead to conflict, and additional work will be done in this area.

## 32. Define Roles (32)

A. Family members were assisted in defining each family member's role within the family.

B. Family members were assisted in clarifying how specific roles have been developed.

C. The pattern of how roles have been changed and/or modified were reviewed and processed.

## 33. Discuss Role Changes Due to Crisis (33)

A. The manner in which the traumatic event has contributed to changes in roles was reviewed.

B. The family was assisted in identifying how roles have been modified due to the traumatic event.

C. Family members were assisted in identifying how changing roles may help to resolve the issues related to the traumatic event.

## 34. Reestablish Routines (34)

A. The family was encouraged to reestablish familiar routines as soon as possible.

B. The family members were assisted in prioritizing the routines and rituals that would help to develop family cohesion.

C. The family has returned to some familiar routines, and the benefits of this familiarity were reviewed.

D. The family has not prioritized familiar rituals and routines, and was reminded about these helpful comforts.

## 35. Ask the Miracle Question (35)

A. The family was asked the miracle question: "If all of you were to awaken tomorrow and by way of a miracle the conflict between you disappeared, how would you know that it was gone?"

B. Family members were supported as they responded to the miracle question.

C. The responses to the miracle question were summarized and processed.

## 36. Use Miracle Question Responses to Identify Changes (36)

A. The family was assisted in defining the changes that must occur in the family, based on the responses to the miracle question.

B. Family members were reinforced as they displayed insight into the changes that must occur in the family to resolve conflict.

C. Family members displayed limited insight into the changes that must occur for the miracle to come true and were provided with additional feedback in this area.

# UNWANTED/UNPLANNED PREGNANCY

## CLIENT PRESENTATION

### 1. Teenage Pregnancy (1)*

A. A teenage, unmarried family member is pregnant.

B. The pregnant, teenage family member has decided to keep her child.

C. The family is in disagreement with the unmarried, teenage girl about her decision to keep her child.

D. As treatment has progressed, the family has resolved their differences in opinion about the decisions regarding the pregnancy.

### 2. Tension about Choices (2)

A. Tension has gradually increased within the family regarding the decision to keep the child out of wedlock, as opposed to an abortion or releasing the child for adoption.

B. Family members' have experienced many arguments regarding the decisions about how to respond to the unplanned pregnancy.

C. Relationships are beginning to deteriorate due to the family members' disagreement about how to cope with the pregnancy.

D. Family members have become more cohesive and in agreement about how to respond to the pregnancy.

### 3. Moral Dilemmas (3)

A. The pregnant teenage family member is experiencing moral dilemmas regarding her consideration of abortion.

B. The pregnant teenage family member is experiencing moral dilemma regarding the consideration of releasing the child for adoption.

C. Family members are experiencing moral dilemmas regarding the decisions to be made regarding adoption and abortion options.

D. Family members have resolved their moral dilemmas regarding the abortion and adoption issues.

### 4. Unexpected Pregnancy for Parent (4)

A. A parent is unexpectedly pregnant.

B. The pregnant parent experiences ambivalence about whether to keep the child, have an abortion, or adopt the child out.

C. The unexpectedly pregnant parents have concerns about their ability to care for the child due to their age, economic constraints, medical/health problems, or other factors.

*The numbers in parentheses correlate to the number of the Behavioral Definition statement in the companion chapter with the same title in *The Family Therapy Treatment Planner*, Second Ed. (Dattilio, Jongsma, and Davis) by John Wiley & Sons, 2010.

D. The family has developed a clear decision about how to respond to the unexpected pregnancy.

### 5. Family Strife (5)

A. Marital problems have developed due to the decision to keep the child within the family, adopt the child out, or abort the child.

B. Family problems have developed due to the decision to keep the child in the family, adopt the child out, or abort the child.

C. Family relationships are more tense and uncertain due to the added stress that occurs because of keeping the child in the family, adopting the child out, or aborting the child.

D. The family has developed better coping skills for the increased stress of keeping the child within the family, adopting the child out, or aborting the child.

### 6. Ignoring the Pregnancy (6)

A. Family members seem to be ignoring the issue of the pregnancy.

B. Family members avoid any confrontation related to the pregnancy.

C. Family members have become estranged due to the pattern of avoiding the issue of the pregnancy.

D. Family members have become more open in their discussion about the pregnancy.

E. Family relationships have improved as the family has worked through the disagreements and emotions related to the pregnancy.

### 7. Divorcing Parents Are Expecting a Child (7)

A. The parents, who were contemplating divorce, now discover that they are expecting another child.

B. The parents feel pressured to attempt marital reconciliation.

C. The parents accuse each other of using the pregnancy as an attempt to manipulate each other.

D. The expecting parents have resolved the divorce issue through reconciliation.

E. The expecting parents have decided to continue with the divorce proceedings.

## INTERVENTIONS IMPLEMENTED

### 1. Encourage Expression of Emotions (1)*

A. A forum was opened for the expression of the feelings of the family members about the pregnancy.

B. All family members were encouraged to express their feelings and were provided support as they did so.

---

*The numbers in parentheses correlate to the number of the Therapeutic Intervention statement in the companion chapter with the same title in *The Family Therapy Treatment Planner*, Second Ed. (Dattilio, Jongsma, and Davis) by John Wiley & Sons, 2010.

C. Family members were questioned about their feelings, such as fear and guilt on the part of the pregnant child, embarrassment and anger by the siblings, and shame and anger by the parents.

## 2. Normalize Emotions (2)

A. Family members were reassured about how their emotions are normal and real.

B. Family members were directed as to how to use their emotions in the decision-making process.

C. Family members were reinforced when they identified their feelings as normal, typical, and valid.

D. Family members were redirected when they tended to invalidate their feelings.

## 3. Stabilize Emotions (3)

A. Family members were assisted in stabilizing their emotions through venting them within session.

B. Family members were helped to clearly define and name their feelings.

C. Family members were encouraged to own their feelings.

D. Family members were reassured that they will eventually obtain solutions to the problems that they are facing.

## 4. Characterize as a Crisis (4)

A. Family members were reminded that their current situation is a crisis and that their emotions may cloud sound judgment during crisis times.

B. Family members were supported as they accepted the likelihood that their judgment can be clouded by their emotions.

C. Family members deny that their emotions were clouding their judgment and were provided with tentative examples of how this can occur.

## 5. Assure about Alternatives (5)

A. The family was helped to define alternative responses to the pregnancy.

B. Family members were reassured that they have time to consider options, rather than make an immediate decision.

C. Family members were reinforced for postponing significant decisions during a cooling-off period.

D. Family members appeared to be acting emotionally to the current crisis and were redirected to put more time between the onset of the crisis and the decisions about how to resolve it.

## 6. Review Options with Pregnant Child (6)

A. The pregnant child was assisted in reviewing the options of adoption, abortion, or raising the baby.

B. The pregnant child was provided with reading material about the adoptions available.

C. The pregnant child was encouraged to read *In Good Conscience* (Runkle).

D. The pregnant child was directed to read *Should I Have This Baby?* (Jones).

E. The pregnant child has reviewed the information about her different options, and the key were summarized.

F. The pregnant child has not reviewed the information about her options and was redirected to do so.

### 7. Review Etiology of Decision (7)

A. An individual session was held with the pregnant child in order to review her decision regarding the response to the pregnancy.

B. It was reflected that the child's decision seems to be reactionary.

C. It was reflected that the child's decision seems to be strongly influenced by others.

D. It was reflected that the child's decision seems to be soundly thought through and consistent with her moral beliefs.

### 8. Encourage Support (8)

A. The family was encouraged to be supportive of the pregnant child.

B. The family was helped to see the pregnant child's fear and struggle.

C. The child's right to choose how to respond to the pregnancy was acknowledged.

D. Family members were verbally reinforced for their support of the pregnant child.

E. Family members did not display much support for the pregnant child and were redirected in this area.

### 9. Review Right to Choose (9)

A. The right of each individual to make life decisions was reviewed.

B. The family was reminded that the individual's decision does not always reflect the other family members' moral beliefs or feelings.

C. Family members were assisted in processing their emotions regarding allowing their child to make important life decisions.

### 10. Explore Parents' Feelings (10)

A. The parents were encouraged to express their feelings about the pregnancy.

B. The parents were probed for feelings of disappointment and loss of control.

C. The parents were asked about their feelings of fear for the pregnant child and the unborn baby.

D. The parents were supported as they described their feelings related to the unplanned pregnancy.

### 11. Promote Discussion about Expectations (11)

A. An option for how to respond to the pregnancy has been selected, and the family was directed to discuss the expectations for the future based on this decision.

B. Family members were assisted in developing a better understanding about what effects the chosen response to the pregnancy may have in the future.

C. Family members were provided with additional ideas about how the chosen response to the pregnancy may affect the future.

### 12. Refer to Peer Family (12)

A. The family was referred to other families who have gone through similar situations.

B. The family was referred to an unwed mother's support group.

C. The family was referred to an adoption agency to connect with families that have made this choice.

D. Family members were encouraged to discuss this issue with acquaintances who have been through a similar experience.

E. The family has connected with other families who have experienced a similar situation, and the benefits of these contacts were processed.

F. The family has not connected with other families who have experienced a similar situation and were redirected to do so.

### 13. Discuss Coping Strategies (13)

A. The family was encouraged to discuss coping strategies for living with each other after the decision has been made.

B. Family members were urged to set guidelines about appropriate versus inappropriate expressions of anger, fear, frustration, resentment, and guilt.

C. Family members were encouraged to use their identified coping strategies as they adjust to the decisions that have been made about how to respond to the pregnancy.

D. Role-play techniques were used to model healthy versus unhealthy responses and expression of emotions.

E. Family members were redirected in situations for which they did not use healthy coping skills.

### 14. Discuss How to Support Each Other (14)

A. Family members were asked to identify the ways in which they can support each other.

B. Family members were asked to identify the ways in which they wish to be supported.

C. Family members were reinforced for providing support to each other.

D. Family members were uncertain about how to support each other, and were provided with tentative examples in this area (e.g., allowing time for venting anger, fear, or sadness).

E. The family was taught reflective listening skills.

### 15. Review Parents' Stand on Abortion (15)

A. A conjoint meeting was held with only the parents to establish and define their beliefs and feelings regarding abortion.

B. Guidelines were set regarding how the parents' beliefs about abortion can be addressed in the course of family therapy.

C. The parents were noted to be very open to the option of abortion.

D. The parents were noted to be ambivalent about the option of abortion.

E. The parents were noted to be strongly opposed to the option of abortion.

## 16. Highlight Respect for Pregnant Child's Choice (16)

A. Family members were prompted to respect the right of the pregnant child to decide how to respond to the pregnancy, regardless of their contrary feelings.

B. Family members were assisted in recognizing that they do not have the final choice regarding how to respond to the pregnancy.

C. Family members were supported as they respected the pregnant child's right to make choices.

D. Family members were provided with factual information about the pregnant child's legal rights.

## 17. Explore Estranged Family Members' Emotions (17)

A. Estranged family members were invited to a therapy session.

B. The thoughts and emotions of the estranged family members in regard to the pregnancy and the decision that has been made were explored.

C. All family members were supported as the estranged family member vented his/her thoughts and emotions about the decisions made in regard to the pregnancy.

D. Family members were redirected when the discussion of the estranged family member's emotions became dysfunctional.

## 18. Facilitate the Expression of Hurt about Rift (18)

A. The pregnant child was allowed and encouraged to express her feelings of hurt and sadness over the rift in the family in reaction to her pregnancy and response decision.

B. Support and redirection were provided to the pregnant child and the family as the hurt and pain of the family rift were discussed.

C. Each family member was asked what he/she can do to reunite the family.

## 19. Discuss Respecting Decision (19)

A. The need for respect for another's decisions even though one may disagree with that decision was discussed.

B. Affirmations of love for one another were solicited, in spite of differences and a stressful situation.

## 20. Review Pros and Cons (20)

A. It was noted that the spouses feel open to discussing the wife's unexpected pregnancy with other family members.

B. The pros and cons of the alternative responses to the unexpected pregnancy were reviewed.

C. The need for sensitivity to the anger of other family members was highlighted.

D. The family was reinforced for their willingness to discuss this sensitive issue.

E. The parents were unwilling to discuss the unexpected pregnancy in the context of the entire family, and this was respected.

## 21. Explore Ambivalence (21)

A. The parents' ambivalent feelings regarding the unexpected pregnancy were explored.

B. The parents were assisted in clarifying the multiple factors and emotions that they see as relevant.

C. The parents were supported as they expressed their feelings regarding their unplanned pregnancy.

## 22. Gather Medical Information (22)

A. Since the pregnant parent's health is at issue, relevant medical information was gathered.
B. Since the pregnant parent's age is at issue, relevant medical information was gathered.
C. The family was urged to gather appropriate medical information.
D. The family was helped to process the relevant medical information.

## 23. Recommend Reading Material (23)

A. Reading material regarding the unexpected pregnancy was assigned to the pregnant parents.
B. *Should I Keep My Baby?* (Zimmerman) was assigned to the parents.
C. The parents have read the assigned material about the unexpected pregnancy, and key issues were reviewed.
D. The parents have not read the assigned material on the unexpected pregnancy, and this resistance was processed.

## 24. Review Feelings and Motives (24)

A. A separate, conjoint interview was held with the parents to discuss their feelings about the wife's unexpected pregnancy.
B. The parents were searched for unconscious motives that may have contributed to the wife's pregnancy.
C. The couple was provided with examples of unconscious motives that may have contributed to the wife's pregnancy (i.e., a fear of drifting apart as the children get older).
D. The parents were assisted in processing their unconscious motives.
E. The parents were noted to have denied any unconscious motives for the unwanted pregnancy.

## 25. Explore the Impact of a Baby (25)

A. Each family member was questioned about how the impact of the new baby would affect him or her individually and as a family.
B. Family members were assessed for underlying feelings of resentment or jealousy.
C. Family members were confronted regarding cognitive distortion or myths that foster feelings of resentment and jealousy.
D. Family members' variety of effects were summarized and processed.

## 26. Use Nondirective Techniques (26)

A. Nondirective techniques were used to help the family express feelings and reduce tension.
B. Metaphors were used to clarify the family members' beliefs and expectations.
C. Family members were assisted in identifying alternative ways of expressing feelings of resentment or discontent with the decision to keep the child.

## 27. Develop Functional Expression of Emotions (27)

A. A discussion was held about alternative ways the family members can express feelings of resentment or discontent with the decision about how to respond to the pregnancy.

B. Role-play and modeling techniques were used to teach respectful use of "I" messages.

C. Family members were reinforced for their respectful use of functional expressions of their feelings.

D. Family members were redirected for their dysfunctional pattern of expression of emotions.

## 28. Discuss Reciprocal Impact of Children and Decision to Divorce (28)

A. The parents were assisted in identifying the impact that the pregnancy will have on the decision regarding whether to continue the relationship.

B. The parents were asked to consider how the decision regarding whether to continue the relationship would impact the children.

C. It was noted that the parents displayed a clear understanding of the impact on the children from the decision about whether to continue the marriage.

D. The parents were provided with additional feedback regarding how the children may be impacted by the decision as to whether to continue the relationship.

## 29. Encourage Interim Steps (29)

A. The couple was assisted in considering interim steps prior to the decision to announce a separation/divorce to the family.

B. The couple agreed to use interim steps prior to announcing a separation/divorce to the family and were assisted in identifying the specific nature of these steps.

C. The couple was provided with examples of interim steps to use prior to announcing a separation or divorce to the family (e.g., separating within the household, traveling to the same location in separate vehicles, engaging in activities that give space in the relationship).

## 30. Review Alternatives to Separation (30)

A. The couple was asked to review all alternatives to separation.

B. The couple was provided with alternatives to separation.

C. The couple was encouraged to participate in conjoint marital therapy rather than opt for separation.

D. The couple has participated in conjoint marital therapy, which has helped to resolve the relationship issues.

E. The couple has not participated in conjoint marital therapy and was redirected to do so.